LORD CHATHAM
AND THE WHIG OPPOSITION

THE MARQUIS OF ROCKINGHAM AND EDMUND BURKE.

From an unfinished picture by Sir Joshua Reynolds at the Fitzwilliam Museum, Cambridge.

LORD CHATHAM

AND THE

WHIG OPPOSITION

D. A. WINSTANLEY

FRANK CASS & CO. LTD.
1966

Published by Frank Cass & Co. Ltd.,
10 Woburn Walk, London W.C.1
by arrangement with Cambridge University Press.

First Edition   1912
New Impression   1966

Printed in Holland by
N. V. Grafische Industrie Haarlem

PREFACE

AN apology, or at least a defence, is perhaps necessary for a work dealing with the struggle between the whig factions and the crown during a very limited period of George III.'s reign ; for the party politics of a bygone age, however great their interest for contemporaries, are apt to be somewhat lacking in life and reality for those who, living at a later date, and absorbed in the political controversies of their own day, are disposed to be somewhat impatient of the details of a conflict long since brought to a final conclusion. It is possible that few would deny that the establishment of the personal influence of the crown by George III. had vital consequences in English history ; but there are probably many who would feel that a close analysis of the means adopted by that king to attain his end, of the circumstances which favoured or retarded his progress, was perhaps unnecessary, and most certainly tedious. It can hardly be hoped that the following pages will provide a refutation of either of these charges ; but the responsibility for the failure rests upon the workman and not upon his material. Many are the accusations which can be brought against the period which lies between the formation of Chatham's ministry in July 1766 and the collapse of the whig opposition to Lord North in the summer of 1771 ; but it can scarcely be accused of lacking in either interest or importance. Within those few years the destinies of the nation were determined and the work of the Revolution nullified.

Never before had the opponents of personal government been given such a favourable opportunity to thwart the execution of the royal schemes; and yet they failed hopelessly. It was the king, and not the whigs, who triumphed; and, as Lord Acton has said, "about the year 1770 things had been brought back, by indirect means, nearly to the condition which the Revolution had been designed to remedy." [1] The consequences which flowed from that royal victory are too well known to need particularisation; and it would be generally allowed that the history of England might have read somewhat differently if Grafton had fallen before the onslaught of the whigs, or if North had failed at the outset of his ministerial career.

A contest so momentous can hardly be without interest; and, therefore, an attempt has been made to give both a record and an explanation of the failure of the whigs. For this purpose it has been necessary to concentrate the attention almost exclusively upon domestic politics, and to omit much well deserving of close consideration. Colonial history and foreign policy have been but very briefly touched upon; and if an exception has been made in the case of the dispute with Spain over the Falkland Islands, this can be justified by the influence which those negotiations exercised upon the parliamentary conflict. Such omissions, however serious they might be in a work claiming to be a history of the period, may perhaps be pardoned in what is more than a study of one particular aspect of the time; and it is to be hoped that if something has been lost in comprehensiveness, something has also been gained in lucidity.

It may not be out of place to say a few words about some of the manuscript authorities that have been used,

---

[1] Lord Acton's *History of Freedom and Other Essays* (1907), 54-55.

well known though they are to all students of the period.
The Newcastle Papers in the British Museum are, of
course, absolutely essential for any understanding of the
politics of the early years of George III.'s reign ; and
historians have reason sincerely to lament the duke's
death in November, 1768. Though neither an infallible
guide, nor free from personal prejudice, Newcastle,
from his position as patriarch of the whig party, and
from his intimacy with the leading politicians of his
time, was the centre of many negotiations and intrigues ;
and his correspondence reveals not a little of the inner
history of the Rockingham party. The Hardwicke
Papers, also to be found in the British Museum, though
perhaps of less importance for this particular period,
certainly cannot be neglected with safety, since they
include many valuable reports of parliamentary debates,
and much of vital interest. Neither the second Lord
Hardwicke, nor his two brothers, Charles and John
Yorke, apparently enjoyed the close confidence of the
Rockingham whigs ; but as politicians, keenly alive
to their family interests and to the critical character
of the warfare going on before their eyes, they are able
to tell us much that we are glad to know. Sufficiently
detached to be able to criticise, and sufficiently interested to care to do so, their judgments are often
sounder than those of the politicians more actively
engaged in the struggle ; and as onlookers, who are
proverbially reported to see more of the game, their
opinions and impressions are deserving of careful study.
Moreover, in the same collection are to be found the two
accounts of the last days of Charles Yorke, compiled
by Lord Hardwicke and Mrs Agneta Yorke ; and
though these have already been used to very good
purpose by Mr Basil Williams for a most interesting
paper published in the Transactions of the Royal

Historical Society, it has been thought permissible to narrate again a story which must ever appeal to those who realise the tragedy of human life and the vanity of human ambition.

Mention should also be made of the Wilkes Papers in the British Museum, and of the Pitt Papers in the Record Office. As might be expected, the correspondence of Wilkes throws little light upon the designs of the various parties ; and his fragment of autobiography is rather a revelation of his private character than of his political activity. The more important of the Pitt Papers have for many years been accessible in the published correspondence of the Earl of Chatham ; but it would be a mistake to imagine that what has not been printed is without value. The unpublished papers can be consulted with advantage and profit, and should not be disregarded.

History, however, even the most imperfect representation of it, is never made from manuscripts alone ; and to the great historians of the eighteenth century a debt of gratitude is owing from all who have profited by their labours. Lastly, my thanks are in a special measure due to my friend, Dr Foakes-Jackson, of Jesus College, Cambridge, who was kind enough to read my manuscript, and bold enough to play the part of the friendly but candid critic. For his advice I am sincerely grateful, and I only regret that the volume is so little worthy of the care which he generously bestowed upon it.

D. A. W.

July 1912

CONTENTS

LORD CHATHAM AND THE WHIG OPPOSITION

1766-1771

CHAPTER I

THE FORMATION OF CHATHAM'S ADMINISTRATION

THE fall of the first Rockingham ministry in July, 1766, brings to an end a well-defined period in the constitutional struggle of George III.'s reign. Barely six years had elapsed since the king had come to the throne, an untried and inexperienced boy, yet determined to regain for the monarchy the influence which it had lost during the reigns of the first two Hanoverian monarchs. It was never his intention to bring about a revolution in the government or to trample under foot the privileges acquired by the nation in its contest with the Stuarts; but he firmly believed, and with some justice, that the politicians, who had driven James II. from the throne and excluded his son from the succession, had never intended to reduce the kingship to a condition of subservience. The constitution had developed on other lines than those laid down by the statesmen responsible for the Revolution settlement; and the royal authority had been usurped by a narrow oligarchy which had taken advantage of a disputed succession and a foreign dynasty to acquire supremacy in the state. The whigs had triumphed over the family which they had placed

upon the throne ; and when George III. succeeded
his grandfather, the royal power appeared to have
reached the very nadir of its fortunes. With some
bitterness, and no little truth, George II. had once
declared that " ministers were kings in this country,"
and the cry was wrung from him by bitter experience.
Towards the close of his reign he discovered that he
was often obliged to take his advisers at the dictation
of the house of commons, and to give the sanction
of his name to a policy which he did not approve.
As long as the ministers enjoyed the confidence of
parliament they were able to prevail against the
court ; and George II. found much food for thought
in the contemplation of the difference between the
theory and the practice of the English constitution.
He informed Lord Waldegrave that " we were, indeed,
a very extraordinary people, continually talking of
our constitution, laws and liberty.   That as to our
constitution, he allowed it to be a good one, and
defied any man to produce a single instance wherein
he had exceeded his proper limits. That he never
meant to screen or protect any servant who had
done amiss ; but still he had a right to chuse
those who were to serve him, though, at present,
so far from having an option, he was not even
allowed a negative." [1]

It was left for George III. to undertake the task
of avenging his grandfather, and to recover for the
crown the authority of which it had been deprived.
For this work he had been trained by his mother,
the dowager Princess of Wales, and her friend and
counsellor, Lord Bute. According to the constitutional doctrines, in which he had been reared, an
English king, though obliged to rule in accordance

[1] Lord Waldegrave's Memoirs (1821), pp. 132-133.

with the national will, had never been intended to become the puppet of the party predominant in parliament. It was the duty of the sovereign to lead rather than to follow, and the functions of the house of commons were those of a guardian, not those of a dictator. It was for the king to choose his own advisers ; and it was incumbent upon parliament to support the ministers of the crown, unless they were guilty of a breach of the law or proved themselves so incompetent as to render their removal a matter of urgent necessity. George III. was not slow to imbibe these tenets, and ascended the throne with a fully formed determination to rescue the royal prerogative from the decay into which it had fallen. He was resolved to govern as well as to reign, and he had not been king many days before his advisers discovered that they were intended to be servants of the crown in something more than name. For the first time, since the accession of the Hanoverian dynasty, the supremacy of the whig party seemed in danger of destruction ; and when all men thought that the power of the crown had passed away, never to revive, the court once more became the spring and centre of political life.

That there should be a reaction against the whig rule is not surprising. Possessed of the charm of youth, dignified in bearing, and graceful in manner,[1] George III. was more likely to be the subject of loyal adoration than his grandfather who had never succeeded in winning the affection of the nation whose welfare, nevertheless, he sincerely sought. The first

---

[1] " The young king," wrote Horace Walpole, " you may trust me, who am not apt to be enamoured with royalty, gives all the indication imaginable of being amiable. His person is tall and full of dignity ; his countenance florid and good-natured ; [his manner graceful and obliging." Walpole's Letters, 4, 449-452.

of his family to be born and bred in this country, the young king could claim to be an Englishman, if not by birth, at least by education ; and the nation, which had long been weary of the undisguised preference of its rulers for their German dominions, welcomed with enthusiasm a sovereign who was at least a master of the tongue of his subjects. The political value of the outburst of loyalty, which usually greets a new occupant of the throne, must not, however, be exaggerated ; and it is perhaps of greater moment that the king could count upon a certain measure of interested support for his design of restoring the royal prerogative. Recruits for the cause were likely to be forthcoming from those who, under the whig domination, had either been driven from office or forced to spend the best years of their lives in the wilderness of opposition. Men of this type were ready enough to rally round the throne in hope of profit or revenge ; whilst there were not a few who, actuated by a purer motive, regarded the subservience of the crown to one political faction as a gross perversion of the English constitution. The supremacy of the whig party had been too oppressive to pass unchallenged ; and Bolingbroke, by his famous pamphlet, " The Idea of a Patriot King," had prepared the way for George III. It is fashionable to decry Bolingbroke's political philosophy, and to depict him as the baffled adventurer seeking to poison the sources of political life; but in the arguments which he advanced, in the most famous of his works, there is more truth and cogency than has often been allowed. It is impossible to deny the justice of his denunciations of the political morality of the age ; and when he called upon the monarchy to rescue the country from the slough of corruption into which it had fallen, it was not with the intention of restoring the absolutism of the Stuarts, but of bringing about an alliance between the crown and the nation, in order to effect the downfall of an immoral system of government. An experienced controversialist and a most attractive writer, Bolingbroke was able to persuade by the lucidity of his argument and the grace of his style; and when George III. came to the throne, men had been taught to expect salvation from the court, and were not surprised to find that their new ruler was disinclined to be content with that narrow sphere of influence to which his predecessor had been restricted.[1]

Yet, when every allowance has been made for favouring circumstances, it remains true that George III.'s initial efforts were rewarded with a far greater degree of success than could possibly have been anticipated by the most optimistic partisans of the royal prerogative. Contemporaries were astonished at the ease with which the youthful sovereign overcame obstacles which had proved too formidable for his more experienced predecessor. His campaign against the whig oligarchy was naturally not unchequered by disaster, and at times he found himself obliged to undergo humiliations which his grandfather had never known; but this is a lot common to those who embark upon novel and dangerous ventures, and the checks which he encountered never caused him to waver in his purpose. His persistence was rewarded with victory. The famous coalition ministry of Pitt and Newcastle, which had raised England to a pinnacle of glory, not attained since the days when the genius of Marlborough had humbled

---

[1] It is intimated," wrote Horace Walpole, three days after the death of George II., " that he means to employ the same ministers, but with reserve to himself of more authority than has lately been in fashion." Walpole's Letters, 4, 444-447.

the pride of the proudest of French kings, fell before
the first assaults of the boy upon the throne. A
victory over such opponents, so early in the reign,
could not but redound to the credit of the crown ;
for Pitt was by far the most popular statesman of the
day, and Newcastle enjoyed a well-deserved reputation
for being one of the most successful of party managers.
Thus it was against experienced veterans that the
king gained his first triumph, and the attack had not
been made merely to demonstrate the strength of the
royal authority. From the day that he succeeded
his grandfather, the king had intended that his
favourite, the Earl of Bute, should be the first
minister ; and when Newcastle was driven to resign
in the spring of 1762, Bute was chosen to succeed
him as first lord of the treasury.

No more striking testimony could have been given
to the new order inaugurated by George III. than the
rapid rise of Lord Bute to high office in the state.
Regarded as an alien by the whig oligarchy which
had hitherto enjoyed a monopoly of power, distasteful,
both as a Scotchman and a friend of the king, to a
nation which has never loved its northern neighbours
and has always been opposed to royal favourites,
Bute rose to supremacy in the cabinet solely through
the influence of the crown. He had few qualifications for administrative office, being neither a ready
debater nor a far-sighted statesman ; and although
his political ability has been unduly depreciated, his
warmest admirers have never contended that it was
of such a character as to justify his meteoric rise to
power. Conscious of his own defects, aware of his
deficiencies in the art of managing men, he shrank
from political responsibility ; and it is to his credit
as a man, if not as a statesman, that it was only

genuine, if mistaken, affection for the king, his master and pupil, that led him to essay a task for which he knew himself to be intellectually unfit. With but a scanty personal following in parliament, the mark for the hatred of the people who regarded him as a Scotch adventurer preying upon the wealth of England, Bute was emphatically the king's minister, solely dependent upon the royal favour.[1] In the reign of George II., Carteret, one of the ablest men in an age when the standard of ability was high, had been unable to maintain himself in office, though warmly supported by the court ; but where George II. had failed, his youthful successor triumphed. The influence of the crown proved sufficient to uphold Bute against attacks in parliament and the virulent onslaught of the opposition press ; and he was able to conduct a difficult and tortuous negotiation with France, which resulted in the conclusion of peace with that country and the withdrawal of England from the Seven Years war.

He has been, indeed, most adversely criticised for conceding, in his anxiety for peace, more favourable terms to France than the course of the war justified ; and not a few historians have been blinded, by their dislike of his policy, to the difficulties of the task which he accomplished. It may be that it might have been better for England if he had never taken office, but he at least succeeded in attaining the goal which he sought, in spite of obstacles which at times threatened to prove insuperable. Without any

[1] As is well known, George III., on the very first day of his reign, offered to make Bute secretary of state ; and when, six months later, the royal favourite accepted that office, it was only with the very greatest reluctance. " Each fond wish of my heart," he informed the king, " crys out against this important change, but duty and gratitude condemns one to the trial. I make it then, but not without violent emotions and unpleasant forebodings." Add. MS., 36797, f. 47.

previous experience of administrative life, intensely
unpopular with the nation, and often obliged to meet
and overcome the attacks of his colleagues in the
cabinet, Bute did not purchase his success cheaply ;
but, if the conclusion of the Peace of Paris testifies
to the perseverance of the servant, it equally bears
witness to the influence of the master. Deprived of
the favour and confidence of the crown, the minister
would have quickly fallen a prey to his many enemies ;
and when he retired in the spring of 1763, it was not
because he was unable to command a majority in the
house of commons, but because his work was done.
He had taken office in order to extricate the country
from an exhausting conflict, and, having attained
his end, he laid down the distasteful burden of
administration.

His place at the treasury was taken by George
Grenville who resembled him in the particular of
being neither the choice of parliament nor of the
nation, but of the king. Politicians, however, even
when they sit on thrones, are often compelled to do
what they can rather than what they would ; and
it was not without serious misgivings that George III.
had selected Grenville as Bute's successor. Tenacious
of power, so lately acquired, the king was resolved not
to fall back into the condition of servitude from which
he had but just emerged ; and, from the moment that
he took office, the new first minister discovered that
he was expected to be obedient to the court which
had created him. His freedom in the construction
of his own cabinet was seriously restricted, and in
Lord Shelburne he was given a colleague whom he
profoundly distrusted and disliked. Moreover, there
was a wide-spread, and by no means unfounded, belief
that Bute, though he had retired from the ministry,

intended to remain the confidential adviser of the crown; and that, if Grenville was the actor on the stage, the favourite was the prompter in the wings. Unconsidered by the nation which regarded him as a pawn in the royal game, and obliged to depend in the house of commons upon a majority supplied him by the court, Grenville was provided with the trappings but denied the substance of power. Uninspired by that personal affection for the king, which had caused Bute to seek no greater happiness than the execution of his master's will, and disinclined by disposition to adopt a deferential or even a conciliatory attitude, he was ill-adapted to acquiesce in a condition of gilded servitude; and it is not surprising that friction soon arose between the crown and the minister. If he had incurred the royal hostility by espousing a popular cause, much would have been forgiven him, and he might have come down in history surrounded with the glory given to those who fail in a noble endeavour; but, unfortunately for his good fame, Grenville was almost as objectionable to the nation as he was to the king. It had once been his wish to become Speaker of the house of commons, and it was in an evil moment for his reputation that he consented to forswear his ambition. Few men were more deeply versed in parliamentary law or more punctual and methodical in the despatch of business; but the very qualities, which would have enabled him to preside with distinction over the debates of the lower house, militated against his success as a statesman. Stiff and unbending in demeanour, a tedious debater, afflicted with a pedantry which encouraged him to regard precedent and law as above reason and good sense, and lavishing upon details a wealth of care and attention which rendered him oblivious to wider and more

important issues, Grenville was not fitted to be the
ruler of a great country, and could never hope to
acquire the approval of either the king or the nation.[1]
No sooner had he taken office than his fall was prophesied ; and, if he continued in power for more than
two years, it was not by reason of his parliamentary
strength or his popularity with the country, but on
account of the difficulty experienced by the king in
finding a suitable successor. Grenville was, indeed,
intolerable, but he was not dangerous ; and George III.
preferred to endure discomfort rather than run the
risk of diminishing his recently acquired authority.

Thus, though saddled with a servant of whom
he would have willingly been rid, the king could
legitimately boast of the success he had achieved. It
was now abundantly clear that, whereas in the past
ministers had been able to coerce the court, they were
now its dependents. The centre of power had been
shifted from the cabinet to the palace ; and the
change had been effected largely by an adroit and
systematic use of the royal patronage. It is difficult
to exaggerate the extent of the resources of bribery
and corruption which remained to the crown in the
eighteenth century, or the frankness with which
politicians of the time were wont to demand a more
substantial reward for their services than the gratitude of the country. It was not only that the
episcopal bench was crowded with men who had
earned promotion by services not strictly ecclesiastical,
and that many a skilful time-server was rewarded by
a place among the peers of England : there were
numberless posts at court which constantly brought

---

[1] Dr Johnson, with his usual sturdy common sense, remarked of Grenville
that " he had powers not universally possessed : could he have enforced payment of the Manilla ransom, *he could have counted it.*"

their holders into close contact with the fount of bounty, and innumerable sinecure places which, once secured, dispensed their happy possessors from the necessity of earning an honest livelihood. Nor was it only by places and offices that adherents in parliament could be purchased : men, who would have been seriously offended if their honesty had been impugned, thought nothing of accepting a money bribe for a vote given in parliament ; and it was not infrequent for a ministry, when closely pressed, to purchase a majority in hard cash.[1] Nor was this torrent of corruption confined within the walls of parliament ; for elections were flagrantly and openly corrupt. A certain proportion of the members of the lower house sat for treasury boroughs, so called because they always elected the nominees of the government ; and in Cornwall, which returned forty-four representatives, and was notorious for electioneering corruption, the influence of the crown was particularly strong. By the end of the century nearly half the members of the house of commons were appointed by private patrons,[2] and borough owners were accustomed to treat their right of nomination as a species of property, saleable to the highest bidder.

Thus it was not difficult for George III., if he was prepared to soil his hands by participation in a disgusting business, to secure a house of commons obedient to his will. He had but to proclaim that the avenue of promotion was obedience to the court, to dispense the royal patronage amongst those who

[1] Thus when during Walpole's administration a proposal was made to settle an income of one hundred thousand pounds upon Frederick, Prince of Wales, it was reported that more money was expended to defeat the motion than "would have answered the demand made for the prince." Hist. MSS. Comm. Carlisle MSS., pp. 178, 179.

[2] Porritt's *The Unreformed House of Commons*, i. 310, 311.

distinguished themselves by their readiness to support the crown, to traffic in boroughs like a huckster, and to dispense the secret service fund himself instead of allowing it to be manipulated by his ministers, and the eager crew of placemen would quickly rally round the monarchy. Neither genius nor statesmanship was required for the formation of a parliamentary party pledged to support any administration as long as it was approved at court ; and the cause for surprise is not that a youth upon the throne should have been able with so little difficulty to attain his end, but that his predecessors should have permitted such a sensible declension in the royal authority. The riddle, however, is not difficult of solution. Both George II. and his father were too little acquainted with English politics and too much attached to their German dominions, to play an active part in what was styled the management of the house of commons. Driven by fear of the tories, whom they suspected of sympathising with the exiled Stuarts, to give their confidence to one political party, the first two kings of the Hanoverian line, in order to safeguard themselves against the jacobites, undermined the foundations of their own authority ; and it was left for George II. to discover that the whigs had used the confidence of the crown to establish a hold upon parliament and secure themselves against the attacks of either the court or the nation. Permitted by the king to dispense the royal patronage, to purchase rotten boroughs, and to buy votes in parliament, the whig ministers had quickly overshadowed the monarchy. Rapacious placemen, intent upon nothing but to keep what they had got, and to acquire more if they could, quickly perceived the drift of events and followed the ministry and not the king ; and George II., at the close of his reign, was mortified to find that he had sold himself into slavery to a few whig nobles who ruled the country in his name.

The most successful of these whig leaders, who had thus reduced the monarchy to subjection, was, undoubtedly, Thomas Pelham-Holles, Duke of Newcastle. An important territorial magnate, descended through his father from an ancient Sussex family, and through his mother from the Earls of Clare, Newcastle was born to a great political position, and, espousing the whig cause, quickly rose to high office in the state. Few English statesmen have enjoyed a more prolonged or less interrupted tenure of political power ; but with posterity he has paid dearly enough for his success, his name having become a byword for inefficient administration and wholesale corruption. Historians have depicted him in graphic language as little better than a dotard who, by dint of a certain low cunning and great wealth, rose to political eminence ; and his contemporaries never wearied of enlarging upon his lack of dignity, his childish inconsequence, his colossal ignorance, and his absurd jealousies. No one would assert that he was in any way a great statesman or deny his many serious limitations. He was often unduly suspicious of his closest and most trusted friends, and was wont to take offence at imaginary slights ; but the greatest statesmen are not without shortcomings, and Newcastle has suffered from being judged by whig historians who have chosen to consider him a disgrace to their party. His incapacity as an administrator has probably been exaggerated, and his unremitting industry, in the discharge of what he believed to be the business of the state, has not received the recognition it deserves. Nor was he without a certain measure of political insight. Long before Burke had preached the necessity of a party system, Newcastle had practised the same doctrine, devoting all his energy to the formation of a strong personal following in both houses of parliament. He understood, far better than many of his contemporaries, that the natural outcome of the Revolution settlement was the dependence of ministers upon parliament rather than upon the crown, and he acted accordingly. He realised that systematic organisation was the secret of political success, and that, unless ministers were able to count with confidence upon the support of the house of commons, they would inevitably tend to fall into submission to the court. Such was his contribution to the practical philosophy of politics ; and, if not the first, he was by far the most successful of party managers. No man was more alive to the value of the loaves and fishes of public life ; and he dispensed them with a lavish, though discriminating, hand. Possessed of estates in nine counties, and the owner of nearly the whole of Nottinghamshire, he was able to control elections over the length and breadth of England ; and few men were more adept in the art of borough-mongering or more eager and persistent in the purchase of adherents.[1] The episcopal bench was crowded with his nominees,[2] and, very often, a wealthy peer and a humble exciseman found themselves strangely connected by a common bond of obligation

---

[1] For a most interesting account of the Duke of Newcastle's electioneering methods see an article by Mr Basil Williams in the *English Historical Review*, entitled " The Duke of Newcastle and the Election of 1734." Vol. xii. pp. 448 ff.

[2] At his first levee, after his fall from office in 1762, only one bishop was present, though in the days of his greatness they had been conspicuous by the regularity of their attendance. When this marked abstention was pointed out to Newcastle, he wittily declared that " bishops, like other men, are apt to forget their Maker."

to the great whig duke.   In return for what he gave, he only asked that the recipients of his bounty should answer to the call of the party and support him in parliament ; and the politicians of the day were not averse to enriching themselves upon such easy terms. Nor was Newcastle left unrewarded for his prescience and industry, for both George II. and William Pitt had occasion to regret the unbounded influence which the duke had been allowed to acquire over the representatives of the nation.

Yet, impressive as was the edifice which Newcastle had reared, its foundations were of sand. He had gained a parliamentary following, not by the ability of his statesmanship or the force of· his personality, but by bribery and corruption ; and was not so much the leader of a party as the captain of a band of mercenaries.   His followers had no common belief, no common political principles, and if they remained faithful to him, it was because they hoped to profit by their loyalty.   Deprived of the right of dispensing the royal patronage, Newcastle would, indeed, be a shorn Samson ; and no sooner had George III. ascended the throne than the duke discovered the insecurity of the foundations upon which his power rested. The placemen, who had fawned upon him in the days of his greatness, now turned to the court, and were as eager to follow the king as they had been in the past to follow the minister. Parliament, which remained as corrupt as before, was now tied by gold chains about the throne ; and, under normal conditions, the king had no call to fear the opposition of the house of commons.   To excuse the change, that had thus been effected, there was much talk of the usurpation of oligarchy, and of the king's right to remunerate his servants ; but the phrases of courtiers and political philosophers were but a scanty veil to conceal the substantial truth that there had been something little short of a constitutional revolution, the significance of which could not be measured by the ease with which it had been effected. No longer could parliament be considered an effective check upon the despotic tendencies of the crown, since the astute policy of George III. had rendered the Bill of Rights and the Act of Settlement, which had been framed with the intention of subjecting the monarchy to the national will, almost constitutionally valueless. Parliament, which had previously been the puppet of the whig nobility, now became the slave of the court. By preying upon the weakness of mankind, and cynically indifferent to the morality of public life, George III. had conquered where better and more scrupulous men might have failed; and, though he may be guiltless of the remark, with which he is credited, that " we must call in bad men to govern bad men," the epigram is a true description of his contribution to the art of government. He had defeated Newcastle with his own weapons, the boasted strength of the whig party had crumbled away into dust; and the royal authority, no longer obscured by the clouds of faction, shone forth in undiminished splendour.

Yet, all men were not blind or indifferent to the policy pursued by the court, and if many were regardless of what was happening or only thought to make use of it to promote their own interests, there was one at least who understood that the constitution was confronted by a danger as great as any as had threatened to overwhelm it in the previous century. It was he who had suffered most by the change. Though defeated, Newcastle remained true to the principles he had professed when in power; and, in opposition, as in place, constituted himself the champion of the party system so deftly attacked by the court. Though it was loudly and repeatedly proclaimed that the country would never know good government until ministers were selected, not on account of their political connections or their following in parliament, but by reason of their capacity for administration, Newcastle was content to adhere to the doctrines which he had learnt in his youth, and practised with so much effect ; and no sooner had he been driven from office than he set to work to form an opposition party to the court, recruiting his followers from the scanty few who were not prepared to sacrifice every conviction on the altar of their own advancement. This little band, which came to be known by the name of the Rockingham whigs, but of which Newcastle was the founder, fought for a constitutional principle which seemed in the way of becoming obsolete. Instead of administrations, lacking in unity, composed of men of widely different political opinions and un-accustomed to work together, Newcastle and his supporters believed that a really efficient government should be representative of one party in the state, and dependent, not upon the crown, but upon its own adherents in parliament. It is true that their conception of a political party was far narrower and more oligarchic than would be tolerated at the present day, and, though willing enough to have the nation on their side, they had little thought of widening the confined aristocratic circle in which they habitually moved ; but it should be remembered that this tendency to exclusiveness was in accordance with contemporary opinion which regarded government as an essentially aristocratic art, and that the vices incidental to oligarchy were blended with real political virtues.

If they can be accused of attempting to wrest power from the crown in order to acquire it for themselves, it ought not to be forgotten that they were contending for a system of government which has become an essential element of parliamentary life. In an age when open war was declared upon the party system, they defended it ; and their efforts have received scanty recognition. It is too often overlooked that if George III. was fighting for a principle, so were his opponents. It was a clash of differing and opposite constitutional ideals, a new phase of the old struggle between the monarchy and the nation.

The contest may be said to have begun in the autumn of 1762, when the preliminaries of peace with France were submitted to parliament and were attacked by Newcastle's recently formed opposition party. The challenge, thus thrown down, was quickly taken up by the court, and the men, who had dared to oppose the peace which Bute and the king approved, were punished for their audacity. Newcastle was deprived of his lord lieutenancies, and a political persecution set on foot, expressly designed to stifle the opposition in its birth. The exercise of the parliamentary function of criticism was treated as a traitorous insurrection against the crown ; and the persecution, which would have been sufficiently iniquitous if confined to those who had taken an active part in opposing the peace, was rendered additionally shameful by being extended to humble dependents of the great whig leaders. Neither great nor small were spared, and holders of small places under government were driven from their employments for no other offence than that they had received their preferment from the men who had dared to rebel against the court. Yet the politicians, who had had the courage to embark upon such a dangerous enterprise, were not to be turned aside by the first disaster ; and for three years Newcastle marshalled, if he did not lead, the forces of opposition to the crown. His allies, though numerically insignificant, were worthy of the cause they had espoused, for among them are to be found some of the most honourable and distinguished statesmen of the day. William Cavendish, fourth Duke of Devonshire, and Philip Yorke, first Earl of Hardwicke, had both played for many years a leading part in the world of politics, and it was no slight blow to George III. that they refused to abjure their principles and enlist under his banner. But, valuable as their services might have been to the opposition in the constitutional struggle, for Devonshire was deservedly renowned for his probity, and Hardwicke justly famous for his extensive legal learning, it was hardly likely, seeing that they were both well advanced in years when George III. ascended the throne, that they would long be able to endure the heat and burden of the battle. Both were taken by death in the year 1764, and the loss, though great, was not unexpected. The future of the party lay with its younger members and its more recent recruits, with those who had never known the whig cause in the days of its greatness, but were prepared to fight for it in the hour of disaster. Youth is the season of heroic opposition and high endeavour, and it is not surprising that many young nobles, removed by their wealth and their social position from the temptation of succumbing to the insidious influence of the crown, elected to join Newcastle in his arduous campaign.

The most important and influential of these allies were the Duke of Grafton and the Marquis of Rockingham. Grafton, very largely because at a later date he was unfortunate enough to incur the vitriolic hatred of Junius, has acquired an evil reputation both as a man and as a politician. As generally depicted, the licentiousness of his private life was only exceeded by his incapacity as a statesman ; and his most partial critics would hardly deny that his defects were many and conspicuous. Yet, at the beginning of his career, he seemed likely to win a name for disinterested patriotism and purity of motive. Careless of the favour of the court, placing his principles above his own advantage, he enlisted under Newcastle's banner, and embarked upon a course of opposition ; but time was to prove him lacking in stability of purpose, and the hopes, which had been based upon his early achievements, were never to find fulfilment. If something far better than the abandoned voluptuary and tyrannical debauchee represented by Junius, his career as a statesman gave sufficient colour to the bitterest charges to render them plausible. Ill-fitted for public life, and condemned to pass through a fiery ordeal which would have taxed the virtue of far better men, Grafton suffered the fate of those who shoulder a burden too heavy for them to bear. Cursed by such anxiety to please as to prefer to do wrong rather than give offence, furnished with few settled convictions, and, though anxious to do his duty, not sufficiently clear sighted to recognise where the path of duty lay, he became a piece of wreckage upon the waste of waters, a prey to the winds and waves of time. He passes down to the political hell by the road of good intentions, and the tragedy of his fall is rendered all the greater by the promise of his beginning.

A happier fate befell the young Marquis of Rockingham who ultimately became the leader of the party which Newcastle had created. Like Grafton,

Rockingham shared many of the tastes of the young aristocrat of the period, and was wont to be at New-market when he ought to have been at the house of lords ; but, though sometimes inattentive to business, he never wavered in his adherence to the whig cause, and was content to spend the greater part of his life in leading a forlorn hope. Wealthy, and acquiring no little distinction from being the only marquis in the English peerage, Rockingham's rise to political eminence was much assisted by his birth and affluence ; but it would be a serious error to dismiss him as an aristocratic dilettante in public life. With every temptation to spend the useless and often vicious life of the fashionable young man of his day, he fought the good fight against the crown, and carried on the work which Newcastle had begun. Scorning the meaner side of public life, so attractive to many of his contemporaries, sincerely desirous of promoting the welfare of the country, and conscientiously convinced of the truth of the constitutional ideals for which he fought, there is much to admire in his career ; but the charm of his private life, and the many attractive traits in his character, cannot obscure the truth that he had many defects as a statesman, and was but ill-fitted to accomplish the task which he had so heroically undertaken. He was not cast by nature to endure the heat and burden of a constitutional struggle, and, in a more democratic age, it is unlikely that he would have ever emerged from comparative political ob-scurity. Shy, and of a retiring disposition, rarely taking part in debate, and always reluctant to stand in the fore of the battle, Rockingham could win re-spect, but was unable to inspire either fear or admira-tion. The courage, which steeled him to persevere in a seemingly hopeless contest, was not always united with the wisdom to select the best mode of attack, or the insight which would have enabled him to see the weak points in his adversary's armour. Though in much superior to Newcastle, he was infinitely beneath him as a party manager ; and when the old duke died in 1768, the whig party suffered a greater loss than has often been admitted. Youth is not inclined to overrate the value of the experience of age ; and, like many a young man, Rockingham was disposed to minimise the dangers which beset his path, and was, therefore, consequently sometimes guilty of serious blunders and tactical mistakes. His greatest admirers have been forced to allow that as a leader he was often singularly ineffective ; and that, though the end at which he aimed was generally right, the methods he pursued were sometimes open to criticism. Nor were his political associates of such eminence as to compensate for the shortcomings of their leader. The Duke of Portland, Sir William Meredith, Sir George Savile, and William Dowdeswell never emerged from the second rank of politicians in which nature had placed them ; and, if in Edmund Burke the party was given a genius of the first order, that great Irishman did not take his seat in parliament until the year 1766, and was too accustomed to dwell in the altitudes of the intellect to be really successful in the rude warfare of parliamentary life.

Thus the opposition, though numbering many bearers of distinguished names, and including much virtue and gallantry in its midst, was not over rich in political sagacity ; and could ill afford to lose the wise counsels of a Hardwicke or a Devonshire. Yet for three years it maintained the parliamentary struggle against Bute and Grenville, championing causes which it hoped would prove popular, and seeking to defend the interests of the nation against a house of commons which had sold itself to the court. The preliminaries of peace with France, the cyder tax, and the use of general warrants were attacked, while Wilkes, that rather sordid champion of freedom, was defended by men who had nothing in common with him save hostility to the personal influence of the crown. Yet the reward of all these efforts was failure, and by the summer of 1765 the party of opposition was weaker than it had ever been before. Defeat following upon defeat had extinguished hope, and even Newcastle gave way to despair, and retired for a short time from the fray. The ranks of the party had been thinned by death and by the desertion which is the inevitable accompaniment of a failing cause, and Charles Townshend was probably not the only member of the band to reflect that " he was a younger brother, and if nothing was to be made out of opposition, or no active measures pursued, he would lie by this summer, and consider himself at liberty to take what part would be most convenient to him." [1]

The causes of the failure are not far to seek. As long as bribery and corruption continued, as long as boroughs were bought and sold, and parliament was crowded with placemen who could be deprived of their livelihood at the royal will, an opposition party was at a very serious disadvantage. Allowing for the political morality of the day, it is little wonder that the bribes and offices, dispensed by the court, proved too tempting for the easy virtue of men who regarded a political career as an easy and expeditious way of filling pockets emptied at Arthur's or White's; and, although reason and good sense were more often than not to be found on the side of the enemies of the crown,

[1] Add. MS., 35361, f. 95.

the government had little cause to fear the force of argument as long as it could count with confidence upon the support of the solid phalanx of placemen. Yet, true as it is that Newcastle and his followers were fighting with weapons of straw against arms of iron, to attribute the success of the ministry solely to the power of the purse, would be to fall into the mistake of explaining by a single cause an event which, indeed, had several. Due account must be taken of the often neglected fact that a systematic opposition to the administration was an irregular and novel feature of the constitutional life of the period. Political traditions die hard, and it was still very generally held that it was in accordance with the best interests of the nation to promote, rather than to hinder, the task of government. To thwart the ministers at every turn, to oppose their measures for no better reason than that they proposed them, to subject them to an incessant shower of criticism, was regarded as playing into the hands of the enemies of England, and as a blameworthy indulgence in that spirit of faction which renders all good government impossible. Thus those who attacked the court in the early years of the reign of George III. endured all the disabilities attaching to constitutional pioneers. The cause for which they fought was destined ultimately to triumph, and an opposition party was to become an indispensable element in the parliamentary life of the country ; but they were not to reap the fruits of their labours, and were compelled to endure the burden of misrepresentation.

Though fully aware of the difficulties of the path which they had elected to tread, the whig leaders had not been without hope that victory might yet be theirs. Recent history had shown that it was sometimes possible for the opposition to carry the day against the court and the ministry. Sir Robert Walpole who, whatever his faults as a politician, cannot be charged with timidity, had been obliged to abandon the excise bill on account of the parliamentary attack upon it, and had been induced by the popular outcry to make war upon Spain against his will and his own better judgment. Moreover, the same opponents, who had induced him to abandon his much cherished policy of peace, succeeded, a few years later, in driving him from office by depriving him of his majority in the house of commons. Historians, rightly impressed by Walpole's sagacity and the recklessness of the opposition party, have dwelt too much upon the enlightened policy of the minister and too little upon the insight of his enemies. Carteret and Pulteney, Walpole's leading adversaries, conquered because they deserved to conquer ; and, though their cause was evil, their skill was great. Understanding the conditions under which the game of politics was played in their day, aware that it was hopeless to expect to prevail by force of argument in a parliament which had sold itself to the government, they had sought to champion causes likely to be popular with the country, and to appeal from an unrepresentative house of commons to the nation at large. Caring little for truth, only anxious to create a public opinion antagonistic to the administration, they used the press to spread their own opinions and to misrepresent those of the ministers. They succeeded in working the country up into a frenzied state of excitement over the excise bill which was represented as an insidious attack upon the cherished liberties of Englishmen, and they did not a little to spread the cry for war with Spain throughout the land. For so doing they may, indeed, be justly blamed, but it would be unfair to deny that they were wise in their generation. If they can be accused of being regardless of the true interests of the country, and of playing, for their own selfish purposes, upon the ignorance of the mob, they at least paid homage to the force of public opinion, and encouraged the belief that the nation is the ultimate court of appeal. They saw that when popular excitement ran high and the conviction spread that the ministers were guilty of inefficiency, if not of something worse, the political system of the day, based as it was on the maxim that all men were to be bought, was apt to suffer a complete collapse. Members of parliament, for once with the fear of their constituents before their eyes, would refuse to sell their votes to an unpopular government, and the opposition party, with an infuriated country behind it, would rise at a bound from insignificance to power. Public opinion was a rare and intermittent force in the politics of the eighteenth century, but its existence is testified by the fall of Walpole in 1742, and Newcastle's similar fate fourteen years later.

It may well be asked why public opinion did not come to the aid of the whigs in their contest with George III., for it would be generally admitted that they were far more deserving of such assistance than Walpole's opponents. It is certain that, in the early years of the reign at least, they advocated a policy more in accordance with the wishes of the people than the measures pursued by the king and his advisers. The peace, which they opposed, was intensely disliked by the populace who believed that a golden opportunity had been missed of crushing for ever England's traditional enemy ; and Wilkes, whom the opposition vainly sought to defend against the animosity of

George III. and Grenville, was the object of a popular admiration which he was too adroit not to use and too clever not to despise. Moreover, the cyder tax threatened to rival the excise bill in the outcry which it evoked ; and yet, in spite of these many advantages, Newcastle and his friends signally failed to win the country to their side. The applause and affection of the people were given, not to them, but to William Pitt who consistently declined to throw in his lot with the party, with which he had much in common, and which sorely needed his help.

Few statesmen have stood higher in popular favour than William Pitt at the accession of George III. ; and that he fully deserved the almost unique position he had won in the affections of his people is shown by the agreement between the judgment of contemporaries and the verdict of history. That shrewd, if cynical, critic of mankind, Frederick the Great, is reported to have said that England had been long in travail but had at last brought forth a man ; and the remark aptly sums up the impression created by the appearance of Pitt upon the stage of European and domestic politics. In an age when public life was marred by rapacity and self-seeking, when ideals had vanished, and enthusiasm was decried, Pitt arose to breathe a new spirit into a nation dying of inanition. His greatest achievement was not the conquest of the new world, but the regeneration of England from a cynical indifference to every true and inspiring impulse. He has been well termed the Wesley of the political world, and if his burning sense of patriotism, more akin to ancient than to modern times, was sometimes tinged with the spirit of conquest, if he was often overbearing towards his colleagues, and lacking in sympathy for those who were not in entire agreement with him, these faults may be forgiven to one who did so much for the country whose interests he always had at heart. At the moment of peril, when England, just entering upon a war with France, seemed likely to succumb to her ancient enemy, Pitt, taking upon himself the burden of government, infused an energy and zeal into the administration, astonishing to a people who had come to expect anything of its rulers except enthusiasm and efficiency. Brooking no opposition, dominating alike the cabinet and the house of commons, and intent upon the overthrow of that Bourbon power which barred the road to English supremacy in the New World and the East, Pitt, by the activity and enterprise with which he carried on a world-waged conflict, gained for himself the admiration of every English patriot and for his country the envy of Europe. Canada was conquered, the French power in India overthrown, and news of English successes were coming from all quarters of the world when George III. ascended the throne. Every fresh battle won, and every new piece of territory acquired for the English crown, served to swell the reputation of the great commoner, as Pitt was affectionately styled. He had once proudly boasted that he alone could save the country, and he had more than fulfilled the pledge; and the nation, grateful for what he had done, and regarding him as the only statesman worthy to be entrusted with the national destinies, placed him upon a pedestal, and fell down and worshipped him.

It was impossible that such a man, legitimately proud of the success he had achieved, and strong in the support of the people, should find it easy to work in harmony with a young king determined to play an active part in politics; and George III. had not been a year upon the throne when Pitt was driven into resignation. Great was the shock of his fall to the nation, convinced that he was the only statesman worthy of a place in the cabinet ; and in the city, the stronghold of Pitt's influence, the storm ran high against the court. It was in vain that the king sought to appease the national indignation and discredit the national hero, by conferring a pension upon Pitt and a peerage upon his wife. Though the unworthy trick had a temporary success, a few words from the fallen statesman sufficed to still the tempest which was rising against him, and to re-establish the people in their idolatry. Though out of office, he was more powerful than any minister ; and, if he had chosen to go into opposition, the early years of the reign of George III. might have been a record of the king's failure instead of his success. Few men have been more favourably placed for leading a parliamentary attack ; and what had been done by Carteret and Pulteney against Walpole, might have been effected far more easily by Pitt against Bute and Grenville. It would have been vain for the ministers to promise offices and dispense bribes if the great commoner had been leading the forces against them ; and, with the keen eye of an experienced party manager, Newcastle read the political situation aright. No sooner had the duke declared himself an enemy of the court, than he perceived the necessity of enlisting the services of Pitt at all cost. Led by the most popular statesman of the day, the Rockingham Whigs could not be denounced as an aristocratic clique ; but, if he stood aloof, there was scant hope that their efforts would receive the approval of the nation. And there was much to induce Pitt to throw in his lot with the men who were so anxious to salute him as their leader.

Like them he believed that Bute was intellectually unfit for high office in the state, and he never ceased to denounce that peace with France, which they had been so cruelly punished for opposing. It is true that on certain questions there was not complete agreement between him and Newcastle's followers, but the difference of opinion was certainly not so great as to render an alliance impossible. And yet, in spite of a harmony of ideas, greater than that which often prevails in a modern cabinet, Pitt, during these critical years, when the necessity of strengthening the attack upon the government was so urgent, claimed the liberty of a free lance, and resolutely declined to place himself at the head of the opposition party. Though at times when the parliamentary contest ran high, when vital constitutional questions, such as the use of general warrants, were under discussion, Pitt, excited by the lust of battle, would talk as though he had thrown his scruples to the wind, and was prepared to enrol himself as a regular member of the opposition, it was never long before he resumed his independent attitude, and blasted the hopes which his utterances had raised. By the autumn of 1764 it had become abundantly clear that he was not to be won, and even Newcastle, who had laboured more strenuously than any other member of the party to gain the indispensable ally, abandoned the quest as hopeless.

For his conduct during this period Pitt cannot escape censure. He stands convicted of having mis-read the signs of the time, and must be judged accordingly; but, though mistaken, his policy was not influenced by sordid or ignoble motives. It was not the fear of losing his pension, as Newcastle and Devonshire uncharitably believed,[1] nor any personal

---

[1] Add. MS., 32946, f. 317, f. 329.

dislike of Newcastle, that deterred him from going into opposition, but a fundamental difference of constitutional opinion.   The Rockingham whigs were the foremost champions of the party system so fiercely attacked by the court, and it was on this point that Pitt was in complete disagreement with them.   Though he had begun his political career as a reckless partisan, having been one of the foremost and most violent of Walpole's opponents, he had come to think of his earlier conduct with sorrow and regret, and to regard the party system as detrimental to the interests of the nation.   That ministers should be selected for the opinions they professed rather than for their ability to rule, and that the crown, in its choice of advisers, should be limited to the party which had a majority in the lower house, now appeared to him to be the negation of good government, and to place the comparatively trivial interests of a faction above the welfare of the state.   It was never his wish that the will of the king should override that of the nation, but, believing the test of good administration to be efficiency, he desired that ministers should be chosen irrespective of their political connections, and frankly avowed that he would proscribe no man, whether whig or tory, whom he thought likely to prove an able ruler.   " Men not measures " became his watchword, and the destruction of the party system his goal ; and thus a wide and unbridgeable gulf separated him from those who, with equal sincerity, believed that the party system was something more than a worthless relic of an age of faction, and that a disunited administration would be unlikely to exercise much influence in parliament or resist the pressure of a court.

It would be grossly unfair to dismiss Pitt's opinions

as idle and fanciful. Experience has shown that the system of party government, even as it is understood at the present day, is not free from serious and obvious defects, and the idea of making administrative capacity the only qualification for admission into office, has always proved irresistibly attractive to a certain type of mind. Statesmen, who are emphatically men of action, who are zealous for the promotion of good government, and desire to get things done, are naturally impatient of an arrangement by which men, in every way qualified, are excluded from office and second-rate politicians often entrusted with duties which they are incapable of discharging. Moreover, party government in the eighteenth century was open to even more serious objections, for a system, which practically restricted admission into the cabinet to the members of a few noble families, was hardly to be discriminated from government by an aristocracy. Few would deny that under the first two Hanoverian kings there was a real danger that the place of the monarchy would be taken by an oligarchy ; and, if Pitt had voiced his protest then, his appeal, though it might have fallen upon deaf ears, would have redounded to his political wisdom. But he was belated in his attack, and at the time he chose to repudiate the party system, the evil to be feared was, not the usurpation of oligarchy, but the restoration of the personal power of the crown. Without the organisation which the party system alone could give, the unreformed house of commons lay at the mercy of the occupant of the throne ; and, while Pitt believed himself to be preparing the way for sound administration, he was really undermining a bulwark against arbitrary power. The Rockingham Whigs, mistaken as they may have been in much, were at least fighting for a constitutional principle of great practical importance in their day, whereas Pitt, seduced by a train of reasoning which, whatever abstract validity it may have possessed, was out of place in the actual conditions of affairs, embraced the cause of the court, and tilted against a danger which had ceased to exist. It is true that Pitt and the king sought to obtain different ends, the former being desirous of ministerial efficiency, and the latter of ministerial servitude; but the means they adopted were identical, both being the declared enemies of the party system; and, widely as they differed, time was to bring about their union.

Six years, however, elapsed before this unhappy and disastrous alliance was concluded. For some time George III. lived in fear that he might have to face a coalition between Newcastle and Pitt; and it was not until June, 1765, that he fully grasped the political situation, and understood how groundless had been his anxiety. But, if slow to understand, he was quick to act, seeing how much would be gained if the most renowned and popular statesman of the day could be persuaded to enter the royal service. Pitt, as a minister, could hardly fail to reflect much credit upon the king who, having incurred no small odium by the promotion of Bute and the prosecution of Wilkes, might hope, by an alliance with the national hero, to acquire the trust of the nation. A speedy and decisive triumph might then be anticipated over the whig oligarchy which was attempting to enslave the monarchy; and, strong in the support of the nation, the king and the minister would be in a position to wage effective war upon the already discredited party system, and confer the blessing of good government upon a grateful people.

It was an attractive programme, and George III.

was not reluctant to rid himself of Grenville whom he had long found intolerable, and only endured lest by a change he might bring greater evils upon himself. For a time he wandered in the dark, carrying on negotiations with the Rockingham whigs and Pitt, whom he believed to be allies ; but his mistakes were not unprofitable, inasmuch as they enlightened him as to the actual political situation. Thus, in May, 1765, ignorant of the fundamental change which had come about in Pitt's opinions, he began a negotiation with that statesman and the Rockingham party ; and, although he failed to attain his end, he acquired information which was not without influence upon his future conduct. The negotiation was brought to an abrupt conclusion by Pitt declining to take office, and, probably, his refusal was dictated by an unwillingness to take his place at the head of an administration which, composed as it would be of the Rockingham whigs, would stand for that very party system which he had so definitely determined to destroy. This interpretation of Pitt's conduct is, at least, supported by the action of the king who, in the following month, made direct overtures to him, leaving Newcastle and his followers to fare as best they might. It is true that this negotiation was no more successful than that which had preceded it, but the responsibility for failure rests this time, not upon Pitt, but upon his brother-in-law, Lord Temple. Though influential by reason of his great wealth, and of an active and intriguing disposition, Temple was of little real importance in the political world, and would have played an even more insignificant rôle, had he not participated to a certain extent in the lustre surrounding the great commoner ; and no little astonishment was caused by Pitt refusing to form a ministry because Temple declined the treasury. It is extremely unlikely that he exaggerated the value of Temple's services, or that he was guilty of misplaced chivalry, sacrificing the country in the cause of private friendship; and it is more reasonable to suppose that he needed Temple, not for what he might do, but for what he might avert. Fearing that the treasury, which his brother-in-law had refused, might fall into the hands of Newcastle, or some other member of that party, Pitt preferred to continue to eat the bread of idleness, rather than play a part in a ministry controlled by politicians with whom he had ceased to be in sympathy. He had staked everything upon Temple's willingness to take office, and, when that failed him, he had no resource but to confess himself defeated. He was the victim of a principle, not of a political necessity.

The country might indeed suffer from Pitt's action, but, for the time being, the king was in the worse predicament. It was impossible for him to return to George Grenville, humble and contrite; for, when on previous occasions the king had struck for freedom, and failed to gain it, that ungenerous minister had displayed a tendency to chastise rather than pardon the repentant sinner; and the punishment would be likely to be increased with the repetition of the offence. Feeling that he had sinned too deeply to be forgiven, George III., pursuing the only safe course, put his pride in his pocket, and began a negotiation with the whig opposition, which resulted in the formation of the first Rockingham ministry in July, 1765. But, though the personal pride of the sovereign had been affronted, it would be a serious mistake to imagine that the whigs received office as the reward of victory. They conquered by their weakness not by their strength; and both in its origin and in its ultimate fate, the Rockingham administration bore eloquent testimony to the influence of the crown. Few cabinets have contained a larger proportion of statesmen genuinely anxious to promote the interests of their country, and their efforts were certainly not entirely fruitless. The stamp act, imposed upon the American colonies by Grenville, was repealed, the obnoxious cyder tax was abolished, and general warrants definitely declared to be illegal ; and, after the fall of the administration, Burke, in a famous pamphlet, proclaimed the great and lasting benefits it had conferred upon the country. The boast was legitimate, but, in a measure, beside the point ; for, when all allowances are made, it remains true that the ministers had failed in their first and greatest duty, that of keeping themselves in power. When they fell, after having been a year in office, the catastrophe was not due to any sudden assault or subterraneous court intrigue, but to their own inherent weakness. As the months passed by, it became abundantly clear that Rockingham and his colleagues were engaged upon a possibly heroic, but a certainly hopeless, undertaking : and when, shortly before the end came, a rumour was spread that the ministers had been dismissed, Lord Albemarle, one of the most active of their supporters, rejoiced to hear that his friends had been relieved from an impossible situation.[1] The king had originally taken them into his service because he knew that they had reached the nadir of their fortunes, and could never hope to prevail against him ; and he had judged aright. Unable to command a majority in the lower house without the placemen who would only lend their support as long as the ministers did what was pleasing to the king, and not daring to

[1] Add. MS., 32975, f. 414.

appeal to the country at a general election unless allowed to use the royal influence on their own behalf,[1] the ministers existed on sufferance ; and when George III. withdrew his favour, declining to create peers at their bidding, or to dismiss placemen who voted against them,[2] their fount of life ran dry.

Yet too much stress should not be laid upon the king's hostility, for it is very generally allowed that the ministry was not so constituted as to inspire confidence, or to ensure a lengthy tenure of power. The Marquis of Rockingham, who occupied the office of first lord of the treasury, was, at this time, comparatively little known in the political world, and was by no means adapted for a task which might have taxed the resources of the greatest statesman ; and, though it is possible that he received invaluable assistance from his secretary, Edmund Burke, it may be doubted whether the genius of the servant compensated for the inexperience of the master.[3] Nor was the Duke of Grafton, the secretary of state for the northern department, likely to supply his leader's deficiencies. He had all Rockingham's inexperience, and, moreover, was but half-hearted in his allegiance to the cause he professed to support. Youthful and impressionable, he had been smitten with an admiration for Pitt, which cast a chill over his earlier enthusiasm for the whig party ; and he had only joined the administration on the understanding that his hero should be

[1] Add. MS., 32969, ff. 390, 392.

[2] Grenville Papers, 3, 253-255 ; Rockingham Memoirs, 1, 347.

[3] " The king surely intends," wrote the second Lord Hardwicke to his brother, Charles Yorke, " to put himself entirely into Mr Pitt's hands, and he as surely means to break up the present administration. If he makes a better, I for one shall not be sorry for it, for I have long had my doubts about the sufficiency of the present, and with all the private regard and friendship which I have for the noble marquis, I have seen the burden too weighty for his shoulders, both in council and parliament." Add. MS., 35362, f. 10.

allowed to enter it whenever, and in whatever capacity, he liked. Undoubtedly the most experienced member of the cabinet was the Duke of Newcastle who, in accordance with a pledge he had given never to hold high office again, took the subordinate post of lord privy seal ; but he was now an old man, beginning to be a victim to the infirmities of age ; and though his advice was often good, as for instance when he took objection to the declaratory act which asserted the right of parliament to tax the American colonies, he failed to exercise much influence over his colleagues, many of whom, having been boys at school when he was managing the affairs of the country, treated his suggestions as the offsprings of senile decay. When, moreover, it is remembered that, besides the defects incidental to what Newcastle rather bitterly described as " an administration of boys," [1] there were members of the ministry, such as Northington, the lord chancellor, and Barrington, the secretary at war, who were frankly out of sympathy with the constitutional ideals of the majority of their colleagues, and firm believers in the extension of the royal authority, the whigs may well be charged with having embarked upon a hopeless enterprise, to which there could be no other issue but disaster.

Plausible as the accusation appears, it would yet be unfair, omitting as it does certain important factors in a very involved situation. Strange as it may seem, the Rockingham whigs had a reasonable hope of success when they consented to take office under the crown. It is true that they had offended the king by their attack upon the peace with France and their defence of Wilkes ; but they might fairly hope that they had washed away their guilt, and earned his

[1] Add. MSS., 32976, f. 325.

gratitude, by coming to his assistance in the hour of his danger, and rescuing him from the clutches of George Grenville. Nor was it only the shadowy hope of establishing a claim upon the royal favour that induced them to set out on what they knew to be a stormy sea. Fully realising their own weakness, they trusted that, once in office, Pitt would come to their aid, and place himself at their head. Upon him rested all their hopes for the future, and they knew that, if he elected to remain in retirement, they could not avert disaster. Only if he was included in the administration could they expect to acquire the confidence of the nation, and thus secure a surer foundation for their authority than the fickle favour of a court; and it is to their credit that they strained every nerve to induce him to accept a place in the cabinet. They sought to gain his approval by promoting his friend, Lord Chief Justice Pratt, to the peerage by the title of Lord Camden, and by beginning a negotiation for an alliance with Frederick the Great, the loss of whose friendship he had never ceased to deplore; but they discovered to their chagrin that the indispensable ally was not to be won. There is no reason to believe that Pitt's disinclination was due to a reluctance to play an active part in politics; for there is ample evidence to show that he was ready, and even anxious, to resume the burden of office, and take upon himself the cares of state. He was wont to enlarge upon the dangers threatening the country, discontented at home and isolated abroad; but, though he believed the national danger to be great, he refused to enter into an alliance or sit in the same cabinet with the champions of the party system. That difference of principle, which had prevented him from co-operating with the

Rockingham whigs when they had been in opposition, precluded him from throwing in his lot with them when they were in power ; and, on the several occasions that he was approached by the ministers for his assistance, he always stipulated for the complete reconstitution of the existing administration. He made it perfectly clear that it must be his ministry, not the Duke of Newcastle's or Lord Rockingham's. The cabinet must be remodelled and transformed ; and the ministers can hardly be blamed for refusing even Pitt's assistance, necessary as it was, upon such terms. They had come into office pledged to uphold the principles of party government, and they would have sacrificed their convictions, and betrayed the trust of their followers, if they had agreed to such conditions. It is to their credit, both as men and statesmen, that they preferred to perish in the hopeless pursuit of victory, rather than purchase security at the price of dishonour ; and no shame attaches to their defeat. They had fought for principles, not for places, and the battle was well worth fighting, even though it ended in a rout.

For the rout was inevitable, and, by the beginning of July, 1766, the Rockingham ministry was tottering to its fall. The Duke of Grafton, offended that Pitt had not been permitted to come into office on his own terms, had resigned the secretaryship of state in the previous April, his place being taken by the Duke of Richmond, an appointment which was difficult of justification unless, as Lord Buckinghamshire affected to believe, the ministers were determined always to have a secretary of state of the race of Charles II.[1] The king disapproved of Richmond's

---

[1] Add. MS., 22358, f. 35. Both Grafton and Richmond were descended from illegitimate children of Charles II.

promotion which he complained had been forced upon him by Rockingham ; and it was in the last degree improbable that the new minister would add to the prestige of the administration. Moreover, it was reported that the members of the cabinet were divided amongst themselves, that Conway, the secretary of state for the southern department, was constantly opposing Newcastle and Rockingham ; [1] and although it is possible that these tales were unfounded, originating in the malice of the enemies of the ministry, they were readily enough believed, and illustrate the popular reputation which the ill-fated administration enjoyed. Thus it might be fairly urged that the king was called upon, in the interests of the nation as well as in his own, to dismiss his advisers ; and George III. was now eager to act upon such advice. He had, indeed, ample cause for self-congratulation, for out of the storm and stress of circumstance he had issued triumphant. What might be styled the rump of the old whig oligarchy had proved itself as ineffective in office as it had in opposition ; and the greatest statesman of the day had declared himself the enemy of the party system, and in political sympathy with the crown. Thus an opportunity was granted to the king, which, if missed, might never recur. The battle over the royal authority had begun on the death of George II., and the time had now come to make the final charge which would complete the overthrow of the enemy.

It was at the end of June that the ministry suffered the blow which was to be the cause of death. When the ministers assembled at Northington's house to discuss a plan for the government of the recently acquired possession of Canada, the lord chancellor declined to proceed with the business in hand, com-

[1] Grenville Papers, 3, 255-258.

plained with some asperity of the treatment he had received, and ominously remarked that he proposed to discontinue his attendance at cabinet meetings.[1] It is extremely unlikely that this declaration was unconsidered, or evoked by a sudden gust of passion. Northington must have long been weary of a government which he disliked for its opinions and despised for its weakness ; and, if his action had not been previously concerted with the court, he was fully aware how heartily it would be approved in that quarter. Visiting his master on Sunday, July 6th, he informed him that he did not intend to remain in office ; and, when Rockingham entered the royal closet after Northington had left, the king told him that the chancellor's resignation was " a very important matter, and must make him consider very seriously what must be done."[2] No further light upon the royal designs was vouchsafed to the prime minister ; and this want of confidence on the part of the crown would not unreasonably have given birth in most men to the gloomiest forebodings. But Rockingham, who was naturally of a sanguine temperament, preferred to look upon the brighter side, and declined to believed that the chancellor's action was the first move in a carefully prepared campaign.[3] Difficult as it might be to fill up the vacancy, he hoped to weather the storm which had thus suddenly arisen. At a meeting of the leading members of the party, held at Conway's house on July 9th, it was arranged that Rockingham and Newcastle, accompanied by the two

[1] Rockingham Memoirs, 1, 350-355.
[2] Add. MS., 32976, f. 19, f. 52 ; Grenville Papers, 3, 255-258.
[3] In a letter to Newcastle, Rockingham remarked: " Indeed, his majesty's manner was exceedingly gracious, but whether this transaction of the chancellor's is on a plan, or a mere effect of passion, I can hardly determine. I should think there is no plan ; a few days must show it." Add. MS., 32976, f. 19.

secretaries of state, should seek an interview with the king, in order to learn the line of conduct he intended to pursue ; and, if it was found possible, gain his consent to the appointment of Charles Yorke as Northington's successor.[1]

Much could be urged in favour of the promotion of Yorke to the woolsack. The son of one of the most distinguished judges who have ever presided over the court of chancery, Yorke himself enjoyed a great reputation in legal circles, and was well known to cherish the ambition of becoming chancellor. Moreover, such a successor to Northington was not likely to be unpleasing to the king, for Yorke, though on intimate terms with the whig leaders, had never been, save for a brief period, a member of the opposition party, and had supported the court in the contention that the arrest of Wilkes for seditious libel was not a violation of parliamentary privilege. When the Rockingham ministry was formed, Yorke, instead of being created chancellor as he had naturally hoped, was obliged to content himself with his old office of attorney-general, but, in order to compensate him for the disappointment which he might legitimately feel, the king had promised him that he should be raised to the woolsack within a twelvemonth.[2] The time had now come for the pledge to be fulfilled ; but George III. paid little heed to a promise which had been given to meet a particular emergency, and which it was now inconvenient to execute. When visited by his

[1] " I found," wrote Newcastle, " that it was my Lord Rockingham's opinion that, if this should appear to be no more than a flight in the chancellor, and that the king would give the seals to Mr Yorke, and make some proper removals, . . . that everything might go on with ease and success; and that the additional strength of having Mr Yorke chancellor, and in the house of lords, would make a very great alteration in favor of the present administration." Add. MS., 32976, f. 69.

[2] Add. MS., 35428, f. 1, f. 94.

ministers he made no mention of appointing a suc-cessor to Northington, and, though courteous and affable, pronounced the death sentence upon the administration by informing his hearers that he had sent for Pitt.[1] The letter of summons had been dispatched on July 7th, the day after Northington's visit to court ; and Pitt was already on his way to town. It was well known, both to the king and to the ministers, that he was coming, not to strengthen, but to destroy the existing government. Having declared war upon a system, not upon individuals, it was probable that he would retain in office some of those who had served under Rockingham ; but the men, whom he selected, might count upon finding themselves associated with colleagues with whom they were in fundamental disagreement.[2]

In summoning Pitt, George III. claimed to have acted upon Northington's advice ;[3] but what the

[1] Add. MS., 32976, f. 52 ; Newcastle's *Narrative*, p. 77.

[2] In the letter summoning Pitt to town, the king remarked : " I cannot conclude without expressing how entirely my ideas concerning the basis on which a new administration should be erected, are consonant to the opinion you gave on that subject in parliament a few days before you set out for Somersetshire " (Chatham Correspondence, 2, 436). Newcastle mentions that Pitt " will form his plan upon the declaration he has made ' to take the best men without distinction of parties or *connections*,' that he will propose to keep as many of the present ministers as he shall think will be attached to him ; and particularly the Duke of Grafton and Mr Conway " (Newcastle's *Narrative*, p. 81) ; and Horace Walpole, who was a good political prophet, remarked that " the plan will probably be to pick and cull from all quarters, and break all parties as much as possible." Walpole's Letters, 7, 12-13.

[3] It is certain that Lord Camden was also consulted. In his letter to Pitt Northington declares, " I have not uttered a word of this business but to Lord Camden." George Onslow informed Newcastle that Camden had played a part in this transaction, and when Newcastle handed on this information to the Duke of Richmond, the latter replied : " Your Grace's information that Lord Cambden (*sic*) and the chancellor negotiated this affair is, I believe, very true and very extraordinary, unless Lord Cambden is to be chancellor and Lord Northington retires with a pension." It is interesting to notice how accurately Richmond had gauged the situation. Add. MS., 32976, f. 65, f. 67, f. 103, f. 107 ; Bedford Correspondence, 3, 340-341 ; Chatham Correspondence, 2, 434-435.

chancellor suggested was so completely in accord with the royal inclinations, that no pressure could have been necessary to induce the king to pursue a policy which he could not but approve. He saw Pitt for the first time on Saturday, July 12th, and probably learnt from him the plan upon which he intended to proceed. Though prepared to take the existing administration as the foundation of his own, Pitt was determined to be governed in the selection of his colleagues, not by their political connections or their constitutional opinions, but by their ability for administration. Efficiency was to be the hall-mark of the new cabinet, and therefore Rockingham, of whom he had thought poorly from the beginning, was to be replaced at the treasury by Temple, and though Conway was to be retained as secretary of state, the Duke of Richmond was to be dismissed.[1] In such a programme there was nothing which could give the king offence, and much which he would find agreeable. No more effective means of breaking up the Rockingham party could have been devised than the admission of some of its members and the exclusion of others; for, by these means, dissension might be sown between men whose union had been a menace to the authority of the crown.

That Pitt had no use for Rockingham's services is not surprising; but that Temple should be chosen to fill the vacant place is certainly not so easy of explanation. Though connected with Pitt by marriage, and by a friendship stretching back to the beginning of their political careers, Temple could hardly lay claim to any great administrative ability; and his

[1] Unfortunately no record survives of this interview, but, on the day following it, Pitt informed Conway of the changes he proposed to make in the administration, and it is improbable that he would have concealed from the king what he revealed to his future secretary of state.

appointment, in any circumstances, to the first place in the cabinet would evoke comment. Nor could it be urged that Pitt was determined to have a first lord of the treasury who was in the closest possible agreement with him, for, as is well known, he and Temple, were divided on the vexed question of the taxation of the American colonies. Pitt had always persistently asserted the illegality of Grenville's stamp act, whereas Temple, not only justified that measure, but was unsparing in his denunciations of the men who, in order to acquire a momentary popularity, were prepared to sacrifice the undoubted rights of the mother country, and to give their sanction to re-bellion. Yet, well aware as he was of his brother-in-law's opinions, Pitt wished to see him at the treasury, for, whatever Temple's faults might be, he had, at least, the merit of not being identified with the Rockingham whigs. He was intended to stand in the new ad-ministration as a type of the change which had been brought about ; and, effective as an emblem, his in-fluence would not be such as to endanger Pitt's supremacy. But such an offer can hardly be styled attractive. Temple was to be condemned to acquiesce in a colonial policy which he disapproved, to occupy a position of dignity divorced from all power, and to receive little or nothing in return for such material concessions. It may be that he was given as much as he deserved, but he had not a lowly estimate of his own ability, and might well refuse to be fed with the crumbs which fell from his brother-in-law's table.[1]

[1] It is, of course, possible to contend that it was against Pitt's will, and in accordance with the royal wish, that Temple was offered the treasury. George III. could not but approve Temple's views on American taxation, and Conway informed Newcastle that Pitt had said that " my Lord Temple was sent for not by him, but insinuated by the king, as he was ; that is by my good lord

Temple arrived in London on the evening of Monday, July 14th, knowing nothing of what had passed, save that a negotiation for a new administration was proceeding, and that his services were required. He did not come, however, to be treated as a pawn in the game of his great kinsman, and it is not improbable that he scented mischief from afar. On his way from Stowe he had an interview with his brother, George Grenville, with whom he was now on most intimate terms ; and it was agreed between them that Grenville's claims to a seat in the cabinet should not be pressed. This was, undoubtedly, a most politic renunciation, for it was improbable that Pitt would consent to the inclusion in his administration of the originator of the stamp act ; and, if the request was made and refused, Temple might feel impelled by loyalty to his brother to decline to take any part in the government.[1] Nor was it only a desire to smooth the way for Temple's acceptance that dictated Grenville's self-denying policy. He might reasonably hope that, with his brother at the treasury, the policy of conciliating America would be abandoned, and the colonists punished for their resistance to the stamp act ; and thus, even if he remained excluded from office, his exile would be sweetened by the triumph of his opinions. Yet the ingenious device proved unavailing, and Temple was not long in discovering that he had journeyed to town in vain. An interview with the king on July 15th, followed by one with Pitt on the day after, left him fully determined to

---

chancellor, the amanuensis of the whole " (Newcastle's *Narrative*, p. 84). This utterance, however, cannot be interpreted as meaning that Pitt was opposed to the step ; and it must be remembered that, only a few months before these events took place, Pitt had demanded the treasury for Temple.

[1] Bedford Correspondence, 3, 340-341 ; Grenville Papers, 3, 376-377 ; Chatham Correspondence, 2, 467-470.

refuse the offered terms. When he learnt that what he contemptuously called " the rump of the last ministry " was to form the foundation of the new, that Conway, who had played so leading a part in the repeal of the stamp act, was to continue as secretary of state, that he was expected to work with men with whom he profoundly disagreed, and that, while as nominal leader he would be exposed to all the attacks levied against the administration, he would have little or no influence over the policy of the government, he declined, to use his own trenchant expression, " to come in like a child to go out like a fool." [1]

In the past, Temple had often been guilty of factious conduct, but on this occasion he appears to have been guided by a sound instinct, and to have acted wisely. The mixed motives of men's actions are always difficult to disentangle, and it would be the height of rashness to assume that Temple was uninfluenced by any jealousy of Pitt's predominance. Possibly aggrieved that he had not been consulted earlier, and as reluctant as Pitt to preside over a cabinet which was not of his own nomination, he might well feel that he had been treated as a subordinate rather than an equal, and resent the assumption that he had no choice but to follow in the wake of his powerful friend and relation. The least captious of men are apt to dislike the undue enforcement of unpleasant truths, and Temple had never been ready to forgive an affront to his pride. Yet it would be easy to place too evil a construction upon his action at this crisis, and, if this were the only blot upon his political career, he would be deserving of more credit than is usually given him.

---

[1] Bedford Correspondence, 3, 340-341 ; Grenville Papers, 3, 263-279, 376 ; Chatham's Correspondence, 2, 441, 442, 448, 467-470 ; Grafton's *Autobiography*, 94-95 ; Add. MS., 32976, f. 161.

Indeed, he could plead ample justification for his refusal to come to Pitt's assistance. Though he disliked the Rockingham whigs for their American policy, he was in entire sympathy with them in their advocacy of party government. Reared in the old political school of the late king's reign, having won his spurs as a member of a party, and fully appreciating the strength which comes from union, he still adhered to the creed which Pitt had discarded, and was not so eager for office as to deny his faith. He preferred to continue in opposition, rather than be obliged to work with colleagues from whom he differed on most of the important questions of the day ; and it is not easy to see where he erred, unless it be a crime to practise what has been called " the doubtful virtue of consistency."

His contemporaries, however, worried little about the morality of his action, being far more interested to discover whether Pitt would consent to form a ministry without him. Judging from what had happened only a year before, it might seem that Pitt was once more to be baffled in the attempt to come to the rescue of the country ; but, if Temple had counted upon history repeating itself, he was doomed to be disappointed. In the previous year his aid had been essential to the success of Pitt's scheme, for, unless he accepted the treasury, that office would fall into the hands of a member of the Rockingham party, who would be certain to introduce into the ministry the poison of the party system ; but, by the July of 1766, Temple had ceased to be indispensable, having a rival in the Duke of Grafton who, if he had not entirely broken with the Rockingham whigs, had at least resigned his place in their administration in order to place himself at Pitt's disposal. Freed from the fetters

of the party system, Grafton was eligible for the office
which Temple had declined ; and it was to him that
Pitt turned for assistance.   The young duke had
indeed few and most imperfect qualifications for such
a post ; and, fully conscious of his own incapacity, he
was sincerely reluctant to undertake a task which he
could not perform : but he struggled in vain against
the fixed determination of the man he had chosen
as his political leader.   With something perilously
approaching cruelty, Pitt told him that, if he refused
to take the treasury, he, himself, would decline to form
a ministry ; and thus driven between the horns of a
particularly cruel dilemma, compelled either to endure
the odium of forcing Pitt to continue out of office,
or undertake duties which he could not adequately
discharge, Grafton pursued the nobler, if not the wiser,
course, and accepted the treasury.   Great as were
the evils which he was to bring upon the country, it
should always be remembered in his favour that, when
he found himself at the cross-roads of his destiny,
he knowingly sacrificed his own political reputation
to what he believed to be the good of the nation.[1]

Having thus made sure of his ground by securing
the services of Grafton, Pitt addressed himself to the
task of forming a ministry, picking and choosing from
the various political camps of the day.   He retained
Conway, undoubtedly one of the most efficient members
of the late government, as secretary of state, but
removed him from the southern to the northern department, possibly in order to restrict his patronage
which, it was feared, he might use to benefit his former
colleagues.   The southern department, wrote the
Marquis of Rockingham, when he heard of the change,
" includes a great patronage, and would have been

---

[1] Grafton's *Autobiography*, 90-91.

of use to our friends, if it had been in a real friend's hands." [1]   Nor was this the only intimation given to Conway that, though continued in office, he was expected to adapt himself to new surroundings and new companions ; and it could have been but with a faint heart that he welcomed the appointment of Lord Shelburne as his successor in the southern department. Still a comparatively young man, Shelburne had begun his political career as a supporter of Bute, and a bitter opponent of the German war ; but, after the effacement of the royal favourite, he had attached himself to Pitt, and loudly proclaimed his hostility to the party system, and his sympathy with America.   When offered a place in the Rockingham ministry, he had declined it, declaring, like his leader, " men not measures " to be the rule of his conduct : and thus it was only fitting that he should be given a seat in an administration which was intended to demonstrate the futility of the party system.   Nor was this, indeed, Shelburne's only claim to high office.   An accomplished debater, and of a very high order of ability, he was one of the most enlightened statesmen of his time, and seemed destined to rise to political greatness.   Yet the promise of these early years was not to be fulfilled, and his career was to be blasted by the reputation which he earned for unparalleled treachery and deceit.   Nick-named " Malagrida " and " The Jesuit of Berkeley Square," denounced by political friends and foes alike, Shelburne was almost universally believed to be admirably adapted for playing the part of the traitor in the camp.   As early as 1763, Henry Fox had denounced him as a " perfidious and infamous liar," and Grenville, in whose ministry he had sat for a short time, had found him intolerable as a colleague ; and

---

[1] Add. MS., 32976, f. 253.

although, when Pitt selected him to be secretary of state, Shelburne did not enjoy the full extent of the evil fame which he was later to earn, he was only too likely to prove an element of discord and disagreement in the cabinet. That he was guilty of the treachery and deceit, so freely attributed to him, it is difficult to believe; but a strained and artificial demeanour, an involved mode of speech, and a preference for rather crooked ways, lent colour to the charge which, however unfounded it may appear to us, was almost universally believed by those who had ample opportunities of forming an opinion.[1]

Almost as much of a foregone conclusion as the appointment of Shelburne to high office in the administration, was the promotion of Lord Camden to the woolsack. In addition to the claims of a friendship dating back to days at school, Camden had won Pitt's approval when, as chief justice of the common pleas, he had ruled that parliamentary privilege covered the offence of seditious libel, and that general warrants were illegal; and Pitt was determined that this champion of the liberty of the subject and the independence of parliament should be made lord chancellor at the earliest opportunity. This resolution had done not a little to embitter Pitt's relations with the Rockingham whigs who had pressed the claims of Charles Yorke; but, now that his friends had been driven from office, Yorke was obliged to relinquish all hope, for the time being, of following in his father's footsteps; and the only obstacle in the way of Camden's promotion was Lord Northington who had been lord chancellor from the first year of the reign. Attached to the emoluments of his office, and never allowing his

---

[1] For an interesting discussion of Shelburne's character, see Lecky's *History of England* (Cabinet edition), v. 132-139.

judicial duties to encroach upon the hours which he reserved for his pleasures,[1] Northington might naturally feel reluctant to resign his place, unless assured of a comfortable and easy retreat ; and it is extremely unlikely that he would have advised the king to send for Pitt, unless he had been prepared to make way for Camden on the woolsack, and confident that he would be rewarded for so doing. Northington was not a politician to take a leap in the dark, and he issued in triumph from the transformation of the ministry. Lord Camden became chancellor, but Northington continued in the cabinet as lord president of the council, the salary of that office being considerably augmented in order to render it attractive to the ex-chancellor who was further gratified by the promise of a pension and the reversion of a sinecure.

Thus the promotion of Camden, upon which Pitt had set his heart, was rendered unexpectedly easy by Northington's adaptability ; and the remaining places in the cabinet were filled without much difficulty. The Marquis of Granby, who had been master of ordnance under Rockingham, was made commander in chief, and Lord Egmont continued as first lord of the admiralty. William Dowdeswell, however, Rockingham's chancellor of the exchequer, whom Pitt despised as a mediocrity, was not allowed to remain in office, his place being taken by Charles Townshend ; and the change was not entirely for the better. Though by no means a brilliant, Dowdeswell was not an inefficient administrator ; and it would have been well for the country if he had been permitted

---

[1] There is a story, the truth of which is not above suspicion, that Northington asked the king's permission to discontinue the evening sittings of the court of chancery because he was always drunk by that time of the day. A more moderate version of the anecdote represents him as urging that an evening sitting prevented him from sitting over his port after dinner.

to continue to serve it. Steady persistence and even dulness are sometimes of greater value than intellectual brilliance divorced from character ; and, in spite of his undoubted ability, it must be admitted that Townshend was not worthy of a high place in any administration. A ready and accomplished debater, with a great reputation for wit in an age critical of such matters, Townshend was cursed by defects which rendered barren his many great gifts. Lacking in stability of purpose, without settled convictions, and always treating life as a game of chance, he never rose above the level of a brilliant political adventurer ; and neither the charm of his conversation nor the ingenuity of his mind can be pleaded in defence of his many and serious political failings. He was too often inclined, we are told by a contemporary, to play the part of harlequin ; [1] and, though eagerly sought after as a companion, he was treated with scant respect as a politician. But for his promotion to be chancellor of the exchequer, it was Grafton, and not Pitt, who was to blame; for the latter only consented with unfeigned reluctance to an appointment which he never approved.[2] In order to mitigate, as much as possible, the evil which Townshend might work, Pitt insisted that he should not be admitted into the inner cabinet ; but even this most salutary restriction was removed in a few weeks, and the most volatile of statesmen joined that small circle of ministers who really ruled the country.[3]

Such were the leading members of the administra-

---

[1] Hist. MSS. Comm., 12th Report, Appendix, Part ix. 340.

[2] Grafton's *Autobiography*, 92.

[3] Lord Egmont reported that Townshend was vexed and disappointed at his exclusion from the cabinet, and, on learning the rumour, John Yorke, a younger brother of Lord Hardwicke, remarked, " I don't much wonder at it, for he was of the cabinet when first commissioner of trade, and Dowdeswell was so when chancellor of exchequer." Add. MS., 35374, f. 305.

tion which Burke aptly compared to a piece of un-cemented tessellated pavement, and it is impossible to quarrel with the description. If Pitt cannot be accused of going into the highways and hedges for his ministers, he may, at least, be said to have drawn them from very opposite and different quarters ; and nearly every possible political opinion was represented in his cabinet. Thus, though Conway and Shelburne agreed on the American question, they had little else in common ; and both Pitt and Camden were opposed to the declaratory act which Conway had supported. The Marquis of Granby had voted against the repeal of the stamp act, and if Charles Townshend had voted for the repeal,[1] he had also supported the measure when it had first been introduced by George Grenville. Moreover, Lord Egmont, the first lord of the ad-miralty, was well known to be antagonistic to the project of an alliance with Russia and Prussia, which Pitt warmly favoured ; and no reliance could be placed upon a political adventurer like Northington, devoid of convictions and unburdened with scruples, who would support the administration as long as it suited his purpose, but no longer. Thus, in accordance with his determination to destroy the party system, and draw into the service of the crown the ablest politicians of the day, Pitt had purposely constructed an ad-ministration which represented everything except an unanimous opinion. It was an experiment of no little daring, and, though its success would reflect great glory upon the man who had dared so much, its failure might well cause it to be conceived as the whim of a madman's brain. Yet there is no evidence that Pitt feared disaster. He, apparently, had no misgivings as to the future, no fear that the team, he had under-

[1] Add. MSS., 35436, f. 31.

taken to drive, might prove too unruly to be controlled. He was confident that, with the royal support, he would prevail in the cabinet and parliament alike, and nothing is more striking than his complete assurance of having secured the favour of the crown. A few weeks after he had taken office, he informed a friend that he " had the king's entire confidence ; and that he had not the least doubt or suspicion that he should lose it ; that he depended so much upon it, that he should go for six weeks to Bath for his health, to return by the meeting of parliament, the beginning of November ; that he should leave those ministers with the king whom he could entirely trust ; that his majesty had such confidence in him that he could propose nothing that his majesty did not immediately agree to ; and that no private gentleman could talk more properly upon all subjects than the king did. That he was very sensible of the run there was against him ; but that did not affect him, nor should alter his conduct ; that if his majesty was pleased . . . to continue his confidence to him, he would never desert the king, but support him in all events, broke and old as he was ; that he has not the least doubt of success ; and that his administration would be a permanent one." [1]

These were strange words in the mouth of one accustomed in the past to look rather to the nation than to the court as the source of his power ; but to use them in order to prove Pitt guilty of being a time-server, of having descended into the rôle of a palace favourite, would be a gross and malicious perversion of the truth. He was as eager as he had ever been for the glory and greatness of England; but, whereas

---

[1] Add. MS., 32977, f. 41. This is taken from an account of the conversation given by a third person to Newcastle ; but there seems no reason to doubt its substantial accuracy.

when he had pursued this end in the past, he had been obliged to stoop to an alliance with Newcastle, in order to acquire the support of the house of commons, he now sought assistance from the crown. Confident of the royal favour, and still the idol of the popular adoration, Pitt might well regard his position as impregnable, and anticipate a speedy triumph over his enemies both at home and abroad. It was, perhaps, this complete faith in the security of the foundation of his power, that encouraged him to take a step which produced something like a panic amongst his followers. In failing health, and unequal to the strain of a great administrative office, he determined to occupy the comparatively unimportant post of lord privy seal, and to such an arrangement there could be little objection. His influence in the ministry would be quite independent of the office he held, and the necessity of exercising a general supervision might be pleaded in favour of an unusual expedient. But, unfortunately for his popularity, and to the amazement of his colleagues, he decided to enter the upper house as Earl of Chatham.[1] That in so doing he was guilty of a serious tactical blunder admits of no denial. It is true that he was probably unequal to the lengthy and fatiguing debates of the house of commons, and was not unlikely to be often prevented by ill-health from attending parliament ; but the populace is governed by imagination more than by reason, and the affection, which had been lavished upon William Pitt, was withheld from the Earl of Chatham. He had acquired the trust and confidence of the nation because he was universally believed to be supremely indifferent to those prizes of political life, which most men so eagerly covet, and the outcry, which had been raised

[1] Grafton's *Autobiography*, 97.

in 1761, when he accepted a pension from the crown, ought to have enlightened him as to the conditions upon which he enjoyed the affection of the people. Unreasonable as the clamour may have been, Pitt selected a most inopportune moment for throwing down the glove of defiance to the nation. In the very hour when he needed all the popularity which he enjoyed, he chose to squander it ; and his colleagues might well be appalled when they heard the news. It is not impossible that Temple was partly influenced to decline a place in the ministry by the knowledge that Pitt was about to become a member of the upper house ; and, if this is so, it redounds to his political wisdom.[1] Few men have been more deserving of a peerage than Pitt, but few men have purchased it at a higher rate. He earned it by the many distinguished services which he had rendered to the country, but he paid for it by the loss of the popular affection.[2]

Thus the preliminaries were finished, and everything prepared for the crusade aimed at the destruction of the party system, and the establishment of the royal authority. Though Pitt, by an act of folly, had

---

[1] It is by no means certain that Temple actually knew that Pitt intended to take a peerage ; but there is a significant passage in his letter to Grenville, dated July 18th, in which he remarks, " Illuminations, city address, etc., all preparing : whether any damp will be cast upon them I know not." Grenville Papers, 3, 267.

[2] In a letter to Lord Buckinghamshire, written in August 1766, Hans Stanley remarked that " Though I have been much confined to my own home, and my personal business, I have seen evident marks of the same unpopularity in administration which you mention as prevailing in Norfolk. The cry about the peerage will, I think, subside, for however unaccountable in point of prudence that step may appear to me, it certainly is not a parallel case with the Earl of Bath who deserted both his opinions and his friends. The fault here has been of a contrary nature, men without merit or pretensions preferred to the highest situations in this country, which I think will very much weaken authority at home and credit abroad. . . . Upon the whole I am thoroughly disgusted with all the late scenes of politics, and nothing but that sentiment could have embarked me in my present undertaking." Add. MS., 22359, f. 52.

thrown away the popularity which might have proved so formidable a weapon in his hands, he still remained a very dangerous antagonist; and it was necessary for the Rockingham whigs to look to their arms, and prepare for the battle, soon to be fought in parliament. It was open to them to go into headlong opposition, and wage unceasing war against the ministers who had displaced them; but, though such a course was possible, both its expediency and its chance of success were open to question. On many of the questions which would come before parliament, they were in substantial agreement with Chatham; and prolonged and systematic antagonism would be difficult, unless they were prepared to suffer the accusation of reckless and factious opposition. Moreover, quite apart from such a consideration, they could not hope to prevail alone, outnumbered as they were by the supporters of the court; and, if they seriously intended to run the administration close upon divisions, and possibly outvote it, they must not flinch before an alliance with the followers of the Duke of Bedford and the adherents of George Grenville. But to such a union there were, seemingly, insuperable and, certainly, serious objections. The faction led by the Duke of Bedford numbered some of the most rapacious and immoral policitians of the day. Bedford, himself, if not a very enlightened, was, at least, a respectable statesman; but, among his followers, Sandwich, Weymouth, and Rigby enjoyed a most evil pre-eminence. While Rigby was the most abandoned and brazen of place-hunters, Sandwich startled an easy-going generation by the immorality of his private life, and Lord Weymouth was reported to divide his affections between play and strong beer. But it was the public conduct rather than the private vices of the leaders of the Bedford party, which rendered it difficult for the Rockingham whigs to coalesce with them. Sandwich had been active in the attack upon Wilkes, and the Duke of Bedford an important member of the administration which had introduced the stamp act; and thus, unless Rockingham was prepared to abandon the American colonists to their fate, an alliance with the Bedford party would be attended by many difficulties. A wider, and even more unbridgeable, gulf separated him from George Grenville who viewed with detestation and disgust the man whom he believed to have sacrificed a principle to expediency; and, though the followers of Bedford might be driven by their hunger for office to discard their convictions, and come to a working agreement with the Rockingham whigs, it was far less likely that the little band, which had sworn allegiance to Grenville and his brother, Lord Temple, would barter their opinions for places in an administration led by Lord Rockingham. Thus there was much to deter Rockingham from immediately embarking upon a career of opposition; and it is to his credit that he declined to be a renegade to his political creed, and to gain a temporary triumph by forming a confederation which could be truly styled factious.

Though opposition, however, might be out of the question, Lord Rockingham and his followers were not dispensed from the necessity of deciding upon a plan of campaign. If they pursued a policy of drift, of idly waiting upon events, they would certainly encounter disaster. Their existence as a party was openly threatened by Chatham who had sworn their destruction; and, if they were to be true to their principles, it was their very life that they had to defend. They sought to do so by securing as many places as possible in the new administration, and by reducing the resignation of their friends to the smallest possible number.[1] It was with the warm approval of their former colleagues that both Grafton and Conway accepted office under Chatham;[2] and great was the rejoicing in the whig camp when the news was brought that Temple had declined to join the ministry. Lord Rockingham declared himself " much pleased, because I now think that the corps will be kept together, which, indeed, I feared was doubtful some hours ago ";[3] and the Duke of Newcastle prophesied that " Pitt must fling himself into us."[4] When Lord John Cavendish resigned his place at the treasury, Rockingham regretted, and Newcastle excused, the action;[5] and the Duke of Portland was told that, if he left the administration, he would " ruin all."[6] It was, of course, impossible that there should not be some exceptions to this general rule, and Charles Yorke, chagrined that he was not promoted to the woolsack, declined to continue as attorney-general;[7] but, for the most part, those members of the

---

[1] Thus Burke writes, " I thought it was a settled point that none should go out without the concurrence of the party." Burke's Correspondence, i, 106.

[2] Newcastle's *Narrative*, 82-87. Newcastle wished Rockingham to remain at the treasury, but this was obviously out of the question. Add. MS., 32976, f. 173.

[3] Add. MS., 32976, f. 161.

[4] Add. MS., 32976, f. 173; see also f. 169.

[5] Add. MS., 32976, f. 253, f. 255, f. 269.

[6] Add. MS., 32976, f. 221.

[7] The king was prepared to continue Yorke as attorney-general, but the latter refused to remain in that office; and his conduct was approved by Lord Rockingham. " Your note of last night," wrote the marquis to him, " surprized me much. I could hardly have believed that you should have been desired to come to his majesty, and no other proposition made to you but so unworthy a one as desiring you to continue attorney-general. . . . If the proposition had been chief justice with a peerage, I should have thought it might require consideration. . . . I am positively clear that you cannot stay in the office of attorney-general, and that no sollicitation should weigh with you to do it. . . . Don't by any persuasions accept the chief justiceship without a peerage." Add. MS., 35430, f. 59.

Rockingham party, whom Chatham was willing to retain, continued to occupy the posts they had held in the late administration.

It is not difficult to discern the motives which inspired this policy. If Rockingham called upon his followers to come into the wilderness of opposition, there was a risk that he might put a greater strain on their allegiance than it was capable of sustaining. There could hardly fail to be many desertions, and thus Chatham would be given a favourable opportunity of breaking up the whig party by winning its adherents with the bribe of office. It was to guard against this danger that both Newcastle and Rockingham encouraged their friends to continue in the ministry ; the new administration, as well as the old, must be representative of the party system. There was no idea of trailing the Rockingham banner in the dust, of breaking up the organisation which had been so laboriously achieved. There must be close and constant communication between those members of the party who continued in office, and those who had lost their places. They must continue to act as a corps, to work together for the attainment of a common end, in the hope that the day would perhaps come when Chatham, realising that he had undertaken more than he could perform, would abandon his principle of "men not measures," and conclude an alliance with the Rockingham whigs. Thus the late ministers hoped to achieve, by patient endurance and studied moderation, more than they could have accomplished by the most carefully designed attack. Chatham had resolved to destroy the party system, and they were determined to maintain it.

The issue of such a struggle could not fail to have important consequences upon the development of the constitution. If Chatham succeeded in the fulfilment of his hopes, the personal authority of the crown would be firmly established, and the ideas promulgated by Bolingbroke realised in practice. The party system, proved to be unnecessary, would pass away and be forgotten, and the ministers of the sovereign be freed from all allegiance, save to their master who appointed them, and the law of the land. But before this attempt to set back the hands of the clock, and undo the work accomplished by the whigs under the first two Georges, could be successful, the various parliamentary parties, the Rockinghams, the Bedfords, and the Grenvilles must be destroyed; and thus upon them fell the burden of maintaining the battle against the court. Time was to show how worthy they were of discharging such a responsible function.

CHAPTER II

THE MINISTRY ON ITS TRIAL

IF it be heroism to set out upon a stormy and dangerous enterprise, in the full assurance of victory, and
oblivious to the possibility of failure, then at no time
of his life was Chatham more truly heroic than when
he began his unhappy crusade against the party
system. Ill and suffering, and confronted with a
task, the difficulties of which might have inspired a
lesser man with fear and a wiser man with caution,
he does not appear to have had any misgivings, any
anxiety for the future, confidently believing that,
whereas in the past he had saved his country from
her enemies abroad, so now he was destined to deliver
her from her foes at home. His self-appointed work
was to still factious strife and political discord, and to
restore England to that proud position among the
powers of Europe, to which he had formerly raised her.
Yet, glorious as the conception was, its execution was
far from easy, for Chatham could hardly count upon
his opponents abandoning the struggle, and laying down
their arms, directly he appeared in the field. Many
obstacles would have to be overcome, and many fierce
contests fought, before the political millennium, as
he conceived it, could be successfully inaugurated ; and
Chatham stands convicted of having seriously under-
rated the difficulties of the undertaking. It is true
that his parliamentary enemies were divided, and that

the prospect of a union between the Rockinghams, the Bedfords, and the Grenvilles, was comparatively remote; but it would have been well if he had remembered that, however little else his opponents had in common, they at least all believed, though in differing degrees, in the principles of party government, and that the time might come when they would elect to drop their differences, and stand united in defence of the one article of faith which they all professed. Should this ever happen, Chatham would indeed be in a perilous situation. Having gone far to extinguish his personal popularity by the acceptance of a peerage, he was no longer the idol of the people whose favour had meant so much to him in the early days of his struggle for power; and it was to the king, rather than to the nation, that he looked for assistance, should be ever be hard pressed. It was not inconceivable that he might find it impossible to reconcile his newly-found devotion for the court with his old preference for the people.

It was not long before he learnt that his path was not to be free from obstacles. On August 13th, Lord Egmont, having come to the conclusion that he could not conscientiously remain a member of an administration whose foreign policy he did not approve, resigned his office of first lord of the admiralty; [1] and, though he was not likely to have materially increased the efficiency or prestige of the cabinet, his resignation was not devoid of importance, since it was a protest against the doctrine of " men, not measures," and, moreover, created a vacancy which had to be filled.[2] Thus, at

---

[1] Add. MS., 32976, f. 423.

[2] " Lord Egmont . . . resigned his own employment in a manner that does him great honor, and is a great blow to this administration, and I know it is felt by Conway."—Newcastle to Portland, August 16th, 1766. Add. MSS., 32976, f. 423.

the very beginning of his campaign, Chatham was confronted with the writing on the wall; but he refused to read the message aright, and determined, in the appointment of Egmont's successor, to maintain the principle which, he thought, would bring salvation to the country. An appeal was made to Lord Gower, one of the most respectable of the members of the Bedford party; but, anxious though Gower was for office, he promptly declined the invitation when he discovered that the offer was confined to himself alone, and that nothing was to be done for his friends and political allies. That he acted wisely cannot be doubted, for it would be a mistake to attribute his refusal to the proverbial rapacity and self-seeking of the faction to which he belonged. George Grenville, who was taken into the confidence of the Bedford party, and played a part in the negotiation, pointed out that " the evident purpose of all this is to break and divide us if possible ";[1] and he was not far from the truth. Gower was to be taken but the others were to be left, and, as first lord of the admiralty, he would be expected to forget his friends, and forswear the party in which he had received his political education. But Chatham was to discover that recruits were not to be so easily won; and, though eager enough for power, from which they had been too long exiled for their own happiness, the Bedfords realised that the best way of bringing the prime minister to acknowledge defeat was to present a united front, and to stand and fall together.[2]

The overtures to Gower having ended in failure, the vacant office was offered to, and accepted by, Sir

[1] Grenville Papers, 3, 302-305.
[2] Bedford Correspondence, 3, 342-344; Grenville Papers, 3, 302-310; Grafton's *Autobiography*, 99-100; Chatham Correspondence, 3, 54, 55.

Charles Saunders, a distinguished seaman, and, politically, in sympathy with the Rockingham party. Though chagrined that Saunders had only been asked when Gower had declined, Rockingham, in accordance with his policy of encouraging his friends to take places in the administration as long as they did not break with the party, approved the appointment,[1] and, indeed, had reason to be pleased with the change; for Egmont, though he had served under Rockingham, cannot be numbered as one of his followers. Far more reliance could be placed upon Saunders, and his appointment strengthened Rockingham in his resolution to refrain from opposition if it could be possibly avoided. " I still continue anxious," he wrote at the end of August, " that we and our friends should be quiet, and that our only object should be to keep up a good-humoured correspondence with those parts of the present system who were parts of ours, and perhaps at some day we may feel the benefit of this moderation " ;[2] and these opinions were re-echoed by Newcastle who affirmed that he would give " no improper opposition to this administration, and even . . . support them if their measures are agreeable to our conduct during the opposition, and to those successful ones which were followed by the last administration."[3] It was a policy of stooping to conquer ; and, if the Rockingham whigs abstained from attacking the ministry, it was not from any love they bore to Chatham and his political principles, but because they were anxious to remain on friendly terms with their former colleagues, especially Grafton and Conway, and to use them as

[1] " I don't think the manner of Lord Chatham doing it was so obliging to Sir Charles as to merit much even from him ; but the appearance is rather reconciliatory towards us, and will be so represented."—Rockingham to Newcastle, August 29th, 1766. Add. MS., 32976, f. 488.

[2] Add. MS., 32976, f. 488.   [3] Add. MS., 32976, f. 511.

an avenue through which they might pass into office.
" I conclude," wrote Newcastle to Lord Rockingham,
" your lordship's view is to engage the Duke of Grafton
and Mr Conway to use all their credit with my Lord
Chatham to convince him that he can have no security
upon which he may depend, but from the friends of
the last administration " ; [1] and such was, doubtless,
the plan approved. Chatham was to be educated
into the belief that the support of the Rockingham
party was essential to his success, in the hope that,
having learned his lesson, he would abandon his war
against all political factions, and, by allying himself
with the Rockingham whigs, re-establish the system
of party government once again.

For the success of such a plan of campaign much
depended upon the loyalty of Conway and Grafton,
and not a little upon Chatham himself. Conway, it
is true, gave entire satisfaction, and appeared anxious
to maintain friendly and intimate relations with his
old whig friends ; [2] but far more doubt was felt about
Grafton who, though he had been secretary of state
in the late administration, had never really been in
complete accord with the party, and appeared to be
now more devoted to Chatham than ever.[3] Youthful
and impressionable, he was dazzled by the glamour
of the doctrine of efficiency, and was inclined to credit
his former associates with preferring the triumph of a
party to the welfare of the nation. The loss of Grafton,
however, could be easily borne if Conway continued

[1] Add. MS., 32976, f. 511.

[2] " Yesterday my Lord Rockingham called here on his way to Bath. I
had a great deal of discourse with him ; he was in very good humour, and
seemed free and open. He gave me a general account of what had passed at
two conversations with Mr Conway, with which he was very much pleased,
as indeed we have all reason to be."—Newcastle to Portland, Oct. 11th, 1766.
Add. MS., 32977, f. 236 ; see also f. 91, f. 215.

[3] Add. MS., 32976, f. 511 ; Add. MS., 32977, f. 91.

faithful, and it was in him that the Rockingham whigs placed their trust. Yet Conway, though able to hold out a helping hand, by no means controlled the political situation, and it rested with Chatham to direct the course of future events. Haughty and dictatorial, never ready to trim his sails to the breeze, it was very possible that the prime minister might drive the Rockingham party into headlong opposition. If he replied to friendly advances by deliberate insults, open war might take the place of an armed neutrality; and the information, given by Conway to Newcastle at the end of September, that " we were to expect some further removals, and that some of them would be very disagreeable," [1] was hardly hopeful of peace in the future. Moreover, the unfavourable impression created by such intelligence must have been intensified by the overtures made by Chatham to the Duke of Bedford when they met at Bath in the month of October.[2] The vague assurances of the minister were by no means sufficient to satisfy the leader of a party which thoroughly understood the art of political bargaining; but the abortive negotiation is of interest, inasmuch as it shows that Chatham had not the slightest intention of throwing in his lot exclusively with the Rockingham whigs, and was as determined as ever to win recruits from all camps.

It would be, however, to inflict a startling injustice upon a great statesman to imagine that Chatham had no other design in taking office than to wage a domestic war, or that he spent all his time and energy in futile negotiations. He had come into the king's service to accomplish greater things than these; and no sooner had he constructed his cabinet than he set to work to repair what he believed to be the most pressing

---

[1] Add. MS., 32977, f. 91.   [2] Bedford Correspondence, 3, 348 ff.

evils of the time. He found much to regret in the position which his country occupied in Europe. When he had retired from the coalition ministry in the autumn of 1761, the nation stood at the very pinnacle of its fame, triumphant over France, and allied with the victorious King of Prussia; but, on returning to power five years later, he discovered that, though the horrors of war had been exchanged for the blessings of peace, England no longer enjoyed that proud predominance which he had formerly bestowed upon her. Though outwardly all was quiet and at rest, the signs of a gathering storm might be read in the political heavens. The two Bourbon countries of France and Spain were now united by the family compact, concluded in 1761; and, as both these powers had suffered many recent indignities and losses at the hands of England, they might be expected to seek revenge upon their conquerer at the first favourable opportunity. No man could foretell when that occasion would arise, but it was necessary for England to be prepared to meet this dread event when it came. Unfortunately, nothing was clearer than her lack of preparation, for she stood isolated in Europe, and, if attacked by France and Spain, might well be overwhelmed by the mere weight of numbers. She had quarrelled with her former ally, Frederick the Great of Prussia, the most renowned general of his time and the leader of an army which might safely be counted upon to hold France in check. Into the rights and wrongs of that quarrel, which had occurred when Bute was prime minister, this is not the place to enter; and Chatham showed no disposition to rake up the ashes of a dead controversy.[1] He looked to the future

---

[1] For a discussion of the rupture between England and Prussia in 1762, see von Ruville's *William Pitt, Graf. von Chatham*, vol. iii. chap. 2.

not to the past, and set to work to free England from
her isolation by beginning a negotiation for an alliance
with Prussia, in which Russia was to be included.
This was certainly no fool-hardy enterprise, for there
was much to encourage him to believe that the English
advances would be welcomed by Frederick the Great.
The King of Prussia was known to retain a grateful
memory of the services rendered him by Pitt during
the Seven Years war ; and, now that his benefactor was
once more in office, it might be anticipated that he
would forget his grievances, and welcome the English
overtures.   This, unfortunately, proved to be a delusive
hope.   Bearing in lively remembrance what he had
suffered at the hands of Bute who, he firmly believed,
had betrayed him in his hour of greatest need, Frederick
was resolved not to enter again into an alliance with
a country in which a change of cabinet might mean
a revolution in foreign policy.   Many ministers had
risen and fallen since George III. ascended the throne ;
and though Chatham was now in power, and able to
lead England where he would, in a twelvemonth he
might be in opposition again, and deprived of any
influence over the destinies of the country.   Nor was
it only a well founded objection to the want of consistency in English foreign policy that induced
Frederick to reject Chatham's advances : an important
change had also taken place in his own situation.   He
had recently become the ally of his former enemy,
Russia, and was already deeply immersed in the tangled
game of Polish politics, playing it with a skill which was
to be rewarded in a few years by the first partition of
Poland.   Engaged upon such work, he was not likely to
receive, nor indeed to need, the assistance of England.
Secure against another attack by Austria who was
not disposed to appeal against the decisive verdict

of the Seven Years war, and with little to fear from France, Frederick had turned his face to the east, and could afford to dispense in safety with the English alliance. England, indeed, needed him far more than he needed England; and, although he kept Chatham in play for some weeks, it was never his intention to come to terms, and, before the year was out, it was perfectly clear that it was useless to continue the negotiation. The disappointment was serious, for, if Chatham had succeeded in concluding the alliance, not only would the country have been removed from her dangerous isolation, but something would have been done towards reviving the glorious memories of his first administration. He had staked not a little, including his reputation, upon a successful throw of the dice, and fortune played him false.[1]

It was hardly a happy beginning for a ministry which, constituted as it was in direct defiance of the political experience of the previous half-century, required to be justified by success; and, unfortunately for Chatham, failure abroad was accompanied by the commission of an illegal, if necessary, action at home. An exceptionally bad summer had ruined the harvest, and consequently raised the price of corn; and in several districts the lower classes, brought to the verge of starvation, and inflamed by the belief that their distress was being aggravated by dealers withholding corn from the market, broke out into riot and disorder, stormed granaries, and, seizing upon supplies of grain, distributed them at low prices amongst themselves. No government could allow such flagrant lawlessness to continue unchecked, but, as coercion might only increase the mischief, it was wiser to dissipate the fear of famine and restore public confidence

---

[1] Von Ruville's *William Pitt, Graf. von Chatham*, vol. iii. chap. 10.

by forbidding any further exportation of corn from the country. To do this, however, the intervention of parliament was legally necessary, for under the existing law exportation continued permissible until the price of corn at home had risen to fifty-three shillings and fourpence a quarter, a level which, in spite of the scarcity, it had not yet attained. As parliament was not then in session, much valuable time would be wasted before the necessary statutory change could be effected ; and the severity of the crisis might be pleaded in favour of a course of action, difficult to justify by the strict letter of the law. Chatham and his colleagues were decidedly of the opinion that no time was to be lost, and, on September 24th, the privy council placed an embargo upon any further exportation of corn from the country. That in so doing the council exceeded its legal authority cannot be doubted, since it had taken upon itself to exercise a power of suspending law, which it certainly did not possess ; but the necessity had been so urgent that it might be anticipated that the ministers would escape hostile criticism in parliament. The Rockingham party was not at all likely to condemn the action of the government, for Newcastle had attended the meeting of the council, and warmly approved all that had been done ; [1] and the Duke of Bedford was equally reluctant to take up the cudgels against the ministers. If it had not been for Grenville and Lord Temple, the administration might have counted upon immunity from attack ; [2] but, though all might remain silent, Grenville, to whose legal and pedantic intelligence such a point proved irresistibly attractive, was

[1] Add. MS., 32977, f. 160.
[2] Add. MS., 32977, f. 332 ; Bedford Correspondence, 3, 353-354 ; Grenville Papers, 3, 337.

determined to bring home to the ministers that, however great had been the necessity, they had been guilty of a violation of the law of the land.

Parliament met on November 11th, 1766. In the king's speech the embargo was mentioned, but there was no reference to its illegal character, and this natural reticence was maintained in the addresses of both houses. It is very probable that the omission was not due to a desire to refrain from giving a point of attack, but rather to a misconception on the part of the ministers of the position in which they stood. At the meeting of the privy council, which had issued the embargo, Camden, the lord chancellor, had declared " that the king's ordinary prerogative did not empower his majesty to do it ; but that by the constitution, and by all constitutions, there must be a power to save the whole, the *salus populi* ; that, if this was the case, if there was such a necessity, then there was that power to do it." [1] Dangerous as such a doctrine was, and suggestive more of the age of the Stuarts than the Hanoverian era, the members of the privy council may be forgiven for accepting their law from the lord chancellor. But, if they believed their action to be legal, they were to be quickly undeceived by parliament ; for, though the addresses passed in both houses without a division, the government was obliged to listen to some very sharp criticism ; and the situation was not improved by Lord Camden repeating the same theory of the constitution as he had expounded to the privy council. Lord Mansfield, playing the very unwonted rôle of a champion of liberty, denounced the embargo as an illegal encroachment upon the freedom of the subject, and Lord Temple demanded that the ministers should introduce

[1] Add. MS., 32977, f. 160.

an indemnity bill to cover their own illegality. In the lower house Grenville, true to his word, branded the king's servants as law-breakers, and it was undeniably fortunate for the government that both the Bedfords and Rockinghams abstained from taking part in the attack. When Grenville found that he was almost alone, he inquired of Rigby what the members of his party were going to do, and received as an answer, "We are to do nothing, but, so help me God, as I am a man of honour, it is not by my advice." [1]

Sharp as much of the criticism had been, Chatham had indeed cause for exultation if he could take the first day of the session as an omen for the future; for the proceedings had been characterised by the entire absence of any co-operation between the enemies of the administration. The Rockinghams and Bedfords had stood aside while Grenville led the attack; and, if each of the various parties continued to act in isolation, the ministers might confidently look forward to a comfortable and easy session. An adept politician would have carefully weighed the parliamentary forces, and framed his conduct accordingly; but Chatham, who was singularly defective in political strategy, and far too careless of details ever to be a really successful parliamentary leader, threw away an advantage, which he ought to have tenderly cherished, by wilfully inflicting an insult upon the men whom he should have conciliated. Two days after the meeting of parliament, he informed Lord Edgecumbe, the treasurer of the household and a follower of Rockingham, that he must resign his office in favour of Shelley, a politician of little account, who had deserted his uncle, the Duke

---

[1] Grenville Papers, 3, 382-384; Walpole's Letters, 7, 72-74; Bedford Correspondence, 3, 354; Hist. MSS. Comm. Stopford Sackville MSS., 1, 114-117.

of Newcastle, in order to attach himself to Chatham.
It is difficult to perceive any sufficient justification for
this treatment of Edgecumbe ; and the treasurer of
the household, justly offended that so worthless a
creature as Shelley was preferred to him, was not to be
appeased by the stately compliments of Chatham who
told him that " his majesty did not mean to show
any slight or disregard to his lordship, but, on the
contrary, he hoped it would be a means of his having
him nearer his person in a more distinguished office,
and that the king for that purpose wished to have him
of his bedchamber." Aware that he was being kicked
upstairs, Edgecumbe was not to be won by fine words,
and caustically remarked that " he thought himself
rather too old to come up three hundred miles twice
or thrice in a year to have the honor of putting
on the king's shirt." [1]

Thus, for no apparently better reason than that
a sycophant should be given a place, Edgecumbe
was told to go ; but insults have a way of recoiling
upon those who inflict them. Chatham had indeed
made a dangerous enemy, for not only might the dismissed treasurer of the household take his revenge
by using his considerable electioneering influence in
the counties of Devon and Cornwall against the
government ;[2] but also, through him, his friends, the
Rockingham whigs, had been insulted, and they might
be expected to resent the affront. Indeed, the time had
come for them to take decisive action, to look to their
arms and means of defence ; for there was good reason to
believe that the dismissal of Edgecumbe was not intended
to be a solitary event, but the opening of a carefully
thought-out campaign. Hints had been dropped that

[1] Add. MS., 32977, f. 394.
[2] Walpole's *Memoirs of the Reign of George III.*, 2, 267,

there might be some unpleasant changes in the ministry, and Lord Monson, another follower of Rockingham, had already been told that he must resign the chief justiceship in eyre, directly a suitable successor could be found.[1]

In view of Chatham's minatory attitude, the Rockinghams can hardly be accused of surrendering to panic if they foresaw danger and disaster looming ahead. Indeed, they would have failed in their duty if they had not seized the occasion to reconsider their policy. It was clear that if, adhering to their original resolution, they continued to give an unconditional support to the administration, they would not only lose their prestige in the political world, and acquire an unenviable reputation for patient endurance of the whips and scorns of the prime minister, but also run a serious risk of complete shipwreck. They might see their friends one by one driven from the government, and all their hopes of winning their way into the ministry through their allies in office brought to nothing. They must check the evil before it had gone too far, and clearly intimate to Chatham that their support in parliament was strictly dependent upon his good-will towards them. Nor were they as powerless against the minister as might superficially appear, for in Henry Conway they had a weapon which, if adroitly enough used, might inflict a mortal wound. If Conway responded to the call of his party, and refused to continue to serve the man who had so wantonly outraged his friends, Chatham might be driven hard to find another secretary of state, and discover too late that, in order to satisfy a whim, he had destroyed his own administration.

Few statesmen have been placed in a more delicate

[1] Add. MS., 32977, f. 198, f. 390.

and painful situation than Conway at this moment, and few have issued more pitiably out of the crisis of their lives. Well equipped in many respects to play a great part in public life, intelligent, conscientious, and industrious, he never succeeded in attaining greatness, and the failure was not accidental. He lacked that faith in himself, that confidence in his own destiny, without which no man can rise above mediocrity ; and, when the time of trial came, Conway revealed his weakness, and, instead of seeking to mould events, allowed them to mould him. Yet, much as there is to condemn in his conduct, it must not be forgotten that it was a cruel and relentless fate which called him to endure such an ordeal. Maintaining cordial and intimate relations with his old whig friends, and still regarding Rockingham as in a certain sense his leader, he was torn between duty to his country and loyalty to his party. If he continued to act under Chatham after the treatment meted out to Edgecumbe, he would lie open to the accusation of treachery towards those by whose side he had once fought and conquered ; and if, on the other hand, he followed Edgecumbe into retirement, he must be prepared to meet the charge of preferring the triumph of a faction to the greatness of his country. Whichever course he adopted, his conduct lay open to misconstruction, and would certainly be misconstrued ; and, fearing to put his fate to the touch, he fell to playing the part of the Hamlet of the political world.

The unhappy situation of the secretary of state was, however, a golden opportunity for his friends to strike a blow at Chatham. Conway first heard of Edgecumbe's dismissal on Monday, November 17th, and at once sent for Rockingham who arrived to

find him horrified and aghast at the prime minister's
conduct, and uncertain what he ought to do.
" General Conway," Rockingham informed Newcastle,
" felt equally this dismission, both in regard to its
being of one of the corps, and also as being of a person
who had enjoyed the late Duke of Devonshire's friendship, and who at my desire had brought into parliament
gratis, not more than six months ago, General Conway's
nephew, Lord Beauchamp " ; and thus a situation,
already sufficiently involved, was further complicated
by considerations of private friendship.[1] What Conway
would do, no one, least of all himself, knew, and if
the Rockingham whigs were to reap the full advantage of the situation, they must drive him into taking
action. Subjected to the right amount of pressure,
properly applied, he might be induced to abandon
office, carrying Chatham with him in his fall;[2] and the
problem before the Rockingham whigs was how
they could persuade their indecisive friend to take
so decisive a step. "What his decision will be I
cannot say," wrote the marquis. "Perhaps his conduct depends upon ours."[3]

It was to deal with this question, and to frame
a plan of campaign, that the leaders of the party
assembled at Rockingham's house on Wednesday,
November 19th. They were informed that " something
must be done to show spirit, to keep our friends together, and to encourage Mr Conway to persist in the
good disposition he was in at present. That, if nothing
was done, the party, and all the friends of the late

[1] Add. MS. 32977, f. 415. Horace Walpole, however, affirms that it was
Rockingham who reminded Conway of his personal obligations to Edgecumbe.
Walpole's *Memoirs of the Reign of George III.*, 2, 267.

[2] Rockingham reported that Conway had threatened resignation to
Chatham, who had replied that in that event he also would retire. Add.
MS., 32978, f. 1.

[3] Add. MS., 32977, f. 415, f. 421 ; Rockingham Memoirs, 2, 19-24.

administration, would be weeded out by degrees, our friends angry and discouraged, and everything left to the arbitrary disposition of my Lord Chatham without any check or control," and the truth of this statement was too obvious to require much explanation or to evoke a lengthy discussion. It was almost unanimously agreed that four leading members of the party, the Duke of Portland, the Earl of Scarborough, the Earl of Bessborough, and Lord Monson should resign their places in the administration, that " further resignations in the house of commons might follow afterwards " ; and that Conway should be informed of what his friends intended to do. Thus the order for retreat was sounded, and it was anticipated that the secretary of state would feel impelled by every instinct of honour to follow his old friends into retirement. If they so publicly repudiated Chatham and all his works, he would seem to have no alternative but to do the same ; and thus Edgecumbe might be avenged by the downfall of the ministry. It was still open, indeed, for Chatham to save himself and his administration, but only at the price of a confession of wrong-doing and the reinstatement of the dismissed treasurer of the household.

In the best laid schemes, however, there must always lurk an element of uncertainty, and the success of this method of attack upon the government depended entirely upon Conway's action. It is true that all present at the meeting, with a single exception, believed that he would retire when so peremptorily called upon to do so ; but that single exception was the Duke of Newcastle who, though he assented to the opinion of the majority for the sake of preserving unity, did not approve the plan. He was as anxious as those, from whom he differed, to keep the party together, and to protect it against the onslaught of Chatham ; but his wider and more varied acquaintance with political life enabled him to perceive dangers hidden from less experienced eyes. He dreaded a fiasco, arguing with no little force that many members of the party, dependent upon politics for a living, might be very loath to resign their places, and that, even if the resignations were successfully executed, Conway, instead of being driven to retire, might take offence at the factious conduct of his friends, and continue in office. If indeed this came about, the last state of the Rockingham party might easily be worse than the first ; for Chatham, deprived of the services of Portland and his friends, and threatened by their avowed hostility, might purchase safety by an alliance with the Bedford party or the adherents of Lord Bute. Time was to prove that Newcastle was not far from the truth ; but his arguments fell upon deaf ears, and it could have been but sorry comfort for him to reflect that he was wiser than his friends.[1]

In accordance with the approved procedure, the Duke of Portland waited upon Conway on Friday, November 21st, and informed him of the storm which was about to burst upon the administration. Though, naturally enough, much agitated by the intelligence,

[1] Add. MS., 32977, f. 445 ; Add. MS., 32978, f. 1 ; Rockingham Memoirs, 2, 19-24. A few days later Newcastle received information which confirmed him in his opinion : " I think myself obliged to acquaint your grace," he wrote to the Duke of Portland, " that I have great reason to fear, and indeed to know, that the resignations will not be received by the party in the manner it was imagined ; nor be generally or at all, followed by those in employment in the house of commons. . . . Lord Rockingham is extremely mistaken as to the behaviour of his friends, and particularly the Townshends upon this occasion. Tommy Townshend of the treasury, Charles Townshend of the admiralty, and George Onslow have agreed to act together ; they were all against resignations, and have now, as I am informed, determined not to resign." Add. MS., 32978, f. 51. It was from George Onslow himself that Newcastle acquired this information, f. 64.

for he saw himself driven to make a final choice between Chatham and the whig cause, Conway evinced
no displeasure; but he pleaded for delay, on the ground
that Grafton had been with him that morning, and
had held out hopes of Edgecumbe receiving proper
satisfaction. The request was reasonable enough,
but, though Portland acceded to it, he very explicitly
explained that " the satisfaction to Lord Edgecumbe
must be immediate, that assurances must be given
to the party of . . . respect and countenance, that
they must stand as forward to be provided for as any
other persons whatever, and that he must be admitted
to that confidence and those communications which
would alone give us security for any promises that
might be made in the present emergency." [1]

To these terms Conway cordially agreed, but he
was well aware how gloomy the outlook was. He had
little reason to hope that Chatham would condescend
to reinstate Edgecumbe, or even to make him suitable
reparation; [2] and yet, unless this was done, the resignations would take effect, and Conway would be forced
to declare himself on one side or the other. With a
sincerity, which cannot possibly be mistaken, he told
Portland that " he had not had a happy moment since
his embarking (I understood) a second time; and that,
if he only consulted his own ease of mind and body,
he should not stay one moment in employment." [3]
Like a drowning man he was ready to clutch at any
means of salvation, and the proverbial straw happened
to float across his path. Lord Bessborough, joint

---

[1] Add. MS., 32978, f. 11; Rockingham Memoirs, 2, 19-24. The letter in
the Rockingham Memoirs is misdated by one day.

[2] The day before he visited Conway, Portland remarked in a letter, " all
that I learn is that Conway has been with my Lord Chatham, and finds him
inflexible." Add. MS., 32977, f. 449.

[3] Add. MS., 32978, f. 11.

postmaster general, and one of the four peers who had agreed to retire in the event of Chatham proving obstinate, suddenly proposed that, in any case, he should give up his office, and that it should be given to Edgecumbe who would thus receive ample compensation for the loss of the treasurership of the household. Much could be urged superficially in favour of Bessborough's suggestion, for there was reason to believe that Edgecumbe would be more than satisfied with such an arrangement; and no time was lost by Conway in submitting the proposal to Chatham.[1] But, if Conway was exultant over the change in the political situation, seeing, at last, a gleam of hope on the horizon, Newcastle and Rockingham were correspondingly despondent. Aggrieved not unnaturally with Bessborough for acting so precipitately without taking them into his confidence, they repudiated his proposal in the name of the party. " This unfortunate step in our friend, my Lord Bessborough," wrote Newcastle, " has quite ruined everything when there were the best appearances " ;[2] and this gloomy judgment was not so very wide of the mark. Edgecumbe might be content to have the post office, and Bessborough willing to put up with the bedchamber which Edgecumbe had scornfully rejected ; but the happiness of these two noblemen had not been the object of an elaborate political intrigue. Bessborough had either forgotten, or had never realised, that Edgecumbe was simply being used as a weapon with which to wound Chatham ; and, though the latter might possibly agree

---

[1] Chatham Correspondence, 3, 130. The letter is dated Friday, November 24th, an obvious slip for Friday, November 21st, the day on which Conway first heard the news. The letter begins, " Having this moment heard a thing," a phrase which he would hardly have used, if his information was already three days old.

[2] Add. MS., 32978, f. 41.

to make Edgecumbe joint postmaster general, such a concession would by no means satisfy the demands of either Newcastle or Rockingham. They desired some guarantee that the prime minister would not continue to inflict insults upon their followers, driving them one by one from the ministry; and any concordat, which omitted this fundamental condition, might well work the destruction of the Rockingham party. Bessborough, in spite of all his good intentions, had indeed been guilty of a serious error in tactics, and his blundering threatened to prevent his friends from effectively stemming the tide of Chatham's arrogance, and to give Conway an easy excuse for continuing in office.

Yet, the alarm aroused in Newcastle and Rockingham was shown to be unnecessary; for Chatham, blind to his good fortune, absolutely declined to consider Bessborough's proposal, or, indeed, to make any concession whatever. All hope of a reconciliation having vanished by November 26th,[1] the four peers resigned their places, and their example was followed by Sir Charles Saunders, the first lord of the admiralty, and two members of the same board, Admiral Keppel and Sir William Meredith. That other resignations did not follow may be attributed to a natural reluctance on the part of politicians, who had secured a comfortable office, to cast themselves once more adrift; but, though numerically more restricted than had been intended, the secession was undoubtedly a striking demonstration against the prime minister's arbitrary conduct. Whether, however, it was to be anything more than a demonstration depended upon Conway. The moment for decisive action had found him as wavering and irresolute as ever. Shortly before

[1] Add. MS., 32978, f. 78.

vacating his office, Portland told Newcastle that " Conway does not resign at present, but tells me he thinks he shall not stay, and seems further to be of opinion that upon the principles Lord Chatham has adopted, it is impossible for the administration to last long " ; [1] but the days passed by, and Conway, a prey to irresolution' and doubt, still continued in office. His brother, Lord Hertford, and his most intimate friend, Horace Walpole, were urgent in persuading him that the whigs were using him for their own selfish ends ; and, from the other side, Rockingham and the Cavendishes were calling to him to resign on grounds of honour and decency. In such circumstances the boldest man might have passed through a period of doubt ; and Conway is worthy of blame, not because he stumbled on the road, but because he never arrived at his destination. Compelled to make a choice between Rockingham and Chatham, he never made it ; he was neither for God nor for the Devil. Though he continued as secretary of state, the thought of resignation was never out of his mind, and twice in the house of commons he significantly described himself as a passenger in the administration.[2] Nor, if Horace Walpole is to be trusted, did he ever forgive Chatham : " the wound rankled so deeply in Mr Conway's bosom, that he dropped all intercourse with Lord Chatham ; and, though he continued to conduct the king's business in the house of commons, he would neither receive nor pay any deference to the minister's orders, acting for or against as he approved or disliked his measures." [3]

Thus, though Conway continued to sit in the cabinet, his value to Chatham was seriously diminished ;

---

[1] Add. MS., 32978, f. 78.   [2] Grenville Papers, 3, 396.
[3] *Memoirs of the Reign of George III.*, ii. 273.

and this was not the only consequence of the dismissal
of the treasurer of the household. The Rockingham
whigs, who had previously been disposed to refrain
from opposing the ministry, were now inclined to
adopt a more hostile attitude. They had sought
peace, and had been insulted for their pains ; and
the natural conclusion to draw was that the time
had come to exchange the olive branch for the sword.
It was necessary to wait for a fitting opportunity for
attack ; but, when that moment came, there would be
nothing to restrain Rockingham and his followers
from entering upon the battle into which they had
been provoked. It was better to perish fighting than
to be led like victims to the slaughter.

Yet, in spite of the threatening danger, Chatham
appeared almost magnificently careless of the future.
Except for the loss of Sir Charles Saunders and Admiral
Keppel, whose services he valued, he troubled little
about the withdrawal of the Rockingham whigs from
the administration. He looked to the court for help
in his time of trouble, assuring Grafton, panic stricken
by the rising storm, that " the closet is firm, and there
is nothing to fear." [1] He was as determined, as when
he had originally taken office, that his ministry should
reflect the opinions of all political parties ; and, to fill
the vacancies caused by the recent resignations, he
began a negotiation with the Duke of Bedford. The
restricted character of his offer, for it was only proposed
that Gower should be master of the horse, Lord Weymouth postmaster, and Rigby cofferer, conclusively
condemned it in the eyes of the Bedfords who coveted
the first lordship of the admiralty, left vacant by the
resignation of Sir Charles Saunders ; but neither
George III. nor Chatham were prepared to forego

[1] Grafton's *Autobiography*, p. 107.

their crusade against the party system for the sake of acquiring the support of the Woburn confederation. " A contrary conduct," wrote the king at this time, " would at once overturn the very end proposed at the formation of the present administration ; for to rout out the present method of parties banding together, can only be obtained by a withstanding their urgent demands, as well as the engaging able men, be their private connections where they will." [1] This might be true enough, but the effect of such a policy was to drive George III. and Chatham into the highways and hedges for ministers ; and, failing to come to terms with the Bedfords, they filled the vacant places, for the most part, with adherents of Lord Bute. It is true that Sir Edward Hawke, who succeeded Saunders at the admiralty, was a most distinguished seaman, and cannot be counted as belonging to any political party ; but both Jenkinson and Brett, who succeeded Keppel and Meredith on the admiralty board, were well-known followers of Bute, and when Bute's heir, Lord Mount Stuart, moved Jenkinson's new writ in the house of commons, members smiled at one another.[2]   But, though men might smile to see Chatham conferring places upon such insignificant politicians, they might well weep when they saw Lord Despenser introduced into the administration in the capacity of joint postmaster general.   Better known by his earlier title of Sir Francis Dashwood, Despenser had not only obtained a widespread and almost un-rivalled reputation for profligacy, but had also given ample proof of his administrative inefficiency during the time that he served Bute as chancellor of the exchequer.   If the consequence of the destruction of the party system was to be that politicians of this

---

[1] Chatham Correspondence, 3, 137.   [2] Add. MS., 32978, f. 168.

stamp were to be given a voice, however subordinate, in the government of the country, wise men might begin to look back with affectionate regret upon the worst days of whig supremacy. It was quite certain that the changes in the ministry were not directed to the promotion of efficiency, nor likely to elicit the confidence of the nation : " The strength the government will acquire by all these promotions," wrote Portland to the Duke of Newcastle, " I leave your grace to judge of ; it cannot want any comment." [1]

Yet, when parliament rose on December 15th for the Christmas holidays, Chatham appeared to have more than held his own, and to have triumphed over his enemies. But, victorious though he had been, the session had not been free from incidents which might have suggested to the more thoughtful supporters of the government that it was time to pause. In order to protect from legal proceedings the custom house officers who, acting under the illegal order of the privy council, had prevented the exportation of corn, Conway had introduced an indemnity bill, thus affording Grenville an opportunity for continuing the attack which he had begun on the first day of the session. Nor were his criticisms without effect. As originally framed, the bill only applied to those who had acted under the embargo ; but, in the course of its passage through the lower house, Conway was obliged to extend it to those who had advised the measure, thus overthrowing Camden's constitutional defence of the ministerial action, and emphasising, somewhat unpleasantly, that the king's servants, however justified they had been by necessity, had been guilty of a breach of the law to which they at first had been unwilling to own. And this was not the only

[1] Add. MS., 32978, f. 135.

change that was made.   In the original preamble to
the bill it was affirmed that the embargo could not
be justified by the strict rules of law, an ambiguous
and undoubtedly misleading statement which did not
escape Grenville's notice, and which was finally
amended by the omission of the word "strict." [1]
Thus, though the bill was carried by substantial
majorities, success had not been achieved without making somewhat damaging concessions ; and, although
the ministers might plume themselves upon a victory,
they owed it in no small degree to the support they
received from the majority of the followers of Bedford
and Rockingham.   But there was little assurance that
such assistance would be continued in the future.[2]
The indemnity bill, save to a man like Grenville bent
upon opposition at all cost, was hardly a contentious
measure ; and the Rockingham whigs, originally well
disposed towards the government, had, in the course
of the session, been driven by Chatham himself to
think more of attack than of conciliation.   They were
biding their time, and, when that time came, they
would not fail to strike.

Thus, in view of the actual situation, Chatham
might have gained applause for his political wisdom
if he had confined his activities within a narrow and
non-disputatious sphere, and carefully abstained from
pursuing a policy likely to provoke opposition or alarm
vested interests.   But, whatever were his faults, and
they were many, he was never deficient in courage, or
wanting in obedience to his sense of duty ; and no man
was less disposed to refrain from action for fear of

[1] Hist. MSS. Comm. Stopford Sackville MSS., I, 114-117.
[2] Edmund Burke and Rigby sometimes joined Grenville in opposing the
government, and if the preamble had not been amended, Rockingham wa
prepared to attack it in the house of lords, and was anxious for Newcastle
to do the same.   Add. MS., 32978, f. 204, f. 208, f. 215, f. 221.

giving a handle to his enemies. He had issued from his retirement into the glare of public life, inspired by no selfish seeking after power, but convinced that there was work to be done for England, which no one but he could do ; and no sooner had he taken office than he addressed himself to a task which, if successfully accomplished, would materially add to his renown, but which was undeniably attended by many and great dangers. This undertaking was no other than an inquiry into the affairs of the East India Company, with a view to revising the existing relations between that corporation and the state ; and the enterprise was not only fraught with dangers and difficulties, but might easily afford an opportunity for an attack upon the government, in which the Rockingham whigs might join and thus revenge themselves for what they had suffered at the hands of Chatham. The minister was well aware of the perils of the voyage on which he was setting out, of the strange and stormy seas he would be obliged to traverse ; but he believed himself called upon to meet an urgent necessity, and took his political life into his hands.

Time had indeed wrought a change in the fortunes of the East India Company, and most impartial men, though differing as to its scope, agreed in thinking that some sort of an inquiry was necessary. Originally a purely trading association, the company had become possessed, more by chance than by design, of territorial power, and, from comparatively humble beginnings, had risen to be the ruler of a vast and increasing dominion. As the result of the Seven Years war, Bengal and the adjacent states passed under its influence ; and the overthrow of the French in India, which was a consequence of the same conflict, removed the last effective barrier to the extension of its authority. With revenues now swelled from other sources than those of trade, connected by treaties with native princes, and deeply immersed in the tangled and tortuous politics of the east, the company was burdened with new and weighty responsibilities which it was not well adapted to discharge. It is proverbial that traders are rarely qualified for the enjoyment of independent political power, since their immediate aim being the acquisition of wealth they are under the temptation to sacrifice everything that stands in the way of the attainment of this end. Nor, indeed, was there any reason to believe that the East India Company would prove an exception to this rule ; on the contrary, every indication existed to show how unworthy it was to be entrusted with the government of what might one day develop into a mighty empire, and that, however successful it had been in trade, it was incompetent and inefficient as a sovereign ruler. A mutiny among the company's native troops in the spring of 1766 pointed a moral which had already become sufficiently clear, and it was seriously anticipated that an empire, which had been acquired by valour and skill, would be lost by mismanagement and corruption. Nor were these the only evils that the state was called upon to redress. The majority of Englishmen, unable to distinguish between public and private gain, and dazzled by the spectacle of men returning, after a comparatively brief sojourn in the east, enriched beyond the wildest dreams of avarice, were led to believe that the company was as wealthy as its servants. As nothing was known, everything was believed, and every nabob, who returned to flaunt his opulence in the face of an envious and credulous public, helped to confirm and spread the legend of the vast and inexhaustible resources of the company. In any civilised community it needs but a spark to fire the gambling spirit latent in all men, and, as speculation in East India stock had already begun, there was no little danger of a repetition of the catastrophe of the South Sea Bubble. It was the imperative duty of the state to check the evil before it attained more dangerous proportions; and therefore, both on grounds of policy and morality, the government was called upon to undertake a scrutiny into the affairs of the company.

The perils attending such an inquiry would, however, be many. Those whose interests were concerned in allowing the company to fill its coffers from the revenues of Bengal, those who thought more of plenty than of power, and were indifferent to what happened as long as their capital earned a substantial return, bitterly resented any interference by the government; and the most determined opposition might be expected from the city, once the stronghold of Chatham's influence. The cry was certain to be raised that the rights and privileges of all corporations were endangered, that the attack upon the East India Company was only the first of a series, and that soon charters would be of no greater value than the parchment upon which they were written. That not a little selfish greed, ignorance, and malice, lay at the bottom of this outcry did not make it any less formidable; but Chatham, though he had used the support of the people as a stepping-stone to power, was not of the order of demagogues who defer to public opinion in and out of season. He emphatically declared that the question of the company was " the greatest of all objects, according to my sense of great," [1] and this was no bombastic utterance but the expression of a fully

---

[1] Grafton's *Autobiography*, pp. 101-102.

formed determination. Action speedily followed upon words ; and, at the end of August, the Duke of Grafton, acting as Chatham's spokesman, informed the chairman and deputy chairman of the company that East India affairs would, in all probability, be brought before parliament in the forthcoming session.[1] The directors, appreciating the significance of the hint, understood that the most politic course to pursue was to refrain from giving any further handle to their critics ; but the proprietors of stock were far less discreet, and at a general court, held on September 24th, a dividend of ten per cent. was declared as a mark of defiance to the government, and in direct opposition to the wishes of the directors. This was a singularly futile proceeding, for it neither inspired the public with confidence nor intimidated the ministers.[2] On November 25th, Beckford, well known to be in Chatham's confidence, introduced a motion into the house of commons for examining into the company's affairs ; and, shortly before parliament rose for the Christmas holidays, it was resolved that copies of the grants made to the company, and statements of the revenues it enjoyed, should be laid before the house.[3]

Thus the attack was begun, and Horace Walpole was able to write that the session had ended " very triumphantly for the great earl."[4] The triumph, however, was but on the surface ; and it would appear that Chatham, however laudable his courage, was guilty of undue haste and precipitation, and failed to obtain success in this daring venture because he did not deserve it. The ministers were divided on the

[1] Chatham Correspondence, 3, 57-60 ; Grenville Papers, 3, 322-323.
[2] Bedford Correspondence, 3, 344-346 ; Grenville Papers, 3, 323-325 ; Chatham Correspondence, 3, 90-93.
[3] Chatham Correspondence, 3, 144, n. 1 ; Walpole's Memoirs, 2, 287-290.
[4] Walpole's Letters, 7, 77-79.

question of the proper policy to be pursued in regard to the affairs of the east, and can fairly be charged with beginning a serious and important undertaking too much in the spirit of haphazard enterprise. Chatham, himself, was convinced that an essential preliminary to any successful negotiation with the company was a parliamentary decision upon its right to the revenues it received as a territorial ruler ; while Charles Townshend and Conway were in favour of leaving this point, which would certainly prove contentious, out of consideration, and coming to terms with the company without delay.[1] Such a fundamental divergence of opinion necessarily brought with it divided counsels, and militated against success ; and this was not the only danger which menaced the future safety of the administration ; for what threatened to be a sword of division to the ministers seemed likely to prove a bond of union to their opponents. It was ominous for the future that in the division, which concluded the debate on November 25th, many of the Rockingham whigs were found in the minority, fighting side by side with George Grenville and the followers of the Duke of Bedford. Both Charles Yorke and Edmund Burke distinguished themselves by the fierceness of their opposition to the government,[2] and their conduct was well pleasing to their leaders. Newcastle declared himself "convinced upon most mature consideration, that the general inquiry into the private state of a great company, acting under a legal charter, without any fact alledged, or the least complaint made, is of most urgent consequence," and was delighted to find that Rockingham shared the same opinion.[3]

---

[1] Grafton's *Autobiography*, p. 109 ; Grenville Papers, 3, 331-336.
[2] Add. MS., 32978, f. 86.   [3] Add. MS., 32978, f. 244, f. 404.

The leaders of the ministry might indeed regard the future with anxiety. Rockingham, driven to abandon his pacific attitude by Chatham himself, was now in favour of what he called a general opposition, though he was careful to explain that by " general opposition he always meant upon such points only as were wrong in themselves." [1] This limitation, however, was not likely to prove very restrictive in practice, and would certainly not prohibit a defence of the East India Company which the marquis and his followers, apparently conscientiously, thought to be unjustifiably attacked. Moreover, in championing the rights of that corporation, they could count upon the assistance of Grenville and Bedford ; and it might reasonably be contended that the time had now come for the different sections of the opposition to unite. However much they differed, they were at least agreed on the East India question which seemed likely to absorb public attention for some time to come ; and, as it was certain that if they continued to fight separately, and without any common plan or organisation, the administration would prevail, it might be well to sink their differences, and unite in defence of what they all believed to be a righteous cause. Newcastle, taught by his rich political experience, was warmly in favour of an alliance with the Duke of Bedford who was rumoured to be quite prepared to come to terms ; but the difficulty in the way was George Grenville.[2] It was extremely unlikely that Bedford would agree to any alliance in which Grenville was not included ; for close and friendly relations existed between their two camps, and they had much in common, especially on questions where they differed from Lord Rockingham.

[1] Add. MS., 32978, f. 404.
[2] Add. MS., 32978, f. 15, f. 27, f. 35, f. 281, f. 285, f. 309.

Grenville had been first lord of the treasury, and Bedford president of the council, in the administration that had imposed the stamp act which Rockingham had repealed; and thus they had the same grievance against the party which had reversed their measure. But Grenville was far more identified than Bedford with the taxation of America, and far more bitterly hostile to the colonial policy of the Rockingham ministry; and it was assumed that, if he was ever given an opportunity, he would continue the work which he had begun with the imposition of the stamp act. Thus Rockingham and his followers were confronted with a difficult situation calling for delicate handling. They were prepared to conclude an alliance with Bedford, and even with Grenville; but it was reported that the latter, in the event of an administration being formed, demanded the treasury either for himself or his brother, Lord Temple,[1] and such a request would, indeed, prove a stumbling block. Valuable as was the support of the Bedford party, the promise of the treasury to Grenville was a very heavy price to pay for it, and Rockingham was able to point out " how strange it would appear to the public . . . to make him a principal, after you had spent a whole session in tearing to pieces all that he had done while in the treasury." [2] That the objection was well founded is undeniable, for Rockingham and his followers would have forfeited the respect of all honest men if they had consented to sit in an administration presided over by Grenville. But it was by no means certain that the Duke of Bedford was prepared to espouse Grenville's claim to the treasury; and Newcastle, understanding that, without some addition to their

---

[1] Add. MS., 35362, f. 48 ; Rockingham Memoirs, 2, 28-29.
[2] Add. MS., 32978, f. 299 ; Rockingham Memoirs, 2, 31-32.

parliamentary strength, it was very dangerous for his friends to begin a contest with the government, pressed for overtures to be made to Woburn ; but to this scheme Rockingham was opposed, favouring postponement in the hope of " making a better bargain about George Grenville." [1] But it was Newcastle's opinion which at first prevailed ; for, though Rockingham still continued to believe that Bedford would demand the treasury for Grenville, and that the wisest policy was to do nothing, it was decided at a meeting, held at Claremont on December 17th, that Lord Bessborough should approach Lord Gower.[2] At the last moment, however, this scheme was abandoned ; for when it was imparted to Portland and Albemarle, they both loudly protested against it, arguing that if overtures were made to the Bedfords, they would gain an exaggerated idea of their own importance, and consequently raise their terms ; [3] and, as Portland and Albemarle were important members of the party, whose opinions could not be safely disregarded, Newcastle was compelled to relinquish his much-cherished project, and seek comfort in the reflection that an alliance with the Bedford party might have driven him and his friends headlong into factious opposition.[4] Rockingham was, naturally enough, well pleased that what he had never approved should not be done ; [5] but, when all that could be said in favour of inaction had been urged, it remained undeniably true that the Rockingham whigs were in an unpleasantly dangerous situation. They had broken with Chatham, and were determined to oppose his East Indian policy; but they were no stronger in parliament than before, and Newcastle

[1] Add. MS., 32978, f. 299.
[2] Add. MS., 32978, f. 404.
[3] Add. MS., 32978, f. 378, f. 414.
[4] Add. MS., 32978, f. 484.
[5] Add. MS., 32978, f. 418.

must have found much sorrowfully to agree with in Bessborough's frank statement that " as things stand at present, you certainly have no plan at all, no system, nor do we know one another's minds : all is afloat, excepting in a very small set of men, who can make but a very small appearance in any division, and though honest and men of honour, yet they make but a very insignificant figure in regard to any material business in parliament, and are, 'tis true, laughed at, and all this arises from a want of knowing one another's minds, and being properly connected, and knowing what to do, for we have neither plan, system, method, or scheme." [1] Hard as these words were, they were only too bitterly true; and though it was easy for Rockingham, ever inclined to look on the bright side of things, to declare that " in regard to the ideas among our friends in the country . . . they are as right as right can be," [2] good intentions, alone, are apt to be of little value when brought into contact with the hard facts of parliamentary life. However great the determination to oppose the evil deeds of the government might be,[3] the ability to render opposition effective remained very doubtful.

Yet, evil as was the plight of the Rockingham whigs, there were some of the ministers who thought their own fate to be but little better. On the rising of parliament for the Christmas holidays Chatham set out for Bath, where he was to remain for many weeks; and, in his autobiography, Grafton deplores that his leader was " not sensible, nor would he be persuaded, of the many difficulties under which his administration labored, though they were viewed

---

[1] Add. MS., 32978, f. 488.   [2] Add. MS., 32979, f. 143.
[3] Add. MS., 32978, f. 436; Add. MS., 32979, f. 143.

with real concern by the nation at large."[1] Nor were the difficulties slow in making themselves felt. In the absence of the prime minister, detained week after week by a more than usually acute fit of gout, it fell to Grafton, as first lord of the treasury, to preside over the cabinet; and, though always " pleased the Almighty's orders to perform," the young duke was certainly deficient in that power which " rides in the whirlwind and directs the storm." He was destined to experience to the full all the evils of a divided and ill-assorted administration, and to become a plaything in the hands of fate and Charles Townshend. For it was now that Townshend, freed from all effective control, and careless of consequences, began to play the part of a mischievous sprite, and to teach the country that too heavy a price might be exacted for the privilege of having a witty and high-spirited minister. Down to its final doom the government passed with headlong force; and, when Chatham returned to London in the spring of 1767, he was to find his ministry in full enjoyment of the discredit which it richly deserved.

It was in the affairs of the East India Company that Townshend first displayed a tendency to pursue a policy independently of Chatham. Believing, unlike the prime minister, that it would be wise to conclude immediately a bargain with the company, and waive the question of its right to its territorial revenues, he found himself favoured by circumstances; for at a general court, held on the last day of the year, 1766, the directors were empowered " to treat with administration upon all such points, in the general state of the company, as they shall judge to be most re-

[1] Grafton's *Autobiography*, p. 109.

quisite and conducive to the extending their commerce, securing their possessions, and perpetuating the prosperity of the company." Acting upon these instructions, the chairman and deputy-chairman presented Grafton on January 8th with a paper, specifying the points upon which they were prepared to treat with the government; and, as might have been expected, while they asked for a renewal of their charter, their right to the revenues they drew from subject provinces was not included amongst the questions for discussion.[1] Chatham, to whom the offer was submitted at Bath, did not conceal his disgust, and rightly attributed the unfavourable turn events had taken "to the unfortunate original difference of opinions among the king's servants . . . which shook the whole foundation of this great transaction."[2] Worse news was to follow; for when East India affairs were under discussion in the house of commons on Tuesday, January 20th, and the following Thursday, Townshend, not only revealed that a negotiation with the company was on foot, but frankly avowed his difference of opinion with Chatham. He roundly declared that "the East India Company had a right to their territorial revenues," and, according to Beckford, "uttered so many kind and comfortable words for their consolation, that the stock rose the next and the succeed-

---

[1] Chatham Correspondence, 3, 149, 163; Hist. MSS. Comm., 12th Report, Appendix, Pt. ix.; Donoughmore MSS., p. 260; Weston Underwood MSS., 401. It is impossible to say with certainty that Townshend had any part in persuading the company to make overtures to the government; but that it should do so was certainly in accordance with his policy, and it is not without interest that on January 7th, Newcastle informed Albemarle that the ministers "are in the highest spirits about their success in the East India affairs. It is certainly all Charles Townshend's doing, who triumphs beyond measure upon it." Add. MS., 32979, f. 107.

[2] Grafton's *Autobiography*, p. 113.

ing day six per centum." Nor was the chancellor
of the exchequer the only mutineer, for Conway
had also declared that he was reluctant to permit
the company's territorial rights to be decided by a
parliamentary vote.[1]

Chatham, delayed by illness at Bath, might well be
appalled at hearing of the conduct of his rebellious
lieutenants ; and he was obliged to acknowledge the
unpalatable truth that they had succeeded in cutting
the ground from under his feet, at least for the time
being. It was impossible to expect the house of
commons, now informed that a negotiation had been
begun, to set to work to discuss an abstract question
of right ; and Chatham, though he did not abandon
his point, was compelled by Charles Townshend's
indiscretion to alter his plan of procedure. " I hear,"
he wrote to Shelburne, " that Mr Townshend has
declared in the house that a proposal from the company was upon the point of being made. After this
declaration, and during the pendency of a transaction
with the company, so avowed, I am clearly of opinion
that a question for deciding the right would not be
duly supported : it is therefore become necessary to
delay going into the consideration in the committee
till the proposal is made; after that, and when the
proposal is before the house, the whole matter will
be under the contemplation and ripe for the decision
of parliament. . . . I have advised Mr Beckford,
by this post, to put off the consideration for a
fortnight." [2]

Thus was Chatham obliged to trim his sails to the
breeze created by his subordinates, and it still re-

[1] Chatham Correspondence, 3, 176; Hist. MSS. Comm. Lothian MS.,
p. 274.
[2] Chatham Correspondence, 3, 181.

mained uncertain whether his government would succeed in weathering the storm. On February 7th, the directors presented their definite proposals to the cabinet, and, encouraged perhaps by Townshend's conciliatory attitude, they did not err on the side of excessive moderation. In return for the payment of the sum of £500,000, and the promise of an annual contribution to the state, they asked for the renewal of their charter for a term of fifty years, and that " their late acquisitions, possessions, and revenues should be annexed by act of parliament to the term to be given in the exclusive trade." [1] However objectionable such proposals might be, and whatever ambiguities they might contain,[2] it was the duty of the ministers, if they were to execute Chatham's wishes,[3] to submit them to parliament before coming to any decision upon them; but both Conway and Townshend were in favour of continuing the negotiation with the company, and waiting, until some final conclusion had been reached, before calling upon parliament for its advice and ratification.[4] In this, however, they were overruled, and it was agreed to lay the company's terms before parliament, even though the negotiation was but barely begun. Accordingly, Beckford, on March 6th, moved that the proposals should be laid

[1] Grafton's *Autobiography*, p. 114 ; Chatham Correspondence, 3, 196.

[2] A good deal of time was occupied by the ministers in clearing up, not very successfully, doubtful points in the proposals. Grafton's *Autobiography*, 118-120.

[3] " I now come," wrote Chatham on February 9th, " to the papers of the 6th of February from the committee of directors. I shall not enter into the merits of the proposal. Parliament is *the only place* where I will declare my final judgment upon the whole matter, if ever I have an opportunity to do it. As a servant of the crown, I have no right or authority to do more than simply to advise that the *demands* and the *offers* of the company should be laid before parliament, referring the whole determination to the wisdom of that place." Grafton's *Autobiography*, p. 116.

[4] Add. MSS., 32980, f. 207 ; Hist. MSS. Comm. Stopford Sackville MSS., I, 118 ; Grafton's *Autobiography*, p. 121.

before the house, and that the papers of the company, which had been already submitted to parliament, should be printed. Both motions were carried without a division, and further consideration of the question was postponed for a fortnight ; but, though the ministers had been apparently victorious, the debate had been not a little damaging to them by revealing their dissensions. Charles Townshend did . not scruple to utter his objections to the course proposed ; and Conway, though more moderate and restrained, argued that, as the proposals had neither been approved nor rejected by the cabinet, the time had not yet come to submit them to the judgment of the house of commons.[1]

If Grafton's anxiety for the future was intensified by the part played by Townshend and Conway in the debate on March 6th, the Rockingham whigs had equally little cause to feel satisfied. There had been an opportunity of attacking the ministry upon a question, on which they were in agreement with the Grenvilles and the Bedfords, and they had failed even to bring the motions to the test of a division. " We are much laughed at," wrote Newcastle, " for our conduct on Friday, and not making use of the advantages we had from Charles Townshend and Conway " ; and he could have been but ill pleased to learn from George Onslow that " yesterday was a great day for the administration ; that they carried their point ; that they have put off the East India affair for a fortnight ; in which time they will make up everything with Charles Townshend."[2] If such was indeed the case, the enemies of the administration

---

[1] Add. MS., 32980, f. 217 ; Grenville Papers, 4, 213 ; Walpole's Letters, 7, 89-92 ; Walpole's Memoirs, 2, 304-305.
[2] Add. MSS., 32980, f. 224, f. 238.

must strike a blow before it was too late ; and fortune favoured them. Rockingham, much to his joy, discovered that the order to print the company's papers, submitted to parliament, was objected to, not only by his friends, but also by the followers of Grenville and Bedford ;[1] and he was therefore encouraged to renew the attack by a reasonable chance of success, and in the hope that something might be done towards promoting a permanent alliance between the parties in opposition. Newcastle, as eager as ever in his old age for the fray, was delighted to see what he took to be the " beginning of concert between Lord Rockingham and the Bedford party," and emphatically and truly enough declared that " nothing can be done without it, either for the publick or the party."[2] Under such favourable conditions a plot was quickly hatched ; and in accordance with an idea, which apparently originated with Rigby, it was arranged that on Monday, March 9th, one of the directors of the company should present a petition to the house of commons, asking that the papers called for should not be printed. The government, taken by surprise, found itself confronted by an exultant and united opposition. Dowdeswell, Burke, Rigby, Grenville, and Charles Yorke all spoke on behalf of the company, and how nearly they approached victory is shown by the fact that the ministerial motion, to adjourn the debate until the following Wednesday, was only carried

---

[1] Add. MS., 32980, f. 220. " I have seen," wrote Rockingham to Charles Yorke, " several who are ready to revive the subject, and oppose the printing, etc. Sir Laurence Dundas, after he had been with me, saw Rigby. Rigby went to G. Grenville, and I met Rigby to-night at Arthur's . Rigby is eager, and assures me that G. Grenville is so, and will support and vote heartily. They have suggested that the best way of bringing the matter on again would be by getting the directors to apply to parliament, begging that the papers may not be printed." Add. MS., 35430, f. 166.

[2] Add. MS., 32980, f. 238.

by the slender majority of thirty-three votes.[1] Even
this, however, was more of a temporary check than a
defeat of the opposition who looked forward to resum-
ing the debate on March 11th, and nursed high hopes
of victory. " I don't think," wrote Lord Rockingham
on the day between the two encounters, " a majority
of thirty-three on a question of adjournment a mighty
matter of exultation for administration. . . . I think,
with some pains, we may add a few more, and I think
the Bedfords and Grenvillites may also add, and I
hope for some out of the 180."[2] But his expectations
were disappointed, for, when March 11th came, the
government frustrated its adversaries by beating a
retreat. It was proposed that only the charters and
treaties, and not the correspondence or accounts of the
company, should be printed, and the opposition,
deprived of a contest, was reluctantly obliged to
allow the motion to pass without a division. The
ministry had triumphed by playing the old game
of defeating your antagonists by embracing their
opinions.[3]

The course of East India affairs had certainly,
up to this point, not run any too smoothly for the
ministers; and, although they had succeeded in remaining afloat, they had not done much more. The
debates in the house of commons had revealed the
dissensions in the cabinet to the outside world; and
it was not only in its handling of this delicate and
intricate business that the ministry had lost in prestige and weight. It had been defeated in the house
of commons on a financial measure. When, on
February 27th, Charles Townshend had proposed that

---

[1] Add. MS. 32980, f. 248 ; Walpole's Memoirs, 2, 306-307 ; Walpole's
Letters, 7, 89.
[2] Add. MSS., 32980, f. 250.   [3] Add. MS., 32980, f. 262, f. 264.

the land tax should be continued at the existing rate of four shillings in the pound, William Dowdeswell, formerly Rockingham's chancellor of the exchequer, brought forward an amendment reducing the tax to three shillings ; and the amended motion, supported by all sections of the opposition, and by not a few country members who, though generally supporting the government, were anxious, with a general election looming in the near future, to please their constituents,[1] was carried against the ministry by eighteen votes.[2] This attack was certainly not due to the inspiration of the moment, for it had been carefully prepared beforehand by the Rockingham whigs.   Hearing that Grenville intended to propose a reduction of the land tax, and alarmed lest he should, in consequence, acquire too much popularity,[3] they agreed to forestall him, and Newcastle was active in whipping up supporters for Dowdeswell's motion.[4] That their conduct was factious, and entirely unworthy of their reputation for honesty and fair dealing must be frankly admitted by all impartial inquirers. It is true that Dowdeswell was able to make out a plausible case for the reduction ; but the best of politicians are only too adept at defending a bad cause ; and the heaviest condemnation of the Rockingham whigs, for their surrender to the desire for mere factious success, came from members of their own party.   Burke, Charles Yorke, and Lord Albemarle,

---

[1] George Cooke, who, though joint paymaster general, voted for the amendment, defended his action to Chatham on the ground that " his particular situation as member for Middlesex, and being chosen by the unanimous and affectionate voice of my constituents, rendered it impossible for me not to vote for the three shillings."   Chatham Correspondence, 3, 222 ; see also 224.

[2] Chatham Correspondence, 3, 224 ; Grenville Papers, 4, 211 ; Hist. MSS. Comm. Stopford Sackville MSS., 1, 119 ; Walpole's Memoirs, 2, 298 ff. Grenville dates the debate February 25th.

[3] Add. MS., 32980, f. 138.

[4] Add. MSS., 32980, f. 147, f. 149, f. 151, f. 153.

all disapproved in different degrees of the action of their friends; and if Admiral Keppel agreed to support the motion, it was only after making the damning confession that, if Dowdeswell proposed the reduction, " he believed he should be for it; but if Mr Grenville moved it, he should certainly be against it." [1]

A ministry, which deserved and enjoyed the confidence of the country, might have afforded to despise such an unworthy triumph; but Chatham's administration was not in a position to endure with safety even a defeat which reflected so little discredit. The land tax was the first important measure lost by a government since the fall of Sir Robert Walpole; [2] and the catastrophe had overtaken a cabinet which was torn by internal dissensions, and was pursuing, in its negotiation with the East India Company, so tortuous a road that it was impossible to guess at its destination. If additional burdens were added to its already heavy load, it seemed that it must collapse under a weight, already far too heavy for its shoulders; and it was an ironical stroke of fate that imposed upon an administration, which had already proved its inefficiency up to the hilt, the exceedingly difficult task of restoring peace and order in America. Unfortunately it is always easier to begin than to stop a revolution, and the colonial policy of the first Rockingham administration has perhaps been credited with a greater success than it actually achieved. The imposition of the stamp act had set ablaze a fire of rebellion in America, which was by no means utterly extinguished by the repeal of that measure. Agitators who had

[1] Add. MS., 35362, f. 63, f. 65 ; Add. MS., 32980, f. 144 ; Hist. MSS. Comm. Stopford Sackville MSS., 1, 119 ; Walpole's Memoirs, 2, 298 ff.
[2] Walpole's Memoirs, 2, 301.

profited by the late disturbances, revolutionary spirits who, while willing to accept all that England had to give, resented every demand of the mother country as a grievance, and sincere devotees of freedom, who believed that the majority of English statesmen harboured a dark design against colonial liberty, all combined to maintain an atmosphere of restless suspicion. Though Rockingham had repealed the stamp act, he had not been able completely to obliterate the past; and his successors in office were soon to learn that the colonial problem had received no final solution. Early in February, 1767, it was known in England that several of the colonies had refused obedience to the mutiny act extended by Grenville to America, that many of the sufferers by the riots over the stamp act were still anxiously awaiting compensation for the losses they had incurred, and that the province of New York had petitioned parliament to be relieved from the main restrictions imposed by the navigation acts.[1]

No wise observer could be blind to the fact that the American problem called for delicate handling, or be surprised that the colonists had not instantly resumed a submissive and deferential attitude towards the mother country. Those who, like Lord George Sackville, believed that the stamp act ought never to have been repealed, of course saw " the fatal consequences of yielding to riot and ill-grounded clamour " ; [2] but more impartial and judicious observers perceived in these events the last dying efforts of a diminishing storm. Yet it would be a mistake to imagine that those, who took the more conciliatory view, were in favour of granting the colonies all

---

[1] Hist. MSS. Comm. Stopford Sackville MSS., I, 118.   [2] *Ibid.*

that they chose to ask, and of winning peace by further and further concessions. As determined as their adversaries to maintain the supremacy of the mother country, they differed from them, more in the means they adopted, than in the end they sought. Their first and greatest object must be to restore the confidence of the colonists in the mother country, and that could be best achieved by a happy blending of moderation and firmness. The storm must be stilled, not forcibly repressed; and, above all, no occasion given to the Americans to believe that they would forfeit their ancient rights and privileges by remaining under English rule.

That such a policy was difficult no one could deny, but that it was impossible would be hazardous to assert. That all the revolutions, which have occurred in history, were inevitable from the beginning may be a convenient doctrine to hold, but it certainly does not bear the test of historical investigation; and, amidst much that is doubtful and open to question, it is abundantly clear that, in the year 1767, an overwhelming majority of the American colonists had never contemplated the idea of severing the connection with the mother country. Though restless and discontented, and only too likely to become the prey of agitators who would, given favouring circumstances, work them up to the revolution level, they still remained for the most part loyal to England; and on this foundation might have been based a restoration of those harmonious relations which had so recently existed. Moreover, with Chatham in power, there seemed a reasonable chance of such a policy being pursued. Not only the prime minister, but Grafton, Shelburne, and Conway, were well known to be favourable to the colonists, and, from his place in the house of commons, Chatham had denounced the stamp act as actually illegal, and had applauded the resistance which it had encountered in America. Drawing a distinction between an external tax imposed for the sake of regulating commerce, and an internal tax levied in the country itself for the purpose of obtaining a revenue, he had declared, while justifying the former class of impositions, that the latter was a gross and unlawful infringement of the liberties of the colonists who could claim, as well as Englishmen, to be free from taxation by any body in which they were not represented.

That the distinction drawn by Chatham had very little ground in fact, and is hardly capable of a serious defence, would be readily allowed at the present day ; for it is impossible to contend that the duties imposed by parliament upon colonial trade were not taxes upon American wealth. Yet, arbitrary and unreal as such a doctrine was, it was not without value at the time it was enunciated ; for, while permitting the mother country to continue to restrain colonial trade in her own interests, it entirely differentiated from such impositions an internal tax levied within the country ; and thus the colonists, happy in the entirely fictitious belief that they were not being taxed by the mother country, might continue to submit quietly to the various commercial restrictions imposed by parliament. The delusion was ruthlessly exposed by Charles Townshend who, on January 26th, 1767, declared in the house of commons that the distinction between internal and external taxa- tion was illusory and nonsensical, that he knew a way of taxing the colonies without giving offence, and that, in order to increase the revenue from America he was prepared to put it into effect.[1]

Few men have been simultaneously so right and so wrong as Townshend on this occasion. In ridiculing the doctrine maintained by his leader, he had scored a sound academic point, and he could justify himself by the undeniable fact that the American revenue had been sadly depleted by the repeal of the stamp act and the removal of certain prohibitive duties upon American commerce ; [2] but anything less statesmanlike or more reckless than his conduct it is difficult to conceive. Without consulting any of his colleagues, or giving them the slightest intimation of his intention,[3] he had not only directly defied the prime minister, but definitely pledged himself to impose taxes upon the colonies with the object of obtaining a revenue ; and the promise was eagerly welcomed by a listening and astonished house. Whether those taxes were internal or external was now of little importance, for Townshend, by his criminal folly, had destroyed a distinction which, however baseless in fact, might have served an useful political turn. The colonists, having eagerly accepted the doctrine of " no taxation without representation," now knew that a commercial duty could be made as productive of a revenue as an internal tax, and that a weapon was being forged for use against them, which, without being open to the same objection as the stamp act, would cut quite as deeply into their purses and their liberty. That they might have been more willing to contribute towards the expenses of the empire, and

[1] Add. MS., 32979, f. 343 ; Grafton's *Autobiography*, p. 126 ; Hist. MSS. Comm. Lothian MSS., 274; Weston Underwood MSS., 402 ; Chatham Correspondence, 3, 176, 182.

[2] Hist. MSS. Comm. Weston Underwood MSS., 402.

[3] Grafton's *Autobiography*, p. 126.

displayed a greater readiness to participate in its burdens as well as in its privileges, may be allowed, but this does not excuse Charles Townshend. His crime is not that he violated a constitutional principle, or sought to fetter the colonies in slavery to England ; but that, at a time when it behoved a wiser statesman to tread warily and with caution, when everything should have been done to disarm American suspicion, he recklessly, and entirely on his own responsibility, fanned into active flame the embers of a dying grievance. His fault was not what he did, but the time he chose to do it.

At the present day, such behaviour in a subordinate would be promptly and justifiably met by dismissal from the cabinet ; but Chatham was secluded at Bath, and, as Grafton sadly admits, "no one of the ministry had authority sufficient to advise the dismission of Mr Charles Townshend, and nothing less could have stopped the measure." [1] Saddled with such a colleague, the youthful first lord of the treasury, still only in his thirty-second year, might well scan the future with anxiety. Whatever business he undertook, whether he dealt with the old world or the new, he was confronted by the chancellor of the exchequer bent upon the pursuit of a policy in direct conflict with the wishes of the prime minister. If worse evils were not to follow, it was time that Chatham returned to piece together the shattered fragments of his authority. Starting from Bath about the middle of February, he was seized on the road by an attack of gout, and obliged to rest at Marlborough. There he remained many days, lying at the inn of the town ; and it was not until March 2nd that he arrived in London. Much had happened during his absence ; and it was no

---

[1] Grafton's *Autobiography*, p. 126.

peaceful prospect that faced him on his return. Ill and suffering as he was, he would be obliged, if his hopes were to be saved from shipwreck, to perform a task which, if successfully accomplished, would rank with his greatest achievements in the past ; but it remained to be seen whether he was equal to such an undertaking.

CHAPTER III

THE RISE AND FALL OF THE OPPOSITION

CHATHAM'S arrival in London, at the beginning of March, 1767, forms a notable landmark in the history of his ill-fated and disastrous administration. No one had more eagerly awaited his return than Grafton who, convinced that his leader would be able to restore order out of chaos, looked to be rewarded for having toiled against hope in the hour of adversity. Nor can his expectation be considered in any way unreasonable or unfounded. Though no longer the object of that almost idolatrous veneration which had once been paid him, Chatham, illumined by the lustre of his past achievements, was still regarded as differing in kind, as well as in degree, from the other politicians of the day, and accounted capable of accomplishing feats which to most men would be well outside the range of possibility. That supreme self-confidence, which had once allowed him to justify his proud boast that he alone could save England, might be expected to nerve him in the present crisis; for surely never did the trumpet-call to action louder sound. Stretched before his eyes lay the ruins of the administration, built by himself according to principles which, though derided by other political architects as eccentric and bizarre, he believed to be just and sound; and it was for him to repair the edifice shattered in his absence. Inspiring by his

114

presence those in whom hope was almost dead, rooting up the evils which menaced the safety of the state, and routing the enemy who had taken heart while he dallied at Bath, he might by these means rejuvenate a ministry which had fallen into the last stage of decay. Few statesmen have been granted a more favourable opportunity of increasing an already glorious reputation; and, if the task was arduous, the prize was proportionately great. Ten years had elapsed since the country, threatened by enemies abroad and incompetence at home, had turned to William Pitt for deliverance; and now again he was needed to repair the mischief which other men had wrought.

But the hopes raised by the prime minister's return to the capital were doomed to a speedy and crushing disappointment; for he came back to his labours a changed and broken man, incapable of performing the work which lay ready to his hand. He stood on the eve of a complete nervous break-down, and betrayed all the wonted symptoms of mental distress. His friends, unaware of the disease which, day by day, was fastening its grip upon him, were astonished to find that all his old vigour and determination had fled. He declared himself unequal to the transaction of business, and, after making a fruitless attempt to remove Townshend from the chancellorship of the exchequer in favour of Lord North, relapsed into a complete state of inaction, rarely seeing his colleagues, and only once visiting the king. For a few weeks he remained in London, doing nothing to set right the disorganised machinery of the government; but it was not long before he finally succumbed, and retired to Hampstead. There, in a house situated in a remote corner of the Heath, and effectively screened from all passers-by, he lived for many months secluded from the world, a prey to an agony which, if they had witnessed it, would surely have moved his bitterest enemies to compassion. Without the power of making the most trifling intellectual effort, the least call upon his energy sufficed to throw him into a paroxysm of distress ; and the statesman, who had controlled and dominated a world-waged conflict, now shuddered at the slightest reference to politics or affairs of state.   Sometimes he might be seen riding out upon the Heath, but it was but seldom that he took such active exercise ; and, for the greater part of the day, he remained within doors, sitting with his face buried in his hands, but rarely speaking, and generally alone.[1]   His contemporaries, unskilled in differentiating between the varying degrees of mental affliction, either thought him mad or shamming madness ;   but he was neither insane nor a hypocrite.   He was but paying the price of a body and mind overtaxed in the past ; and outraged nature took her revenge at the moment most inopportune for the country's welfare.

Thus the restoration of the ministry, so confidently expected by many, was not to come to pass ; and if Charles Townshend had cause for exultation in the removal of the one man who could have kept him in check, the burden of disappointment fell upon the unfortunate first lord of the treasury. What had promised to be the dawn of salvation suddenly turned into the midnight of despair ; and Grafton was left to preside over a ministry which he had already shown that he could not control.   It would have been well for the country, and well for his own political reputation, if he had declined the task thus imposed upon him ;   but it should always be remembered to his credit that it was no unworthy craving for power

[1] Grenville Papers, 4, 118.

that induced him to remain at his post. It was impossible to predict the hour when Chatham would have
sufficiently recovered to resume command, and Grafton
believed it to be his duty to keep the ministry together,
waiting his leader's return. If he had resigned, he
might have acquired peace and security, and escaped
the censures of historians ; but, ignorant of what the
future was to bring forth, he feared by retirement to
destroy the administration, and thus cast Chatham
once more adrift in political life. If he acted wrongly,
he, at least, had the courage to persist in a noble, if
fatal, journey along the path of greatest resistance.
With all the fervent devotion of a young man, he
sincerely, almost passionately, believed that Chatham
alone was capable of bringing salvation to a distraught
nation, and shrank from a course of action which might
effectively prevent his hero's return to power. If
he had viewed the situation from a more critical, and
less partial, standpoint, if he had thought less of
Chatham, and more of his own incapacity to rule, it
would have been better ; but, whatever were his faults,
they were those of the understanding, not of the heart.

Yet, much as he idolised Chatham, even that devotion might not have sufficed to steel him to undertake the task if he had fully known its magnitude ;
and the tragedy of his career lies in the fact that he
so completely failed to attain the end for which he
endured the distasteful burden of power. Chatham
was destined never to return to office ; and, though
Grafton continued as first lord of the treasury, it
was Charles Townshend who ruled in the cabinet,
and dictated the ministerial policy. Thus the stone,
which the builder had wanted to reject, became, in
that builder's absence, the head of the corner ; and, in
a famous passage in a famous speech, Burke, referring

to Chatham's temporary eclipse, has described "how even before this splendid orb was entirely set, and while the western horizon was in a blaze with his descending glory, on the opposite quarter of the heavens arose another luminary, and for his hour became lord of the ascendant." That luminary was Charles Townshend ; and England has deep cause to regret that ever such a star shone in the political heavens. Playing politics as a gambler might play a game of cards with no money on the table, " unfixed in principles and place," brilliant in debate, and ready to say anything which would serve his turn at the moment,[1] he could inspire every sentiment except confidence, and be everything except consistent.

Nothing could possibly be a severer condemnation of the practical application of Chatham's much-vaunted principle of "men, not measures" than the only too apparent fact that, with the single exception of the prime minister, there was not a member of the cabinet capable of staying Townshend in his erratic and perilous course. Grafton might, indeed, bare his breast to the storm, but only to be overthrown and swept away like a piece of wreckage. Conway, quite apart from the fact that on certain points he was in agreement with his turbulent colleague, was far too uncertain of his own opinions, too prone to waver and hesitate, to withstand an antagonist who had at least the merit of knowing what he wanted ; and, moreover, there was little inducement for Conway to plunge into such a fray, as he had already determined upon retirement at the end of the session.[2] Lord Shelburne, the other secretary of state, was indeed made of

---

[1] He did not scruple to encourage the Rockingham whigs to believe that he was about to throw in his lot with them. Add. MS., 32980, f. 296, f. 333 ; Chatham Correspondence, 3, 240.

[2] Add. MS., 32980, f. 300 ; Chatham Correspondence, 3, 240.

sterner stuff, amply furnished with convictions, and the least likely of men to submit to the will of another ; but, instead of battling against the storm, he preferred to discontinue his attendance at cabinet meetings, confining himself to the duties of his office.[1] Thus, with no one to say him nay, Townshend was able to strike for independence, and reap to the full all the advantages which might be gleaned from Chatham's illness.

If, at such a moment, the ministry, bereft of its leader, and shaken to its foundations by one too powerful member, had been called upon to meet the attack of a united opposition, the end might have been quick indeed in coming. Nor was the danger so remote as has sometimes been imagined. No settlement had yet been reached with the East India Company, and it was not improbable that a common sympathy for that threatened corporation might serve as a bond between Rockingham, Grenville, and Bedford, leading them to form a permanent alliance against the government. There is no doubt that all three leaders were in favour of a parliamentary union if certain difficulties could be accommodated ; and a negotiation was set on foot about the end of March. But, though all might be convinced that they could never succeed, unless they organised themselves for the battle, it was by no means easy to plan the distribution of the spoils which would follow upon the hoped-for victory. Rockingham was determined that neither Grenville nor any of his followers should be given the treasury ; and, although at first there seemed to be a fair prospect of success, Grenville showing himself unexpectedly conciliatory, the sky quickly

[1] It was after the meeting on March 12th that Shelburne ceased to attend the cabinet. Lord Fitzmaurice's *Life of Shelburne*, ii. 58.

became overcast. In George Grenville's heart burned a steady flame of suspicion of the men who had reversed his American policy; and, imagining that they intended to use him as a tool for their own ends, he raised his terms, and, after asking for the treasury for Lord Temple, allowed the Bedfords to demand it for himself. The request, objectionable as it might be to those to whom it was made, was emphatically not unreasonable, for Grenville had better claims than Rockingham to the first place in the government. A more varied experience of political life, a far more extensive knowledge of parliamentary procedure, a far greater readiness in debate, and an equally unsullied reputation for honesty and integrity, could all be pleaded on behalf of the contention that he should lead and Rockingham should follow. Yet, if he was right to ask, the young whig marquis was equally right to refuse, and to break off the negotiation when he understood that the demand would not be withdrawn. It was no personal spite, no petty or selfish impulse, that led him to abhor the prospect of Grenville at the treasury; but a deep-rooted and well-founded conviction that the statesman, who had introduced the stamp act, might, if given a favourable opportunity, revive it. When Rockingham stipulated that his own party must have a majority in any cabinet that was formed, that Grenville must be rigorously excluded from all dealings with the colonies, and that the policy of the late administration towards the trade and commerce of America must be continued, he revealed what he feared from an alliance with the men whose work he had undone.[1] Between

---

[1] Add. MS., 32980, f. 450. For the negotiation generally, see Add. MS., 32980, f. 374, f. 376, f. 384, f. 386, f. 398, f. 410, f. 418, f. 424, f. 438, f. 440, f. 450, f. 454 ; Add. MS., 32981, f. 1, f. 24 ; Grenville Papers, 4, 218-220.

him and Grenville lay a clear and fundamental divergence of opinion on a question still unsettled ; and it is to their credit that they refused to sacrifice principles, which they believed to be true, to a policy which they knew to be expedient.

Yet, though the negotiation had proved abortive, the different parties in opposition were prepared to work together against the government ; for, whatever their differences might be, it was to the interest of all to overthrow the existing ministry. The demand of the treasury for Grenville had been declined in friendly and polite terms ;[1] and no little pains were taken to maintain amicable relations between those who had failed to arrive at a common understanding. Grenville assured Lord Mansfield, who quickly passed the information on to Newcastle, that he intended to refrain from proposing any measure, in regard to the American colonies, which would clash with Lord Rockingham's views ;[2] and although Bedford was reported to be angry at the negotiation having failed, and to have said that, had it succeeded, " he would have done nothing upon the American affairs that could be disagreeable to us ; but that being over, he will push his own opinion as far as he can " ; in conversation with Newcastle he displayed a more conciliatory spirit, declaring himself in favour of a " solid, cordial agreement and union " between all parties in opposition.[3] Newcastle, himself, was strongly of the same opinion. " We have," he wrote in April, " three parties ; one, the administration, I will have nothing to do with ; the remaining two I most sincerely wish united for the sake of the nation and the whig cause. I am not clear that either party is much pleased with

[1] Add. MS., 32981, f. 1.   [2] Add. MS., 32981, f. 28.
[3] Add. MS., 32981, f. 65, f. 156.

me for my way of thinking . . . which is to try to have
it in my own way, and that of my friends, if I can ; but
if not, if the union is necessary, as I think it is, I wish
it made any way almost rather than no way." [1]   A
few weeks later, he repeated the same sentiments,
affirming his belief in a " coalition and union which
I think can alone save this country " ; [2] and even
Rockingham, who appeared to be so hostile to Grenville's influence,[3] began to think more kindly of a
possible combination of forces.[4]   Newcastle, indeed,
in his anxiety for union, went further than Rockingham and a good many other members of the party ;
but there were some who agreed with him, and amongst
them was Sir William Meredith.   " He differs," wrote
Newcastle to the Duke of Portland, " more with our
friend, the marquess, about union and coalition, than
your grace and I do.   He thinks it so necessary, that
he intends (as he says) to sit by George Grenville in
the house of commons, to use himself to it," [5]—a
self-denying ordinance which was a doubtful compliment to Grenville.

Thus, though no formal alliance had been concluded, the parties in opposition were inclined to sink
their differences for the time being, and to unite against
the ministry ;   and the parliamentary conflict might
well prove arduous and exhausting for a government
rent by internal dissensions and deprived of its leader.
The inquiry into the affairs of the East India Company,

---

[1] Add. MS., 32981, f. 254.   [2] Add. MS., 32982, f. 148.
[3] " I know no news," wrote Newcastle to Lord Grantham on April 17th,
" and am not very curious about any.   My Lord Rockingham made me a
visit. . . . I showed him my account of what passed with the Duke of Bedford.
He said not a word upon it ; neither seemed pleased nor displeased : but
stopped at every place where George Grenville was named, against whom
and my Lord Temple . . . he seems more picqued than ever."   Add. MS.,
32981, f. 197.
[4] Add. MS., 32982, f. 148.   [5] Add. MS., 32982, f. 146.

and the condition of the American colonies, offered many easy points of attack ; and the members of the cabinet could not but regard the future with some degree of trepidation. But to stand still was impossible, and the papers of the East India Company were discussed and examined by the house of commons. After a lengthy and tedious inquiry, there occurred, on April 14th, the first important struggle between the government and the opposition, since Chatham's return from Bath. The battle was opened by Sir William Meredith who moved that an end be put to the committee on the affairs of the company. If he carried his motion, the ministry would, indeed, suffer a crushing and humiliating defeat. It would be compelled, at the dictation of its enemies, to abandon a task over which it had expended much time and trouble, and which Chatham had placed in the very forefront of his programme. The laborious examination of the company's papers had been undertaken in order to furnish Beckford, who was recognised as Chatham's mouthpiece in this question, with information upon which to found the resolutions he was prepared to submit to the house ; and, if Meredith triumphed, this intention would be frustrated, and the company secured from all further molestation. No more direct challenge to the administration could possibly have been contrived, and it had all the defects of a frontal attack. The ministers strained every nerve to avert defeat on so final an issue, and it was hard for impartial men to believe that the examination had revealed nothing to justify further proceedings ; and yet, unreasonable as Meredith's proposal essentially was, it was not until after a lengthy discussion, continuing until the early hours of the following morning, that a ministerial motion, adjourning the debate until May 1st, was carried by a majority of fifty-six.[1]

But, though the opposition had been defeated, there was no reason why despair should prevail in its ranks. The minority had numbered one hundred and fifty-seven, no inconsiderable number on what was described as so " unfavourable a proposition " ; [2] and there was, therefore, a hope that, if more favourable ground was selected for the next conflict, a victory might even be won. Moreover, there was another, and indeed a weightier, reason for the enemies of the government, to persevere in the attack : while they had stood united, the ministerialists had clearly revealed their internal differences. Voicing the avowed sentiments of the absent leader, Beckford had announced that his resolutions would deal with the legal right of the company to the territories it had acquired, while Townshend and Conway had maintained their old contention that the question of the right should be waived, and a speedy and amicable settlement be made.[3] The moment was indeed critical. If Beckford moved his resolutions, he would encounter the hostility, not only of the opposition, but also of two leading members of the administration ; and it might well be that he would incur defeat, and, perchance, inflict a mortal wound upon the ministry. Grafton believed in the policy which Chatham and

---

[1] Hist. MSS. Comm. Stopford Sackville MSS., 1, 122 ; Walpole's Memoirs, iii. 1 ff.

[2] Grenville Papers, 4, 10.

[3] Hist. MSS. Comm. Stopford Sackville MSS., 1, 122 ; Weston Underwood MSS., May 2nd, 1767 ; Walpole's Memoirs, iii. 1 ff. It is nowhere actually stated that Conway and Townshend said what is attributed to them in the text ; but Walpole records that they took part in the discussion, and Lord George Sackville states that " in the course of the debate, the ministry thought proper to disclaim all violence and hostility against the company, and seemed to decline the question of right."

Beckford favoured ; but, if he was true to this conviction, he ran the risk of destroying the administration
which, he was sincerely convinced, it was his duty
to uphold until Chatham's return. It was no easy
decision which he was called upon to make, for both
surrender and defiance could be supported by arguments based upon principles ; and no blame attaches
to his final resolution to surrender to his colleagues, in
order to avert a disruption in the cabinet, and to
deprive the opposition of a formidable weapon against
the government. He may have erred, but it was
from no unworthy motive, and the heavier guilt lies
upon the shoulders of his rebellious subordinates.
But it was they who enjoyed the triumph of the hour.
When, on May 1st, the house of commons met, expect-
ing to hear Beckford move his resolutions, Boulton,
one of the directors of the company, announced that
fresh proposals had been made by his company to the
government, which seemed likely to result in a final
settlement ; and he therefore asked the house to
delay the discussion of East Indian affairs for another
week, in the hope that by that time terms might have
been arranged, which could be submitted for its approval. The motion, supported as it was by Townshend and Conway, was carried ; and consequently
the opposition was deprived of the privilege of falling
tooth and nail upon Beckford's resolutions.[1]

The terms offered to the government were not such
as Chatham would have approved, deviating as they
did from that " right forward road " which he had
always wished to tread.[2] In return for certain commercial concessions, the company undertook to make

[1] Hist. MSS. Comm. Weston Underwood MSS., 405 ; Walpole's Memoirs,
11-13.
[2] Grafton's *Autobiography*, p. 125.

an annual payment of £400,000 to the state for a term of two years. No mention was made of the vexed question of the territorial rights of the company, which was still left as open as it had been when Chatham first put his hand to the plough ; and the most favourable of its critics could hardly have regarded the agreement as a permanent settlement of a difficult problem. In character not unlike a huckster's bargain, nothing could have less resembled the policy which Chatham had outlined when he took office ; and, if Grafton had saved the ministry, he had equally betrayed the opinions of his leader. Moreover, he was to discover that what he had striven to avert was yet to come to pass. As though pursued by a malign destiny, he was to be robbed of much of the benefit he had anticipated from his surrender, by an unforseen incident which was to delay a final settlement for many weeks, and once more plunge the ministry into internecine strife. When it became known that the company had undertaken to make an annual grant to the state of so substantial a sum as £400,000, the proprietors of stock began to fear a sensible reduction in the dividends, and displayed all the customary greed of shareholders. Thinking of nothing but their own pockets, and of no one but themselves, the general court of the company, at a meeting on May 6th, voted a dividend of 12½ per cent. for the ensuing half year, and, in so doing, bade open defiance to the directors and the state.[1]

The bearing of such an incident upon the course of the negotiation can be easily appreciated. It was as clear as noonday that if the company continued to enjoy the right of voting what dividends it pleased, the annual payment to the state would be seriously

---

[1] Walpole's Memoirs, 3, 16.

imperilled. The proprietors of stock would be driven by every impulse of self-interest to secure themselves against financial loss, and only a small minority could be expected to be tenacious of the honour of the corporation. What they had already done, they might well repeat in the future ; and, therefore, every consideration of wisdom and foresight dictated that, before any final settlement was arrived at with the company, its power of voting dividends should be restricted within reasonable limits. The actions of politicians are seldom guided, however, by the light of pure reason, and when, on May 8th, Jeremiah Dyson asked leave to introduce a bill, providing that the dividends of the company were not to exceed ten per cent. until the next session of parliament, that veteran placeman discovered that he had started a hare which many were eager to hunt ; and, though the bill was ultimately carried in both houses, its passage was not unattended with difficulty. In the house of commons both Conway and Townshend frankly avowed their dislike of a measure which they regarded as tyrannical ; [1] and in the house of lords the leaders of the opposition, deprived by the action of the government of bigger game, took their revenge by attacking the dividend bill.[2] Yet, supported by the king, Grafton prevailed ; and, after the bill had been passed, the terms agreed upon between the ministry and the company were embodied in an act which received the sanction of parliament.

Thus a lengthy and troublesome business was brought to a temporary conclusion ; but the ministry had little cause for triumph in the very moderate

[1] Grenville Papers, 4, 224 ; Hist. Comm. MSS. Weston Underwood MSS., 405 ; Stopford Sackville MSS., 1, 123 ; Grafton's *Autobiography*, p. 125 ; Walpole's Memoirs, 3, 36.

[2] *Ibid.*, and Add. MS., 32982, f. 148, f. 192, f. 194.

success which it had achieved. Divided and dis-
cordant counsels, the absence of the prime minister,
and the recklessness of certain members of the cabinet,
had marred the execution of a great work ; and, if
Grafton and his colleagues had done nothing more
during the session, they would still have borne ample
testimony to their incapacity to rule. Unfortunately,
however, for the ill-fated first lord of the treasury,
he was called upon to deal with the American colonists
who were showing a fixed determination to resist
what they regarded as the aggressions and encroach-
ments of the mother country. The assembly of New
York refused to enforce the mutiny act, on the ground
that that measure, by compelling the provincial
assemblies to arrange for providing the troops with
quarters and a few of the common necessities of life,
was in reality a tax in kind if not in money, and New
York did not stand alone in rebellion ; for the assembly
of Massachusetts took upon itself to grant an indemnity
for all offences committed during the popular agitation
against the stamp act, and in so doing certainly passed
beyond the limits of its legal authority.

Such were the facts as they lay before the ministers,
and seldom has any government been confronted
with a more delicate and responsible task. If a
policy of inaction was pursued, if nothing was done,
and open defiance met by passive acquiescence in the
seemingly inevitable, the colonists would be led to
believe that they could ask for nothing which would
be refused. The repeal of the mutiny act would follow
the repeal of the stamp act, and be followed by the
repeal of the navigation laws, against which complaints
had already been raised : each concession would
form a precedent for the next, and America acquire
her independence at the hands of a government which

was neither firm nor conciliatory, but only weak. It is possible to contend, at this distance of time, that such a solution of the difficulty would have been by far the wisest and happiest ; but it was certainly not a course which recommended itself to any statesman of the period ; and nothing is more unfair than to judge the men of the past by the ideas of the present. Whatever may be said of morality, political wisdom is certainly ambulatory.   Yet, if a stand was made against rebellion, and a clear intimation given that the repeal of the stamp act was to be the exception and not the rule of English policy, no little care would have to be taken to keep within the limits of absolutely necessary coercion.   If an unduly peremptory attitude was adopted by the English ministers, the colonists, already dangerously alienated in sympathy from the mother country, might easily be precipitated into rebellion.   The cry would be raised that England denied to her sons across the seas that liberty which she had acquired for herself at home ; that American freedom would soon be but a glorious memory of a bygone age ; and that the generations to come would never forgive the men who, from a craven love of peace and quiet, had allowed the fetters of tyranny to be riveted upon themselves and their children.   Unfair as such an outcry might be, it would be none the less potent ; for men, and above all the champions of freedom, are often swayed by windy sentiment and bombastic declamations ; and it behoves wise statesmen to consider how their policy will appear to imaginations aglow with excitement and rhetoric.

Thus, both coercion and conciliation presented dangers, and the wisest, though not the easiest, course to pursue was, probably, a judicious mixture of both. Such, indeed, was the method adopted by the cabinet when it met on Thursday, March 12th. It was decided to introduce a bill prohibiting the governor, the council, and the assembly of New York from passing any bill until the mutiny act had been complied with; and all the ministers present, with the single exception of Conway, approved of this proposal. Grafton, in after years, described it as a "temperate, but dignified proceeding, and purposely avoiding all harsh and positive penalties"; [1] and Shelburne, the friend of America, has left it on record how at this time he believed that "some measures . . . ought to be taken of so bold and decisive a nature, as to convince the Americans that the long patience of Great Britain has been by no means owing to timidity, and yet the ends of those measures should be so manifestly just and important, as to leave no room for jealousies and fears in the minds of the sober and well-disposed, and thereby give no pretence for common measures of resistance, and it would be still more desirable if these measures could be directed against a particular province." [2]   Camden, the lord chancellor, who had formerly denounced the stamp act not only as inexpedient but as actually illegal, was now in favour of a stand being made against the colonists' demands, hinting, in a speech in the house of lords, that his opinions might not be as lenient as they previously had been; [3] and though Chatham was not present at this meeting of the cabinet, it is probable that he quite approved the decision of his colleagues.   On first learning of the resistance offered by the New York assembly, he roundly denounced such conduct. "America," he wrote, "affords a gloomy prospect. A spirit of infatuation has taken possession of New

---

[1] Grafton's *Autobiography*, p. 126.   [2] *Shelburne's Life*, 2, 50-55.
[3] Walpole's Memoirs, 2, 318.

York : their disobedience to the mutiny act will *justly* create a great ferment here, open a fair field to the arraigners of America, and leave no room to any to say a word in their defence." Nor was he any more sympathetic towards the New York merchants who had petitioned to be relieved from certain restrictions upon their trade, describing the request as " highly improper : in point of time most absurd ; in the extent of their pretensions most excessive ; and in the reasoning, most grossly fallacious and offensive " ; and, when informed of the indemnity granted by the Massachusetts assembly, he oracularly remarked : " New York has drunk the deepest of the baneful cup of infatuation, but none seem to be quite sober, and in full possession of reason." [1] These were trenchant utterances in the mouth of one who had openly proclaimed his joy at the resistance offered by the Americans to the stamp act ; and it is clear that, whatever Chatham had thought in the past, he now believed that the time for concession was past. This change in his opinions, if change it can be called, was not long in becoming known. Early in April, Newcastle informed Rockingham that the prime minister favoured the adoption of strong measures against the colonies ; and the Duke of Bedford was apparently convinced that, in pressing for the punishment of those who had dared to resist the authority of parliament, he could count upon the sympathy of Chatham.[2]

Thus, with the exception of Conway, the ministers, from the leader downwards, were in favour of checking the growing spirit of turbulence in the plantations ; and it is hard to accuse them of wrongdoing. While

[1] Chatham Correspondence, 3, 188, 190, 193-4.
[2] Add. MS., 32981, f. 34, f. 65.

the Americans were justified in throwing off a yoke which crippled and fettered their development, the English ministers would have been more than human, and something very different from what they actually were, if they had been willing to accept, without a struggle, the lesson which it was destined that they should receive at the hands of the colonists. Every step along the road of liberty is an innovation upon what already exists ; and, at this critical juncture, Grafton and his colleagues, trained in the old school of colonial policy, conceived it to be their duty to maintain the traditional relations between England and the American plantations. The interpretation which condemned the mutiny act as a violation of the principle of no taxation without representation, was capable of very indefinite extension ; and, if the action of the New York assembly was condoned, fresh and more exacting demands might be anticipated upon the patience of the mother country. Nor, with any show of reason, can the measure adopted by the ministry be viewed as unduly tyrannical or oppressive. A provincial legislature had defied the supremacy of the English parliament, and the offence called for punishment. The penalty, touching as it did the legislative powers of the rebellious assembly, and leaving untouched the life and property of those who had not participated in the crime, was confined in its operation to the actual offenders ; and, though Conway might plead for conciliation, proof is lacking that such a policy would have earned any greater measure of success. Indeed, it might be argued, as it actually was by Shelburne, that " if Great Britain does not in some shape put forth her dignity on this occasion, she may end by losing all credit and reverence in America, and lose likewise her power there, which is, and must be, in a great measure, founded on opinion." [1]

Yet, however reasonable the ministerial proposal might be, parliamentary criticism must be expected; for an opposition, which had harried the government upon the affairs of the East India company, would not be likely to remain quiescent when the colonies were under discussion. But the danger, which confronted the enemies of the administration, was that they might fail to agree upon a programme of attack; for between Rockingham and Grenville lay a difference of opinion on colonial policy, which could not be easily bridged. But a yawning chasm, which cannot be crossed, can sometimes be avoided; and Grenville and Bedford, aware of the necessity of standing united against the government, had already assured the followers of Lord Rockingham that they would refrain from making proposals likely to offend the men who had repealed the stamp act.[2] For a little time Rockingham declined to show his hand, leaving his supporters, as Newcastle somewhat bitterly remarked, to shift for themselves; [3] and the evil consequences of such untimely reticence were not long in making themselves felt. On April 10th, the Duke of Bedford moved in the house of lords that the king should be addressed to instruct the privy council to consider the legality of the indemnity granted by the assembly of Massachusetts; and, although all his hearers were agreed in thinking the indemnity illegal, the Duke of Grafton, interpreting the motion as a vote of want of confidence in the government, moved the previous question, and carried it by a substantial majority of twenty-seven votes. There is no doubt that the Rockingham whigs were

---

[1] *Shelburne's Life*, 2, 55. [2] Add. MS., 32981, f. 28, f. 65.
[3] Add. MS., 32981, f. 65.

largely responsible for the ease of the ministerial victory. With no instructions from their leader, with no definite plan of campaign, they knew not what to do, and were as sheep without a shepherd. Rockingham, himself, supported the government ; others, including Lord Grantham, voted with the Duke of Bedford ; and Newcastle, Portland, Albemarle, and Bessborough were amongst those who went away, before the division was taken, in order that they might not be compelled to oppose their friends.[1]

Such was not a favourable opening for the opposition campaign which demanded union as an essential condition of success ; and Grenville and Bedford, after the assurances they had given, were, naturally enough, somewhat chagrined at the conduct of the Rockingham whigs. Nor was Newcastle any less disappointed, for he bitterly regretted the loss of such a golden opportunity of placating the Duke of Bedford.[2] The mischief, however, was not irreparable ; and, four days after the debate in the house of lords, Newcastle called upon the Duke of Bedford in order to apologise for the conduct of his friends. His excuse was that, as Bedford had not communicated his intentions, Rockingham and his followers were taken unawares, and each man obliged to do what was right in his own eyes ; but, in reply, Bedford pointed out that, if there had been communication, Conway, who was known to be in frequent and intimate intercourse with many members of the Rockingham party, might have got wind of what was intended, and revealed the plot to his colleagues in the cabinet. The hit was palpable, but Newcastle was far too experienced a negotiator

---

[1] Add. MS., 32981, f. 112, f. 125 ; Grenville Papers, 4, 222 ; Walpole's Memoirs, 2, 322, 323.
[2] Add. MS., 32981, f. 127.

to be driven away by the first rebuff. " I insisted strongly," he reported, " that for the future proper previous communications should be made on both sides during the remainder of the session, in which I thought His Grace entirely agreed." [1]

Newcastle, in the course of a long life, had often been doomed to go on many fruitless errands, but on this occasion, at least, he was rewarded by success ; for Bedford was as good as his word. On Sunday, May 3rd, Lord Gower, happening to meet Rockingham at Arthur's, informed him that, on the following Wednesday in the house of lords, the ministers would be asked to explain what they had done in the matter of the Massachusetts assembly ; and Rockingham assured him that he thought " it very fair and very right." The fruit of this communication was seen on Wednesday, May 6th, when Lord Gower moved for an account of the proceedings of the privy council upon the action of the Massachusetts assembly. The ministers opposed the motion, alleging that the business would not be finished until the end of the week ; but though they carried the day, it was only by nine votes. The increase in the numerical strength of the opposition arose from the Rockingham whigs having thrown in their lot with the Bedfords and the Grenvilles ; and thus Newcastle could congratulate himself upon a timely and successful visit to Bedford House.[2]

[1] Add. MS., 32981, f. 156.
[2] Add. MS., 32981, f. 313 ; Grenville Papers, 4, 11. Grenville gives the government a majority of ten. It is nowhere distinctly stated that the Rockingham whigs voted in the minority, but the assumption is justified by their subsequent conduct, by the increase in the numbers of the opposition, and by the approval which Rockingham had extended to Gower's plan. It would be, moreover, a mistake to imagine that Rockingham was inclined to be sympathetic towards the action of the Massachusetts assembly. In a letter, dated May 11th, 1767, and addressed to a collector of customs at Boston, he mentions his dissatisfaction " with the behaviour of the assembly in

The united attack upon the government, having once begun, was not relaxed ; and it was in the upper house that the surest hopes of victory for the opposition lay. Bedford and Newcastle had carefully scrutinised the different parties in the assembly to which they belonged, and agreed that they "had a majority, or very near it, in the house of lords against my Lord Bute and my Lord Chatham " ; [1] and thus there was every inducement to continue the struggle. Nor were they to be stayed by any concession on the part of the ministers. Though the privy council had annulled the indemnity, and though a record of the Council's proceedings was to be submitted to the house, this was not enough to satisfy an opposition determined upon attack. The indemnity, though annulled, had not been declared null and void *ab initio*, and this omission supplied an excuse for an onslaught upon the ministry on May 22nd. All was carefully arranged beforehand ; [2] and the contest, when it came, was exciting enough, a motion by Lord Gower being only defeated by six votes. Rockingham and Newcastle fought side by side with Bedford and Temple, and the ministry was brought within an ace of defeat. The opposition just failed to attain success, but Newcastle was almost as much delighted with the result as if it had been a victory. " I hope you have not suffered," he wrote to Lord Rockingham on the following day, " by your long attendance yesterday. The good appearance we made has done me so much good that I have not been so well, or slept so well, of some time as I did last night. If all of us take

regard to tacking of their indemnity bill to the compensation bill. The power of pardoning crimes of the nature of which the assembly has done, is not only much beyond the limits of their constitution, but, in fact, would be dangerous for themselves," Grenville Papers, 4, 12.

[1] Add. MS., 32981, f. 156.   [2] Add. MS., 32982, f. 32.

proper care, we shall beat them in the committee on Tuesday, if the court don't bring down greater numbers than they did yesterday." [1] Newcastle's high hopes, however, were to be disappointed; for, in the debate on the following Tuesday, the ministry just succeeded in holding its own, though only by the very narrow majority of three votes.[2]

These proceedings in the upper house are not unworthy of attention, and it is much to be regretted that our information concerning them is so scattered and fragmentary. We know enough, however, to be certain that Bedford, Rockingham, and Grenville had agreed to sink their minor differences, and to act together against the government; and, in so doing, they gave an useful lesson in the art of constitutional opposition. Instead of intriguing in the royal closet, as statesmen in the previous reign had so often done, they sought to expel the ministers by depriving them of parliamentary support, and thus paid indirect homage to the sovereignty of the people. Moreover, there is no reason to believe that Rockingham sacrificed a single principle in order to gain the assistance of Bedford or Grenville; for such an accusation can only be supported on the assumption that he was in favour of conciliating the colonists at all costs, and conceding all their demands. But such was certainly not the case. If he was opposed to that system of direct taxation which Grenville had introduced, and he had abolished, he was equally opposed to compliance with every request that the Americans chose to make. He has left on record his views on the situation as it existed in the year, 1767 : " a system of arbitrary rule

---

[1] Add. MS., 32982, f. 95, f. 99 ; Grenville Papers, 4, 224 ; Walpole's Memoirs, 3, 34.
[2] Walpole's Memoirs, 3, 34.

over the colonies," he wrote, "I would not adopt
on this side; neither would I do otherwise than strenuously resist when attempts were made to throw off
that dependency to which the colonies ought to submit, not only for the advantage of this country, but
for their own real happiness and safety." [1] Thus
thinking, he was able to unite with Grenville and
Bedford in demanding the nullification of the Massachusetts act of indemnity, and, at the same time,
retain a man's most precious possession, his moral
integrity.

The united opposition, which had thus come into
being in the house of lords, also existed in the house
of commons which, on May 13th, was the scene of a
great debate upon the preliminaries of the ministerial
bill suspending the legislative powers of the New
York assembly. For many days before, it was known
that such a measure was in contemplation, and Rockingham was not willing to allow such an opportunity
for an attack upon the government to slip. "I
understand from the Duke of Richmond," he wrote
on May 4th, "that the intention of administration
to-morrow in the house of commons is to propose a
bill to direct all the governors in North America not
to give their assent to any bill from their respective
assemblies until the assembly has made provision for
the due compliance in the quartering bill. Some
time ago, his grace mentioned this when Mr Charles
Yorke was here, who then seemed to think the mode
improper. I hope to see him to-day, and that he will
continue of that opinion. I mentioned this report
at that time to Lord Mansfield, who also seemed to
disapprove it. I hear General Conway much dislikes
this, but this is a secret. If so, and the different corps

[1] Grenville Papers, 4, 13.

concur in thinking the mode etc., improper, to-morrow may be a curious day." [1]

It is clear from this declaration that Rockingham was anxious for his party to attack the bill when it was submitted to the house of commons; and there was indeed much to encourage him to organise an opposition. The hostility of Bedford and Grenville to a measure, which in their eyes would not go far enough along the road of coercion, could be counted upon; and it would be a fatal mistake for the Rockingham whigs not to lend their support to their old comrade Conway when he was in conflict with the rest of his colleagues. Yet, favourable as the occasion might, superficially, appear, Lord Rockingham and his followers found themselves in a somewhat dangerous situation. Grenville and Bedford were opposed to the bill because it did too little, and Conway because it did too much; and the Rockingham whigs, anxious to maintain their union with Grenville and Bedford, and most reluctant to give needless offence to Conway, sought for a comprehensive plan of attack, in which all opponents of the government's proposal might take part without scruple. It is to the credit of their political strategy that they discovered a way of reconciling the seemingly irreconcilable. At a meeting at Rockingham's house on May 12th, attended by Dowdeswell, Sir George Savile, and Sir William Meredith, it was decided that objection should be taken to the bill and that Dowdeswell should propose that the mutiny act be amended and enforced. The ingenuity of this plan cannot but evoke admiration, for to Dowdeswell's proposal Conway, and all sections of the opposition, could subscribe in equal good faith.

[1] Add. MS., 32981, f. 287. It will be noticed that Rockingham was mistaken in believing that the bill was to be introduced on May 5th.

Those who believed that the mutiny act should be modified, and those who believed that it should be rendered more exacting, could all agree in the vague proposition that it should be amended and enforced; comprehension, indeed, could no further go.[1]

The debate on May 13th was opened by Charles Townshend who submitted to the house the three resolutions which had been agreed upon by the cabinet two months before. He moved that the province of New York had been disobedient, that the act of its assembly was void, and that the governor of that colony should not give his assent to any bill until after " a complete and entire submission to, and execution of, the billeting act throughout the province." Debate centred round the last of these three resolutions. Grenville, as might have been anticipated, declared that such a penalty was far too light, arguing that when resistance was offered to the authority of parliament there should be no question of mercy. He taunted the ministers with fearing to use against the provincials that force which they had used at home to prohibit the exportation of corn, and asserted that, if he had his way, not a single person in America should ever be allowed to hold an office unless prepared to swear to the superiority of Great Britain. Charles Yorke and Sir George Savile argued on the same lines, declaring that no punishment could be too severe for rebellion while Conway, separating himself from the other ministers, constituted himself the champion of America, and spoke on behalf of mercy and forgiveness. In accordance with the plan previously agreed upon, Dowdeswell urged that the mutiny act should be amended and enforced, and this proposal was moved as an amendment by George

---

[1] Add. MS., 32981, f. 365.

Grenville. On a division being taken the ministry was victorious by eighty-two votes; but in the minority were to be found Conway and the adherents of Bedford, Grenville and Rockingham. Thus a question, which might easily have plunged the opposition into internecine strife, was diverted by skilful handling into a bond of union, and this diplomatic triumph must have sensibly mitigated the sting of the parliamentary defeat.[1]

Townshend's resolutions having been reported to the house on May 15th, the promised bill was introduced, and became law before the end of the session.[2] Of the debates, which it occasioned in both houses of parliament, we know next to nothing, and the same obscurity hangs over an even more important measure for which the chancellor of the exchequer must bear almost all the responsibility. As has been mentioned before, on January 26th, he had informed an eagerly listening house of commons that he regarded the distinction drawn between internal and external taxation as illusory and absurd, and that he knew of a way of taxing America without giving offence. In response to pressure from Grenville he went further, and pledged himself to provide a revenue from the colonies, and, unhappily for this country, he fulfilled his promise. At the cabinet meeting on March 12th he informed his colleagues that, unless he was allowed to levy taxes upon goods imported into America, he would resign his office; and they reluctantly submitted to the will of one whom they were powerless to control. Early in April, he told the house of commons that " he had formed his opinion for assert-

[1] Add. MS., 32981, f. 375; Grafton's *Autobiography*, p. 176; Walpole's Memoirs, 3, 21 ff.

[2] *Parliamentary History*, vol. xvi.; Grafton's *Autobiography*, p. 179; Walpole's Memoirs, 3, 29, 30.

ing the superiority of the crown, and endeavouring to
lay a foundation for such taxation as might in time
ease this country of a considerable burden " ; [1] and, in
the course of the debate on May 13th, he, for the first
time, gave specific details of his plan. He announced
that " he was clear in opinion that this country had a
power of taxation of every sort, and in every case.
That he could never distinguish between internal and
external, but that such taxation should be moderate
and prudent . . . Would mention some taxes, not as
chancellor of the exchequer, but as a private man,
for the future opinion of this house in a committee
of ways and means " ; and he then proceeded to out-
line a scheme for the levy of import duties upon various
articles, and for the establishment in America of a
board of customs, charged with the collection of the
revenue arising from these imposts.[2] Unfortunately,
we know nothing of the debates upon these proposals
when the house sat in a committee of ways and means ;
the degree to which they were opposed, or by whom.
Alterations were indeed made, other articles being
added to those originally named by Townshend ; but
our information is limited to the resolutions approved
by the house on June 2nd. On that day it was resolved that duties of varying amounts should be laid
upon paper, glass, red and white lead, and painters'
colours imported into the colonies, that a duty of
threepence a pound should be imposed upon all imported tea, and that " the said duties, to be raised
in the said colonies and plantations, be applied in making a more certain and adequate provision for the
charge of the administration of justice, and the sup-

---

[1] Add. MS., 32936, f. 321. This paper is wrongly endorsed April 3rd, 1762.
[2] Add. MS., 32981, f. 375 ; Grafton's *Autobiography*, p. 176 ; Walpole's
Memoirs, 3, 21 ff.

port of civil government, in such of the said colonies and plantations where it shall be found necessary; and that the residue of such duties be paid into the receipt of his majesty's exchequer, and there reserved, to be, from time to time, disposed of by parliament, towards defraying the necessary expenses of defending, protecting, and securing, the said colonies and plantations." [1]

Such was the final form of Townshend's unhappy project, and, for what he did, he has stood in the pillory for nigh upon a century and a half. Upon him has devolved the main load of the responsibility for the loss of the American colonies. He stands accused of having rendered more critical an already critical situation; but the greatest criminals are seldom without some defence, and the chancellor of the exchequer could plead a certain measure of justification for his action. He had not imposed these new taxes, as Grenville had imposed the stamp act, to assert a right, but to meet a necessity. It was undeniably true that the American revenue was insufficient to meet the financial requirements of colonial government, that the new taxes were far from oppressive, and that every penny which they produced was to be spent upon the country on which they were imposed. Though he had originally intruded his scheme without notice, and in a measure forced it upon his colleagues, they had, at least, sanctioned it, and their acquiescence did not spring entirely from fear. " The right of the mother country," wrote Grafton in his old age, " to impose taxes on the colonies was then so generally admitted, that scarcely anyone thought of questioning it, though, a few years afterwards, it was given up as indefensible by everybody." [2] There is no evidence

---

[1] *Parliamentary History*, xvi. 376.
[2] Grafton's *Autobiography*, p. 127.

that Lord Rockingham and his followers attempted to stay Townshend in his headlong course, and most men warmly approved a plan which promised to relieve the mother country of what might, in the near future, become an intolerable burden. Where we see blind wilfulness and reckless vanity, contemporaries detected enlightened statesmanship ; and Edward Sedgwick was certainly not alone in applauding the chancellor of the exchequer " for having provided for the expense of the whole civil administration in the colonies, and made the several officers concerned in it independent of the people." [1]

Yet, in spite of all that can be urged on his behalf, in spite of the approval of contemporaries, it remains true that Townshend was guilty of a fatal and irre-trievable blunder. He forgot that government is an art as well as a science. It was clear that the relations between England and her colonies had undergone a change, that the stamp act had provoked an entirely new attitude in America towards the mother country, and that, if peace was to be maintained, coercion and conciliation must go hand in hand. The suspension of the powers of the New York assembly, and the nullification of the Massachusetts act of indemnity, however justified such measures of repression might be by necessity, could hardly fail to fan the flames of discontent in the colonies ; and yet this was the moment selected by the chancellor of the exchequer for reviving the question of taxation. His action was essentially untimely and also unnecessary. Better would it have been for England to have continued to bear more than her fair share of the financial burden of colonial government. It was of little account that the new taxes were import duties, for

[1] Hist. MSS. Comm. Weston Underwood MSS. 406.

they were sufficiently differentiated from such imposts in the past by being imposed for the sake of revenue ; and Townshend must have been strangely ignorant of human nature if he believed that the colonists would be reconciled to these new exactions because they could be described on paper as external taxes.   Indeed, they would be driven to further aggressions ; for, if both external and internal taxes could be made to yield a revenue, and violate the principle of no taxation without representation, these custom dues must follow the way of the stamp act.   If the English ministers thought to chop logic with the Americans, they would discover that the latter were not in a mood to abide by delicate distinctions, and cared too much for their freedom to be mindful of their consistency.

Thus the seed of conflict and dissension was sown, destined to produce a plentiful crop of mischief in the future ; but, for the time being, Grafton thought less of the gathering storm in the colonies, and more of the parliamentary struggle at home, which threatened the safety of his administration.   By the end of May it was common gossip that the ministry was being hard pressed, especially in the house of lords where it sometimes only carried divisions by very narrow majorities.   The opposition appeared to be as united on colonial policy as it had been on East Indian affairs ; and, while harmony prevailed among its enemies, the ministry was torn asunder by strife and distrust. Shelburne, who had ceased to attend the meetings of the cabinet, was not unnaturally regarded with suspicion by his colleagues [1] ; and both Conway and Townshend had not scrupled to act in opposition to

---

[1] The king, in writing to Chatham on May 30th, refers to " the great coldness shown those three ministers (Grafton, Camden, and Northington), by Lord Shelburne, whom they, as well as myself, imagine to be rather a secret enemy."   Chatham Correspondence, 3, 260-262.

the rest of the cabinet. Though, so far, the ministry had escaped actual defeat, its prolonged existence, threatened as it was by dissensions within and attacks without, seemed very problematical; and Grafton, fearing that at any moment he and his colleagues might be engulfed in the rising storm, turned for advice to the prime minister in his gloomy seclusion at Hampstead. He asked for permission to visit him, but the request was promptly refused, Chatham replying that " nothing can be so great an affliction to him as to find himself quite unable for a conversation, which he should otherwise be proud and happy to embrace." [1] Grafton, however, was convinced that the time for half measures was over, and, accompanied by Northington, visited the king on May 28th, to warn him of what might happen if a policy of drift was pursued. The two ministers drew a sufficiently lurid picture of the actual situation. They elaborated the evil circumstances of the administration, " in one house acting, from the beginning of the session, in direct contradiction to all cabinet decisions : in the other, by the prevalence of faction, brought to such a crisis, as to carry questions in a very full house, by majorities of three only, and even those made up by the votes of two of the king's brothers, and some lords brought down from their very beds." [2] This doleful tale, enforced by a threat from Grafton that he would not continue in office unless something was done, had the desired effect, and the king undertook to ask Chatham to grant the first lord of the treasury an interview. The royal letter was in the true heroic vein. After referring to the narrow ministerial

---

[1] Chatham Correspondence, 3, 255 - 256; Grafton's *Autobiography*, pp. 132, 133.

[2] Grafton's *Autobiography*, p. 134.

majorities in the upper house, and the discord within the cabinet, the king struck the note of defiant confidence : " My firmness," he declared, " is not dismayed by these unpleasant appearances ; for, from the hour you entered into office, I have uniformly relied on your firmness to act in defiance to that hydra faction, which has never appeared to the height it now does, till within these few weeks. Though your relations, the Bedfords, and the Rockinghams, are joined with intention to storm my closet, yet, if I was mean enough to submit, they own they would not join in forming an administration ; therefore nothing but confusion could be obtained. I am strongly of opinion with the answer you sent the Duke of Grafton ; but, by a note I have received from him, I fear I cannot keep him above a day, unless you would see him and give him encouragement. . . . Be firm, and you will find me amply ready to take as active a part as the hour seems to require. Though none of my ministers stand by me, I cannot truckle." [1]

Such an appeal was enough to stir all the old warrior spirit left in Chatham's veins. The suggestion that the monarchy was on the point of being enslaved by the whig oligarchy risen from its ashes, that Grafton was about to retire and, perhaps, precipitate a dissolution of the ministry, and that once more faction would resume its sway over the destinies of the country, induced him to make a great effort. He consented to see Grafton who visited him on the last day of May.[2] It was the first time that Grafton had seen his leader since his retirement to Hampstead, and he was dismayed to find how broken and prostrate was the great

---

[1] Chatham Correspondence, 3, 257-262 ; Grafton's *Autobiography*, pp. 134-5.

[2] Grafton's *Autobiography*, pp. 136-139.

statesman who had once caused Europe to tremble.
Every dictate of human sympathy inclined the duke
to refrain from entering upon the discussion of business
which could not but cause additional pain and grief
to one already in the depths of affliction ; but, compelled to speak when he would gladly have been silent,
he sketched the events of the last three months,
and earnestly implored Chatham for " his advice as
to assisting and strengthening the system he had
established, by some adequate accession, without which,
they were confident, it could not, or ought not, to
proceed." Yet, explicit as such a declaration was,
Chatham seemed to fail to understand in what a
parlous way were the affairs of the state. Aware
that his ministry still enjoyed the favour of the king,
he despised, as he had done from the first, the danger
that might arise from an union of the parties in opposition ; and he was far more exercised at the prospect
of Grafton's resignation. All the little energy that
remained to him he used in dissuading his first lord
of the treasury from taking such a fatal step, arguing
that if he, Northington, and Camden, did not retain
their offices, " there would be an end to all his hopes
of being ever serviceable again as a public man."
To such a plea, coming from so great a man thus
circumstanced, the most selfish and stony-hearted
of politicians could not have listened unmoved ; and
Grafton, the ready victim of a generous impulse,
did not hearken undisturbed to so direct and personal
an appeal. It is true that he did not pledge himself
to remain in office, but he urged that, if he was to
continue to bear the irksome burden of unwelcome
power, the administration must be strengthened.
" A junction with the Bedfords or the Rockinghams,"
he states in his account of this interview, " appeared

to me to be the only steps that could now be effectual : to which his lordship assented, though he inclined to prefer entering into negotiation with the former."

Thus ended a meeting, indescribably painful to both parties ; and Grafton returned to London with his leader's permission to enter upon a negotiation with the Bedfords. That Chatham should have given the preference to that faction is not surprising, as the Rockingham whigs were the foremost champions of that party system whose destruction he had vowed ; and though the king, fearing perhaps that the Bedfords might demand the treasury for Grenville, from whom he had suffered too much in the past to wish to have him again as his first minister, favoured overtures being made to the followers of Rockingham,[1] Chatham's wish was religiously observed, and Lord Gower was approached.[2] At the outset it was rendered clear that, though the Bedfords were to be admitted into place, Grenville and his friends were not to be included in the negotiation; and Gower, aware that the aim of the ministers was to divide the opposition, refused to discuss such a restricted offer. For the time being, nothing more was done, and Grafton continued, until the end of the session, without the assistance which he, himself, had declared to be essential. And, as is not surprising, the outlook grew more gloomy as the days passed by. The ministry, indeed, was not so hard pressed in the upper house as formerly [3] ; but the danger of a dissolution of the cabinet waxed perceptibly greater. Conway had for some long time declared that he would resign at the end of the session, and his hour was almost come ; Northington, having

---

[1] Grafton's *Autobiography*, p. 139.

[2] Walpole's Memoirs, 3, 41, 42.

[3] " The majority in both houses being now very handsome." The king to Lord Chatham, June 25th, 1767. Chatham Correspondence, 3, 275-6.

undermined his health by a lifelong devotion to port, was anxious to quit his employment ; Townshend declared that he would not be left to perish in the wreck which seemed fast to be approaching ; and Grafton, having abandoned all hope, only continued in office because Chatham's words rang in his ears.[1] Again the king appealed to Hampstead for instructions how to meet the tempest ; and all that the prime minister could advise was that, if the threatened resignations took effect, men, agreeable to Grafton, should be chosen to fill the vacant places. " The very little my state of nerves enables me to offer," he wrote, " is, that if the Duke of Grafton can be prevailed upon to remain at the head of the treasury, with such a chancellor of the exchequer as is agreeable to his grace success to your majesty's affairs would not be doubtful ; this being, in my poor opinion, the vital part, and indispensable."[2]

Such was the political situation when the session was brought to a conclusion on July 2nd ; and, on the same day, Grafton presented the king with a paper composed by Northington and himself.[3] This document stated that it was hopeless to fill the expected vacancies

[1] Chatham Correspondence, 3, 275-6.

[2] Ibid., 3, 277-8.

[3] As the paper in question is not over lucid, it may be worth while to reproduce it, in order to support or disprove the interpretation placed upon it in the text. " The President and the Duke of Grafton, after the most serious consideration and explicit conversation in the closet, having fully urged the impracticability for them to form, in the critical circumstances of this country, a temporary administration from any collection of individuals which they should think fit to recommend to his majesty, it becomes now essential for his majesty, though unwillingly, to ask of the Earl of Chatham, whether he can devise any plan, by which the immediate execution of government can be carried on ; for they cannot with honour make any application to any divisions of men, unapprized of his lordship's ideas thereupon ; which, with the resignations in effect made, must leave this country without any government." Chatham Correspondence, 3, 267. This paper is dated June 2nd, but for the reasons to believe that the proper date should be July 2nd, see Grafton's Autobiography, p. 150, n.

in the cabinet with wanderers in the highways and hedges of political life, that an appeal must be made to one of the parties in opposition, and that Lord Chatham should be asked for his opinion upon such a proceeding. Thus, urged by his advisers, the king again wrote to Chatham, and in even stronger terms than before. " I earnestly call upon you," he wrote, " to lay before me a plan, and also to speak to those you shall propose for responsible offices. You owe this to me, to your country, and also to those who have embarked in administration with you. If after this you again decline taking an active part, I shall then lie under a necessity of taking steps, that nothing but the situation I am left in could have obliged to." Fervent, and even minatory, as such an appeal was, it failed to rouse Chatham from his despondency, and once more he implored " compassion and pardon from his majesty, for the cruel situation which still deprives him of the possibility of activity, and of proving to his majesty the truth of an unfeigned zeal, in the present moment rendered useless." [1]

Thus Chatham, in the clutch of a fell disease, showed himself a broken reed ; and, denied his counsel, the king, as he, himself, had said, lay " under a necessity of taking steps, that nothing but the situation I am left in could have obliged to." Throughout a long reign George III. was to show that, whatever his faults might be, he was not lacking in courage ; and never was he more courageous than at this moment. Chatham, in whom he had placed his trust, was lost, for a time, perhaps for ever, to political life ; his ministers threatened to desert him ; and, from afar, he could hear the shouts of an united opposition

---

[1] Chatham Correspondence, 3, 266 ff. These letters are also antedated by a month.

clamouring to be admitted into place and power.
Yet he never blenched, never thought of surrender.
To give up his servants, because they had been attacked
in parliament, would have been to destroy all that he
had so laboriously achieved since the beginning of
the reign, and to submit once more to that condition
of servitude under which his grandfather had fretted.
Whatever he might be called upon to endure, that
humiliation, at least, he was determined to avoid ;
and he is deserving of whatever credit attaches to
high resolve and steady purpose, for his conduct in
a crisis which would have strained the nerves and
taxed the ingenuity of the most adroit and experienced
of politicians.   Dark and devious were the ways
he trod, but the royal gaze, however circuitous the
course, never wandered from the goal upon which it
had been set from the first.

The problem, confronting him at the beginning
of July, was simple enough to state, but exceedingly
difficult to solve.   If Grafton was allowed to resign,
the ministry might fall, and the opposition storm the
cabinet at the point of the sword.   This, the worst
disaster that could happen, must be averted at all
cost, and Grafton must continue in power in order
to preserve the government.   But, time and time again,
Grafton had declared that he would retire unless the
administration received an accession of parliamentary
strength ;   and therefore the king found himself
obliged to sanction a negotiation with those in opposition.   The danger of such a proceeding is sufficiently
obvious.   During the session just concluded,
Rockingham, Grenville, and Bedford had fought side
by side against the government ;   and it might well
be that, when approached by the court, they would
refuse to be separated, and demand the construction

of a ministry representative of all parties in opposition. To allow this, would be for the king to make an abject surrender to what he deemed the forces of faction ; and this he was certainly not prepared to do. But, no longer an inexperienced boy, he detected the weak link in his adversaries' armour. Convinced that the union of the opposition leaders was essentially unreal, the offspring of an occasion and not the result of community of principles,[1] he determined to break up the alliance which threatened his safety. On Saturday, July 4th, he commissioned the Duke of Grafton to inquire from Lord Gower whether there was any hope of the Duke of Bedford and his followers joining the administration. Taking profit by Gower's attitude a few weeks before, the king no longer confined the offer to the Bedford party alone, being willing that both Temple and Grenville should be given places in the cabinet. But, though this much was conceded, it was expressly stipulated that Grafton must remain at the treasury ; and the object of this condition is not hard to understand. With Grafton continuing at his post, any changes, which might be made, would " bear the appearance of an accession to, and not a defeat of, the present administration " ; and thus it could never be said that the king had surrendered to his enemies.[2]

Armed with the royal authority, Grafton visited Gower without delay, and found him in a conciliatory mood. He seemed to think that both Bedford and Temple would be ready to discuss terms, and would raise no objection to Grafton continuing at the treasury ; and, if no more had been said, a negotiation might have been actively begun. But Gower was

[1] Chatham Correspondence, 3, 260, 262.
[2] Grafton's *Autobiography*, p. 151.

careful to add that whatever place Temple might accept in the cabinet, he would claim equal authority with Grafton ; for, continued Gower, " how can he think of having less weight in this, than in one last year, which he would not enter into unless *pari passu* with Lord Chatham ? " [1] It is clear that this new and somewhat unexpected demand alarmed both the king and Grafton when they discussed the situation together on Sunday, July 5th. It would be of little profit that Grafton should continue at the treasury if he was obliged to share his supremacy with Temple ; and George III. was quick to see that, if such terms were granted, the transformed cabinet would be far less the old re-cast than a new administration presided over by Temple. He did not take long to make up his mind, and Grafton was dispatched to inform Gower that his terms had not been approved at court. Before, however, the first lord of the treasury left the royal presence, the king intimated that he desired to see Conway.[2]

This wish was not due to the idle whim of the moment. Having come to the conclusion that it was vain to expect assistance from the Bedfords, he was anxious to discover what " possibility there might be of finding Lord Rockingham's friends practicable " ; [3] and he knew that Conway could give him the information he sought. For, like the cautious political archer that he was, George III. had been careful to have two strings to his bow ; and, at the same time that a formal offer was made to Lord Gower, a more or less subterraneous negotiation was being carried on with the Rockingham whigs. On Friday, July 3rd, Conway informed Rockingham that

---

[1] Grafton's *Autobiography*, pp. 146, 151 ; Grenville Papers, 4, 33, 36.
[2] Grafton's *Autobiography*, p. 152.   [3] *Ibid.*

he and his party would probably be approached by Grafton if they could pledge themselves not to demand either the removal of Camden from the woolsack or Lord Granby from the post of commander-in-chief ;[1] and, though no mention was made of the king's name, it is impossible to believe that such a message was given without the royal sanction or approval. Neither Grafton nor Conway would have dared to have taken such a step on their own authority ; and, in approaching the Rockingham party in this informal way, the king displayed no little craft and cunning. If the negotiation with the Bedfords proved successful, he could easily disavow what Conway had done, since his name had not been mentioned ;[2] and, if Gower and his friends proved obdurate, then it was open to the king to continue what Conway and Grafton had begun. And great was the advantage which George III. might reap from a negotiation with the Rockingham party. If brought to a successful conclusion, Conway, delighted at being reconciled to his old friends, would almost certainly remain in office ; and all might not be lost even if the negotiation should prove abortive. In the event of failure it would be to the royal advantage to throw all the blame upon Lord Rockingham and his followers, to represent their demands as excessive, and their aim as the enslavement of the monarchy rather than the safety of the nation ; for then, Conway, disgusted at such factious conduct, might consent to remain in office, even though his friends continued in opposition. It was a bold game, and boldly did the king play it.

[1] Newcastle's *Narrative*, pp. 104, 108.
[2] " Nothing that has dropped," wrote Rockingham on July 4th, " seems to go further than towards a treaty with us ; and nothing drops in regard to his majesty, but only as the Duke of Grafton's opinion that his majesty's preference is to us." Add. MS., 32983, f. 55.

Rockingham lost no time in imparting to his supporters what Conway had told him ; and a few of the leading members of the party,[1] together with Conway, dined at his house on the evening of July 3rd.   To reject the overtures, without further parley, would be unduly precipitate, and most certainly hazardous, for Rockingham had been given a hint that, if he and his allies " were shy, and would not show a readiness to treat, the probability was that the treaty might be carried on elsewhere " ;[2] and it did not need much insight to understand that the reference was to Woburn.   No more effective spur could have been applied.   " I think, if the negotiation is thrown into our hands," wrote the Marquis to Newcastle, " we may possibly succeed in persuading the Duke of Bedford's friends to take part with us.   If, on the contrary, the negotiation is thrown into the Duke of Bedford's, etc., they must of course naturally make their point George Grenville ; and in that case George Grenville and Lord Temple will take the lead in administration."[3]   The reasoning was just, and all gathered round Rockingham's table agreed in thinking that it would be a great mistake abruptly to refuse to treat.   The demand that Granby must be retained as Commander-in-chief could be easily fulfilled, for Lord Albemarle, the only member of the Rockingham party who might justly aspire to that office, was quite prepared to forego his claims ;   and although Charles Yorke, baffled once more in the hope of obtaining the greatest prize of the legal profession, might well be offended if Lord Camden continued as lord chancellor, it was suggested that he might be consoled by a peerage and

---

[1] The Duke of Portland, Lord Winchelsea, Lord Albemarle, Dowdeswell, Lord John, and Lord Frederick Cavendish, were the guests.

[2] Add. MS., 32983, f. 55.

[3] Add. MS., 32983, f. 55 ; Newcastle's *Narrative*, p. 104.

the office of lord president of the council.[1] Yet, though unwilling to make unnecessary difficulties, the Rockingham whigs displayed no feverish anxiety to accept whatever the court might choose to offer. All concurred in thinking that as yet too little information had been given to enable a definite answer to be framed, and that no further steps could be taken until it was ascertained " whether a general and solid plan was the object." [2] If it was only intended to change the occupants of two or three offices, keeping the administration much as it was, they agreed that they " would much prefer seeing any set, or sets, undertake administration, on such a foot, than be the undertakers ourselves." [3]

This cautious reserve concealed a well-founded suspicion that the king was sounding his way by separate negotiations with the different parties in opposition,[4] so as to break up that union which threatened the safety of the ministry ; and the Rockingham whigs were determined not to be trapped in the royal snare. The experience of the last two years had impressed upon them the inadequacy of their own parliamentary strength, and the necessity of an alliance with the Bedford party ; and Rockingham quickly communicated what Conway had told him to Gower and Weymouth.[5] He acted wisely in so doing. Such frankness was certain to assist in maintaining the friendly relations which

---

[1] Add. MS., 32985, f. 55. Newcastle, however, was less sanguine. " The two points insisted upon," he wrote to Rockingham, " of Lord Granby and the chancellor, are, I believe, the Duke of Grafton's own. As to the first, if my Lord Albemarle is satisfied with it, I can have no objection to it. As to the other, your lordship knows more of the Yorkes than I do ; but so much I think I know that they will never be satisfied till Charles Yorke has the great seal." Add. MS., 32983, f. 59.

[2] Add. MS., 32983, f. 59 ; Newcastle's *Narrative*, p. 104.

[3] *Ibid.*   [4] *Ibid.*   [5] *Ibid.* ; Newcastle's *Narrative*, p. 108.

had existed between the two parties during the parliamentary session, and might possibly lay a foundation for further action. Uncertain of much else, all those, with whom Rockingham had taken counsel, were of the opinion that if they were expected to form a ministry, they must "talk with the Bedfords." [1]

Such was the political situation when, on Sunday, July 5th, the king determined to abandon the negotiation begun with Lord Gower, and sought information from Conway. It may be surmised that the secretary of state's report was favourable,[2] for, on the day following Rockingham learnt that Grafton would see him on July 7th, " and," added Rockingham, " as I understand, authorised by his majesty." [3] When they met, Grafton inquired whether Rockingham and his friends were ready to " come into administration along with the remains of the present administration," and, if so, the king desired that they would submit a plan of government. On inquiring whether the offer extended to the Bedford party, Rockingham was informed that it did ; but the same favour was not shown to Grenville and his friends who were subjected to what Rockingham described as an " implied exclusion." When the treasury came under discussion, Grafton mentioned that Rockingham might have that office, and that he himself would sit in the cabinet or remain outside " according as it might appear to us advantage-

---

[1] " That it was wished by us to know whether a general and solid plan was the object, and in which case (though under no engagements) we should desire to talk with the Bedfords." Add. MS., 32983, f. 55 ; Newcastle's *Narrative*, p. 104 ; see also p. 109.

[2] In his memoirs (3, 46) Walpole gives a jejune, and not very trustworthy, account of this interview. Conway is represented as informing the king that Rockingham would expect to be given the treasury ; but he could not have learnt this at the meeting on July 3rd, for no specific demands had been made.

[3] Add. MS., 32983, f. 125 ; Newcastle's *Narrative*, p. 110.

ous for the administration." [1] Nothing indeed could have been more gracious and yielding than Grafton's behaviour at this interview; but a distinguished politician, who knew well the race of which he was so illustrious a member, has told us that speech was given to men to conceal their thoughts; and it is well nigh impossible to believe that the king really intended that Rockingham should have the treasury. Such a concession was contrary to his fixed determination that any changes, that were made, must " bear the appearance of an accession to, and not a defeat of, the present administration "; and it is far more probable that Grafton, weary of office, either gave the promise on his own responsibility or with the sanction of the king who hoped that the occasion would never arise when he would be called upon to fulfil it.[2] Nor was this the only hidden obstacle, for the " implied exclussion " of the Grenvilles was pregnant with mischief. Both the king and Grafton must have been well aware that the permission granted to Lord Rockingham to include the Bedford party in the negotiation was indeed a barren gift if Grenville and his followers were to be excluded; and even Rockingham, generally

[1] Add. MS., 32983, f. 127; Add. MS., 35430, f. 85; Newcastle's *Narrative*, p. 110.

[2] Certainty on this point is unfortunately out of the question. There is no doubt that Rockingham was quite convinced that he had been offered the treasury (Add. MSS., 32983, f. 127; Add. MS., 35430, f. 85). When, however, on July 22nd, he thanked the king for the offer, the latter replied, " that it was not an offer; that the Duke of Grafton might understand it so, but the king did not mean it as such." On the day following, Grafton explained to Rockingham " that his majesty meant to convey that he had not offered the treasury (which he could not do out of delicacy to the Duke of Grafton) but that there was no mistake in understanding it as intended " (Rockingham Memoirs, 2. 50; Newcastle's *Narrative*, pp. 150, 154). It is difficult to weave a consistent tale out of these cryptic and conflicting utterances. It is possible that the king may have said that if Grafton persisted in his determination to resign, Rockingham might succeed him: thus the promise was only conditional upon Grafton's resignation which the king was resolved to prevent.

so optimistic, was troubled by the vague phrase, " the remains of the present administration." When pressed for further explanation, the first lord of the treasury explained the remark as having special reference to Lord Camden, but he was careful to add that there must be " much caution in regard to others, by way of preventing at this moment it being said that his majesty gave up A, B, or C, etc." When the interview was over, Rockingham was frankly puzzled over the extent of the authority which had been granted him, informing Newcastle that he could " consider this only more as an opening, than as yet anything on which a judgment can be formed. The material matter is, how far his majesty will incline to allow us to introduce a number sufficient to give real strength. If that can't be, I own, I shall have no desire to be a part." [1]

Time would have been saved, and much future trouble averted, if Rockingham had cleared up his doubts before proceeding further ; but thinking that there was a sufficient chance of success to justify action, he sent off an express to Lord Albemarle, who was staying at Woburn, informing him of what had passed, and instructing him to impart the news to his host.[2] Moreover, he held a meeting of his followers at his house on the evening of July 7th, when discussion, for the most part, centred round the proscription which had been placed upon George Grenville ; and, although few of the Rockingham whigs had any love for Grenville,[3] they realised that the Bedfords would never move without him. Understanding, as they did, that Grenville had been proscribed in order to render an alliance between the Bedfords and them-

---

[1] Add. MS., 32983, f. 127 : Newcastle's *Narrative*, p. 110.
[2] Newcastle's *Narrative*, p. 110.   [3] *Ibid.*, p. 109.

selves impossible, two courses were open to them—
they might either refuse to enter upon the negotiation
unless Grenville was included in it, or they might
disregard the restriction imposed by the court. Unfortunately, they chose the latter alternative, and,
although no formal understanding was arrived at, it
was more or less generally agreed that, if the Duke
of Bedford pressed the claims of Grenville and Temple,
they should be given places in the cabinet, provided
that neither of them was first lord of the treasury or
secretary of state for the southern department which
included the American colonies.[1]

Such a decision, justified though it might be by
necessity, certainly laid the Rockingham whigs open
to the charge of exceeding the limits of their instructions ; but the hope of once more coming into office
inclined them to minimise the obstacles which lay
between them and their goal. And, for the time being,
there appeared to be every indication of ultimate
success. From Woburn Lord Albemarle wrote that
" the Duke of Bedford most sincerely wishes to join
with you in the great plan of removing the favourite
and his friends from court. This end, his grace
thinks, cannot be attained without the junction
and hearty concurrence of Mr Grenville, and asked me
if you would have any objection to treat with Mr
Grenville. I ventured to say that you certainly would
not, provided it was through his grace as one of his
friends. He is very sanguine in his wishes. The
treasury they look upon as yours." [2]   Such reassuring

---

[1] Newcastle's *Narrative*, pp. 111, 118, 120. Portland and Newcastle were
in favour of Grenville and his party being included whether Bedford pressed
their claims or not, on the ground that it was very doubtful " whether a *total*
exclusion of my Lord Temple, and his brothers, and of my Lord Lyttelton,
will quite answer the view and plan of settling a lasting administration which
should go on with ease and success."

[2] Rockingham Memoirs, 2, 46 ; Newcastle's *Narrative*, p. 130.

information decided Rockingham to visit Woburn in person; but, before leaving London, he was visited by Rigby who undertook to convey to Grenville that the Bedford party was quite prepared to allow Rockingham to have the treasury, and to endeavour " to prevail upon him to support, if not to take a part in, an administration formed of the Duke of Bedford's and your grace's friends." A safer envoy than Rigby might, perhaps, have been chosen. He had always favoured Grenville rather than Rockingham as the suitable ally for his leader, the Duke of Bedford, and he frankly declared himself in favour of Grenville's colonial policy.[1]

With Rigby at Wotton, and Rockingham at Woburn, the negotiation was transferred from London into the country. On Friday, July 10th, Rigby discussed affairs with Grenville who declared that, though he would not take office himself, he was ready to give his support to any administration which pursued a colonial policy he approved;[2] and, when he heard what Grenville had said, Rockingham was more sanguine than ever. He seems to have paid little attention to the reference to America, which might justly have alarmed him, and to have been more than satisfied that Grenville was prepared to support the ministry when formed, and cherished no designs upon the treasury. He must have been still more elated when Rigby, who had been sent over to Stowe for the purpose, returned with the information that Temple had declared his readiness to unite " in a plan to extirpate the influence of Lord Bute, though neither he nor his brother were thought on by the king to be at the head of this new administration." [3]

---

[1] Newcastle's *Narrative*, pp. 126, 130 ; Grenville Papers, 4, 227 ff.
[2] Grenville Papers, 4, 48 ; Bedford Correspondence, 3, 365.
[3] Bedford Correspondence, 3, 365.

On Sunday, July 12th, Rockingham was back again in London, delighted at the progress that had been made. " I can only now say," he wrote to Newcastle on his arrival, " that appearances are more and more favourable. The Duke of Bedford most cordial, and the result of Rigby's visit at Wooton and Stowe adds much to the general promising aspect." [1] " Lord Rockingham," Hardwicke informed Charles Yorke, " is come back with flying colours from Woburn, a most successful negotiation." [2] But the real tussle was now to begin, and the clear divergence, between what Rockingham desired and the king intended, to be revealed. At an interview with Grafton on July 15th, Rockingham requested to know whether the king was prepared to allow him to form an administration on a comprehensive plan, and to grant him a preliminary audience for the discussion of details. Grafton started at the word comprehensive, pointing out that, if the Rockinghams, the Bedfords, and even the Grenvilles were to be admitted into office, this was hardly consistent with " his majesty's most gracious opening to his lordship where the remainder of the present administration, together with the chancellor, was to be the foundation of it." Rockingham apparently allowed the force of this contention, but still asserted that neither he nor his followers would join any ministry without " Bedford and his friends, such of Mr Grenville's also as chose to come into office ; for as to particular determination thereupon of Lord Temple or his brother personally, his lordship did not take it upon him to answer." [3]

Grafton might well start at the word comprehensive, for grave was the situation which confronted him and

[1] Newcastle's *Narrative*, p. 133.   [2] Add. MS., 35362, f. 129.
[3] Grafton's *Autobiography*, p. 146 ; Grenville Papers, 4, 54, 58.

his master, threatened as they were, apparently, by a union of all the different parties in opposition. What they had schemed to avert [1] seemed to have come to pass in defiance of all their efforts. If they had hoped, as indeed they almost certainly had, that the proscription of Grenville would prove an insurmountable barrier to an alliance between the Bedfords and the Rockinghams, great must have been their disappointment at the turn events had taken. Moreover, they might feel justly aggrieved; for, if there was a breach of faith, it was on the part of Lord Rockingham. He had included Grenville in the negotiation after he had been forbidden to do so; and he had acted on the assumption, which he well knew to be at least unproven, that an entirely new administration was to be formed.[2] But, however threatening might be the aspect, George III. was resolved to defend his closet against those who thought to take it by assault, and never to forego his royal right of choosing his servants in accordance with his own will, not at the dictation of parliament. " After having delivered to his majesty the answer which your lordship communicated to General Conway and myself this morning," wrote Grafton to Rockingham, " I was commanded to acquaint your lordship that the king wishes your lord-

[1] " In the present moment," wrote Charles Yorke to Hardwicke on July 11th, " the court means to divide the opposition which they see cementing, and which, in consequence of that cement, will prove as formidable in the house of commons hereafter as it showed itself in the house of lords at the close of the session. And they believe the points of power to be irreconcilable, and the rocks on which the opposition will split." Add. MSS., 35362, f. 126.

[2] " I have just seen the marquess," wrote Lord Weymouth on July 15th, " who did not see the Duke of Grafton till this morning. He told him what was agreed at Woburn, and said that he now hoped to be able to form a ministry upon a comprehensive plan ; but as this differed a little from the first proposal of his grace, he could not properly desire an audience till he knew whether his majesty was disposed to receive a plan on this comprehensive idea." Grenville Papers, 4, 58.

ship would specify the plan on which you and your friends would come into office in order to extend and strengthen his administration." [1] This was a polite way of intimating to Rockingham that he had exceeded his instructions, and that he had never been called upon to construct a new ministry; but, confident that he could count upon the support of Grenville and Bedford, he still adhered to his original demands. " I hope your grace will do me the honour," he wrote in answer to Grafton, " to explain to his majesty that the principle, on which I would proceed, should be to consider the present administration as at an end, notwithstanding the great regard and esteem which I have for some of those who compose it. If his majesty thinks it for his service to form a new administration on a comprehensive plan . . . I should then humbly hope to have his majesty's permission to attend him, in order to receive his commands, it being impossible to enter into particulars till I have his majesty's leave to proceed upon this plan." [2]

Thus, the antagonists stood face to face, each able to take the measure of the other's sword; but the king never wavered in the determination to save his ministry from overthrow. Yet, if he absolutely refused Rockingham's demands, Conway, affronted that his

---

[1] Grafton's *Autobiography*, p. 144. This letter was composed by Conway, his brother, Lord Hertford, and Grafton, and submitted to Horace Walpole, who objected to it. He argued that the opposition, knowing that they would disagree when it came to a discussion of details, wanted an excuse for breaking off the negotiation, and that this letter, by indirectly refusing the demand for the formation of a comprehensive administration, gave them the opportunity they sought. He therefore drafted a letter in which Grafton was made to say, " that the king wishes your lordship would specify to him the plan on which you and your friends would propose to come in, in order to form an extensive and solid administration "; but this revised version, though approved by the ministers, was rejected at the last moment, probably because the king withheld his sanction. Walpole's Memoirs, 3, 51, 52.

[2] *Ibid.*

friends had not received better treatment, would execute his threat of resignation, and Grafton would almost certainly follow him into retirement. Thus it would appear that, whichever course the king took, the dissolution of the ministry would come to pass ; but he was by this time too experienced a politician not to know that there is always more than one way out of a difficulty. The loophole of escape lay in pursuing a policy of stooping to conquer. It might be well to grant Rockingham the desired permission to form a comprehensive plan, for that might turn out to be the most effective way of shattering the opposition alliance into fragments. There was a reasonable prospect that, when the opposition leaders came to discuss details, they would fall out both over men and measures, and fail to agree upon the much vaunted comprehensive scheme. If they were allowed this rope to hang themselves, Conway could feel no grievance, and might even consent to remain in office ; and thus, what force could not accomplish, guile might effect.[1]

It is in the light of this policy of craft that one must view the change in the attitude of the court, which took place at this juncture. Apparently abandoning his previous position, Grafton, in a letter to Rockingham on July 17th, declared that " the king's gracious sentiments concur with your lordship's in

---

[1] " I understand," wrote Grafton to Northington on July 19th, " that they are now employed in making out their plan to be offered to his majesty's consideration, a work which, before it can be brought to birth, seems open to so many accidents, that I am, I own, not without thinking it possible that it may disunite parties freshly and loosely cemented, and that some one among them may find it for their interest, as well as credit, to fall in honorably with the present administration. If resentment comes in aid on account of too little consideration shown to some, or too much power grasped at by another, this event may still be the more likely." Grafton's *Autobiography*, pp. 146-8.

regard to the forming of a comprehensive plan of administration, and that his majesty, desirous of uniting the hearts of all his subjects, is most ready and willing to appoint such a one as shall exclude no denomination of men attached to his person and government." [1] No surrender could have been, superficially, more complete, and Rockingham immediately set to work to prepare a plan which he could submit to the king. On the evening of Monday, July 20th, most of the leading politicians in opposition assembled at Newcastle's stately residence in Lincoln's Inn Fields. The Rockingham party was represented by its leader, Newcastle, Richmond, Dowdeswell, and Keppel ; and the Duke of Bedford was accompanied by Sandwich, Weymouth, and Rigby. Neither Grenville nor Temple was present, but they were represented in their absence by Rigby, and had no reason to complain of his zeal. When all had assembled, Rigby read a letter from Grenville couched in a haughty and menacing tone. He demanded that steps should be taken to assert and establish the sovereignty of Great Britain over the colonies, that, though neither he nor Temple desired to take office, their friends should have a becoming share of employments ; and that a certain number of places must be left vacant, which they would divide among their followers if they approved of the general plan agreed upon. It is not surprising that such demands provoked a fierce and heated discussion. If, in order to conciliate Grenville, the Rockinghams agreed to assert and establish the authority of England over the colonies, they might find themselves committed to the revival of the stamp act ; and weighty arguments were

---

[1] Grafton's *Autobiography*, p. 144. The letter was actually composed by Horace Walpole. Memoirs, 3, 53.

urged against the fulfilment of so unreasonable a request. Rockingham, anxious to keep the peace, contended that no such declaration was needed, and that " future differences on that head might be avoided." " Such a declaration," he continued, " might have been expected if they were treating with Lord Chatham and Lord Camden, but he and his friends had repealed the stamp act in the particular circumstances of the crisis, with the strongest *salvo jure* imaginable." Dowdeswell, endeavouring to pour oil upon the troubled waters, suggested the substitution of " maintain and support " for " assert and establish " ; and the Duke of Bedford, also on the side of peace, endeavoured to mitigate the acerbity of Grenville's declaration. Finally, after a lengthy debate, general approval was given to a form of words drawn up by Bedford who was instructed to submit his amended draft to Grenville ; but at this point Rigby again intervened, asserting that Bedford's compromise would never be accepted by Grenville. Weary of a discussion which had lasted nigh upon four hours, it was decided to leave the question unsettled, and to pass on to the distribution of the ministerial offices.

The change of topic did not bring with it, however, a more conciliatory spirit. Rockingham was justly indignant at Grenville's outrageous demand that a certain number of places should be left vacant for his friends to take or refuse, inquiring of Newcastle whether, in all his rich and varied experience of political negotiations, he had ever known such a request advanced. More trouble was caused, however, by Rockingham's declaration that, in the ministry about to be formed, Conway must be secretary of state and leader of the house of commons. The Duke of

Bedford at once stoutly opposed such an arrangement, and refused to listen to Rockingham when he urged that, if he was to be first minister, the leader of the lower house must be one whom he could implicitly trust. His arguments fell upon deaf ears, Bedford contending that Conway was a bad leader, that he did not approve his policy, and that it had never been intimated to him that such an arrangement was in contemplation. For hours the wrangling continued, and it was not until two o'clock in the morning that the meeting broke up, nothing having been settled.[1]

Those skilled in reading the signs in the political sky must have known that little hope remained of arriving at a pacific settlement ; and, on the morning after the meeting, Rockingham and Bedford agreed in regarding "the negotiation as absolutely at an end."[2] Yet, in order that no stone should be left unturned, Newcastle, Rockingham, Dowdeswell, Bedford, and Rigby, met again at Newcastle House on the evening of July 21st ; but with no better results than before. Though a somewhat softer note was struck in the discussion of colonial policy, Rockingham still insisted that Conway must remain the leader of the house of commons, and Bedford and Rigby still asserted that to this they could never agree. Thus, no settlement was possible, and the meeting was brought to a conclusion with an announcement by Lord Rockingham "that each party was from that time discharged from any engagement to each other, and at full liberty to take whatever

---

[1] Add. MS., 32984, f. 130 ; Add. MS., 35362, f. 139 ; Grenville Papers, 4, 71, 80 ; Bedford Correspondence, 3, 382 ; Rockingham Memoirs, 2, 50 ; Newcastle's *Narrative*, p. 141 ; Phillimore's *Life of Lord Lyttelton*, 2, 726.

[2] Newcastle's *Narrative*, p. 147.

part they pleased " ; and to this declaration Bedford assented.[1]

Nothing more remained for Rockingham to do than to inform the king that he had failed to accomplish what he had hoped ; and on Wednesday, July 22nd, he visited the court for that purpose. There was little left for him to say, save to explain how he came empty-handed,[2] and the tidings he brought could not have been but welcome to the king. For George III. now enjoyed his moment of personal triumph. He had played for high stakes and had won ; what he had hoped might happen had actually come to pass, and he was now able to reap the fruit of his prescience. Rockingham came to court a humiliated man. The very foundations on which he had built, the support of Grenville and Bedford, had proved as shifting and unstable as sea-washed sand ; and, convinced by hard realities of a truth to which he had long been blind, it seemed possible that he might now consent to that which he had formerly scorned, and throw in his lot with the existing administration. The king, indeed, did not broach this question to the whig leader at the interview on July 22nd, but the omission was probably due to forgetfulness ; [3] for, on the day following, Rockingham was summoned to meet Grafton once more at Conway's house, and, when he arrived, was informed that " the treasury was again open, that it was wished that I and our friends would come in, that it was his majesty's desire; and the Duke of Grafton wished I would open and try whether with him and General Conway some plan could not be hit off that might bring

<hr>

[1] Grenville Papers, 4, 71, 80 ; Rockingham Memoirs, 2, 50 ; Newcastle's *Narrative*, 147 ; Phillimore's *Lyttelton*, 2, 726.

[2] Rockingham Memoirs, 2, 50 ; Newcastle's *Narrative*, p. 150.

[3] Newcastle's *Narrative*, p. 150.

our friends into administration." [1] But Rockingham, even in this moment of despair, refused to forsake the principles he had enunciated from the very outset of the negotiation. He could not forget what he had suffered when, two years before, having no support but his own comparatively scanty following in parliament, he had come to the king's assistance ; and he was resolved never to repeat the experiment. Determined that when he next came into power it should be at the head of a party which would make him independent of the intrigues of the court, he refused to link his fortunes, and those of his followers, with the existing administration, and politely declined Grafton's offer. [2]

Yet, as though to reward him for the courage with which he had faced his adverse situation, fortune continued to smile upon the king; for Conway consented to remain as secretary of state. Ever since the beginning of the month, that unhappy man had been on the rack of self-torment. Every dictate of reason and honour called upon him to withdraw from a ministry whose policy he disapproved ; but, as always happens, the arguments were not all on one side. He knew that Grafton would follow him into retirement, and that, therefore, upon him would rest the responsibility for the downfall of the government ; but even this did not cause him to alter his determination. He still pined for the society of those with whom he had fought the good fight against Grenville, Bute, and the phalanx of placemen in the pay of the court ; and it had been in the hope that he would consent

---

[1] It should be noticed that the treasury on this occasion was not offered to Rockingham, but was only mentioned as " open," which may be interpreted as meaning that Grafton still contemplated immediate resignation.

[2] Add. MS., 32984, f. 34 ; Newcastle's *Narrative*, p. 154.

to remain, if his friends were admitted into office, that the negotiation with the Rockingham whigs had been begun. On the failure of that negotiation, Conway, if he had been true to his original resolution, would have promptly retired ; but, in an evil moment for his fame, he listened to the counsels of his brother, Lord Hertford, and his friend, Horace Walpole. They presented to his dazzled eyes a highly coloured and distorted picture of what had recently happened. They urged that Rockingham had now thrown in his lot with Bedford and Grenville, the very men most bitterly antagonistic to Conway, that he had sought to storm the closet at the point of the sword, and that, when an offer had been made to him that he and his party should join the government, he had unhesitatingly refused it. Surely, these advisers were able to urge, Conway was now absolved from all allegiance to a leader who had so frankly identified himself with the forces of faction ; and, hearkening to their advice, he consented to remain.[1] That he was uneasy about his conduct is shown by his refusal to continue drawing the salary of his office ; [2] but such scruples of conscience mattered little to the king, flushed with a great triumph. The Duke of Grafton, assured that Conway would still be his colleague, abandoned all thought of resignation; and thus, out of the turmoil of the conflict, George III. emerged victorious over his

---

[1] "On the Wednesday Lord Rockingham asked an audience—as everybody did, and must think to offer his services. . . . The marquis behaved sillily and impertinently, and *then* wondered he was not pressed to accept. Great offence was taken at his behaviour ; and yet there was coolness and prudence enough left to permit another offer to be made. This condescension did the business. The weak man took it for weakness, and thinking that he should force more and more, lost all. In short, he refused—and then Mr Conway found himself at liberty. He and the Duke of Grafton have jointly undertaken the administration." Walpole's Letters, 7, 123-125.

[2] Chatham Correspondence, 3, 286 ; Walpole's Letters, 7, 141-144.

enemies who had thought to take advantage of his hour of necessity.

While the king triumphed, the opposition was busily employed in allotting the blame for the catastrophe. Reflecting in after years upon this abortive negotiation, Lord Hardwicke came to the conclusion that it was Lord Rockingham who was to blame. "I have always thought," he wrote, "that Lord Rockingham managed it ill. He differed with the Bedfords for the sake of Mr Conway . . . and he never came close enough to the point with the Duke of Grafton to have seen what he could make of that." [1] Newcastle was much of the same opinion, declaring that "jealousy and suspicion of Mr Grenville, artfully worked up by young men, and particularly one forward young man, in our house,[2] have brought that good young man, the marquess, into this final resolution"; [3] and, in a note to the Duke of Portland, he pathetically described the failure as "our own doing, and God forgive those who are the occasion of it" [4] He informed Rockingham that the breach was entirely due to the "insisting upon Mr Conway"; [5] and to the Archbishop of Canterbury he declared that, however much Bedford and Rockingham might have differed about details, they ought to have agreed upon a plan of administration for presentation to the king; for "if his majesty had been advised to reject that plan (as most probably he would), the union would then have remained entire, and would have been strengthened by the refusal on the part of the court; whereas it now breaks off from my Lord Rockingham insisting at our last meeting that Mr

[1] Add. MS., 35428, f. 1 ; Harris' *Hardwicke*, 3, 459-460.
[2] Unfortunately, it is impossible to identify this forward young peer.
[3] Add. MS., 32984, f. 1.   [4] Add. MS., 32984, f. 14.
[5] Add. MS., 32984, f. 36.

Conway should remain civil minister in the house of commons, contrary to what everybody understood to have been his own intention and frequent declaration." [1] If, however, Hardwicke and Newcastle agreed in thinking that Rockingham had blundered, Lord Albemarle and Rockingham himself believed that George Grenville was the culprit,[2] a compliment which the latter was not behindhand in returning;[3] and, while the Duke of Richmond could not be persuaded " of the propriety of not accepting the late offers, or at least of not having gone further than you did, so as to put all the ministers in the wrong, by driving them to avow more of a closet system than they would willingly profess to the world," Burke was emphatic in his declaration that it was the sincerity of the court that was at fault.[4]

Thus, mutual recriminations followed upon defeat ; but contemporaries are not always the best critics, and, suffering under the smart of a recent disappointment, Newcastle and others might take a somewhat jaundiced view of the motives and actions of those whom they held responsible for the downfall of their hopes. That Rockingham was guilty of undue precipitation may be allowed. He built too much upon impressions gleaned from a flying visit to Woburn, and thought too little of that significant remark dropped by Grenville that he would only support an administration which pursued a colonial policy which he approved. Nor can he escape blame for exceeding the authority entrusted to him ; for it was never contended that, in the first instance, the king had

---

[1] Add. MS., 32984, f. 62.

[2] Add. MS., 32984, f. 8, f. 10 ; Bedford Correspondence, 3, 387 ; Newcastle's *Narrative*, p. 155.

[3] Hist. MSS. Comm., Various Collections, vol. vi., pp. 250-252.

[4] Burke's Correspondence, 1, 132-144.

authorised him to construct a new ministry in the place of the old. Neither George III. nor Grenville was perhaps guilty of the degree of insincerity in this transaction with which they have sometimes been credited. Extravagant as were the demands presented by Grenville at the meeting on July 20th, there is no evidence that he purposely exaggerated them in order to ruin all chance of agreement; and the king, though descending to deceit in the last stages of the negotiation, cannot be convicted of never having seriously intended to give office to Rockingham and his followers. Indeed, the cause of failure lay far deeper than the Machiavellian schemings of factious politicians; success did not reward the laborious endeavours to attain it, for the simple, though not at the time obvious, reason that the impossible was being attempted. In the purely destructive work of parliamentary criticism, it had been comparatively easy for the various parties in opposition to sink their differences, and to unite in an attack upon the government; but, when they approached the work of constructing a ministry and a policy, harmony was quickly succeeded by discord. George Grenville and his followers still regarded Rockingham as the statesman who, frightened by a few riots and seditious speeches, had bartered away the control of the mother country over the colonies; and they had, not unnaturally, demanded that he should formally renounce principles which they deemed pernicious. Nor was the suspicion entirely on one side. Rockingham had not forgotten that it was Grenville who had supported the peace of Paris, had defended the cyder tax, had prosecuted Wilkes, had strained every nerve to prevent general warrants being declared illegal, and, to fill the cup of his iniquity, had introduced the stamp act ; and it was because he so profoundly dreaded the influence of the man, against whom all these misdeeds could be charged, that he was so persistent in the demand that Conway should be leader of the house of commons. If Conway was not given that post, there was no one who could compete for it with Grenville ; and Rockingham, not unreasonably, feared what such a lieutenant in the lower house might do. Separated as they were by measures rather than by men, divided by the yawning chasm of the American question, neither Rockingham, Grenville, nor Bedford had any cause to blush for their conduct : each did what was right in his own eyes; and, if they failed to come to an understanding, it was largely because they were fighting for principles not for places.

Thus, the unhappy dispute with the American colonies had plunged a poisoned dagger into the very heart of the parliamentary life of the country ; and, when every allowance has been made for the king's courage, his perseverance, and his capacity for intrigue, it still remains true that he could hardly have accomplished what he actually did, had it not been for the divisions among his enemies. The men, who should have stood united against the crown, drew their swords upon one another at the critical moment ; and Newcastle, who had more political wisdom than has sometimes been allowed him, understood that, unless those swords were quickly sheathed, the royal victory was assured. In the moment of despair and disappointment he still continued to preach unity and concord : and it was because he cherished such a lively fear that Rockingham might fall apart for ever from Grenville and Bedford, that he so bitterly regretted the former's farewell words at the meeting on July 21st. " The great thing, my lord, that hurt

me the most," he wrote to his leader, " was the strong
declaration your lordship made to the Duke of Bedford,
and his grace's assent to it, that each party was at
full liberty to take what part they pleased, without
consulting or considering what the sentiments of the
other party might be " ; [1] and to the Duke of Portland
he deplored the " unfortunate end that is put to an
union and connection between the Bedfords and us." [2]
Lord Albemarle, with equal emphasis, asserted that
all would be lost unless friendly relations with the
Bedford party were maintained, implored Rockingham
not to break off intercourse with Bedford, and, rather
unnecessarily, pressed the same advice upon Newcastle :
" For God's sake, my dear lord," he wrote, " don't
lose sight of the Duke of Bedford." [3] Nor were
Newcastle and Albemarle mere voices in an otherwise silent wilderness. Rigby assured Lord Albemarle
that the Bedford party was eager for opposition and
for union with the Rockingham whigs ; but, and
the inquiry was significant, he expressed great anxiety
to know whether Rockingham was " clear of Mr
Conway and all connections with the present administration." Albemarle was, naturally, unable to give
a final answer to such a query, and could only say
that he hoped Rockingham was free from such en-
tanglements ; but to Newcastle he confided that it
would be " very necessary to have that point thoroughly
known before any steps can be taken towards a renewal of the negotiation with the Duke of Bedford
and his friends." [4]

Necessary it might be ; but some time was to
elapse before Rockingham clearly showed his followers
what line he intended to take. A few days after his

[1] Add. MS., 32984, f. 36.   [2] Add. MS., 32984, f. 14.
[3] Add., MS., 32984, f. 8., f. 10.   [4] Add. MS., 32984, f. 356.

interview with the king, he politely informed Newcastle that he was desirous of keeping up a good understanding with the Duke of Bedford, though he was unwilling to be " too courting " ; [1] but such a declaration was capable of very different interpretations, and, at the end of August, Newcastle was alarmed to learn that Burke, whose influence over Rockingham was notorious, was not in favour of breaking off all relations with Conway.[2] Convinced that no greater catastrophe could befall his party than to lose touch with the Bedfords, and that this dire event would surely happen unless it was clearly demonstrated that Conway was no longer the protégé of the Rockingham whigs, Newcastle, without delay, dispatched a letter to the marquis, inquiring about plans for the future.[3] About a month elapsed before Rockingham, who was a dilatory correspondent, replied ; and Newcastle occupied the interval in picking up intelligence from different quarters, endeavouring to smooth away difficulties, and complaining not a little of his treatment by certain members of the party. Meeting Bedford at dinner at Gunnersbury House, he was delighted to find the duke " cool, dispassionate, and reasonable," anxious for a union with the

---

[1] Add. MS., 32984, f. 49.

[2] " I long to have the honor," wrote Newcastle to Lord Albemarle on August 29th, " of seeing your lordship to acquaint you with a very long conversation that I have had this morning with Mr Bourke, I am sorry to say as totally different from my sentiments, and what I apprehend also to be your lordship's, as is possible.   He thinks my Lord Rockingham's honor concerned in not dropping Mr Conway, as he calls it, or suffering him to go out to the army. . . . I despair, as it is so, to find things mend much at Wentworth, for, if my Lord Rockingham was in honor obliged to support Mr Conway in the manner he did, I should apprehend that his lordship will continue to do the same, tho' indeed Mr Bourke did make a distinction between that time and the present time."   Add. MS., 32984, f. 358.

[3] No copy of Newcastle's letter has apparently survived, but its general drift can be gathered from Add. MS., 32985, f. 306, f. 406 ; Burke's Correspondence, I, 144.

Rockinghams, but still as determined as ever that Conway should not be secretary of state or leader of the house of commons.[1] A few days later, however, Newcastle was in the depths of despair over the conduct of Lord Frederick and Lord John Cavendish, who were opposed to any union with the Bedfords; and still more chagrined when he learned that Rockingham had definitely declared that he would have nothing more to do with Grenville. " If so," cried Newcastle in his sorrow, " it is vain for his lordship to think of an union with the Duke of Bedford." [2]

While Newcastle was thus alternately rejoicing and despairing, Rockingham, withdrawn into the country, was thinking over a plan for his future conduct. He informed the Duke of Portland that, as the policy of the party in the past had always been directed towards restraining the influence of Lord Bute, and preventing Grenville from acquiring supremacy in the state, he believed that those principles should dictate their actions, in the future ; and he confided

[1] " I dined yesterday at Gunnersbury with the Duke and Dutchess of Bedford, and my Lord and Lady Waldegrave ; and when her royal highness and when the ladys were retired, I had a great deal of very material conversation with the Duke of Bedford upon the present situation. I found his grace in the very disposition that I, and every true friend to this country, could wish. Cool, dispassionate, and reasonable upon every point. Expressing the same ardent zeal for a most thorough union and friendship with my Lord Rockingham and all our friends : talking in the most proper manner upon the subject of George Grenville, and instead of imagining that Mr Grenville intended or wished to break off the negotiation with Lord Rockingham, mentioned some circumstances to me that shewed that George Grenville was determined to acquiesce, even tho' Lord Temple should not so easily come into it as he did. In short, the simple point is Mr Conway." Add. MS., 32985, f. 13.

[2] Add. MS., 32985, f. 88. On September 19th, Lord Frederick Cavendish, writing to Newcastle to excuse himself for not having called at Claremont on his way to Goodwood, remarked : " I am afraid my excuse will be worse than my fault. I went with Mr Secretary Conway, and returned with him, and, so circumstanced, I fancy your grace will not think I judged much amiss not to call." Add. MS., 32985, f. 136.

to Lord Frederick Cavendish that " the thing he wished
was an union with Bedford House, not totally exclusive
of our old friends ; but if that could be attained by no
other means than by making Mr Grenville the minister,
he would never subscribe to it, and in that case he
should stay all the winter in the country and mind
his farming, which was much better funn " (sic).[1]
Yet, though determined that Grenville should not be
" the minister," which may be taken to mean that
he should neither occupy the treasury nor lead in
the house of commons, Rockingham was, apparently,
willing to allow him a place in the cabinet, and even
to abandon Conway.[2] Grenville was not to be proscribed, but it was clearly intended that he should
not control; and this resolution was reiterated by
Rockingham when, on his arrival in London at the
beginning of October, he penned the long-delayed
reply to Newcastle's letter. " I came to town," he
wrote to the duke, " about nine o'clock, and have

[1] Add. MS., 32985, f. 136 ; Rockingham Memoirs, 2, 57.

[2] " Let us see," wrote Portland to Newcastle on October 20th, " whether
the mischief can be remedied, and whether such an union can be formed as
may be able to withstand the influence of Lord Bute, and restore peace,
stability, and dignity, to government. For the effecting which desirable
purpose, I think nothing can be more conducive than the plan laid down by
your grace in the end of your letter of August 7th, viz., ' That Lord Rockingham should give the Duke of Bedford to understand at a proper time that he
desists from his proposal relating to Mr Conway, and that he should talk over,
coolly and dispassionately, the affair of George Grenville with the Duke of
Bedford only.' 'Tis that conversation, that kind of conversation, that I wish,
and recommended strongly to the marquis the morning I went over to him at
Wentworth, where I found him in the very disposition your grace and his
real friends could have desired. Conway was given up by everybody, fully
and explicitly, except Lord John Cavendish, who was silent. A desire for
union, nay, even the necessity of union, was as strongly urged . . . and, in
short, every preliminary agreed to that might engage the Duke of Bedford
and his friends, and prove to them our wishes of uniting and becoming a
corps. A considerable employment was talked of for George Grenville, and
I rather think Lord Rockingham himself mentioned, and certainly acquiesced
in, the idea of the cabinet for Mr Grenville with or without office." Add. MS.,
32986, f. 58.

been with Lord Albemarle, who I found looking as well or indeed much better than I expected. I much wish for a long and full conversation with your grace, and I shall then go through the letter I had the honour to receive from your grace, which has given me much concern, because I differ almost throughout, not only on the manner of stating things which have passed, but also upon the reasonings and arguments drawn from them. I hope to be able to convince your grace that I am not wrong in differing from many parts of the contents of that letter, and I shall try and do it with calmness, tho' I confess I felt some warmths at parts when I first read them, because I thought them injurious. In regard to what is now to be done, I should think the first step among ourselves is to fix firmly in our minds what were, and what I hope and trust are, the fundamental principles on which we have acted. I must beg to lay stress upon principles in the plural number, because I think the publick are very near equally interested in our adherence to the same line of conduct which we have always held against the power of Lord Bute, and also in the prevention of the return of power into the hands of one who, when minister, had his measures opposed by us, and, when we were ministers, whose measures were corrected much to the publick security and advantage." [1]

Whatever may be urged against the attitude adopted by Rockingham, it was at least rational and consistent ; he had thought over the situation, and, seemingly, arrived at a definite conclusion. Essential as the assistance of the Bedford party might be, he was determined never to purchase it by giving the treasury to George Grenville. To do this would be publicly

[1] Add. MS., 32985., f. 306.

to deny all that he had fought for in the past, to abandon his principles for the sake of power. Nor, indeed, did Newcastle desire him to make such a sacrifice ; and the anxiety of the duke was caused, not by the opinions which Rockingham professed, but by the fear of what he might actually do. That Rockingham cherished something approaching to a personal dislike of Grenville seemed undoubted ; and it was impossible to foretell how far that dislike would carry him. When he paid his promised visit to Newcastle, he took strong objection to a passage in the duke's letter, which referred to Grenville's acquiescence in a coalition between the Bedfords and the Rockingham whigs, roundly declaring that " Mr Grenville's acquiescence was not his object, or even what he wished." [1] Such utterances as these made the old duke almost despair of ever bringing about that alliance with the Bedford party, upon which he set so great a store ; nor was he any happier about his leader's relations with Conway. He had, indeed, been told by the Duke of Portland that Rockingham was prepared to abandon Conway, but he feared that, when the occasion arose, the threat would never be executed. " Mr Conway has winning ways with him," he reflected, " and strong hold of our friends, the Cavendishes " ; [2] and it might well happen that Rockingham's antagonism to Grenville would drive him to adhere to Conway, in spite of what that fidelity had cost him in the past. If such, indeed, proved to be the case, slender was the hope of a united opposition facing the government when parliament met in November ; and Newcastle had gloomy forebodings as to what the future might bring forth. [3]

Yet, continuing to hope against hope, he never

---

[1] Add. MS., 32985, f. 406.   [2] Add. MS., 32985, f. 458.   [3] *Ibid.*

relaxed his efforts to secure success. He was rejoiced to hear from Lord Albemarle, who was a visitor at Woburn, that the Duke of Bedford was as warm as ever in favour of an alliance with Rockingham, if only the marquis could overcome his unfortunate partiality for Conway ;[1] and from Lord Mansfield he learnt that " the Duke of Bedford . . . was very civil, personally, in everything he said of Lord Rockingham."[2] Rigby, moreover, who dined with Newcastle on Sunday, October 11th, " talked very well, his sole point is now opposition to the present ministers,"[3] and all this intelligence Newcastle passed on at different times to Rockingham.[4] And, as the day for the meeting of parliament drew near, his activity increased. Admiral Keppel was sent to Woburn to learn what Bedford intended to do, so that Rockingham, who had again retreated into the country, might be furnished, on his return to London for the session, with the latest information ; and Keppel reported that Bedford, though now almost blind, was coming to London on Friday, November 20th, eager for the parliamentary fray, " very hostile to the present

---

[1] Add. MS., 32985, f. 358, f. 360.   [2] Add. MS., 32985, f. 421.
[3] Add. MS., 32985, f. 453.
[4] On one material point, however, Newcastle maintained a significant silence. In conversation with Lord Albemarle, Bedford had remarked " that the treasury was the great and material object . . . which should be determined by the king." In his reply to Albemarle, Newcastle argued that by this remark Bedford meant nothing more " than he did originally, that the king having decided for Lord Rockingham, that was a reason for Mr Grenville and them to acquiesce." This interpretation, however, was far too favourable, and when Rigby dined with Newcastle on October 11th, he told the duke " that the Duke of Bedford's leaving the treasury to the king's decision did mean (as I imagined it did) that if the king should name Mr Grenville . . . that my Lord Rockingham should acquiesce and support in the same manner that Mr Grenville and his friends should support my Lord Rockingham if he should be named." It was this by no means unimportant gloss upon Bedford's words that Newcastle concealed from Rockingham. Add. MS., 32985, f. 358, f. 360 ; Add. MS., 32986, f. 1.

administration, and hopes to find our friends in the same disposition." [1]

Bedford, Newcastle, and others might lust for the battle to begin, but it was clear beyond all possible doubt that, unless the opposition agreed upon a concerted plan, victory would fall to the ministry. Though Northington, in his cups, might talk gloomily of the prospects of the administration,[2] Grafton was reported to be counting upon a larger ministerial majority in the upper house than he had been accustomed to during the previous session; [3] and it was no small gain to the cabinet that it no longer stood in fear of Charles Townshend. That restless and perturbed spirit had ceased to disturb the politics of his age. For a brief season he had blazed like a comet in the political heavens; and it was when he appeared to be at the very height of his power that death summoned him to leave the arena of party strife. He died, early in September, of an inflammation of the bowels;

[1] Add. MS., 32986, f. 391 ; Add. MS., 32987, f. 37. Newcastle's idea of the proper conduct of opposition is worth noting. "I am persuaded," he informed Keppel, "that neither the Duke of Bedford nor Lord Rockingham would think of giving opposition upon points that would not bear it. That would be only to expose us to the nation, and give handles against us at the next election. Our plan, in my humble opinion, both in and out of parliament, ought to be that which may best carry the publick with us, and, consequently, be the more likely to be of service to our friends in the choice of the next parliament, for there must ultimately end all our endeavours. It is from the next parliament that this country must be saved, and the cause of those, who wish it best, supported." Add. MS., 32986, f. 391.

[2] "I heard a few days ago," wrote Sir Matthew Fetherstone to Newcastle, "by a gentleman who dined at Lord Northington's in Hampshire, that his lordship got extremely drunk, and in his cups said many things he ought not. That everything was tending to confusion, that this was an age of the utmost profligacy and corruption, that his M—y was a much honester man than his whole Pr—y C—l put together ; and that the present adm—n had made no acquisition of strength since last session ; all of which was affirmed with a volume of oaths." Add. MS., 32986, f. 311.

[3] "I hear," wrote Newcastle to the Princess Amelia, "the Duke of Grafton says they shall carry it in the house of lords by a majority of forty. In that I believe his grace is mistaken. He does not reckon, I suppose, the bishops, where we have a chance of sixteen to ten." Add. MS., 32986, f. 243.

and those whom he had opposed, even those whom he had deceived, spoke kindly words of him, now that he was no longer to astonish them by his brilliance, and amuse them by his wit. When Newcastle heard of the event, he remarked that the dead statesman, with all his faults, " was very good-natured and very entertaining " ; [1] and it may be surmised that such an epitaph would have been approved by Townshend himself. Yet these attributes, enviable and attractive as they are, do not constitute all that is expected of a chancellor of the exchequer, and in Townshend they were mingled with much that rendered him unfit either to rule or to serve. His loss was an undisguised boon to his colleagues who had suffered more from the evil than benefited by the good in his composition ; and the new chancellor of the exchequer, Lord North, who only accepted the office after some hesitation,[2] was likely to be far more serviceable both in parliament and in the cabinet. Possessed, like Townshend, of a happy wit, and endowed with a temper so sweet that it was wellnigh impossible to make him angry, North was of a pliant disposition, ready to yield to pressure, and averse to giving pain. This lack of resolution in his character was destined, at a later date, to work dire mischief to his country and himself ; but it was of less moment as long as he remained a subordinate member of the cabinet ; and, though many

---

[1] Add. MS., 32985, f. 31. During Townshend's life-time, Lord Buckinghamshire remarked of him that " he often puts his parts in motion, but never stays long enough to give them a consistency. What genius, what imagination, what knowledge, what abilities, what occasionally exquisite feelings : how greatly the first are misused, how soon he forgets the last." Add. MS., 22359, f. 4.

[2] Grafton's *Autobiography*, pp. 166, 167 ; Add. MS., 32985, f. 53 ; Grenville Papers, 4, 167. Writing on September 22nd, Newcastle remarks : " I have heard of the terms to be given to Lord North, a reversion of his father's pension when he comes to be Earl of Guilford, with an estate of 12 or 14,000£ per ann. My God ! where will this end ? " Add. MS., 32985, f. 190.

were his defects as a politician and statesman, he could at least never be the occasion of discord and strife that his predecessor had been.

So, whatever were the prospects of the opposition, the ministry was not ill prepared for the conflict which would begin on November 24th, the day on which parliament was summoned to meet. Yet, on the very eve of the encounter, no one could predict its course ; for not a little depended upon the action of the three opposition leaders. One may be sure that gossip was rife, some saying that the opposition parties would settle their differences before they entered upon the battle, others that the ministers would easily carry the day against men who differed too fundamentally ever to unite even in attacking a government which they all hated ; but no one, not even the leaders themselves, knew for certain the exact turn events would take. Bedford had proclaimed that he intended to continue the onslaught upon the government ; and Rockingham, when he arrived in town on November 21st, announced the same policy for himself and his party.[1] In these circumstances common prudence would have suggested a meeting between Bedford and Rockingham to agree upon a plan of campaign against the court ; and for such an interview Rockingham was quite prepared.[2] It is probable that Bedford was the unwilling party. An eminent French historian has told us that " politics are a conflict of which chance is incessantly modifying the whole course " ; and the truth of this saying is amply proved by the events of the four days preceding the meeting of parliament. When Bedford came to London on November 20th, he had been quite pre-

[1] Add. MS., 32987, f. 75 ; Add. MS., 35430, f. 87.
[2] Add. MS., 32987, f. 75.

pared to co-operate with Lord Rockingham, if they were able to come to a friendly understanding on questions where they differed ; but, soon after his arrival, he heard that Rockingham had told the Duke of Bridgewater that he would never sit in a cabinet in which a Grenville had a place. Bedford may well be excused if he gave way to anger on learning this information. It was the first time that he had been informed that Rockingham intended to proscribe the Grenville party in this fashion ; and he must have concluded that he had been grossly deceived by Newcastle and Albemarle, who had, apparently, so sedulously concealed their leader's intention from him. No time was lost in handing on the information to George Grenville who was told on the evening of November 23rd.[1]

On the following day parliament met. As though anticipating what was to follow, the king, in the speech from the throne, was made to advise the members of both houses to cultivate a spirit of harmony and concord ; and never was advice so much needed or so flagrantly disregarded. George Grenville, having brooded over what he had been told the night before, had come down to the house with hatred in his heart against Lord Rockingham and his supporters, and determined publicly to repudiate the men who had, as he thought, secretly repudiated him. After Dowdeswell had spoken in the debate on the address of thanks, " confining himself to the exact line on North American affairs, which had been approved of by those who met at your grace's on the memorable Tuesday night," [2] George Grenville rose and delivered his soul. He informed the house that he was more

---

[1] Grenville Papers, 4, 234 ; Phillimore's *Lyttelton*, 2, 734.
[2] July 21st.

convinced than ever of the necessity of enforcing the authority of the mother country over the colonies, that he was astonished that any man, and much more that a member of parliament, should hold and publish such sentiments as Dowdeswell had expressed, that he would never unite, either in opposition or in power, with men who held such opinions; but, on the contrary, would keep " the same distance from them that he would from those who opposed the principles of the Revolution." [1]

While these defiant words were issuing from Grenville's mouth, the Rockingham whigs sat aghast, outraged, and dismayed; and Grenville was not the only occasion of their anger. They were equally disgusted with the followers of the Duke of Bedford, none of whom spoke a word on behalf of the party thus so grossly insulted, and, indeed, by their silence appeared to acquiesce in all that had been said. Rockingham was, not unnaturally, deeply chagrined when he heard what had happened, and, in the very early hours of the morning following the debate, wrote an indignant letter to the Duke of Newcastle. " It is no comfort to me," he bitterly remarked, " to have had this full proof that my ideas had not been ill-founded for some time past; and I well see the confusions which may arise. I am happy to have acted with the greatest sincerity and fullest honour towards the Duke of Bedford and his friends. If our friends should now think right to call for a most full and explicit declaration and explanation from the Duke of Bedford's friends, it must produce either a thorough and fixed cordiality or will have the contrary effect." [2]

---

[1] Add. MS., 32987, f. 87, f. 113; Walpole's Memoirs, 3, 81 ff; *Parliamentary History*, xvi. 379 ff.

[2] Add. MS., 32987, f. 87.

The anger of the leader was shared by the majority of the followers, but mere anger would not obliterate the wrong which had been inflicted. A reconciliation with Grenville was clearly out of the question, for he had sinned too deeply to hope for forgiveness, even if he had desired it ; but it was possible that a breach with the Bedfords might be avoided. They lay under the dark suspicion of having given a silent approval to Grenville's bitter denunciation ; and Newcastle was instructed by his party to demand of the Duke of Bedford a full and satisfactory explanation of such doubtful conduct. No envoy could have been chosen more convinced that no greater evil could befall the Rockingham whigs than a rupture with the Bedford party ; and, before Newcastle departed on his errand, he was significantly warned by Rockingham that it would be far better to have " a firm and decisive issue to this affair than a superficial healing which may only entangle and deceive." [1] Newcastle discovered that this opinion was shared by Bedford who argued that, as Grenville had been provoked to make such a declaration by learning what Rockingham was reported to have said to the Duke of Bridgewater, he could not be called to task for his conduct, until Rockingham had given a satisfactory explanation of the remark attributed to him.[2] Such an explanation Rockingham was not prepared to give. " Upon the whole state of what has passed," he wrote, on learning from Newcastle what Bedford had asked, " I cannot but see the improbability of that junction between the Duke of Bedford's friends and ours, which we have so long wished, and to attain which we have taken such pains and acted so fairly. Mr G. Grenville has succeeded fully in his object of

[1] Add. MS., 32987, f. 109, f. 111, f. 125.   [2] Add. MS., 32987, f. 123.

dividing us and them.   Indeed, the apology he makes
by saying that his conduct arose from warmth which
he felt on supposed words of mine is, as your grace
well observed, but a flimsy argument, as that could
not justify him in making an absolute rejection of all
the great and considerable persons with whom I
have acted, and particularly fixing his objection to
them in their having supported systems and principles
in which they still express themselves as determined
upon as he can upon his contrary and opposite system." [1]
Thus, Rockingham decided to refuse the explanation
demanded, and consequently doomed himself and his
party to political isolation.   All the strivings of
Newcastle were rendered useless ; and the old duke
was not slow to recognise that his labours had been
in vain.   " I am sorry to find by your lordship's letter,"
he wrote in reply to Rockingham, " that all further
negotiation or concert with the Duke of Bedford is
now over.   I had before determined that I would
be desired to be excused, and have nothing more to
do in it.   I shall send an answer to his grace, that I
had made a faithful report of what had passed, and
have nothing to trouble his grace with upon it, and
desire to have no further concern in it, since I see no
prospect of being able to do any good." [2]

Seldom has there been a more effective " curtain "
in the drama of party politics.   Until this time an
alliance between the Bedford and Rockingham camps
had always been within the range of possibility ; and
now, by what might appear to be a freak of fortune,
the Rockingham whigs were once more cast adrift,
and forced to depend, in their contest with the ministry,
upon their own meagre parliamentary strength.   That
it was their leader who was responsible for driving

them into a situation, seemingly so unenviable, cannot be denied ; yet it should not be lightly assumed that he acted wrongly. His refusal to comply with Bedford's demand for an explanation does not prove that he was guilty of having made the remark attributed to him by the Duke of Bridgewater. It may well be that Rockingham conceived that the time had come definitely to repudiate Grenville, and to compel Bedford to choose between that statesman and himself. Most will agree in thinking that it is better to know the worst than to live in daily expectation of a catastrophe ; and Rockingham elected to court misfortune rather than continue in a state of doubt. He could have cherished but faint hopes that Bedford, driven to make a decision, would reject George Grenville's friendship in favour of an alliance with the Rockingham whigs, separated as he was from them by many far-reaching differences of opinion. Whenever he had been approached during the past twelve months, Bedford had always consistently refused to contemplate a union which did not include Grenville and his party ; and there was no reason why he should abandon this policy. Thus, in breaking with Grenville, Rockingham destroyed, once and for all, the hope of a united opposition.

The subsequent conduct of the Bedfords amply proves that their action at this crisis was not influenced by any mistaken idea of chivalrous devotion to a friend ; for, having suspended relations with Lord Rockingham, they were by no means prepared to link their fortunes with George Grenville in what appeared to them to be a lost cause. Deprived of Rockingham's assistance in parliament, they would cut but a poor figure in the contest with the government which they could never hope to drive from power; and by a logical, if somewhat unprincipled, train of reasoning, they were brought to the conclusion that it was now time for them to make terms with the ministry. Having thrown over Rockingham for the sake of Grenville, they now threw over Grenville for the sake of office. Only a few days after Newcastle's interview with the Duke of Bedford, they made their first overtures to Grafton who eagerly caught at such a favourable opportunity of strengthening the administration and weakening the opposition; and by the middle of December terms had been agreed upon. It was arranged that Lord Gower should be president of the council in place of Northington who was ready to retire; that Conway, though continuing a member of the cabinet, should resign the secretaryship of state in favour of Lord Weymouth; and that Lord Hillsborough should be created secretary of state for the colonies which were thus transferred from the southern department.[1] 'Lord Sandwich, who had once been secretary of state, was now obliged to content himself with the subordinate position of postmaster;[2] and Rigby succeeded to the vice-treasurership of Ireland.[3]

Thus, the alliance was concluded, and Grafton could indeed congratulate himself upon his achievement. He had taken the tide of fortune at the flood; and had no longer reason to fear the parliamentary opposition which he would have to encounter in the future. Secure of a majority in both houses, he could safely defy the efforts which Grenville or Rockingham

[1] Lord Shelburne, the secretary of state for the southern department, though he acquiesced in this arrangement, did not certainly approve it. Chatham Correspondence, 3, 300.

[2] The king was reported to have refused to make Sandwich a secretary of state, on the ground that he would " make no more sweeps as he has done." Add. MS., 32987, f. 315. For evidence that Sandwich was discontented, see Add. MS., 32987, f. 397.

[3] For a detailed account of this negotiation, see Walpole's Memoirs, 3, 84 ff.

might make to unseat him, able as he now was to count with confidence upon the combined support of the crown and parliament. Nor, indeed, had Bedford cause to regret the bargain that he had concluded. Old and almost blind, he had not sought office for himself, but he had safely established his followers in power ; and whatever may be thought of the morality of his action, its wisdom was undoubted. Neither he nor his followers were men to lose their lives in a doomed cause ; and it needed no great political experience to understand that the opposition was doomed, sentence of death having been passed upon it at the meeting between Bedford and Newcastle on November 25th. Dull and stagnant were the debates in parliament, and quite early in December many members, weary of watching the ministers carry everything before them, began to leave town.[1] On December 5th, Lord Lyttelton reported that all opposition was at an end,[2] and the same tale was told by George Onslow who informed Newcastle that " our house is the quietest place in the world." [3] Convinced that the battle was over, the Bedfords concluded that the best thing was to come to terms with the victorious administration, and acted in accordance with their convictions.

Thus, Grafton had triumphed over the forces which at one time threatened to overwhelm him. With no little courage he had toiled against adversity, and had been rewarded for his perseverance. It now remained to be seen to what use he would put his victory.

[1] " The number of people gone out of town," wrote West to Newcastle, " is so great that the seamen were voted with barely forty members in the house. . . . Mr Grenville comes down alone, and never communicates with anyone. Administration seems perfectly easy, and opposition perfectly indolent." Add. MS., 32987, f. 149.

[2] Add. MS., 32987, f. 171.   [3] Add. MS., 32987, f. 218.

CHAPTER IV

THE RESIGNATION OF CHATHAM

THE admission of the Bedford party into the administration marks the beginning of a new chapter in Grafton's troubled and unfortunate ministerial career. From the time that Chatham had withdrawn into gloomy seclusion at Hampstead, the youthful first lord of the treasury had been playing the game of politics with the dice loaded against him. Persuaded, against his own inclination and better knowledge, to accept a responsibility beyond his capacity, he had been compelled by the breakdown in Chatham's health, which he could not have foreseen, to take command ; and can, indeed, claim a certain measure of pity as the victim of a malicious destiny, driving him where he was unwilling to go. Nor was he able to reflect that his audacity had been rewarded with success. Hard pressed in the parliamentary conflict, especially in the upper house, unable to make his will prevail in a cabinet of which he was the nominal leader, driven to live, politically, from hand to mouth, and the prey of men stronger than himself, he had every inducement to abandon a task which he would never have undertaken, had he thought only of his own happiness and good fame ; and if he continued at the post of danger, facing the full fury of the battle, it was because he was prepared to sacrifice his comfort and reputation to his affection for Chatham and his

194

loyalty to the king. Imbibing the constitutional doctrines of the man whom he had chosen as his political leader, he defended the royal closet against the rush of factions opposed to the court; and, failing in much else, succeeded in accomplishing this part of the appointed task. At the cost of bringing much evil upon the country and himself, he successfully averted the threatened union of the enemies of the administration; and, by the alliance with the followers of the Duke of Bedford, provided the government with a working majority in both houses of parliament.[1] But it is typical of Grafton, and of the policy of helpless drift which he pursued, that this accession of parliamentary strength was purchased by the sacrifice of the constitutional principles which Chatham had avowed and not yet repudiated. With the entry of the Bedfords into the government, the party system came to its own once more, Grafton, in order to avoid shipwreck, having thrown himself into the arms of one of the very political factions which Chatham had set out to destroy. It was in vain that he sought to minimise the change effected, and asserted that the terms of the treaty were such as Chatham could approve.[2] The surrender was far too complete to admit of effective disguise. The party system had triumphed over those who had vowed its destruction; and the Bedfords joined the ministry, not as isolated individuals enlisting under a new banner, but as a

---

[1] " In the house of lords this accession of strength was essentially felt; and damped every expectation which the other parts of opposition might have formed to have embarrassed the administration." Grafton's *Autobiography*, p. 183.

[2] " Besides, the conditions, now proposed and accepted, were short of those which Lord Chatham would have agreed to, either in the conference he had himself with the Duke of Bedford in December, 1766, or in that I had with Lord Gower in June, 1767." Grafton's *Autobiography*, p. 173.

political organisation, possessed of an identity of its own.   Driven, by force of circumstances, to resort to a desperate remedy, Grafton had been obliged to admit both Weymouth and Gower into the cabinet, to give office to Sandwich and Rigby, and to promise that some of the less influential members of the party should be "noticed at the time, or as soon as could be arranged " ; [1] and the granting of such terms registers the failure of the constitutional experiment inaugurated by Chatham.   The ministry could no longer be compared to a piece of uncemented tessellated pavement, being rather a coalition between the Bedford party and the relics of the original cabinet ;   and contemporaries, appreciating the significance of such an alliance, amused themselves by speculating which section of the administration would gain the mastery. The game was easy enough to play, no great prophetic insight being required to foretell that the victory would ultimately lie with the Bedfords.   Lord Weymouth and his friends were proverbial for their skill in converting an inch into an ell ; and, having once entered the cabinet, would not be likely to rest content until they had secured predominance there, even if it meant actively intriguing against the first lord of the treasury.   Their success was almost certain, for Grafton and his colleagues had far too little in common to resist the steady pressure of politicians adept in the art of acquiring an unfair advantage.   Lord Shelburne, already profoundly discontented with his situation and the policy pursued, would not lift a hand in Grafton's defence ;   and it was vain to depend upon Conway and Camden in the hour of need.   The future, undoubtedly, lay with the Bedfords ; and when, after a little hesitation, the king extended to them his

[1] Grafton's *Autobiography*, p. 182.

confidence, their victory was assured. It was some
little time before George III. could forget that his
new servants had been the allies of George Grenville
both in and out of office; and, bearing this fact in
mind, he warned Grafton to be on his guard against
the new recruits ; but in time such distasteful
recollections were obliterated, and " the engaging
manners of the two lords overcame by degrees all
the prejudice there might have been against the whole
party." [1]

Thus, in order to frustrate the designs of the opposition, Grafton had undermined the foundations of his
own authority ; and although such a sacrifice would
have been well worth the making, if productive of an
efficient and popular administration, there was little
indication that such a happy consequence would flow
from the accession of the Bedfords to office. Inasmuch
as the new ministers were pleasing to the king, they
were unlikely to win the approval of the people or to
promote the welfare of the nation. Though Lord
Sandwich was not without industry or ability, and

[1] Grafton's *Autobiography*, p. 183 : " It seems to me clear," wrote
Whately to George Grenville, " that the Duke of Grafton means to gain the
Bedfords entirely : whether the consequences will be that he will get them
as an accession to his party, or they get him as an accession to theirs, is, I
think, very doubtful : circumstances, which neither can command, must
determine ; but without the intervention of particular circumstances, I should
be inclined to think that the party of the Bedfords being of more real weight
than the individual Duke of Grafton, they would rather draw him to them,
than he them to him." John Yorke, a younger brother of Lord Hardwicke,
remarked that he was unable to " understand why the late changes have
been made, and I do not wonder they should be not disapproved at Stowe
and Wotton. They may lead to more, and bring things round to where they
were at the Peace. It is impossible to suppose that the fiery duke and his
friends should be long quiet and contented. Lord Shelburne is half out
already, and Con—y more than half. The house of commons, under the
conduct of Lord North, may easily be played into the hands of G. G., by
accident if Lord Guilford should die, or by management if the Duke of Bedford
lives. But in all events I think the Duke of Grafton has surrendered about
half his powers at least." Grenville Papers, 4, 248-249 ; Add. MS., 35374,
f. 340.

could justly boast considerable experience of administrative life, he enjoyed an unenviable reputation as the most notorious profligate of a very profligate age; and even if the mob had been prepared to overlook the shortcomings of his private life, they would not readily forget that he had basely betrayed Wilkes, the boon companion of his disreputable leisure hours. By this act of infamy he had earned his well-known nickname of " Jemmy Twitcher," which branded him for ever as lacking in generosity, so often the last relic of virtue in a thoroughly depraved nature. It is true that Lord Weymouth had a far less sullied reputation, but his comparative respectability was not so much a tribute to his character as a reflection upon the laxity of the times. Furnished with good natural abilities, and a fairly effective debater, he might have made himself a capable administrator if he had given to statecraft a tithe of the time he devoted to gaming and drinking. George II. had remarked of him that he cared for nothing but cards and strong beer ; and to the satisfaction of these passions he sacrificed both his fortune and his health, politics being merely an interlude in a headlong career of dissipation. Rarely leaving the card-table before six o'clock in the morning, and, consequently, seldom rising before noon, his life was one long drawn-out debauch ; and, shattered by his nightly excesses, he was frequently compelled to leave the business of his office to be transacted by subordinates. Not all the new ministers, however, could boast an equality in vice with Sandwich or Weymouth. Lord Gower, the new lord president of the council, was undoubtedly their moral superior ; and, although he rarely rose above the level of respectable mediocrity, he could boast a fund of good humour and tact, sufficient to make him a useful member of any administration.[1] Unfortunately, these happy attributes were not shared by Lord Hillsborough, the new secretary of state for the colonies. More of a courtier than a statesman, Hillsborough had not been cast by nature to be a ruler of men, and, in after years, George III. frankly avowed that he had seldom encountered a man of less judgment.[2] An impressive presence and agreeable manners, which might have served him in good stead in an office of dignity rather than of business, were but a sorry equipment for the task he had actually undertaken to perform; and, in view of the critical relations between England and her colonies, no appointment could have been more unwise or, indeed, more disastrous.

The reconstructed administration, therefore, was but the old writ large, with old faults exaggerated and new defects introduced; and neither Grafton nor the nation had reason to rejoice over the change which had been effected. The real victor was George III. It was he who had triumphed, for he had secured advisers after his own heart, and no longer had cause to fear that he might be compelled to choose his ministers at the dictation of parliament. By the surrender of the Bedford party to the court, he was more than compensated for the loss of Chatham who, though he had served a useful turn in the overthrew of the Rockingham ministry, was far too great a statesman, and too little of a time-server, to be entirely agreeable to the king. It mattered nothing to

---

[1] Henry Fox, a shrewd and not a lenient judge of his fellow creatures, once told Bute that Gower was " of a humour and nature the most practicable, and if any man could do the office of southern secretary without either quarrelling with Charles Townshend, or letting down the dignity of his own office, he would." Fitzmaurice's *Shelburne*, I, 187.

[2] Hist. MSS. Comm., 10th Report, Appendix, Part vi. 15.

George III. that the ministry was notoriously weak, the country discontented, and the colonists slowly, but surely, heading towards revolt. It was of far greater moment to him that he had taken the sting out of an opposition which might have subdued him to its will, and that the danger, which had threatened him during the year 1767, had been dissipated by a successful negotiation. Even if Grenville, forgetting old and recent grievances, joined hands with Rockingham against the court, it was extremely unlikely that their united forces would prevail against the ministerialists and placemen in both houses of parliament ; and if Rockingham, despairing of the future, had decided to abandon a struggle, from which all hope had apparently departed, he could not have been blamed. Ever since his loss of office in July, 1766, he had toiled in defence of those principles of party government, which he had upheld when in power, and had not forsaken in opposition ; and it seemed as if the hour had now struck for him to relinquish a contest which could never end in victory. Deserted by Bedford, and come to an open breach with Grenville, he knew that, weak as he had been in the past, he would be still weaker in the future : nor was it certain that he could continue to count upon the fidelity of his followers. Wearied by repeated defeat, men's hearts began to fail them, and that apathy, which is so often the accompaniment of failure, began to rear its head in the ranks of the whig opposition. On the occasion of an important debate in the upper house on February 5th, some of Rockingham's supporters did not trouble to appear, and others went away before a division was taken ; [1] and such indifference is hardly to be wondered at, springing as it did from a conviction that, the

[1] Add. MS., 32988, f. 170, f. 186.

cause being doomed, the time had come to beat a retreat.

It is greatly to Rockingham's credit that, adverse as the situation was, he refused to be intimidated into a surrender, and his courage was not misplaced. Deficient as he was in many of the arts of statesmanship, of no great ability, and often lacking in foresight, it must never be forgotten that throughout his life he fought for principles which he refused to sacrifice to expediency or personal profit ; and, nerved by the conviction that right must ultimately triumph, he encouraged his followers to endure the heat and burden of the battle, in the sure and certain hope that the men, who came after them, would reap the fruit of their valour. " I firmly believe," he wrote to Dowdeswell in the autumn of 1767, " that no set of politicians ever acted a more unbiassed part in point of interest than we and our friends have done ; and I firmly hope and trust we shall always adhere to it. You know I never disguised to our friends, on trying occasions, that I considered them a forlorn hope, but that the maintenance of character and credit was in honour incumbent upon them, and would, in the first place, be a comfort to their own minds, and, though it might appear improbable at present, yet it was not impossible but that such conduct would ultimately prove the best policy." [1]

<hr />

[1] " The Memoir of the Right Honourable William Dowdeswell," printed in *The Cavendish Debates*, vol. i. p. 575 ff. A few weeks later, Rockingham informs Dowdeswell that " our line of conduct is nice, and requires much consideration. I think, as a general rule, we should constantly look back to what it has been, and adhere to the same line in future. I think we, and we only, of all the party now in opposition, are so, on system and principles—that we ought to avail ourselves of other parties now in opposition, in order to effectuate good purposes; and that we should be cautious not even to throw the appearance of leading into hands, whose principles we have no reason to think similar to our own, and whose honour we have no reason to. confide in." *Ibid.*

Thus, the despair, which enervates and destroys, had not entered into Rockingham's heart, and, in his resolution to persevere, he was ably supported by the aged Duke of Newcastle. A serious illness, at the close, of the year, 1767, gave Newcastle timely warning that the sands of his long life were at last running out, and he was reluctantly compelled to abstain from active participation in political life. Yet, though the strength had failed, the interest never flagged, and he continued eagerly to watch the fray which had been both his business and his pleasure for more than half a century, calling upon his friends to rally round Rockingham, as they had formerly rallied round him. " As the Duke of Newcastle," he instructed his friend, West, " has entirely withdrawn from all politics and publick affairs, he is very desirous that all his friends should concur with my Lord Rockingham in such measures as he shall take for the support of the whig cause . . . and for the true interest of the nation. He, therefore, will be extremely obliged to Mr West if he would take a proper opportunity to convey these, his sentiments and wishes, to the Duke of Newcastle's friends in the city, . . . and also to my Lord Archer, my Lord Plymouth, my Lord Winterton, and Mr West's son-in-law, Mr Archer." [1]

It is beyond all question that the leaders of the party were right to give the word for the struggle to continue. In a few weeks parliament was to be dissolved, and the country plunged into the turmoil of a general election, and Rockingham's followers would fare but ill if they presented themselves to the electors as beaten men, openly confessing to failure. Under the most favourable conditions they

---

[1] Add. MS., 32988, f. 23. A similar message was conveyed to Newcastle's Sussex friends.

could hope to make but little headway against the
torrent of bribery and corruption which would flow
from the court directly parliament was dissolved ;
but their fate would be worse still if, by an untimely
surrender of their principles and their courage, they
forfeited the respect of the people.   Only by acquiring
the confidence of the country could they expect to
gain ultimate victory ;   and although little success
had attended their efforts hitherto, it was their duty
to continue to appeal to the nation against an inefficient administration and a corrupted house of
commons.   No man could say when the dawn would
come, and the banner of the party must not be trailed
in the dust before the verdict of the people had been
taken.

Therefore, during the last session of the expiring
parliament, Rockingham and his friends, rightly refusing to recognise the full force of the crushing disaster
they had sustained, continued their opposition to the
government, though it must be admitted that not a
little of their energy was expended in vain.   Once
more they championed the cause of the East India
company which they conscientiously believed to be
the victim of unjustifiable interference by the state.
The act, limiting the dividends of the company to
ten per cent., expired in the autumn of 1767 ;   and
when its renewal was proposed by the ministry, the
Rockingham whigs, modelling their conduct on what it
had been in the past, sallied forth again as the defenders
of the rights of chartered corporations.   In the house
of commons Burke and Dowdeswell were foremost in
the struggle, but neither the eloquence of the one nor
the activity of the other exercised any appreciable
influence upon the divisions.   Both the second and
final readings of the bill were carried by substantial

majorities, and once in the report stage the opposition
only numbered twenty-five on a division ;[1] while
in the house of lords, though the bill did not pass
without debate and the registration of a formal protest, the ministry never came within a measurable
distance of defeat.   The ease of the victory was largely
due to the disruption effected by Grafton in the
ranks of the opposition.   The Bedfords, so lately the
defenders of the company, were now the allies of the
court ; and though Bedford, Gower, Sandwich, and
Weymouth, fearful of the charge of interested inconsistency, voted against the bill, the less important
members of the party, not so careful of their reputation,
supported the government ; and if Weymouth gave
his vote against the Duke of Grafton, he was careful
to express his regret at so doing, and the hope that he
would never again differ in opinion from his leader.[2]

It is true, of course, that the followers of Grenville,
being in no wise connected with the ministry, had no
need to put a rein upon their inclination to oppose
the bill ; and in the upper house both Temple and
Lyttelton spoke strongly against the government,
the former, with characteristic acrimony, inveighing
against corruption, declaring that " the times were
bad indeed, that in his youth he remembered Sir
Robert Walpole's times, which he then thought bad,
but that they were perfection compared with the
present." [3]   The example of these two lords was
not, however, followed by Grenville himself, who,
during the passage of the bill through the lower house,
played a rather more ambiguous part.   He expressed
his disapproval of the measure by speaking and voting

---

[1] Add. MS., 32987, f. 301 ; Add. MS., 32988, f. 58, f. 74 ; Grenville Papers,
4, 240.
[2] Add. MS., 32988, f. 170.   [3] *Ibid.*

against it on the second reading;[1] but, having thus made his protest, he withdrew from the fray, and the same course was pursued by a good many of his followers.[2] Thus, the burden of the battle fell upon the Rockinghams, and they could hardly have concealed from themselves that they were fighting in vain. The nation was unlikely to be stirred to its depths by a limitation of the rights of a powerful corporation, and it must have been small consolation for them to reflect that, badly as they had fared, they would have fared still worse if they had adopted a policy of inaction.

A happier fortune attended their efforts to right a wrong inflicted upon one of themselves. The Duke of Portland, a distinguished and most loyal member of the Rockingham party, had recently fallen a victim to the hatred and cupidity of Sir James Lowther, a great territorial magnate in the north of England where Portland was also possessed of extensive estates. It is difficult to give any adequate description of Lowther, save in terms which savour of caricature. Intoxicated with pride, in love with the exercise of power, passionate to the verge of frenzy, and totally unable to brook the slightest opposition to his will, he exercised a tyrannical and almost feudal rule over his tenants and dependents, being wont to display his authority by denying justice to those who were too weak to resist and too proud to submit.[3] A son-in-law of Lord Bute, and, therefore, an ardent supporter of the government, Lowther had extensive political influence in the counties of Cumberland

---

[1] Add. MS., 32987, f. 301 ; Grenville Papers, 4, 240.

[2] After the bill had been sent up to the upper house, Rockingham remarked to Newcastle how " George Grenville, Sir Fletcher Norton, and that set kept away in the house of commons." Add. MS., 32988, f. 81.

[3] For a curious and interesting account of Lowther, see Rockingham Memoirs, 2, 69-72.

and Westmoreland, his only rival in that field being the Duke of Portland who was as justly popular as he was justly detested. Infuriated at the prospect of his supremacy over the voters in the district being disputed at the approaching general election, Lowther applied to the treasury for a lease of Inglewood Forest, which, though originally part of the royal domain, had been in the possession of the Portland family for many years, and, if of small monetary value, was highly prized as including within its boundaries a large number of freeholders possessed of the franchise. Willing enough to gratify a supporter and to damage an antagonist, the ministers acceded to his request ; and they were able to justify their action by the strict letter of the law. The old adage, *nullum tempus occurrit regi*, still held good in law, and it was, unfortunately, impossible for Portland to prove that the territory in dispute had ever been formally granted to his ancestors by the crown. It is true that every obstacle was placed by the government in the way of the establishment of such a claim ; but, even if the most liberal facilities had been granted, it is open to question whether Portland could have proved his right. All that could be urged on his behalf was that his family had held the land, now leased to Lowther, in undisputed possession for many years past ; but such an argument had more moral than legal force ; and even Rockingham, deeply incensed though he was at the wrong inflicted upon a loyal supporter, was compelled to admit that, according to the most favourable construction of the existing law, it was necessary to prove continuous possession for more than two hundred years, in order effectively to bar the claims of the crown.[1]

---

[1] Rockingham Memoirs, 2, 73-74.

Thus, arbitrary and unfair as the ministerial action was, it was not illegal; nor, indeed, was it unprecedented. We learn from Horace Walpole that "it was common, particularly in Wales, for private jobbers to apply to the treasury, and offer to make out the title of the crown to certain lands which had been usurped from the domain, under pretence of having been grants, though often the grantees had occupied much more than had been granted. On these occasions a new grant was the condition and reward of the informer." [1] Walpole's testimony is of interest, but its importance should not be exaggerated. The prevalence of an iniquitous practice does not render it any less iniquitous, and supported though the confiscation of Inglewood Forest might be by precedent and law, there were special circumstances connected with it which rendered it of peculiar and exceptional interest. It was abundantly clear that Portland's political opinions had marked him out for attack, and that the whole transaction was nothing but an unscrupulous move in an electioneering game. Law and justice had been evoked to cloak a thoroughly nefarious business, and the social rank of the victim, his justly respected character, and the infamy of his accuser, were certain to attract general and unwelcome attention to what the ministers had done. A highly obnoxious practice, tolerated in the past because the sufferers had been few, and, for the most part, insignificant, was thus dragged into the light; and landowners, who had hitherto believed themselves immune from any interference by the crown, now began to fear a scrutiny into their title deeds, and to wonder whether the resumption of Inglewood Forest was only the beginning of an organised crusade against private

---

[1] Walpole's Memoirs, 3, 102.

property. "The Duke of Portland himself," wrote Rockingham in January, 1768, "is the only person whom Lord Rockingham has seen, either in town or country, who is cool upon the subject. The duchy courts of Lancaster have, within the last year or two, made several attempts to revive and make out old claims . . . which in the northern counties had already made great uneasiness. This event in the Duke of Portland's case . . . makes the greater impression there, from their minds being already agitated by these circumstances." [1]

If this was true, a private misfortune might become a public benefit, and the Rockingham party profit by the sufferings of one of their number. It was incumbent upon the Rockingham whigs to make use of whatever agitation existed in the nation against the government; and so, influenced by policy as much as by sentiment, they determined to espouse the cause of their injured friend, and, not unnaturally, hoped to receive the support of the landed interest both in and out of parliament. "I heartily wish," wrote Rockingham, at the beginning of February, "that nothing may prevent our agitating a matter which, in my belief, will do so much real publick service . . . and will do us so much honour, at all events, to be the movers in"; while a little later he remarked that, though the "success the motion may have in the house may be doubtful, . . . I am fully persuaded that out of doors it will be most exceedingly relished." [2] Thus, convinced that fortune at last smiled upon them, the followers of Rockingham set to work to prepare a plan of campaign, and the task was not quite so easy as it might at first sight appear. It was imperative that the personal note should not

[1] Add. MS., 32988, f. 31.   [2] *Ibid.*, f. 134, f. 333.

be unduly stressed, the point of the attack being rather to evoke opposition to the government among the landed classes, than to redress the private grievances of the Duke of Portland ; and, if the opposition contented itself with the demand that the Duke should be reinstated in his lost possessions, leaving the rest of the landed gentry to the tender mercies of the ministry, there would be little enthusiasm either in parliament or in the country. The danger was sufficiently obvious to be avoided ; and, after a few meetings of the leading members of the party, it was arranged that Sir George Savile, who undertook the task reluctantly, should propose in the house of commons the enforcement and amendment of an act of parliament, entitled "for quieting the minds of those possessed of crown lands," which had been passed in the reign of James I.[1] The move was skilfully contrived, for such a motion, designed as it was to avert the evil of arbitrary action by the government in the future, could hardly fail to win the support of the country gentry ; and the ministers might well find that the loyalty of many of their habitual supporters was not proof against the competition of self-interest.[2]

Wednesday, February 17th, was the date fixed for the opposition attack, and, until that day came, the greatest secrecy was observed, in order that the government might be taken by surprise. So elaborate, indeed, was the conspiracy of silence, that when notice of Savile's motion was given on February 15th, it was intentionally couched in such vague and misleading language that the ministers failed to gain the slightest

[1] Add. MS., 32988, f. 204, f. 264, f. 288.
[2] Thus Rockingham hoped that the "real goodness of the question will operate strongly on any persons in the house, who may have the least inclination of favour towards us." Add. MS., 32988, f. 307.

inkling of the line that their opponents intended to take.[1] Hopes ran high, Rockingham and his friends being indefatigable in beating up supporters, and their energy was not expended totally in vain; for, when Savile introduced his motion on the appointed day, the government only prevailed by the slender majority of twenty. Indeed, all the arguments, and a great deal of the eloquence, were on the side of the defeated opposition, and the ministerialists, fearing, on the eve of a general election, directly to oppose a proposal so obviously just and so deservedly popular, were driven weakly to urge that the time was inopportune, and that so important a question ought not to be settled by an expiring parliament. This was but a sorry line of defence, a trumped up principle incapable of sustaining investigation; and it is little wonder that Rockingham, who watched the debate until its close, was delighted with the day's work. Burke, Dowdeswell and Charles Yorke were foremost in the attack, and Sir William Meredith spoke with so much fervour and earnestness that " he fairly exhausted himself of bodily strength, but not before the strength of his arguments had made real impression." Nor was the glory confined exclusively to the followers of Rockingham; for even George Grenville acquitted himself well as a defender of property,[2] and although only two members of the administration, Lord Palmerston and Augustus Hervey, voted with the opposition, there were many deserters from the rank and file of the ministerial party.[3] " I will venture

---

[1] Add. MS., 32988, f. 134, f. 222.

[2] Rockingham, at all events, approved of Grenville's conduct, though Horace Walpole affirms that he " trimmed with all his art, not to offend Lord Bute and Sir James Lowther." Walpole's Memoirs, 3, 115.

[3] Add. MS., 32988, f. 357, f. 369: Hist. MSS. Comm. Carlisle MSS., 243-245 ; Walpole's Memoirs, 3, 114 ff.

to ensure success to our motion on renewing it at the opening of the next session of parliament," wrote Rockingham in true prophetic vein; "and I think I may also add that the landed interest in England will highly approve our attempt, as it will secure them against the odious revival of long dormant claims of the crown . . . on private landed property." [1]

Such jubilation, justified in a measure though it might be, was, unhappily, somewhat exaggerated. It is true that the Rockingham whigs had played a creditable part in parliament, and had succeeded in materially diminishing the ministerial majority; but there their victory ended. They had failed in the most important part of their task, namely in arousing a popular agitation throughout the country against the government; and for this they are not to be blamed. There was no time, on the eve of a general election, to carry the conflict from Westminster into the counties, to educate small and large landowners into the belief that their cherished possessions were in danger; and, like the gambler, prevented from reaping a golden harvest from a sudden turn of luck by the closing of the gaming tables, Rockingham and his friends were driven to appeal to the country at the very moment they would not have chosen. On the 10th of March, parliament, having completed its legal term of seven years, acquiring in the process a thoroughly deserved reputation for ignoble subservience to the court, was dissolved, and its epitaph was composed by Horace Walpole. "Thus ended," he wrote, "that parliament, uniform in nothing but in its obedience to the crown. To all I have said I will only add, that it would have deserved the appellation of one of the worst parliaments England ever saw, if its servility

---

[1] Rockingham Memoirs, 2, 73-74.

had not been so great, that, as the times changed, it enacted remedies for the evils it had committed with the same facility with which it had complied with the authors of those evils. Our ancestors, who dealt in epithets, might have called it the impudent parliament." [2]

Evil as the parliament had been, it was, unfortunately, only too likely that its successor would continue in the same path. If the opinion of the country had been really taken, it is probable that George III. might have discovered how far he had strayed from the road in which Bolingbroke had appointed him to walk ; but, in the eighteenth century, the populace had to be deeply stirred to make its voice prevail over the raucous cries of borough-brokers and their like ; and the general election of 1768 was no exception to the common rule. Few political contests have been more disfigured by bribery and corruption, the destiny of a great kingdom being bought and sold in the open market. Even contemporaries, accustomed to a degree of venality which would make the most hardened political cynic of the present day shudder at the depravity of mankind, were astonished at the brutal and fierce competition for seats. " Elections here have been carried to a degree of frenzy hitherto unheard of," wrote Chesterfield to his son ; " that for the town of Northampton has cost the contending parties at least thirty thousand pounds a side, and George Selwyn has sold the borough of Luggershall to two members for nine thousand pounds." [2] Nor is Chesterfield the only witness to the fury of the competition, for we find Rockingham deploring the very large number of men, qualified in every way for a place in parliament, who were prevented, by

---

[1] Walpole's Memoirs, 3, 116.   [2] Chesterfield's Letters, 3, 1375-1376.

lack of means, from satisfying a legitimate ambition ; [1]
and it is somewhat astonishing to find a borough,
for which two thousand pounds was asked, being
regarded in the light of a bargain to be snapped up
without delay.[2]

This general anxiety on all sides to acquire seats
effectively stimulated corruption and intimidation ;
and we may be certain that the stories, which have
come down to us, are but a few of the many in circulation among the politicians of the day. Perhaps the
most flagrant and cynical abuse of the franchise was
afforded by the mayor and corporation of the city
of Oxford, who threatened to unseat their two representatives unless they pledged themselves to redeem
the debt incurred by the corporation in the maintenance of a luxurious and expensive table ; [3] and this
was no solitary instance of intimidation. The curate
of Aldborough, in the county of Suffolk, was active in
bringing illegal pressure to bear upon the voters of
that town ; but, as he worked in the interests of the
government, he was more fortunate than the offending
mayor and corporation of Oxford, escaping a parliamentary conviction.[4] Great noblemen were also

[1] " The great expences of elections have indeed too much . . . deterred the
prudent and proper persons from attempting to come into parliament. Gentlemen possessed of 2 or 3000£ per ann. estates feel that their fortunes will not
bear an extraordinary outgoing of 3 or 4000£ for a seat in parliament, and the
additional expences incurring by a long residence in London." Add. MS.,
32986, f. 329.

[2] " The Duke of Newcastle also acquaints my Lord Rockingham that he
has a friend of his, upon whom he can depend, that has offered him a sure
borough for any friend of his, for £2000, but the answer must be given immediately." Add. MS., 32988, f. 196.

[3] Hist. MSS. Comm. Weston Underwood MSS., 410-411 ; Carlisle MSS.,
235-240 ; *Parl. History*, xvi.

[4] " Bennet, the curate of Aldborough," wrote a member of parliament to
Lord Hardwicke on February 28th, 1768, " appeared at our Bar on Tuesday,
his council Dunning, and George Leigh Tonnereau had no assistance. . . .
His two witnesses clearly proved the fact and uniformly kept to it after repeated examinations. . . . They were not quite so exact in a multitude of

active in the sordid contest. Lord Edgecumbe, who had great influence in the county of Cornwall, counted upon returning six members to the new parliament, and Lord Clive reckoned upon having seven representatives [1]; but Clive and Edgecumbe were but amateur dabblers compared with the Duke of Newcastle who, though crippled by disease and age, plunged, with almost youthful ardour, into what was to be his last electioneering campaign. Many weeks before parliament was dissolved, he had been engaged in the congenial occupation of distributing representatives between the various boroughs under his control, and complaining bitterly of the interference he suffered at the hands of the Duke of Grafton. " I am attacked in a most cruel manner by his grace, the Duke of Grafton," he confided to Lord Mansfield. " He is, I hope, quite defeated at Rye, but he told George Onslow that he had settled Hastings, a town which never was, or ought to be, a treasury burrough . . . a town where, ever since the year 1714, I have constantly chose both the members to this very day." [2] Yet, in spite of Grafton poaching upon what Newcastle regarded as his own private preserve, the old duke's labours were rewarded with a fair measure of success. " For my part, upon the whole," he informed Lord George Cavendish, " I have succeeded pretty well, having carried all my members everywhere, except for that ungrateful town of Lewes " ; [3] and if he failed

collateral questions put by the council, some of them quite forein (*sic*) to the business. This was called gross prevarication. Upon this the advocates rested their defence, and upon this the House acquitted Bennet, about one in the morning, by 155 to 39. . . . 'Twas natural it must be owned that such an inquiry should be opposed, considering whither it led, had it been rigorously followed up." Add. MS., 35608, f. 114.

[1] Add. MS., 32987, f. 202.

[2] Add. MS., 32985, f. 88 ; see also, f. 358 and Add. MS., 32986, f. 391.

[3] Add. MS., 32989, f. 232.

at Lewes it was not for want of trying. "I expected to have heard from you before now," he wrote to his agent in that town, early in March, "how the state of our affairs stands at Lewes. By the enclosed letter I find we shall still have some difficulty with the dissenters. However, they will have a very strong letter from the body of dissenters here, pressing them to support my interest . . . I hear that Morris, the butcher, who has taken so much money of me and my family, is engaged to Colonel Hay. I am determined to know my friends, and they shall be known, not only to the whole country, but to all the world. . . . Stand a poll I will and will know my friends from my enemies. If gratitude and honour won't prevail with them, I hope interest will ; and the tradesmen of Lewes ought to consider how much money my friends, and particularly my cousin, Pelham of Stanmer, and my Lord Gage spend amongst them. My cousin, Pelham of Stanmer, alone pays out £1100 a year amongst them, and he will not lay out less by having above £40,000 left him by his father in-law, Mr Frankland. In short, if they will proceed with violence, I will use violence towards them, and will know who are my friends, and who are not."[1]

It would be a mistake to imagine that intimidation was the only weapon that Newcastle used : his correspondence reveals that there was another and a lighter

[1] Add. MS., 32989, f. 113. On Miller failing to be elected, Newcastle instructed his steward, Abraham Bailey, " to give notice to such of my tenants at Lewes who did not vote for the election of Mr Hampden and Mr Miller at the last election there, the 16th of March last, to quit their several houses at Michmas next. Also that my said steward do call in the bills of such tradesmen at Lewes, who have been usually employed by me, and did not vote as above, and not employ them again on my account." It is doubtful, however, whether these drastic orders were executed ; the Duke of Richmond protested against them, and Newcastle agreed to talk the matter over with him. Add. MS., 32990, f. 165, f. 196 ; f. 200.

side of electioneering business. Sir John Miller, the
father of the defeated candidate at Lewes, relates how
" Sir Ferdinand intends to roast a little ox on the
day of election," and adds, feelingly, that " the service
is rather severe ; I have been up three nights and,
I can assure you, I can jump, dance, run, sing and
hollow as well as ever I did." [1] Nor were such
festivities confined to the town of Lewes ; and, from
the Duke of Richmond, Newcastle heard how, at
Chichester, " we drank your grace's health in a bumper,
with many huzzas, the very first toast after the Royal
family, the county, and the city. We then went
on with the marquis, the Duke of Portland, Sir George
Savile, and no *nullum tempus*, etc., etc., etc., till we
were all completely finished." [2]

Great as was the energy displayed by Newcastle,
he was not the only member of the opposition to toil
to increase the numerical strength of the party in the
new parliament. Rockingham used his great political
influence in Yorkshire to good effect,[3] and nowhere
was the contest fiercer than in the counties of Cumberland and Westmoreland, where the antagonists were
the Duke of Portland and Sir James Lowther. The
political rivalry of these two great landowners having
been embittered by personal hate and spite, the struggle
could not fail to be keen ; and it was rumoured that
Lowther, having defrauded Portland of an estate, was
now intent upon his financial ruin.[4] He failed, indeed,
to attain this sinister end, but he was at least successful
in making Portland spend money lavishly, the duke's

[1] Add. MS., 32989, f. 163.　　　　[2] Add. MS., 32989, f. 230.
[3] Add. MS., 32989, f. 232.
[4] It was reported that the Duke of Bedford had stated, in a public room
at Bath, that Lowther had asserted that he " would at any time spend twenty
thousand pounds to make the Duke of Portland spend fifteen, for I know I
can hold out longer than he can, and my meaning is to ruin him." Add.
MS., 32990, f. 21.

expenditure being estimated at forty thousand pounds. Extravagant as such an outlay was, it did not go un-rewarded ; for if Lowther secured his own return as one of the members for the county of Cumberland, he was destined to be speedily unseated on an election petition ; and Portland had every reason to be pleased with the success of the candidates he favoured. " The election for this place," he wrote to Newcastle from Carlisle, " is appointed on Wednesday next, and I am pretty confident that neither promises, threats, nor money in hand, can prevent my giving you as satisfactory an account of it as that of Wigan. I was met at my entrance into the county, and on my arrival here, by some thousands who, to my honour and satisfaction, . . . crowded in from every part of the county to testify their regard and attachment to me, and their abhorrence and determined resentment of an act so injurious to private property. The eight guilds of this city would all have met me with their colours flying, if they had not been stopped by my friends who thought it more prudent for them to wait in turn, and salute me only as I passed by." [1]

Thus Newcastle, Rockingham, and Portland were all able to congratulate themselves upon the success they had gained ; but it must not be imagined that they, and the principles they represented, had really triumphed. They had held their own, but had done no more, having failed materially to reduce the majority of the government ; and, when the new parliament met, the ministers were able to count with safety upon a substantial following in both houses.[2] Nor,

[1] Add. MS., 32989, f. 206.
[2] " In the meantime the parliament was chosen to the consent of the court, though by the inactivity of the Duke of Grafton, and the unpopularity of their chief friends, the majority was not greater than in the last assembly." Walpole's Memoirs, 3, 135.

indeed, was there any sign that the Rockingham whigs were the chosen of the people, the heroes of the country ; and it was because they were so lightly considered by the nation that they failed to stem the tide of bribery and corruption running against them. That there was little or no love in the country for an administration, which had proved its inefficiency up to the hilt, is beyond all question; but the affection, which the people withheld from the advisers of the crown, was bestowed neither upon the followers of Rockingham nor of Grenville, but upon that restless demagogue, John Wilkes who, having already proved himself a thorn in the side of one ministry, was to be a source of unending trouble and confusion to another.

It was certainly as no unknown man that Wilkes appealed to the English people in the general election of 1768, for he had already posed as the champion of the freedom of the subject, and played with conspicuous success the martyr's rôle. Few men have burst more suddenly into political fame, or risen from more sordid and degraded surroundings. At the beginning of George III.'s reign, his only reputation was that of a clever and debauched man of fashion, notoriously addicted to the most vicious pleasures, and the boon companion of the most dissolute men of the time. Politically in sympathy with the whig opposition to Lord Bute and the court, he but rarely took part in debate, confining his energy, for the most part, to his journal, *The North Briton*, which he used as a vehicle for the most bitter and unscrupulous attacks upon the ministry and the Scotch nation. There was little to discriminate him from the needy herd who eked out a precarious livelihood by the dissemination of slander and falsehood ; and it is possible that, had it not been for the indiscretion of Grenville and the folly of George III., the name of Wilkes would have been unknown at the present day, save to curious inquirers into the shady bypaths of eighteenth-century history.   For a violent attack upon the king's speech at the close of the parliamentary session in the spring of 1763, Wilkes was arrested under a general warrant, an expedient of very doubtful legality, and charged with the offence of seditious libel.   Discharged by Chief Justice Pratt who ruled that the prisoner was protected by his parliamentary privilege, Wilkes only obtained his freedom to fall a victim to the hatred of the ministers and the court, who renewed the attack when parliament met in the autumn.   After prolonged debates, he was expelled from the house of commons in January, 1764; and, having fled the country to escape his persecutors, was convicted in his absence of publishing a seditious libel and an obscene poem, and, on failing to appear to receive sentence, was condemned to outlawry.   In exile he remained for two years, wandering through France and Italy, and finding consolation in the charms of the courtesan, Corradini.   Deserted by his mistress, and hungering to play once more a part in public life, he visited England in May, 1766, in the hope that Lord Rockingham, then in power, would repair the wrong which had been inflicted by his predecessor in office. Disappointed in this expectation he returned to Paris ; but in the autumn of the same year he was again in England, having been encouraged to believe that, now that Chatham was prime minister and Grafton first lord of the treasury, the years he had spent in exile would be taken as an expiation of his guilt, and that he would be pardoned for an offence which might with advantage have been left unpunished.

Such an expectation was certainly neither rash

nor unfounded. Chatham, while unhesitatingly disclaiming any sympathy with the man whom he characteristically described as the libeller of his king and the blasphemer of his God, had affirmed his belief that the offence of seditious libel was covered by parliamentary privilege; and, now that he was in office, might be expected to redress the wrong which had been inflicted. Grafton, moreover, had sought admission to Wilkes when a prisoner in the Tower; and Conway, deserting the court of which he had formerly been a supporter, had fought on his behalf in the parliamentary battle. From such ministers Wilkes naturally expected forgiveness; and his appeal to Grafton was couched in studiously moderate language. " I now hope," he wrote, " that the rigour of a long unmerited exile is past; and that I may be allowed to continue in the land and among the friends of liberty. I wish, my lord, to owe this to the mercy of my prince. I entreat your grace to lay me with all humility at the king's feet: with the truest assurances that I have never, in any moment of my life, swerved from the duty and allegiance I owe to my sovereign; and that I implore, and in everything submit to, his majesty's clemency." [1]

Much trouble in the future would have been averted if this prayer for pardon had been granted, and it was little short of a catastrophe to the administration that a favourable opportunity of rendering Wilkes innocuous was missed. As in duty bound, Grafton submitted the outlaw's appeal to both the king and Chatham. George III., who was a good hater, and never ready to forgive those who had wounded his pride, remained ominously silent; and Chatham,

[1] Almon's *Memoirs of John Wilkes*, 3, 178-180; Grafton's *Autobiography*, pp. 192-193.

complaining that it was a troublesome business, advised Grafton not to take any decisive step. It was hardly necessary to give such advice to one who had all the love of a weak man for inaction ; and Wilkes was justifiably chagrined on receiving, in answer to his letter, only a verbal message from Grafton, recommending him to apply to Chatham. Such a response could only mean that the ministers were not prepared to embroil themselves with the court for the sake of the man who had wrongly thought them to be his friends ; [1] and, as a sojourn in England on sufferance [for he could be arrested at any moment as a returned outlaw] was no part of Wilkes' programme, he departed again for Paris, to brood over the new wrong he had suffered, and to meditate a revenge upon the men whom he hated all the more bitterly from having being deceived in them.

It is difficult to avoid the conclusion that Chatham had missed a great opportunity, and committed a blunder which was to bear a plentiful crop of mischief. Worthless as Wilkes was in many respects, he had undeniably endured many undeserved hardships, and had earned a pardon, not by his own merits, but by the wrong-doings of his enemies. The warrant under which he had been originally arrested had been declared illegal by the chief justice of the common pleas ; he had been expelled from the house of commons by a majority in the pay of the court ; he had been tried and convicted in his absence, and had suffered attack by every weapon which authority, spite, and chicanery could use against him. If he had sinned, he had also been deeply sinned against ; and a royal pardon would have been an act of atonement as well as a

---

[1] Almon's *Memoirs of John Wilkes*, 3, 184 *seq.* ; Grafton's *Autobiography*, p. 193.

politic exercise of the prerogative of mercy. To have pardoned Wilkes would have been the most effective way of destroying his influence, for the populace might be trusted quickly to forget that the man, who had deigned to profit by the clemency of the crown, had once been the victim of royal oppression and the champion of the freedom of Englishmen. Nothing perishes so easily as a demagogue's reputation, and the far-seeing statesman would have advised the king to extend to his adversary the pity akin to contempt. By taking refuge in inaction, Chatham stands convicted of having failed to do his duty as adviser of the crown. No man was better fitted to plead the cause of Wilkes before the throne ; and to treat it as a troublesome business, best left alone, was to push caution to the verge of timidity and sloth. A golden opportunity was missed, and the peace of English political life was to be rudely disturbed, because an administration, which had no support but the royal favour, did not dare to thwart the personal wishes of the king.

The consequences of the blunder were not slow in revealing themselves. The unforgiven Wilkes did not forgive, and was lavishly equipped by nature for the work of revenge. All that a bitter tongue, a ready pen, and a brazen audacity could effect was within his power, and, having nothing to lose and everything to gain, he was prepared to push the contest to the bitter end. For a while he kept silence, and it was not until December, 1767, that he declared open war upon the ministry, his ultimatum taking the form of a letter to the Duke of Grafton. Throwing prudence and moderation to the winds, he returned in this epistle to that virulent style which best suited him, and by which he had first won a name. Upon Chatham he emptied the vials of his wrath, denouncing him as a " proud, insolent, overbearing, ambitious man," insensible to the charm of private friendship, the " first comedian of our age," and so odiously hypocritical as to condemn in public the obscenity which he loved in private.[1] These baseless accusations give the measure at once both of Wilkes' anger and veracity ; but, with all his defects, he was of too high a spirit to use the weapon of slander alone ; and, a few weeks after dispatching the letter, he started for England, arriving there in February, 1768.

Such an advent boded no good for the ministers ; and, though they had their adversary within their power, they were by no means eager to begin the conflict. They were well aware that the most effective and expeditious way of reviving the dimmed lustre of Wilkes' popularity would be to renew the attack upon him ; and, neither prepared to pardon nor to persecute, they took refuge in the middle, and rather futile, course of doing nothing. The days passed by, and no hand was raised against the returned outlaw who was thus threatened with the oblivion which is worse than the tomb for the heroes of the popular fancy. Against a less adroit and accomplished antagonist this policy might possibly have been crowned with success, but Wilkes was far too experienced an adventurer to fall headlong into the first trap laid in his path. Realising that nothing could be more dangerous than the precarious and somewhat contemptuous immunity that he enjoyed, he determined to precipitate a conflict by challenging the government to open combat : and he had not long to wait before throwing down the glove. The opportunity he needed was given by the general election, and, with characteristic effrontery, the returned outlaw came forward

---

[1] Almon's *Memoir of John Wilkes*, 3, 184 *seq.*

as one of the candidates for election by the city of London. His audacity served him well, for, though he failed to be elected, he once more brought himself before the public, and was given ample assurance that he could still confidently count upon the popular favour. Though regarded with scant goodwill by the wealthy city magnates, he was enthusiastically supported by the mob and the more humble of the electors ; [1] and, encouraged by his experience, he stood for the county of Middlesex which returned him in triumph at the head of the poll. Great as such a victory was, Wilkes had done far more than simply secure a seat in the new parliament : once more he was the hero of the hour, the darling of the rabble who expressed, as usual, their enthusiasm for the principles of liberty in riot and disorder. For two nights the metropolis was in the hands of a mob, hoarsely shouting for " Wilkes and Liberty," and wreaking vengeance against all who refused to participate in their rejoicings. The Austrian ambassador, the staidest and most ceremonious of men, was dragged from his carriage to have the sacred number, forty-five, chalked upon the soles of his shoes ; and householders who, in-fluenced either by frugality or their political opinions, refrained from illuminating in honour of the popular victory, were punished by having their windows broken. Against the Scotch, whom Wilkes had so bitterly and so ungenerously attacked, the mob was particularly violent. An assault was directed against Lord Bute's house ; and the beautiful Dowager Duchess of Hamilton, having loyally refused, as the widow of one Scotchman and the wife of another, to illuminate in honour of the enemy of her adopted nation, was compelled to stand a siege of three hours,

[1] Walpole's Memoirs, 3, 126.

during which the assailants broke down the outer gates, poured into the courtyard, and hammered upon the closed doors and shutters.[1]

This popular demonstration was a significant warning to the ministers of the difficulties of the situation into which they had been driven by their cunning and unscrupulous adversary. Wilkes was now more popular than ever, and through him the people had voiced their discontent against the government. By a profligate expenditure of money, the administration had rendered itself invulnerable against attack within the walls of parliament ; but one of the most important constituencies in the kingdom had declared for the man who had nothing to recommend him save that he was an enemy of the court and the ministry ; and the choice was invested with a deep constitutional significance. " Mr Wilkes' success," wrote the Duke of Richmond, " is an event which, I think, must produce something. . . . For my part I confess that, although I hate a mob that rises against order, and acts by force, I am not sorry that the ministry should see that there is in the people a spirit of liberty that will show itself on proper occasions, as in the choice of their members. For whatever men may think of Mr Wilkes' private character, he has carried his election by being supposed a friend to liberty ; and I think it will show the administration that, though they may buy lords and commons, and carry on their measures smoothly in parliament, yett (sic) they are not so much approved of by the nation." [2] Almost identically the same sentiments were echoed by Newcastle who declared that " it should be known that the nation is not satisfied with the

---

[1] Walpole's Memoirs, 3, 128 ff. ; Letters, 7, 176-179.
[2] Add. MS., 32989, f. 294.

present proceedings; and when that is universally known, which appears very plainly now, I doubt not but by the present complexion of the new parliament, there will be spirit enough to take up the causes of the present dissatisfaction in a proper legal and effectual manner." [1]

Thus, armed in the panoply of popular applause, Wilkes proceeded to wage war against the ministry; but, before he could strike a really effective blow, it was necessary that he should pay homage to the law of the land which he daily defied by his presence in England. No sooner had he been returned for Middlesex than he surrendered to his outlawry, and appeared before the court of king's bench on April 20th. Great was the popular excitement, and every precaution was taken by the authorities to guard against a riot. Addressing the court in a carefully prepared and written speech, which he afterwards published, Wilkes pleaded for the reversal of his outlawry on the ground that it was technically invalid, and also contended that he had been wrongfully and illegally convicted of libel. As it happened, he might have spared himself the fatigue of this lengthy exposition, for Lord Mansfield ruled from the bench that the court could take no cognisance of the case, the prisoner having been guilty of the gross informality of a voluntary surrender to his outlawry instead of waiting to be arrested by a writ issued by the attorney-general.[2] This paradoxical situation of a refugee from

---

[1] Add. MS., 32989, f. 299.

[2] "After some arguments about the outlawry," wrote George Onslow to Newcastle, "Lord Mansfield and his three associates declared against the manner of his appearance there, and, by what I hear, bore hard upon the attorney-general for not having issued his capias against him, on his first appearing in England, and all agreed that the court was not the proper place to issue any order for his seizure. There may be more law in that than there

justice vainly endeavouring to secure a trial was not, however, of long continuance ; and, the necessary writ having been issued, Wilkes was promptly arrested, and committed to prison. The question of his outlawry was argued before the king's bench on May 7th ; but again the matter was left in suspense, Lord Mansfield deferring judgment until the following term.[1]

Unpleasing as such delay was to Wilkes who, unless his outlawry was reversed, had nothing to look forward to but life-long imprisonment, it was almost equally objectionable to the ministers who, until they were more precisely informed as to Wilkes' exact legal position, were precluded from taking any action against him. That they were indignant at the outrage which he had inflicted upon them is beyond all doubt. Even Lord Camden, who was afterwards to play a very different rôle, was aghast at Wilkes' effrontery ; [2] and both the king and the Bedford party in the cabinet clamoured for the offender's immediate expulsion from parliament.[3] It is, therefore, quite probable that the attack upon the member for Middlesex would have been begun directly the new parliament assembled, had it not been for Lord Mansfield's delay which rendered it difficult to assign a cause for his expulsion. Not until the outlawry had either been confirmed or reversed was it possible to proceed with the further question of the legality of Wilkes' conviction ; for,

is reason, but the consequence was Wilkes went unmolested out of court." Add. MS., 32989, f. 367 ; see also Add. MS., 32989, f. 363 ; Walpole's Letters 7, 184-186; Walpole's Memoirs, 3, 134.

[1] Add. MS., 32990, f. 25.

[2] " A criminal flying his country to escape justice—a convict and an outlaw—that such a person should in open daylight thrust himself upon the country as a candidate, his crime unexpiated, is audacious beyond description." Grafton's *Autobiography*, pp. 199-200.

[3] Correspondence of George III. with Lord North, 1, 2 : Walpole's Memoirs, 3, 142 : Grafton's *Autobiography*, pp. 199-200.

as Camden pointed out, " Mr Wilkes stands at present convicted only by verdict : and if there shall appear to be any material defect in the record . . . the judgment must be stayed : in which case he must be discharged, and he becomes a free man upon this prosecution, as much as if he had never been convicted."[1] There was, therefore, a possibility that Wilkes might be restored to his full rights as an English subject ; and if the ministers, refusing to await developments, proceeded against him as an outlaw and a criminal, they might find themselves brought into summary conflict with the judgment of the court.   Thus, every sound argument was on the side of politic procrastination ; and, in spite of the protests of the followers of Bute and Bedford,[2] it was decided, at a meeting held on May 7th at the house of Lord North, who had superseded Conway as leader of the house of commons,[3] that no action should be taken against Wilkes until the autumn session.   This policy was approved by Camden, Grafton, Conway, and Granby, among the ministers,[4] and, indeed, by all men except those who were prepared to incur every risk in order to gratify their malice ;   and   when   parliament,   which   had assembled early in May, was prorogued from June 21st until the following autumn,[5] no hostile action had been taken against the man who had so openly braved the anger of the administration.

---

[1] Grafton's *Autobiography*, pp. 200-201.

[2] Add. MS., 32990, f. 71, f. 83 ; Walpole's Memoirs, 3, 142.

[3] On January 1st, Whately, in a letter to Grenville, repeated a rumour that North, not Conway, was to lead the lower house ; and although Walpole asserts that Conway " remained, as much as he would, a leader in the house of commons," it is quite clear that that minister retired more or less into the background, and that the business of managing the house was entrusted to the chancellor of the exchequer.   Grenville Papers, 4, 240-249 ; Walpole's Memoirs, 3, 107.

[4] Add. MS., 32990, f. 63, f. 71 ; Walpole's Memoirs, 3, 142.

[5] Grafton's *Autobiography*, pp. 202-203, 209-211.

If the adherents of Bute and Bedford professed disgust at what they conceived to be the cowardice of the government, the Rockingham whigs were more genially disposed, and had no fault to find with the policy of delay. Indeed, it suited their purpose well enough; for, though Richmond and Newcastle might hail Wilkes as the morning star of freedom, both they and their friends knew quite well that he had already once proved himself a fruitful source of discord in their ranks, and might well do so again. Aware that the first session of the new parliament would not be of very long duration, they desired to refrain from active opposition;[1] and their fear had been that Wilkes might be used as a whip to drive them into the open against their will. Meeting Grafton at Newmarket, Rockingham endeavoured to glean from him the plan of the ministerial campaign; but received so cryptic an answer that, to quote Lord Hardwicke, " if any English could be picked out of what he did say, it was that nothing was fixed."[2] The suspense continued until the meeting of parliament; but when the speech from the throne made no mention of the member for Middlesex, the significant omission was rightly interpreted as meaning that nothing was to be done for the present. " I must most seriously congratulate your lordship," wrote Newcastle to Rockingham, the day after the meeting of parliament, " upon the happy conclusion of this short session (for I look upon it as over) without doing any mischief. I think my Lord

---

[1] " I have thoroughly examined and considered the state of all the new members," wrote Newcastle to Portland on April 11th, " and if we can avoid doing any business upon the return of the writs, except chusing the speaker; and consequently entering upon the affair of Wilkes, upon which there will certainly be differences of opinion, even amongst ourselves, we shall, I think, the next sessions make a very good figure." Add. MS., 32989, f. 319.

[2] Add. MS., 32990, f. 1; Rockingham Memoirs, 2, 67-68; see also Add. MS., 32989, f. 319.

Bute . . . has met with the greatest disappointment that ever favourite met with. His view certainly was to have blown up this little session with the affair of Wilkes; whereas, as it now stands, Wilkes' affair need not give us any trouble, except next winter we should make it our own choice. Wilkes will be half forgot before that time." [1]

On this occasion Newcastle did not show himself a sagacious political prophet, for Wilkes was not to fall into the oblivion to which Grafton and the Rockingham whigs would have so readily consigned him. He had all the genius of the successful demagogue in keeping himself prominently before the public; and his very misfortunes gave him the notoriety which he so eagerly coveted, and which he was to use with such deadly effect.

By the end of June the court of king's bench had pronounced judgment upon him. His outlawry was reversed upon technical grounds; but, failing in his attempt to secure the quashing of his previous conviction, he was sentenced to imprisonment for two years and the payment of a substantial fine. Thus, his legal position was defined, and when the ministers met parliament in the autumn session, they would have no excuse for further delay, and would be compelled to decide upon a definite course of action. Policy, as well as generosity, dictated that they should refrain from inflicting any further penalty upon the man who had already been more than sufficiently punished; but, with the king and the Bedford party clamouring for expulsion and talking vainly about the dignity of parliament, it was almost inevitable that revenge

---

[1] Add. MS., 32990, f. 39. Rockingham, however, was not quite so sanguine, remarking, in his reply to Newcastle, "I don't yet think but that the business of Wilkes in some shape or other may still come on, but it is doubtful. By Monday night we may know." Add. MS., 32990, f. 45.

should triumph over wisdom. Grafton, lacking in stability and conviction, would bend once more to the storm ; and the placemen and pensioners in the pay of the court would eagerly join in the hunt of one who, whatever his faults, was not at least so base as the majority of his pursuers. Yet the most elementary foresight ought to have made the ministers pause before attacking the man who had so deftly struck the popular imagination. The re-appearance of Wilkes had been the signal for riot and disorder which had not been confined to the ranks of his supporters ; and it needed no prophet to foretell that his expulsion from parliament would increase the odium in which the government was held. An administration, well-established in the confidence of the country, renowned for its strength, and illustrious by its achievements, might well have hesitated before undertaking such a task ; and there is something tragic in the circumstance that, while Grafton and his colleagues were girding their loins to punish the man who had dared to appeal to the nation, they were simultaneously displaying, as fully as their bitterest enemies could have desired, their complete inability to maintain the influence and prestige of England abroad. Largely by reason of their weak and faltering foreign policy, their divided counsels, and lack of harmony, Corsica, which had rebelled against the Genoese rule, was allowed to pass into the hands of France ; and, though not annexed to the Bourbon kingdom until 1769, all hope of preserving its independence had vanished before the end of the year 1768. It has been urged that the importance of this acquisition has been unduly magnified, and it is possible to advance many sound arguments in support of such a contention ; but, at the same time, it ought not to be forgotten that most Englishmen viewed with suspicion and alarm every increase in the influence of France ; and it is not altogether without importance that, in the conquest of Corsica, Choiseul saw some compensation for the loss of Canada.

Of far greater moment, however, than the subjugation by France of an island in the Mediterranean, was the course of events in the colonies. There the seed sown by Charles Townshend in his haste was beginning to bear a bitter and deadly crop ; and, what anyone might have foreseen, had come to pass. Townshend, making the mistake of a clever man, thought that he had driven the Americans into a corner by showing them that external taxation, to which they had professed themselves ready to submit, could be made to yield a revenue ; but they, wisely realising that freedom was a far greater thing than logic, promptly repudiated a theory so skilfully converted into a weapon against their liberty. When the inhabitants of the town of Boston learnt that the revenue bill had become law, and that officers had been appointed to enforce it, they assembled in a town meeting, and, entering upon a non-importation agreement, pledged themselves to discourage in every way the importation of commodities from abroad. This shrewd blow, aimed at the English merchants who would thus be deprived of a profitable trade, was followed up by the assembly of Massachusetts petitioning the king and parliament against this new infringement of the principle of no taxation without representation ; and, what was of far more questionable legality, addressing a circular letter to the other colonial assemblies, calling upon them to unite in resisting the aggressions of the mother country.

Thus, the conflict begun by Grenville's ill-advised

stamp act was renewed, and the evil wrought by Charles Townshend, during his brief career as chancellor of the exchequer, lived after him. Once more the authority of the mother country was called into question, and the ministry can hardly be blamed for seeking to quell the spirit of resistance by stern measures of repression ; for no other course was open to them, unless they were prepared to treat the declaratory act as so much wastepaper, and to allow that England had no right to take a penny out of the pockets of the colonists without their consent. Such a surrender of principle, however, was hardly possible ; for even those, who sympathised with the colonists, and had assisted to repeal the stamp act, were taken aback by the action of the Massachusetts Assembly, Newcastle mournfully reflecting that " these New England people always were a refractory people," and Sir George Savile almost coming to the opinion " that George Grenville's act only brought on a crisis twenty, or possibly fifty, years sooner than was necessary." [1] Yet, if a coercive policy had to be adopted, it would be of little use unless it was successful in securing obedience ; and it was a disaster for the ministers that their measures failed to attain the end for which they were designed. The Massachusetts assembly met the demand of the government for the withdrawal of the circular letter by a definite refusal, and paid the price of its disobedience by being dissolved ; but this was no solution of the colonial problem, and that the ministry recognised how critical the situation was is shown by the dispatch of two regiments to Massachusetts Bay. The most superficial observer could hardly fail to perceive the magnitude of the danger, for the unrest in the province

[1] Add. MS., 32990, f. 340 ; Rockingham Memoirs, 2, 75-76.

of Massachusetts might easily spread to the other colonies ; and the money market revealed the state of public opinion.   Stocks began to fall, and capitalists, distrustful of the ability of the government to cope with the evils of the day, preferred to allow their money to lie idle at the bank rather than run the risk of investment.[1]

Threatened thus by troubles abroad as well as at home, Grafton must have viewed with little satisfaction the approach of the autumn session, when his conduct might be subjected to a searching criticism ; and it is not surprising that he resolved to remove, before the meeting of parliament, a dangerous element of dissension from the cabinet. The victim marked out for sacrifice was Lord Shelburne. For many months past Grafton had regarded him with a growing antipathy which was fully shared by the king and the Bedford party in the cabinet ;[2] and if this antagonism was partly due to Shelburne's unfortunate capacity for inspiring distrust and suspicion in the minds of those with whom he came into close contact, it must also be remembered that he profoundly disagreed with the majority of his colleagues on most of the important questions of the day, and had endured slights and indignities more than sufficient to wound a man of less pride and temper. Studiously abstaining from attendance at cabinet councils, he had watched in silence, but not without indignation, the triumph of a policy which he did not approve. Deploring the failure of the ministry to defend Corsica against French aggression, and now convinced that all modes of taxing America were illegal, he had little in common with his fellow ministers ; and, as early as the month of Septem-

---

[1] Grenville Papers, 4, 359-360 ; see also 321-322.
[2] Grafton's *Autobiography*, 213, 215 ; Walpole's Memoirs, 3, 150-151.

ber, 1768, Grafton had determined upon his removal at the first convenient opportunity.

In considering the practicability of this resolve Grafton realised that no opposition would come from the court or the Bedford faction in the cabinet ; but if he thought that the expulsion would be unattended with difficulty, he reckoned without the absent leader of the government, Lord Chatham. Secluded at Hayes, whither he had gone when wearied of Hampstead, Chatham was gradually, though very slowly, recovering from that mental depression which had driven him into isolation ; and, as he slowly struggled back to health, he watched with anger and dismay the course pursued by his subordinates. His silence is no indication that he was ignorant of what was happening ; and bitterly did he resent what he believed to be a betrayal of trust on the part of Grafton. By his admission of the Bedfords into the cabinet, by his failure to check French ambition, and by permitting the revival of the colonial dispute, Grafton had filled his cup of iniquity to the brim ; and the determination to remove Shelburne was the overflowing drop in the already too well-filled flagon. On nearly every point where Shelburne differed from his colleagues he was in agreement with Chatham ; and the latter, confronted with the prospect of losing one of the only two men in the cabinet who possessed his confidence, resigned his office of privy seal, his example being followed by Shelburne who thus, by a timely retreat, escaped the ignominy of expulsion.

So, in attempting to set his house in order, Grafton had seriously loosened the fabric of the structure ; and, indeed, had lost far more than he had gained. The removal of Shelburne might promote a greater degree of ministerial unity, but it would also have the effect of throwing more power into the hands of the Bedfords, with whose colonial policy Lord Rochford, the new secretary of state in place of Shelburne, was to show himself in entire sympathy.[1] The resignation of Chatham, moreover, was, inevitably, a serious blow to the prestige of the administration. It could not be explained away as arising from ill-health, for he had long been incapacitated from attending to business ; and the only possible interpretation was that it was a public repudiation of the ministerial policy, and a declaration of war against the government of which he had laid the foundations. No explanation, however skilful, could disguise the fact that the greatest and most popular statesman of the day had disowned his own creatures ; and the administration, already shaken to its foundations, and confronted with a gigantic task, was still further discredited in the eyes of the nation.

The Duke of Grafton might well feel deeply hurt and chagrined at such a public rebuff by the man whom he had striven faithfully, if mistakenly, to serve ; but he was not the only member of the cabinet who had reason to regret Chatham's action. Lord Camden could not but be deeply affected by the loss of his old schoolfellow and life-long friend ; and, for a short time, it seemed likely that a new lord chancellor would have to be discovered. For many weeks past, Camden had, been discontented with his situation, complaining, somewhat bitterly and pathetically, to Grafton that

[1] Lord Rochford, whose abilities were unduly depreciated by Horace Walpole, does not appear to have belonged strictly to any of the political parties of the day. " I want particularly to speak to you about your friend, Rochford," wrote Newcastle to Albemarle on September 16th. " I hear it is reported that he is to be secretary of state. He is the fittest for it of any man in England ; but I would have him come in with our friends, and not with the present ministers, who will endeavour to get him ; but that your lordship must prevent." Add. MS., 32991, A, f. 107.

" the administration, since Lord Chatham's illness, is almost entirely altered, without being changed ";[1] and only with doubt, and after much hesitation, had he consented to the project of expelling Shelburne.[2] In this state of despondency and uncertainty it was not unnatural that he should be deeply distressed by the withdrawal of Chatham. " To me I fear," he wrote on first learning the news, " the blow is fatal, yet I shall come to no determination. If I can find out what is fit for me to do in this most distressed situation, that I must do : but the difficulty lies in forming a true judgment." These are the words of a man distracted with doubt; and, a few days later, he was still a prey to hesitation, telling Grafton " that nothing could give me so much satisfaction as to join with your grace in one line of conduct; and yet I see plainly, that our situations are different, and the same honour, duty to the king, and regard to the public, operating upon two minds equally aiming at the same end, may possibly draw us different ways." [3]

A modern statesman in Camden's place would have promptly retired from the cabinet, but a mistaken sense of duty to the king and Grafton, and the fear that he might be held guilty of deserting a losing cause, induced him to act against his own convictions, and to remain in office. Well would it have been for his reputation if he had listened more attentively to the appeal of his reason. With little in common with his colleagues, and sincerely convinced that all taxation of the colonies was inexpedient [4] it was

---

[1] Grafton's *Autobiography*, p. 214.   [2] *Ibid.* pp. 214-217.
[3] *Ibid.* pp. 224-225.

[4] " I submit," he wrote to Grafton, early in October, " to the declaratory law, and have thought it my duty upon that ground, as a minister, to exert every constitutional power to carry the duty act into execution. But, as a member of the legislature, I cannot bring myself to advise violent measures to support a plan so inexpedient and so impolitic. And I am very much

indeed time for him to withdraw from an administration with which he had long ceased to be in sympathy, and which by his presence he rather weakened than strengthened.

Yet Camden continued to be of the body though not of the soul of the ministry, a discontented member of a body which gave ample cause for discontent ; and if the government had been called upon to meet a formidable parliamentary opposition, it is by no means impossible that it would have fallen to pieces at the first blow. But the prospect of such a contingency appeared comparatively remote on the eve of the session. No steps had been taken to heal the breach between the followers of Grenville and Rockingham, and no man could tell whether the renewal of the parliamentary struggle would widen or diminish the gulf between them. Ancient bitterness might be renewed by the revival of the colonial dispute, and new hostility created by the resurrection of Wilkes to political importance. Nor was the possibility of still further drifting apart from Grenville the only danger which threatened the Rockingham whigs : they had to beware of divisions in their own ranks, and to fear the day when Chatham, restored to health, would plunge again into the political fray, for none could foretell the course which that erratic warrior would pursue.

The danger of internal dissensions was by no means remote ; and Newcastle was not entirely the prey of an old man's nervous fancy when he thought that

afraid (I speak this confidentially to your grace) that if a motion should be made to repeal the act, I should be under a necessity to vote for it. . . . I am very sensible that a difference of opinion on a subject so serious and important may be prejudicial to the administration . . . but I do fear most exceedingly that upon the American question the Bedfords and myself will be too far asunder to meet." Grafton's *Autobiography*, pp. 215-217.

he detected in some of his friends a growing preference in favour of a coercive colonial policy. " I doubt," he wrote to Rockingham, " by great mismanagement the measure of conquering the provinces, and obliging them to submit, is become now more popular than it was. It is certainly the measure of administration ; and I am afraid some of our own friends are a little tender on that point " ;[1] and, a little later, he expressed his alarm " that the ministerial measure of forcing the colonies may be . . . adopted by some of our best friends," and the hope that he might be mistaken.[2] With Rockingham the old duke was well enough pleased ; but he feared that the more violent members of the party might be prone to judge too harshly the men who had dared to resist the authority of parliament.

Newcastle, however, was not spared to see the future of the party, whose interests he had so much at heart, for he died at his house in Lincoln's Inn Fields on November 17th, a few days after the meeting of parliament. On hearing the news, Chesterfield, who was the duke's junior by one year, remarked, " I own I feel for his death, not because it will be my turn next; but because I knew him to be very goodnatured, and his hands to be extremely clean."[3] Such an epitaph from such a man is not without value. Newcastle, indeed, has paid to the uttermost farthing the penalty of his success. He has been represented as the typical leader of a corrupt and inefficient oligarchy, consumed with a frenzied passion for the most sordid and repulsive side of political life, thinking of nothing but the extension of his parliamentary influence, and preferring to be a huckster rather than

[1] Add. MS., 32991, A, f. 94. [2] Add. MS., 32991, A, f. 206.
[3] Chesterfield's Letters, 3, 1380-1381.

a statesman. Nearly every historian of the eighteenth
century has cast a stone at him. Macaulay, depicting
him as the cunning dotard who by dint of low craft
proved more than a match for far abler men, compares
him to the miser, Trapbois, in the " Fortunes of Nigel ";
and Smollet has drawn a never to be forgotten picture
of the duke, with a shaving cloth under his chin, and
his face well lathered, slobbering over the astonished
ambassador of the Dey of Algiers. Yet, though there
is much truth in these indictments, they do not contain the whole truth ; and Newcastle was something
better than a babbling inconsequential fool. His
faults were many and conspicuous. He betrayed
Walpole in 1742, and Pitt in 1761 ; he was the victim
of a jealousy which often led him to distrust his most
faithful friends ; he was often incompetent in the
transaction of business ; and he thought far too much
of the management of the house of commons and far
too little of the government of the country. But
these glaring defects ought not to obscure his real
merits both as a man and as a statesman. Possessed
of a personal piety which, if it did not lead him to
great acts of Christian devotion, was, at least, sincere,
a faithful and passionately affectionate husband, and
absolutely regardless of all pecuniary profit, he laboured
throughout a long life in what he conscientiously
believed to be the interests of the nation ; and, though
often lacking in wisdom and foresight, was never found
wanting in industry and application. Nor was he
by any means so deficient in political ability as he has
sometimes been represented. Towards the end of his
life, when misfortunes crowded thickly upon him, he
revealed a greater understanding than he had ever
displayed in the hour of his omnipotence. It was
largely by his indefatigable industry and zeal that

the Rockingham party had been founded and maintained; and his advice, though sometimes rejected, was generally well worth taking. It was he who had urged that the assistance of Pitt should be secured at all cost, who had impressed upon his friends the necessity of union, and had warned his supporters against a policy which could only end in a rupture with the colonies; and, if neither a hero of romance nor a heaven-born statesman, Newcastle was something more than a gilded nonentity, and in him the Rockinghams lost a counsellor whom they could ill afford to spare.

CHAPTER V

THE FALL OF GRAFTON

THE meeting of parliament had been fixed for November 8th, and Grafton must have viewed the approach of a new session with apprehension and dread. He was aware that any further postponement of the Wilkes question was out of the question, that the ministry would be arraigned both for its foreign and colonial policy; and that his strength had waned in almost exact proportion to the increase of his difficulties. He seemed to have touched the very nadir of his fortune, to have reached the goal to which he had been aimlessly, but inevitably, drifting from the very moment that he had accepted office at Chatham's dictation. The sport of adverse chance and doom, he had failed to grasp the law of his own soul's progress; and, in a vain endeavour to do right, had consistently passed from bad to worse. Failure had dogged his most conscientious efforts, and, if he had dared to look back, he would have seen how far he had strayed from the course on which he had originally started. The Rockingham whigs, his earliest political associates, were now his open and declared enemies; Chatham, for whose sake he had borne the brunt of the battle, had recently disowned him; no reliance could be placed upon Camden, who had not scrupled to publish to the world his dislike of the administration; [1] and

[1] A few weeks after the meeting of parliament Camden informed Wedderburn " that as to the present administration, he (the chancellor) hated and

neither Gower nor Weymouth were likely to raise a
finger to save Grafton in the moment of peril.   Thus,
separated from old friends and new allies, the prime
minister was doomed to a dreary isolation in the cabinet
over which he presided but did not direct ; and his
experience of administrative life must have served to
intensify his preference for the existence of a country
gentleman, and to deepen his dislike of the cares and
anxieties of a public career.   He would have been
wise to abandon a task which he had clearly shown
that he could not perform ; but, if he elected to continue
attempting the impossible, he was but pursuing the
path which he had conscientiously followed from the
first.   Still retaining the confidence of the court, and
secure of a majority in the house of commons, he was
not called upon, by the constitutional practice of the
day, to resign because he had forfeited the goodwill
of the nation ; and, indeed, had he abandoned office
at this critical juncture, it is not improbable that
George III. would have charged him with desertion.
Believing himself to be the minister of the king rather
than of the people, Grafton remained in office to defend
the crown against the factions which threatened its
independence ; and it is to his credit that he continued
to bear the burden of which he would so gladly have
been rid.

And the burden, heavy enough when he first took
it up in 1766, had become perceptibly heavier with the

despised them, and thought himself in many instances personally ill-used by
them. . . . He repeated many times, with infinite grief, the hard charge of
ingratitude laid against him, saying his conduct in the transaction with Lord
Bristol could only arise from thinking it was conformable to Lord Chatham's
wishes, since he could not mean by it to serve the administration whom he
hated, nor would he do it as a means to preserve that bauble (pointing to the
mace) which possibly he might not hold a week longer.   He left Mr Wedderburn at liberty to tell this to whom he pleased, wishing rather to have it told
than concealed."   Grenville Papers, 4, 404 ff.

passage of the years ; and at no time was the weight greater than in the autumn of 1768. Yet, confronted though they were with problems clamouring for solution, with the colonies speeding towards rebellion, and a discontented nation at home, neither the administration nor the Rockingham whigs were apparently furnished with a plan of campaign. Shortly before the meeting of parliament, Lord Sandwich, who as a member of the ministry would have excellent means of obtaining information, told a friend that " as to Wilkes . . . government were not inclined to propose his expulsion, if he himself was quiet, but if his friends attempted anything in his favour in parliament, that then every advantage would be taken against him " ; [1] and Lord Chesterfield reported that when one minister inquired of another what was to be done with Wilkes, the answer was returned, " I do not know." [2] This is merely the policy of waiting upon events ; and the same attitude of doubt and hesitation is to be detected in the Rockingham party. Those champions of a lost cause were of the opinion, it is true, that the time had come to make a resolute attack upon the government ; but we are left very much in the dark as to the exact plan of the onslaught. Early in October, Rockingham declared that no doubt existed as to " the general idea of what our conduct should be," [3] but details were left over to be decided by the leaders of the party, who were to gather in conclave before the meeting of parliament ; and it is difficult to avoid the impression that it was this part of the work of preparation which was least effectively performed. From what we know of these conferences it seems that, though it was decided to re-introduce the *nullum tempus*

---

[1] Add. MS., 35608, f. 286.　　　　[2] Chesterfield's Letters, 3, 1380.
[3] Add. MS., 32991, A, f. 244.

bill, to contest the validity of Sir James Lowther's election, and, if opportunity offered, to propose an amendment to the address relating to foreign affairs,[1] nothing was determined upon the far more important questions of Wilkes and the colonies.[2]   This was neither a satisfactory nor a comprehensive programme ; and the Rockingham whigs, like the ministers, are open to the charge of neglecting the maxim that victory goes to the man who knows what he wants, and plans to get it.

It may well be, however, that both the opposing forces were wise in their generation, and that, by carefully shunning an over-elaboration of policy, they sought to avert a pressing danger. The lack of preparation by the ministers is not surprising, seeing how few and comparatively unimportant were the questions upon which they were really in agreement ; and Grafton, unwilling to go as far as the Bedfords in coercing the colonists, and aware how little Camden approved of what had been done in the past or might be done in the future, probably felt that only in an atmosphere of vagueness and indecision could his administration continue to exist. It is also possible that the Rockinghams were encouraged to adopt the same attitude of expectancy, lest, by nailing their colours too promptly to the mast, they might not only cause dissension amongst themselves, but also widen the gulf which lay between them and Grenville.

---

[1] The proposed amendment ran as follows : " To thank his majesty for such information as he has been graciously pleased to give his parliament concerning the doubtful state of this nation in regard to foreign powers, and to assure his majesty that his faithful commons, when more fully informed on these matters, will immediately take the same into their most serious consideration, and humbly offer such advice, and cheerfully give such support, as may be most for the honour and dignity of his majesty's crown, the welfare of his majesty's subjects, and the preservation of the peace and tranquillity of Europe."   Add. MS., 32991, A, f. 401.

[2] Add. MS., 32991, A, f. 375 ; Add. MS., 35430, f. 120.

Separated as were the two wings of the opposition by the unhappy dispute with the colonies, they might be driven still further asunder if, in headlong haste, the Rockinghams espoused the cause of Wilkes. For it was while Grenville was in office, and in entire accordance with his wishes, that Wilkes had been originally expelled from parliament ; and it might be expected that he would view with approval and exultation a renewal of the attack upon his victim. Reasonable caution, therefore, dictated to the Rockinghams to tread carefully on what could not but be dangerous ground ; and care was far more necessary than even they realised. It was not only that Temple had begun to hint at a reconciliation, telling Charles Yorke that he had always been well disposed towards a union and connection with the Rockingham party, but " if that was impossible, we might and should agree in measures " : [1] what was of far greater moment was that the whole political situation had been transformed by the withdrawal of Chatham from the ministry. Once more that great statesman was a free lance, and it might not be many months before he had rallied his strength sufficiently to take once again a part in the conflict. When he reappeared in the political arena, it was certain that he would attack an administration which he had disowned ; but whether he would lend his aid in the encounter to the Grenvilles or the Rockinghams, or, as he had done on a former occasion, fight in splendid isolation, no man could prophesy. The time, the mode, and the consequences of Chatham's return were all uncertain ; and it behoved cautious politicians to walk warily, for fear of dooming themselves, by undue haste, to disaster in a distant and obscure future.

[1] Add. MS., 32990, f. 368.

Such was the atmosphere in which the parliamentary struggle began on November 8th. In the speech from the throne there was an indirect reference to the unfriendly attitude of France, and a pointed censure of the spirit of faction in the American colonies, but no mention of Wilkes, an omission which may be taken to signify that the ministers had not yet determined upon the punishment to be meted out to that offender. In the upper house there was little discussion, no amendment being proposed to the address of thanks ;[1] but in the house of commons there was a lengthy and animated debate. Lord Henley, the eldest son of Lord Northington, in moving the address, strongly inveighed against the colonists, declaring that " we shall be ever ready to hear and redress any real grievances of your majesty's American subjects ; but we should betray the trust reposed in us, if we did not withstand every attempt to infringe or weaken our just rights ; and we shall always consider it as one of our most important duties, to maintain entire and inviolate the supreme authority of the legislature of Great Britain over every part of the British empire." Henley, moreover, did not stand alone in his violence, the same unconciliatory tone being adopted by the seconder of the address, who contemptuously referred to the " insolent town of Boston," and contended that " men so unsusceptible of all middle terms of accommodation, call loudly for our correction." These were emphatic enough statements, and most of the speakers, who took part in the discussion, breathed the same spirit of hostility towards the colonists. George Grenville expressed his rooted abhorrence of any course of action which might encourage the Americans to persevere in their ill-advised resistance ; Lord

[1] Add. MS., 32991, A, f. 406.

Barrington stigmatised them as " worse than traitors against the crown—traitors against the legislature of this country " ; North vehemently declared that he would oppose any attempt to repeal the revenue act ; and an amendment, proposed by Dowdeswell, and supported by Burke and Barré, calling upon the government to explain the steps that had been taken " for maintaining peace and good order in his majesty's colonies in North America," was abandoned without being put to the vote.[1]

The violence of the debate on the first day of the session was unfortunately only too true an indication of what was to follow later ; and, until parliament rose in May, 1769, its time was mainly occupied with discussion of colonial business and the attack upon Wilkes. In the intervals between the battles on these questions, the opposition was successful in unseating Sir James Lowther, and in carrying the *nullum tempus* bill ; but these victories were due in no small measure to the politic generosity of the ministers who took little pains to defend an adherent notoriously guilty of having purchased his seat by the worst kind of corruption, or to oppose a bill which approved itself to the landed gentry throughout the country.[2] If

---

[1] *Cavendish Debates*, I, 30 *seq.*

[2] The popularity of the *nullum tempus* bill rendered opposition by the ministers unwise, and little resistance was made to it in either house of parliament. Add. MSS., 35362, f. 237, f. 238. The corruption attending Lowther's election can be gathered from a letter by the Duke of Portland to Newcastle. " At last the poll is closed for this county," wrote the Duke on April 23rd, 1768, " and the high sheriff, after having rejected 373 during and since the close of the poll, has found out that Sir James Lowther has a majority of two above Mr Fletcher ; and has consequently, upon the following state, returned him and Mr Curwen contrary to all law, reason, and justice. The numbers according to his discovery stand thus : Curwen, 2139 ; Lowther, 1977 ; Fletcher, 1975 ; Senhouse, 1891. Besides the rejection, in which I can safely assure your grace, there was not a single questionable vote, he was, for the infamous purpose above mentioned, obliged to admit upwards of one hundred votes for Sir James Lowther, and Mr Senhouse, who really had no pretence

they had utilised the strength thus saved in devising some means of restoring the old harmonious relations with the colonies, they would have deserved the gratitude of all Englishmen ; but this they neither accomplished nor even attempted ; and it cannot be pleaded in their defence that they were ignorant of the danger which was threatening the mother country. They must have known that the resistance started at Boston was rapidly spreading throughout America ; [1] for, no sooner had the session begun, than parliament was inundated by petitions from indignant colonials, encouraged, by the example of Massachusetts, to protest against what they thought to be an infringement of their natural rights. A remonstrance from the assembly of Virginia was followed by a petition from the province of Pennsylvania, which in its turn was succeeded by a petition from a body styling itself the " major part of the council of Massachusetts." [2] Not the least striking, and certainly the most ominous, characteristic of these appeals was the comparatively slight and unimportant differences between them. They unanimously denounced the revenue act as a gross violation of that traditional English freedom which the colonists had not forfeited by their journey across the seas ; and, in so doing, implicitly called upon the king and parliament to abandon an unlawful practice disguised as a legal right.

It was no small demand to make, but it would be a mistake at once to come to the conclusion that its

---

in the world to offer themselves, and who are guilty of the most wilful and corrupt perjury. The freeholders, actuated by the same spirit that has led them hitherto, are determined not to bear this insult ; and, at their own expense, to petition the house of commons, and prosecute the offenders." Add. MS., 35638, f. 262 (copy).

[1] Grenville Papers, 4, 408-409.

[2] *Cavendish Debates*, 1, 49 seq., 82 seq., 185 seq.

fulfilment was impossible. Statesmen have sometimes to pay a very heavy price for the mistakes committed either by themselves or their predecessors in office; and, as has been well said, if guilt be expiated in another world, the wages of folly are often paid here below. And few would now deny that the English ministers had been guilty of great folly, with no one but themselves to blame for the impasse in which they were. The beneficial effects to be expected from the repeal of the stamp act had been partly discounted by the declaratory act, and totally obliterated by Townshend's revenue bill; and the colonists can hardly be blamed for believing that the home government was determined, under one pretext or another, to extract money from their pockets without their consent. Passions and interests had been deeply stirred, and men's minds loosened from their ancient moorings; and it is arguable that only by the surrender of the right of taxation, however humiliating it might be to the pride of a great country, could England have won back the love and loyalty of her American children. Concession is not always a sign of weakness, and more has been lost by pride than by humility.

If, indeed, such a policy was the only solution of the difficulty, the situation was truly tragic; since something in the nature of a miracle was needed to bring salvation. Save for Chatham and Camden, hardly any of the leading politicians of the day were in favour of the repeal of the declaratory act. It is not likely that the Rockingham whigs would approve the removal from the statute book of a measure for which they were responsible; and the king, the Grenvilles, and the majority of the cabinet, would certainly object to what might be construed as an unworthy concession to rebellion. All parties in parliament might, therefore, be expected to oppose what was perhaps the only effective remedy for an urgent evil ; and the ministers can hardly be censured for having failed to act, not only against their own convictions, but also against those of their opponents. Yet they by no means stand completely exonerated from blame; for, impracticable though the wisest course might be, it was still their business to devise a policy for the emergency ; and it might have been well for them if, following the example of the Rockingham ministry, they had repealed Townshend's act, leaving untouched the right of the English parliament to levy taxes for purpose of revenue upon America. Such a programme might, possibly, have failed to placate the colonists, but it would at least have been a step in the direction of conciliation, and might have been taken without any fear of evoking a formidable parliamentary opposition. Grenville, of course, ever sensitive upon the point of American taxation, could be relied upon to oppose such a proposal ; but the Rockingham whigs, on the other hand, might be expected to welcome the unexpected vision of the ministers advancing with an olive branch in their hands. When in power themselves they had repealed the stamp act on account of the resistance it had encountered ; and Burke may be taken to have voiced the sentiments of his party when he declared in the house of commons that " if the question was whether we should repeal or whether we should enforce the act in question, I have no hesitation in saying, repeal." [1]

If, however, conciliation was to take the place of coercion there must be no delay. The oil of forgiveness must be poured upon the troubled waters of rebellion before the tempest had reached its height ; the pardon

[1] *Cavendish Debates*, 1, 398-399.

must appear to flow from kindness not from fear ; and the goodwill of the colonists fostered before it had entirely evaporated. Unfortunately, however, the ministers were too blind to perceive the force of such a consideration ; and, when the parliamentary session came to an end, the revenue act was still un- repealed. Truly disastrous as such procrastination was, it is not necessary to imagine that it was due to a settled conviction in the cabinet that Townshend's measure must stand for ever, or to a callous dis- regard of the critical character of the situation ; far more probably it was based upon an intelligible, if wrong-headed, policy. Apparently the administration believed that the repeal of the act must be deferred until a demonstration had been made of the displeasure of the mother country ; and the ministers, overlooking the fact that they were expected to behave like states- men, decided to act like schoolmasters who find it easier to exercise the rules of discipline than to practise the arts of management. In accordance with this pedagogic conception of government, Lord Hillsborough, on December 15th, 1768, moved eight resolutions in the house of lords, couched in a minatory tone, denouncing the illegal pretentions of the Massachusetts assembly and the disorderly conduct of the citizens of Boston ; and he was followed by the Duke of Bedford who moved an address to the king, approving the steps taken to maintain order in the colonies, and petitioning the crown to revive an obsolete statute of the reign of Henry VIII., under which colonists, suspected of treason or misprision of treason, could be brought over to England to stand their trial.[1]

Possessing the advantage of looking back across

---

[1] *Parl. Hist.*, xvi. 476 *seq.*; Hist. MSS. Comm., 14th Report, Appendix, part x.

the years, and knowing what was to be the issue of the
unhappy dispute, we need no great insight to perceive,
at a glance, the hopeless futility of such proceedings.
There was much to be said for a policy of instant
conciliation, and something to be said in favour of
consistent coercion ; but to steer a middle course
between the two, to do nothing towards a solution of
the problem, and yet, at the same time, to cause needless
offence, was but to court disaster. Empty resolutions
such as these were not likely to intimidate, and only
too certain to aggravate, a disturbed continent; for the
Americans would have been either more or less than
human if they had not deeply resented the iniquitous
proposal to revive a law, passed in a tyrannical
age, under which every colonist suspected of treason
could be dragged from his home to stand his trial in
a distant land. Such arguments, however, would
carry little weight with the well-paid supporters of the
court ; and the resolutions and the address were
carried in both houses. In the house of lords the
debate was languid and ineffective, few of the peers,
with the exception of the Duke of Richmond, offering much objection ; [1] but in the commons there was
a fiercer and more animated discussion. Both Dowdeswell and Burke denounced the proposal to revive a
treason law passed in a century hateful to every good
whig ; and although Grenville refused to oppose the
resolutions and address in their final form, for fear
that he might be held guilty of countenancing
rebellion, he was bitterly, and indeed justly, contemptuous of the ministers 'whom, he declared,
" were holding out angry words on the one hand,
and giving no remedy on the other." " Do not
let us stand," he vehemently cried, " shiffle-shuffle

[1] *Parl. Hist.*, xvi. 476.

between two measures . . . you are absolutely doing nothing." [1]

Grenville was true enough; and his point of view, perverted though it might be by doctrinaire and pedantic conceptions of government, was at least more statesmanlike and enlightened than that of the ministers who elected to occupy a whole parliamentary session in offensively marking time. Yet the situation was too critical even for the government indefinitely to postpone a solution; and on May 1st, a few days before the end of the session, the ministers met in cabinet council to decide upon a course of action. Nine members were present, the only absentee being Sir Edward Hawke, the first lord of the admiralty, who was prevented from attending by illness, a circumstance which was destined to have important and unfortunate consequences. Convinced that the time had come to abandon a hopeless position, Grafton proposed that the revenue act should be totally and entirely repealed, and was supported by Camden, Conway, and Granby. Late as such a proposal was, since the repeal, if agreed upon, could not be carried into effect until the next parliamentary session, there is no doubt that it was by far the wisest, and indeed the only, course that could be pursued, unless the government was prepared to quell rebellion by force of arms. Wisdom, however, is not always triumphant in the affairs of this world, often failing to overcome her enemies, prejudice and unenlightened self-interest; and so it was on this occasion. The other five ministers present—Gower, Weymouth, Rochford, North, and Hillsborough—believing that so complete a surrender would be construed as weakness, insisted that while the duties upon paper, glass, and colours should be

---

[1] *Cavendish Debates*, i. 190.

repealed as commercially unsound, that upon tea should be retained to testify that England had not abandoned the right of taxation ; and, profiting by the absence of Sir Edward Hawke, they carried their point by one vote. Thus, by the smallest possible majority, did a radically unsound policy prevail ; and the pride of England was saved to her own ultimate undoing. The colonists would think little of the duties remitted, and a great deal of the duty which remained ; the tax upon tea would stand as a sign of a hated principle, as a testimony to the fact that England still claimed the right of extorting money from her children across the seas, and as a perpetual incitement to colonial rebellion.[1]

Thus, the forces of darkness prevailed, and Grafton had once more cause to reflect upon the little influence he was able to exercise in his own cabinet. The evils of delay were aggravated by imperfect concession ; and in its American policy the ministry steadily and persistently pursued the road of failure. Nor was the darkness relieved by gleams of light elsewhere ; for, if in their treatment of the colonists the ministers stand convicted of stupidity and misunderstanding, in their handling of Wilkes, and the questions to which he gave rise, they were guilty of a violation of the law of the land. That inveterate disturber of ministerial peace was, indeed, to lead his pursuers a weary chase before being run to earth and to enjoy by far the greater share of the sport. Confined though he was as a convicted criminal to the king's bench prison, he was admirably equipped for making war upon the adminis-

[1] Grafton's *Autobiography*, pp. 229-233. Lord Camden was also further aggrieved because certain conciliatory expressions, which had been agreed upon at the meeting, were omitted from the circular letter in which Lord Hillsborough communicated the intention of the cabinet to the Colonies. *Ibid.*

tration, having lost nothing of the popularity which he had recaptured by his appearance at the poll. He was still the popular hero, the champion of liberty; and the tedium of his seclusion was much alleviated by the attentions of his many admirers. The "Sons of Liberty" of Boston complimented him by an address in which he was hailed as a martyr in the sacred cause of freedom; and this was but one of the many testimonies of respect he received from corporations as well as individuals. Nor was more material recognition lacking from thoughtful admirers who had the wit to understand that the body as well as the soul of the martyr needed sustenance. A well-wisher, resident in Rotterdam, presented him with a dozen of the best Burgundy; a native of Shropshire provided a collar of brawn, and had the forethought to pay the carriage; and the gentlemen of the Cave in Covent Garden, indignant at "the dangerous and unconstitutional manner with which Mr Wilkes has been treated, and as a small token of their abhorrence thereof," requested his acceptance of twenty guineas and "a hamper of their best liquor." [1]

Such gifts were doubtless acceptable enough; and if Wilkes had been the ordinary type of adventurer, he might have rested content with the disturbance he had already caused, and waited, until his term of imprisonment was over, before renewing his attack upon the administration. If he had been satisfied to profit by the generosity of his admirers, and rest upon his oars, it is possible that the ministers might have left him alone, and permitted him to remain a member of parliament, at least until he emerged from his confinement. He was well known to be a dangerous antagonist; and the royal advisers do not appear to have framed

[1] Add. MS., 30870, f. 45, f. 56, f. 81, f. 90.

any definite plan of campaign against him before the beginning of the session, being, on the whole, rather inclined to refrain from any hostile action, if Wilkes, on his part, abstained from giving new offence ; and we have it on fairly good authority that he received a private message from the Duke of Grafton to the effect that if he remained quiet no attack would be made upon him.[1] But, though the ministers might propose, it was Wilkes that disposed ; and tamely to acquiesce in accomplished facts was not in accordance with his nature or, indeed, with his interests. Fully alive to the fickleness of the mob who need to be constantly reminded of their heroes, he realised that the price of leisure and inactivity would be the loss of his popularity and, consequently, his own destruction. Such a mistake he could not afford to make, and he determined to renew the battle which at least some of his opponents would have gladly brought to an end.

It was on Monday, November 14th, that Sir Joseph Mawbey, a politician who claimed to be above party, but who was known to be a friend of the imprisoned senator, presented a petition from Wilkes, asking for redress of grievances. The petition, though suffered to lie upon the table, was not heard for many weeks ; and it is not improbable that the delay was intentional.

---

[1] Almon, in his *Memoirs of Wilkes*, denies the report that the ministers had decided upon a policy of expulsion before parliament met, and the assertion, as has been seen, is supported by independent evidence. " The report never had any foundation in truth : the editor here speaks from his own knowledge. There was no engagement made, nor resolution taken, to expel Mr Wilkes till he presented his petition. On the contrary, it was the wish of the Duke of Grafton that Mr Wilkes should take his seat without any obstruction at the end of his imprisonment or, perhaps, sooner." Almon then states that on November 10th, 1768, he received a message from the Duke of Grafton, through Mr Fitzherbert, asking him to tell Wilkes that " if he would not present his petition, the duke assured him, upon his honour, no attempt should be made in parliament against him " ; and that Wilkes refused to pay any heed. Almon's *Memoirs of John Wilkes*, 3, 293 *seq.*

Neither the ministers nor the opposition were probably anxious to plunge headlong into the fray, wisely preferring to see their way more clearly before taking decisive action. Rockingham had not been taken into Wilkes' secret counsels, having only heard of the petition forty-eight hours before it was presented,[1] and Grenville was studiously careful to conceal his opinion.[2] For Wilkes, however, to be ignored was worse than to be attacked ; and the petition having failed to provoke the desired storm, he resolved to precipitate a crisis, and goad his enemies into the path of persecution, by making a personal attack upon a. leading member of the cabinet.

On April 17th, 1768, Lord Weymouth, in his capacity of secretary of state, had addressed a letter to Daniel Ponton, one of the Surrey magistrates and chairman of the quarter sessions at Lambeth, giving warning of the spirit of riot and disorder which was abroad, and recommending both him and his fellow magistrates not to hesitate to call upon the military for assistance in the event of a serious tumult. The advice was neither untimely nor unnecessary. For many days disorderly conditions had prevailed in the metropolis ; and on May 10th, the day of the opening of parliament, a mob, which had gathered in the neighbourhood of the king's bench prison, in the hope of seeing Wilkes proceed to the house of commons, had vented their disappointment in disorder, threatening to take the prison by storm, and to drag their incarcerated hero in triumph to parliament. The riot act was read, and

---

[1] Add. MS., 35430, f. 130.

[2] " It is very odd," wrote Lord Hardwicke in November, " what Lord Lyttelton told me, that George Grenville would not impart to any of his friends what part he intended to take, and he described the debate in the house as the strangest he ever heard, and that administration seemed to have no settled plan any more than opposition." Add. MS., 35362, f. 235.

the soldiers summoned upon the scene ; and the tumult not subsiding, the order to fire was given, with the result that about five or six persons were killed. Popular indignation, already sufficiently kindled against the government, was intensified by this incident which was represented as a wanton massacre of innocent citizens ; and political capital was made out of the entirely immaterial circumstance that the soldiers employed on this occasion had been mainly drawn from Scotch regiments. Wilkes, always unscrupulous in regard to the choice of weapons, and ever ready to hurl a stone at the government, having obtained a copy of Weymouth's letter, published it in the *St James' Chronicle* on December 8th, with an introduction in which the affray of May 10th was represented as the outcome of a deliberate plot on the part of the ministers. " I send you," he wrote, " the following authentic state-paper, the date of which, prior by more than three weeks to the fatal 10th of May, shows how long the design had been planned before it was carried into execution, and how long a hellish project can be brooded over by some infernal spirits, without one moment's remorse." [1]

These were strong words and bitterly untrue ; and it is difficult not to believe that by this stroke of malice Wilkes intended to force the hand of the government. On any other hypothesis it is almost impossible to explain why he should launch this bolt when his petition was under consideration by the house of commons ; and, if the assumption be correct, he can be counted to have succeeded. The hearing of the petition had been postponed until January 27th, 1769 ; but from the moment that the letter appeared in the *St James' Chronicle*, the ministers, discarding the reserve

---

[1] Almon's *Memoirs of Wilkes*, 3, 273 ff. ; *Cavendish Debates*, 1, 106-107.

which had hitherto characterised their conduct, declared war upon their adversary, and determined upon his expulsion.   In spite of the protest of Lord Camden, who would have preferred that pardon rather than punishment should be meted out to the offender,[1] the cabinet agreed upon a policy of retaliation ; and although this decision was destined to lead to great disaster, it must be allowed in fairness that a certain amount of justification could be pleaded in support of it.   The king and the Bedford party in the cabinet, who had always been in favour of a drastic procedure, could now urge that it was vain to try and come to terms with a desperate man intent upon mischief ; and their contention had sufficient plausibility to make it difficult to resist.   It required great insight to perceive that, since he sought persecution, the most effective punishment for Wilkes would be forgiveness ; and Grafton was hardly the man to disentangle the threads of a complicated situation, and to adhere to a policy unintelligible to the average mind.   The victory of Wilkes was a victory of intellect over common-sense.

The attack was begun in the house of lords, which promptly voted the introduction to Weymouth's letter an insolent, scandalous and seditious libel ; and this resolution having been communicated to the house of commons by means of a conference, Lord North, in frank disregard of all principles of equity and justice, at once moved the concurrence of the lower house.

---

[1] " I do wish," wrote Camden to Grafton, early in January, ". . . that the present time could be eased of the difficulties that Mr W.'s business has brought upon the government : a fatality has attended it from the beginning, and it grows more serious every day.   Your grace and I have unfortunately differed. I wish it had been otherwise.   It is a hydra multiplying by resistance and gathering strength by every attempt to subdue it.   As the times are, I had rather pardon W. than punish him.   This is a political opinion, independent of the merits of the cause."   Grafton's *Autobiography*, p. 201.

Such precipitancy, however, was too much even for the seared and easy-going political conscience of the eighteenth century, no witnesses having yet been examined by the commons to prove the authorship of the libellous introduction ; and a revolt took place in the ministerial ranks. Recovering for the moment some of his old independence of spirit, Conway dared to oppose North, contending that " the great point we are now agitating is matter for grave discussion, and should be postponed "; and, much to North's disgust, a similar protest was made by Dunning, the solicitor-general.[1] The same cry was echoed by the speakers on the opposition side : Burke and Grenville united to deprecate such unnecessary and unconstitutional haste, and the former significantly inquired whether the house was prepared to model itself upon the court of star chamber.[2] For mere argument, however convincing, North cared little enough, but, fearing that he might be borne down by sheer weight of numbers,[3] he abandoned his motion, and it was agreed that evidence should be taken. In accordance with this resolution, witnesses were examined by the house on December 19th, and, after their testimony had been heard, it was agreed to postpone further action until January 27th, the day already appointed for hearing Wilkes' petition.[4]

This was, however, but a momentary check to the government, and when parliament re-assembled after the Christmas holidays, the attack was promptly renewed. It was, of course, a foregone conclusion that Wilkes' petition would be dismissed, and although

---

[1] Grafton's *Autobiography*, pp. 227-228.

[2] Almon's *Memoirs of Wilkes*, 3, 273 ff. ; *Cavendish Debates*, 1, 106-107 ; Add. MS., 35430, f. 136 ; Harris' *Hardwicke*, 3, 425-429.

[3] Add. MS., 35430, f. 136.

[4] Add. MS., 35608, f. 309 ; *Cavendish Debates*, 1, 111 ff.

three days were occupied in discussing it, this was but a concession to decency, with little relation to reality. The petition having been rejected on Wednesday, February 1st, the way was clear for further and more decisive action, and, on the day following, the house promptly set to work upon the introduction to Weymouth's letter. The evidence given in the previous December clearly pointed to Wilkes as the author ; but any difficulty, that might have arisen in establishing the proof, was averted by the victim himself. Summoned to the bar of the house, Wilkes avowed himself the author of the offensive introduction, and then proceeded, with characteristic effrontery, not only to describe the secretary of state's letter as " a bloody scroll," but to apologise to his hearers for using so mild and inadequate an expression. It was not, however, sufficient to prove that Wilkes was the author in order completely to justify further action : another obstacle in the path was the not unimportant question whether the house of commons was the proper body to take cognisance of the offence. The libel in question had been directed against a member of the house of lords, and it might reasonably be contended that it was the business of the peers, not of the commons, to punish the offender. Such was the line of argument adopted by Grenville who inquired whether it was intended that, whenever "a libel against any of his majesty's ministers in the other house is sent to this, we are to take it up," and the point was of a nature to appeal to Grenville's legal caste of mind, though hardly likely to strike a responsive chord in the average man not enamoured with precedents. The ministerial action was more against reason than law, and Burke spoke truly, and in the spirit of prophecy, when he declared that what was being done would go far to make Wilkes the most dangerous member of the state, and endear him still more to the riotous elements in the nation. " As I will ever pray," he said in conclusion, " for the peace of Jerusalem, so I say, let those who pursue these measures answer for the consequences." [1]

In spite, however, of Grenville's learning and Burke's wisdom, the big battalions carried the government to victory, the introduction being voted an insolent, scandalous, and seditious libel. If action had been stayed there, much harm might have been avoided; but, as all men knew, all that had been done hitherto was but a preliminary to the expulsion which had been decreed. On February 3rd, Lord Barrington moved that " John Wilkes, Esq., a member of this house, who hath at the bar of this house, confessed himself to be the author and publisher of what this house has resolved to be an insolent, scandalous, and seditious libel; and who has been convicted in the court of king's bench of having printed and published a seditious libel, and three obscene and impious libels, and, by the judgment of the said court, has been sentenced to undergo twenty months' imprisonment, and is now in execution under the said judgment, be expelled this house." Seconded by Rigby, one of the most abandoned members of the Bedford party, the motion was fiercely debated until three o'clock on the following morning; and in the course of the discussion much good advice was tendered to the ministers, which they would have done well to accept. A certain number of the speakers on the opposition side pointed out that, if the motion was carried, the house of commons would certainly lose a member whose popularity outside the house was unequalled, and that it was the business of the parliament to interpret, not to thwart, the will

[1] *Cavendish Debates*, i, 139.

of the nation. The speech of the evening, however, was made by George Grenville.[1] Carefully disclaiming all connection with either the ministry or the Rockingham party,[2] he announced that he was impelled by his conscience to stand up in defence of the man he had formerly attacked ; and, having made this personal confession, proceeded to riddle the rather thin ministerial armour with well-aimed shafts. It was comparatively easy for him to show the wanton iniquity of Barrington's motion, combining as it did four separate reasons for Wilkes' expulsion in one resolution. " Is it not evident," he inquired, " that by this unworthy artifice, Mr Wilkes may be expelled, although three parts in four of those who expel him should have declared against his expulsion upon every one of the articles contained in this charge." In clear and vigorous language he explained how some members would think his imprisonment sufficient ground for expulsion, others his conviction for libel, and others his attack upon Weymouth, and that the resolution would be carried by a majority unable to lay any claim to unanimity of opinion. Then, proceeding from the general to the particular, he enumerated singly the charges brought against Wilkes, and showed how insufficient they were to justify expulsion. He pointed out that it was not the business of the house of commons to punish a libel upon a peer of the realm, that imprisonment had never been reckoned a disqualification for a seat in the lower house, and that to expel Wilkes for his libel upon the king's speech and the " Essay on

---

[1] " My brother made," wrote Temple to Lady Chatham, " what was universally deemed the best speech he ever made against expulsion." Chatham Correspondence, 3, 349-350.

[2] " I am," remarked Grenville, " under no restraint either from this or that side of the house ; I know and feel my own independence on (sic) both." Cavendish Debates, 1, 159.

Woman " was a gross violation of that sacred principle of justice by which no man can be punished twice for the same offence. In conclusion he predicted the consequences of the expulsion, and his prophecy was only too literally fulfilled. " In the present disposition of the county of Middlesex," he said, " you cannot entertain a doubt, but that Mr Wilkes will be re-elected after his expulsion. You will then probably think yourselves under a necessity of expelling him again, and he will as certainly be again re-elected. What steps can the house then take to put an end to a disgraceful contest, in which their justice is arraigned, and their authority and dignity essentially compromised ? You cannot, by the rules of the house, rescind the vote for excluding Mr Wilkes in the same session in which it has passed, and I know but two other methods which you can pursue. They have both been the subject of common conversation, and are both almost equally exceptionable. You may refuse to issue a new writ, and by that means deprive the freeholders of this country of the right of choosing any other representative, possibly for the whole term of the present parliament. . . . If you do not adopt this proceeding, the other alternative will be to bring into this house, as the knight of the shire for Middlesex, a man chosen by a few voters only, in contradiction to the declared sense of a great majority of the freeholders on the face of the poll, upon a supposition, that all the votes of the latter are forfeited and thrown away, on account of the expulsion of Mr Wilkes." [1]

Thus spoke Grenville, to the astonishment of many who believed that in him Wilkes had a relentless enemy, and that his words carried some weight can be seen by the marked reduction of the usual ministerial

[1] *Cavendish Debates*, I, 151 ff.

majority, Barrington's motion being only carried by eighty-two votes.[1]   If this, however, had been the only consequence, the victory over Wilkes could be counted to have been easily and cheaply won : unfortunately, for the ministerial peace of mind, the events of the third of February were only the beginning of a long and arduous campaign.   Grenville had not long to wait before his prediction was fulfilled, and from the king's bench prison Wilkes contrived to draw the administration further and further into a morass from which they were never really to emerge.   All the advantage of the game lay with him, for he could rely with absolute certainty upon the loyalty of his constituents, and he would have been little short of a political craven, instead of a man of unusual courage, if he had accepted his first expulsion as a final defeat. Appealing once more to the faithful county of Middlesex, he was re-elected a member of parliament on February 16th, only to be again deprived of his seat on the following day when Lord Strange moved and carried that " John Wilkes, Esq., having been, in this session of parliament, expelled this house, was, and is, incapable of being elected a member to serve in this present parliament " ; and he encountered the same fate when he was elected for the third time in the month of March.   That he should be deprived of his place in parliament almost as soon as he became entitled to it, mattered little enough to him, for he could plume himself upon covering the administration with ridicule ; but it ought to be remembered that, futile as such proceedings were, and illegal as Lord Strange's motion was,[2] the royal advisers were in a situation

---

[1] Hist. MS. Comm. Weston Underwood MSS., 412.

[2] This motion was, of course, not legally sound, since it was beyond the power of either house, acting alone, to declare any man, not disqualified by law, incapable of being elected.

of no little difficulty. Wilkes could not be allowed to take his seat in the same session in which he had been expelled, for this would be to reduce the punitive powers of the house of commons to an idle sham ; and there were not a few politicians who, while firmly convinced that the original expulsion was a fatal and irretrievable error, were yet of the opinion that the house was bound by its own irrevocable decree. Thus George Grenville, while affirming that he would always resist " the expulsion of any man, unless I hear better reasons than any I have heard given for the expulsion of Mr Wilkes," declared that " the house has come to a resolution, that this gentleman is inadmissible : in this session, therefore, he cannot take his seat amongst us." [1] The reasoning was just, and in accordance with the custom of parliament ; and both Burke, who had protested so strongly on February 3rd, and Conway, who had stayed away rather than do his conscience wrong by voting with his colleagues,[2] were in agreement with Grenville.

Custom and precedence, however, are not always in accordance with the claims of common-sense ; and it was difficult to disguise the truth that the house of commons was in a thoroughly false position. Manacled by fetters of its own contriving, the house was obliged to sanction an evil because it could not repair it ; and with that broad and comprehensive grasp which characterises so many of his utterances, Burke explained the fundamental issues of what might, superficially, appear to be a rather idle controversy. " The honourable gentleman," he remarked in the course of one debate, " who moved the present resolution, has put it upon its true footing : he has described it as a contest of five hundred and fifty-eight members of

---

[1] *Cavendish Debates*, I, 348. [2] *Cavendish Debates*, I, 351-352.

this house against the county of Middlesex ; a contest between the electors and the elected ; the electors looking upon themselves to be the root of power. If ever that contest should spread beyond the county of Middlesex, it will be a contest between five hundred and fifty-eight members of this house and several millions of people. I do not say it is so ; but it is our business to show it is the contrary. This house has had contests with the crown ; this house has had contests with the house of lords ; but this is the first time it has had a contest with the people. Such a contest would be the most destructive civil war ever carried on." [1]

This was the constitutional, and therefore the most important, aspect of the struggle ; and into this dilemma had the house of commons been driven by a clever rascal and incompetent ministers. Both parties in the contest could claim in a measure that the law was on their side ; and therefore, if neither would give way, the controversy was legally insoluble. Though in asserting that Wilkes was incapable of being elected, the house had clearly exceeded its powers, it was impossible to deny the right of either house to inflict the penalty of expulsion ; but equally beyond dispute was the right of a constituency to elect as its representative any man not disqualified by law for a seat in the house of commons ; and neither conviction for libel, imprisonment, nor even expulsion, had ever been reckoned as a bar to re-election. Thus it seemed likely that, until the end of the session, Wilkes would be repeatedly elected by the county of Middlesex, and repeatedly declared incapable of sitting by the house of commons, and it is beyond all doubt that in this idle game the ministers would be the sufferers. What

---

[1] *Cavendish Debates*, I, 348 ff.

little dignity they still retained, and it was little enough, would be entirely lost in such an ignoble and ludicrous contest, and they decided to extricate themselves from a farcical situation by a flagrant violation of the law of the land, thus adding crime to folly. The first fruits of this determination were seen in April when Wilkes, standing for election for the fourth time, found himself opposed by Colonel Luttrell, a man of very doubtful reputation, who had been persuaded by the ministry to come forward as a candidate. Naturally enough, Luttrell failed to secure election, Wilkes being victorious over him by more than eight hundred votes ; but this by no means meant that the government had failed in its enterprise. The ministers had neither expected nor intended to defeat Wilkes at the poll ; and the inner meaning of Luttrell's candidature was revealed when the Middlesex election came for the fourth time under the consideration of the lower house. In accordance with what was by this time a well-established precedent, Wilkes, on April 14th, was expelled from the house ; but on this occasion this was but a preliminary move, for on the following day George Onslow moved that Luttrell should be declared to have been duly elected for the county of Middlesex. The motion was carried ; and when, a few weeks later, a petition, signed by fifteen freeholders of Middlesex protesting against such an infringement of their legal rights, was discussed in the house, it was again resolved that " Henry Lawes Luttrell, Esq., is duly elected a knight of the shire to serve in this present parliament."

That such a solution of the problem was illegal there is no doubt, and it was not rendered any less illegal by the fact that there was no court in the land which could call the house of commons to account for its action. It is clear that the lower house had the right

of deciding contested election, and of expelling its own
members ; but in the exercise of these functions it
acted as a judicial, not as a legislative body, concerned
not with the making but with the execution of law. It
is an axiom of the constitution that neither house of
parliament acting alone has any legislative power ;
yet the recognition of Luttrell as the member for
Middlesex was a legislative rather than a judicial act,
for it could only be justified on the ground that Wilkes
was legally incapable of being elected, a contention
not supported by existing law. Eligibility for election
to parliament was emphatically a legal right, based
upon statute and common law ; and therefore, in
passing over Wilkes in favour of Luttrell, the house
of commons took upon itself to make a new disqualification, and thereby to create law. Plausible arguments
were, indeed, urged in support of the ministerial action,
more than sufficient to confuse men unversed in legal
subtleties and not trained to think clearly ; but they
were one and all fallacious, resting upon a confusion
between legislative and judicial power. " The lawyers
for the court," wrote Burke to his friend, Lord
Charlemont, " were, as they have generally been for
some time past, bold and profligate. The chief arguments which they insisted upon, were, that when a court,
having competent jurisdiction in a cause, has determined, its determination is the law of the land until
it is reversed ; that we had jurisdiction in all causes
relative to election ; that we had already determined
this point ; it was therefore against order, to debate it
again, and against law to contradict the determination
of a court from whence no appeal lay. That the house
had a power to qualify or disqualify without any other
rule than their own discretion ; and Blackstone went
so far as to say that ' if he affirmed that we could make

laws, he could support himself by respectable authorities.' " [1]

If such arguments were sound, a single house of parliament could override law, saddle constituencies with members which they had never elected, and exercise a despotism almost as unchecked as that of a Tudor monarch ; and such a doctrine had only to be advanced to encounter sincere and emphatic protest. Fierce and protracted were the debates in the lower house ; and the weakness of the government's position is attested by the reduction in its majority.[2] Indeed, all the weight of argument lay with the opposition, and the debates, barren as they were in practical effect, are rich in expositions of true constitutional doctrine. " The man," exclaimed Grenville on April 15th, " who will contend that a resolution of the house of commons is the law of the land is a most violent enemy of his country; be he who or what he will " ; and the same sentiments were expressed by Burke, Dowdeswell, Wedderburn, Barré, and, indeed, by nearly every speaker who raised his voice in protest against the violation of the law.

Undoubtedly, the hero of this parliamentary contest was George Grenville ; and against his many short-comings as a statesman, his conduct at this national and constitutional crisis ought to be remembered. As will be seen later, his enemies were prepared to give the most sinister explanation of his defence of Wilkes ; but it is not necessary to believe that politicians are always swayed by the basest motives, and there was nothing inconsistent in the course of

---

[1] Hist. MSS. Comm., 12th Report, Appendix, Part x., 293-294.

[2] On April 15th, the numbers on a division were 197 to 143; and on May 8th, 221 to 152. For a general account of the two debates, see *Cavendish Debates*, 1, 366 ff., 406 ff; Hist. MSS. Comm., 12th Report, Appendix, Part x., 293-294 ; Chatham's Correspondence, 3, 357-359.

action which Grenville pursued. He fought for the supremacy of the law rather than for Wilkes ; and a reverence for law had always been a dominating passion in his rather narrow mind. Indeed, the same insistent belief in principle which led him to tax the American colonists in 1765, impelled him to stand up in defence of Wilkes four years later ; and his true greatness lay in successfully overcoming the prejudice which he must have contracted against the man who, at one time, had been a thorn in his flesh. But the appearance of Grenville in the unaccustomed rôle of a champion of freedom had a greater importance than as merely effecting his own personal reputation ; and it was only natural that the Rockingham whigs, or at least some of them, beheld in him at this moment a very Daniel come to judgment. To some of the more sanguine it seemed that Wilkes, who had threatened to be a cause of still further division, might prove to be a bond of union between the two parties in opposition ; and that the politicians, who had quarrelled over the government of the colonies, might unite in defence of the English constitution. While the fight in parliament was still continuing, and before the law had been actually broken by the government, it was rumoured that an alliance had been concluded between Grenville and the Rockingham whigs ; [1] and though the report had no foundation in fact, it witnesses to the popular opinion as to the probable outcome of the struggle on behalf of Wilkes. Indeed, the time had come round again for another attempt at a rapprochement between the two sections of the opposition ; and in true English fashion a dinner was fixed upon as the best means of laying the foundations of future harmony. Accordingly, when on May 8th the Rockinghams and

[1] Grenville Papers, 4, 412-414.

the Grenvilles were gathered together in the same division lobby, Dowdeswell seized the occasion to suggest that they should dine together on the following day at the Thatched House Tavern. The proposal was agreed to, and on May 9th more than seventy of the opposition met at the appointed tavern, George Grenville, as well as the leaders of the Rockingham party, being included in the number. A formidable list of twenty-one toasts, beginning with, " The king and constitution ; the right of electors ; the law of the land," and ending with " To our next happy meeting," was conscientiously worked through ; and under the mellowing influence of good food and drink, old hostilities were forgotten and new hopes born. " The whole meeting," in the words of Temple who, though not present, probably received an account of what passed from Grenville, "appeared to be that of brothers, united in one great constitutional cause " ; and another opponent of the government remarked, in a letter to a friend, that " it is to be hoped from the occurrences of the day that all the sub-divisions of the minority will be consolidated into one grand constitutional party." [1]

Such, indeed, was the hope of many ; but serious obstacles would have to be overcome, before it could be brought even near to realisation. The need for such an union was certainly greater than it had ever yet been ; for, the parliamentary session having ended on May 9th, the time had now come for the defenders of Wilkes to appeal to the country against a law-breaking house of commons, and to bring popular pressure to bear upon the ministry and its supporters. Nor were they likely to appeal in vain, the administra-

[1] Chatham Correspondence, 3, 357 ff. ; Walpole's Memoirs, 3, 242 ; Hist. MSS. Comm., 12th Report, Appendix, Part x., 294.

tion having by this time become more discredited than ever. The mysterious Junius had already begun the publication of those virulent epistles which, whatever their defects, will always rank high in the annals of vituperative literature ; but it hardly needed his vitriolic pen to arouse the wrath of a nation aflame with indignation against a house of commons which had defied it. There is no shadow of doubt that Wilkes had won the stakes for which he had played ; and any inconvenience he may have suffered was amply compensated for by the popularity he enjoyed. His sufferings, often grotesquely exaggerated, formed the theme of conversation in obscure villages and hamlets, and he enjoyed true fame since his name was a household word to many who had not the slightest idea of the cause of his imprisonment or expulsion.[1] Neither Wilkes nor his supporters were likely to make the mistake of allowing such a favourable soil to go untilled ; and the popular agitation on his behalf began many weeks before the parliamentary session came to an end. A meeting of his principal supporters was held on February 21st at the London Tavern, at which a subscription for the relief of his financial necessities was started, and a society formed, styled " The Supporters of the Bill of Rights," and pledged to

[1] Writing to Lord Dartmouth in August 1769, the Rev. John Newton states how " a few months I heard that some of them in their prayers at home had been much engaged for the welfare of Mr Wilkes. As the whole town of Olney is remarkably loyal and peaceable with regard to the government, I was rather surprised that gentleman should have partisans amongst our serious people. Upon inquiry I found they had just heard of his name, and that he was in prison ; comparing the imperfect account they had of him with what they read in their Bibles, they took it for granted that a person so treated must of necessity be a minister of the gospel, and under that character they prayed earnestly that he might be supported and enlarged. Your lordship will perhaps be surprised that in this time of general ferment the whole story of Mr Wilkes should be utterly unknown to many people in a market-town within sixty miles of London. But this is the fact." Hist. MSS. Comm., 15th Report, Appendix, Part i., 190-191.

maintain the English constitution.[1] This new organisation was not slow in getting to work, drawing up,
shortly after the intrusion of Luttrell into the house
of commons, a petition to the king, rehearsing the
popular grievances and calling for the dismissal of
the ministers.[2] After being widely signed, the petition
was presented to the king on May 24th, and was received
in contemptuous silence by the monarch who, at the
outset of his reign, had professed to make war on
faction in the name and in the interests of his people.[3]

Nor was this the only manifestation that not an
inconsiderable proportion of the nation had declared
for Wilkes, and against George III. and his advisers.
Various counties and boroughs began to send instructions to their representatives in parliament,
directing them to support Wilkes and the English
constitution ; and although the adherents of the court
engineered counter-addresses, professing unbounded
loyalty to the court and faith in the government, it
was notorious that these were sometimes only obtained
with very great difficulty ; and they could hardly
fail to be discredited by the obviously artificial character
of their origin.[4] Indeed, the great pains taken to
create the impression that the ministry enjoyed the
favour of the country was in itself a proof that the
reverse was true ; and the wisest amongst the supporters of the court must have realised that they had
taken a plunge into deep waters from which they
might not possibly emerge in safety. Men, acquainted
with the history of the previous century, were reminded,
by what they saw going on around them, of the days of

---

[1] Walpole's Memoirs, 3, 225.
[2] Hist. MSS. Comm. Weston Underwood MSS., 415 ; Walpole's Letters,
5, 162, 163.
[3] Bedford Correspondence, 3, 409.
[4] Walpole's Memoirs, 3, 225, 227, 231.

Charles II. when the country was divided up into petitioners and abhorrers ; and the parallel was by no means far-fetched.[1] Yet the misfortunes of the state are sometimes the benefits of a political party ; and if, before the next session, Rockingham and Grenville could settle their differences and rally the country to their side, they might return to parliament as the leaders of an united party approved by the nation, and use their newly-acquired strength to destroy the administration, and fight their way into the royal closet at the point of the sword. Divided and leaderless, the ministry could hardly withstand an onslaught pressed to the very end.

If such was the outcome of the dinner at the Thatched House Tavern, those who had attended that convivial gathering would have ample cause for self-congratulation ; and it was not only Burke who understood that " if we mean to get redress, we must strengthen the hands of the minority within doors, by the accession of the public opinion, strongly declared to the court, which is the source of the whole mischief." [2] What the Rockinghams had so eagerly and, hitherto so vainly, waited for, the approval of the people, now appeared to be within their grasp; and it was not necessary for them so much to create an agitation against the government as to use one already in existence. No sooner was parliament prorogued than the king and his ministers began to be inundated with a flood of petitions which, though varying in violence, agreed in denouncing the admission of Luttrell as a gross breach of the constitution. A most violent petition by the Livery of London, rehearsing past as well as present

---

[1] " Does not all this nonsense on all sides," wrote Lord Hardwicke, " put you in mind of the dregs of Charles the 2nd's reign with addressing and abhorring." Add. MS., 35362, f. 240.

[2] Burke's Correspondence, 1, 179-183.

grievances, was carried almost unanimously at a crowded meeting at the Guildhall on June 24th; [1] and, a few weeks later, the electors of Westminster, going still further, petitioned the king to dissolve a parliament which had betrayed its trust by violating the rights of the freeholders of Great Britain. [2] The example

[1] " It is in substance," wrote Burke to Rockingham, " the same as that from Middlesex ; but I think it brings it more home to the king's ministers, not the present only, but the past ; and calls for redress in very strong terms. . . . On the question for the petition there was not a 'single hand against it. One man, indeed, attempted to make a speech in opposition to it, but his voice was drowned in a cry to throw him off the hustings." Rockingham Memoirs, 2, 96-101.

[2] An interesting, though not an impartial, account of the meeting which approved the Westminster petition is given by a correspondent of Lord Hardwicke. " I attended," he writes, " the meeting at Westminster Hall this morning. The company began to assemble soon after ten o'clock, and kept increasing till twelve, about which time came into the hall Sir Robert Bernard, Dr Wilson, Prebendary of Westminster, and Mr Jones, who has been President of the Bill of Rights Society, who, together with Humphrey Cotes, were all the people of note that I could learn of. They were received into the hall with the shouts of between 2 and 3000 people, to say the most, (tho' those who were fond of the meeting estimated them above double that number), and proceeded on to the middle of the hall against the court of common pleas, where a chair was placed upon a sort of carpenter's work-board, which was filled by Sir Robert Bernard. The company were then addressed by Mr Jones who told them the occasion of their meeting was to consider of a petition to his majesty for redress of grievances, which petition Sir Robert Bernard had in his hand, and would read to them if agreeable. To which they shouted consent, and Sir Robert accordingly read it, having first recommended it by a short speech for that purpose ; and it was received with violent shouts of applause, both of huzzas and clapping of hands. The petition was seconded by (some say) Mr Martin, Sergeant Glynn's Attorney, but others say it was one Lycett, an upholsterer in Golden Square. The subject of the petition was the violation of the privileges of the freeholders of Middlesex, who, having elected Mr Wilkes by a very great majority, the parliament, being corrupted and influenced by the ministry, had set him aside, and declared Colonel Luterell to be duly elected. They, therefore, pray that his majesty would dissolve his parliament, and cause a new one to be elected as soon as possible. There were several copies of the petition drawn out upon large sheets of parchment, and carried to different parts of the hall for all those to sign who could write their names, and chose so to do ; for I found that was all that was required ; no place of abode or profession being added. The majority of the assembly were rather well dressed, creditable-looking people, most of which, I believe, were there, like myself, out of curiosity, for that part of the company who seemed eager for signing were of the shabby sort." Add. MS., 35609, f. 32.

of London and Westminster, moreover, was followed in more distant parts of the kingdom, various counties petitioning for a redress of grievances. When the petition of the county of Wiltshire was presented for approval to a meeting at Devizes, the clergyman of the parish and the eldest son of Lord Holland were the only dissentients ; [1] and although we are told that the Worcestershire petition was " received but coldly by the major part of the county," the information comes from a hostile and not very well-informed source.[2] " The spirit of petitioning," wrote Burke at the end of July, "extends and strengthens," [3] and the best testimony to the success of the movement is afforded by the strenuous efforts of the ministerialists to check and restrain it. Had it not been for the active intervention of certain adherents of the government, it is highly probable that many more counties would have presented addresses of complaint. It was due to Rigby that no petition came from Essex, and the same service was rendered to the government in Norfolk by the Townshends and the Walpoles, who mustered in strength at the Norwich assizes, ready to oppose a petition should one be presented.[4] The aged Duke of Bedford, though now almost on the verge of the grave, endured the fatigue of a journey into Devonshire in order to use his influence in that county against a petition,

[1] Add. MS., 35609, f. 34.

[2] " At this distance," wrote Charles Cocks to Lord Hardwicke, " I can give but a poor account of the Worcestershire petition. It was first proposed by a shattered brain fellow, Holland Cooksey (who is chairman, to the disgrace of the county), at the Session. A meeting was afterwards advertised at the Assizes which, nothing being then done, was adjourned to the race week ; it was again accordingly proposed and signed by a few gentlemen (after being corrected by Mr Dowdeswell) and by some freeholders, but I have understood, from time to time, that it has been received but coldly by the major part of the county." Add. MS. 35609, f. 43.

[3] Burke's Correspondence, I, 179-183.

[4] Hist. MSS. Comm. Lothian MSS., 286-287.

and was rewarded for his self-sacrifice by being set
upon by the mob, both at Exeter and at Honiton.[1]

Thus, the contest was transferred from the parliament to the country at large ; and it is by no means
easy to estimate the success of Wilkes' supporters.
Horace Walpole, an unfavourable critic both of
Rockingham and Grenville, sneeringly remarks in his
Memoirs that the opposition " had polled the nation,
and the majority by far was against them. Not a
dozen counties, and only a few boroughs, had petitioned.
. . . The greater part of England, all Scotland to a man,
and Wales, were against them." [2] This judgment,
however, is somewhat jaundiced, and certainly cannot
be accepted without reservation. It is necessary to
remember, not only that the government must often
have been able to use local influence to suppress the
real opinion of a county, but that the organisation
for the expression of public opinion was very different,
and decidedly inferior, to what is at the present day ;
and that the men, who appealed to the country on
behalf of Wilkes, suffered from the disabilities which
must always hamper the activities of constitutional
pioneers. The mere fact that nearly twelve counties
had united in protesting against the government was
in itself evidence of wide-spread discontent, and, at
least, a favourable beginning if nothing more ; and
the opponents of the administration would have been
little deserving of success if they had despised and disregarded the assistance which the people offered them.
They had, however, been too well schooled by adversity
to fall into this blunder, and were quite prepared to
profit by the favouring turn of circumstance. Nor
were they unmindful of the necessity of healing their

---

[1] *Cavendish Debates*, 1, 621 ; Walpole's Memoirs, 3, 251-252.
[2] Walpole's Memoirs, 4, 28.

internal dissensions before renewing the attack in parliament. Early in July, Edmund Burke informed Rockingham that at least an appearance of union with Grenville was essential to the safety of the party,[1] and it did not seem that such an alliance was so entirely outside the range of practical politics as it had hitherto appeared. Temporarily sinking old grievances, Grenville and Rockingham had joined in defence of Wilkes and the constitution, and both approved of the policy of appealing to the nation, though on this point there was far greater eagerness on the part of Grenville than Rockingham who, with true aristocratic prejudice, only gave a very reluctant approval to what he disliked as a popular agitation.[2] Both working for the same end, it might be expected that the two leaders, forgetting ancient discord, would unite in harmony; but the path of party politics is no smoother than that of love, and the situation was fundamentally changed in the twinkling of an eye by the reappearance of Chatham upon the political scenes.

Ever since his resignation in the previous October, Chatham had been slowly but perceptibly mending in health, and by the summer of 1769 he had almost completely shaken off that depression of spirit which had for so long clouded his brain, and was once more ready to play a part in public life. For nigh upon two years secluded at Hayes and Hampstead, he had

---

[1] Burke's Correspondence, 1, 168-172.

[2] Burke's Correspondence, 1, 173-179. Grenville is far less undecided, informing Lord Buckinghamshire that " if the body of the freeholders are dissatisfy'd, and think that their rights . . . are violated by the late determination in the house of commons, they may certainly remonstrate against it in the proper manner, and I take it for granted will do so. . . . If they do, they will give weight to the resistance which has been made to that measure in the house of commons, and prevent the like measure for the future." Hist. MSS. Comm. Lothian MSS., 287-288.

been, in a measure, forgotten ; and great was the excitement when on July 7th he visited the king. Politicians, reminded of the days when the appearance of William Pitt at court had generally intimated that a ministry was tottering to its fall, circulated wild reports of impending changes ; but Charles Yorke spoke more truly when he declared that Chatham's " visit at court was a phenomenon which occasioned a good deal of unnecessary speculation, being only a necessary and decent ceremonial on the recovery of his health." [1] The arrival of Chatham in London certainly did not mean the instant fall of the Grafton ministry, but, from his discourse to the king, it was abundantly clear that he bore no goodwill to the ministers. Expressing his disapproval of the compact with the East India Company, and hinting his dislike of the attack upon Wilkes, he frankly asked the royal forgiveness in the event of his being compelled to go into opposition.[2] From the point of view of George III., no conversation could be less satisfactory. In former days Chatham had shown what a dangerous enemy he could be ; and, if he embarked upon a career of opposition, supported by a discontented country, it was only too likely that the ministers might be intimidated into surrender, and the king, driven to abandon a right for which he had fought, be compelled to take his advisers at the dictation of his people.

Nor was it only George III. who had cause to fear the consequences that might flow from Chatham's resumption of political activity : the Rockingham whigs had equally good reason to be alarmed. They had not forgotten, and were not likely to forget, that their fall from office in 1766 had been largely due to him, that he had consistently rejected their friendly

[1] Add. MS., 35362, f. 249.　　[2] Grafton's *Autobiography*, p. 237.

overtures, and that, while his health had lasted, he had waged increasing war against that party system which they believed to be the mainspring of ordered political life.[1] They had no reason to suppose that his old animosity had expired or even diminished, and could not but know that a deadly weapon of attack lay ready to his hand. Chatham had appeared at the critical moment when the Rockinghams and the Grenvilles were converging towards an alliance ; and it seemed within his power to blast the hope of such an union being formed. If he still cherished his antagonism to Lord Rockingham and his followers, he might easily frustrate their plans by throwing in his lot with his two brothers-in-law, Grenville and Temple, thus constituting a family party which would be equally opposed both to the Rockinghams and the ministry.

Such was the danger presented by the restoration of Chatham to health, and it was certainly neither remote nor fanciful; for the foundations upon which the Grenville brotherhood might be reconstituted had been laid many weeks before the summer of 1769. As far back as the autumn of the previous year, Temple had paid two visits to Hayes within the space of a fortnight ; and, unusually privileged, had been permitted to see and converse with Chatham. Contemporaries at once jumped to the conclusion that this incident had a political significance, that the differences, which had separated between the two kinsmen, now no longer existed, and that Chatham, having dissociated himself from the ministry, was now resolved upon an

---

[1] Burke's hatred of Chatham was revealed in his comments upon the latter's audience with the king. " If he was not sent for," he wrote, " it was only humbly to lay a reprimand at the feet of his most gracious master, and to talk some significant, pompous, creeping, explanatory, ambiguous matter, in the true Chathamic style, and that's all." Burke's Correspondence, I, 173-179.

alliance with two of his most bitter political enemies.[1] As generally happens, public opinion, in its lust for excitement, overshot the mark, and favoured a theory which the actual facts did not support. There was no evidence that politics were introduced into the conversation at Hayes, and, as Temple had undertaken the first journey to his brother-in-law in response to an invitation from Lady Chatham, it is reasonable to imagine that the visit was more of a friendly than a political nature. Yet, to fly to the other extreme, and to view the reconciliation which took place as exclusively domestic, would be to draw too hard and fast a line between the private and public lives of politicians. Temple was far too alert an intriguer not to realise that, while obeying the dictates of his heart, he might yet be laying the foundation of an invaluable parliamentary alliance ; and his remark to Grenville, who, it was rumoured, was about to visit Hayes [though apparently the project was never executed], " to keep his mind void of suspicion," is not without significance.[2] It would seem as though Temple realised that the sooner a family compact was signed the better ; and that a triumvirate consisting of Chatham, Grenville, and

[1] " I have the joy to find," wrote Lord Temple in an undated letter to Lady Chatham, but which from internal evidence appears to have been written shortly after his first visit to Hayes on November 25th, 1768, " my first visit of Friday gives either universal satisfaction or alarm ; the first affords me the most solid pleasure, tho' the latter is not without its delights." Chatham MSS., P. R. O., 1st series, vol. lxiii.

[2] Whether Grenville actually visited Hayes at this time is a point in dispute. We know that Temple went there on November 25th and December 5th ; and that on November 28th Lord Hardwicke told Charles Yorke that Grenville intended to visit Hayes that day. Relying upon a statement of the Prussian Ambassador, Dr von Ruville asserts that Grenville dined at Hayes on November 29th ; but this is, at least, open to doubt, for in a letter written in July, 1769, Lord Hardwicke states that " Mr Grenville was to come over from Wotton, which will have been his first interview with Lord Chatham since the last breach amongst them." Add. MS., 35362, f. 235 ; Rockingham Memoirs, 2, 102-103 ; Von Ruvilles' *William Pitt, Graf. von Chatham*, 3, 274 ; Grenville papers, 4, 403, 404, 406.

himself, might effectively restore the shattered fortunes of the country. In a letter written to Lady Chatham during the parliamentary struggle over Wilkes, he relates how he has returned to London " perfectly well recovered by the salutary air of Hayes, and was at the Horse-Guards by thirty-five minutes past one. I am not, however, quite so well this day as yesterday, but am setting out for the field of battle, well replenished with my dinner. I had a long conversation last night which ended most fraternally and amicably, so that I have nothing left to wish on that score." [1] More direct evidence is afforded by a letter written to the same lady on January 24th, 1769, in which Temple relates, with obvious jubilation, how he has been assured " that if the king would call for the assistance of a certain triumvirate, the whole would stop in the twinkling of an eye, and rage be converted into joy and approbation, with every testimony of it that could be wished. This, I believe, is not far from the true mark." [2]

Scattered and fragmentary as these hints may appear to be, they are, at least, sufficient to justify the assumption that, whatever was passing through the mind of Chatham, Grenville and Temple were at least intent upon securing his assistance ; and men began to suspect that something was in the air. Thus by suspicious politicians, Grenville's defence of Wilkes was regarded as a sop for Temple who seems to have known of Chatham's disapproval of the policy of expulsion. [3]

---

[1] Chatham MSS., P. R. O., 1st series, vol. lxii. [2] *Ibid.*

[3] The Wilkes' Papers in the British Museum include an undated letter from Almon to Wilkes which runs as follows : " Last night my Lord Temple read to me a letter he had just received from Lady Chatham, assuring his lordship that Lord Chatham was strongly against the measure of expelling Mr Wilkes. These are her ladyship's words." A note in another hand, states, " This letter was written a few days previous to Mr Wilkes' first expulsion, which happened on the third day of February, 1769." Add. MS., 30870, f. 107.

" But, above all," wrote a member of parliament concerning the debates on Wilkes, " it would astonish me that Mr G. G. should be one of that minority, if I did not recollect his late reconciliation and now perfect intimacy with Lord Temple," [1] and the judgment, though in reality superficial enough, must have been fairly widely accepted, being the easiest though not the truest, explanation of the apparent inconsistency of a doctrinaire statesman. Nor were men left long in doubt as to the degree with which Chatham was prepared to identify himself with the Grenville party. On July 28th, Burke saw him pass through Beaconsfield on his way to Stowe, accompanied by his wife and four children, and followed by a train of " two coaches and six, with twenty servants, male and female." [2] Thus, in true patriarchal fashion did Chatham proceed on his journey, and that the visit had a political significance is beyond all doubt. While he sojourned at Stowe, Grenville came over from Wotton expressly to pay his respects ; and the compliment was returned, Chatham visiting Wotton where he remained for two or three days. Unfortunately, we know nothing of the questions that were discussed at these meetings ; but it may be safely assumed that politics were by no means forbidden. " I made a visit," wrote Hardwicke to Charles Yorke, " . . . to Stowe. . . . The noble owner was very polite and obliging. He expected Lord and Lady Chatham as yesterday, and seemed pleased with the idea of a perfect agreement, private and public, in that family." [3] Moreover, we know that Grenville was well enough pleased with the union which had been effected, in-

---

[1] Hist. MSS. Comm. Weston Underwood MSS., 412.
[2] Burke's Correspondence, pp. 179-183.
[3] Rockingham Memoirs, 2, 102-103.

forming a friend that " whatever effect it may have
in the political world, where it may possibly occasion
much speculation, I am persuaded that our friends
will be glad of an event which will contribute so much
to our domestic happiness ";[1] and Lord Lyttelton,
wishing Temple joy of " your endeavours for the
reunion of your family, which is the great step towards
the reunion of the nation," advises the three brothers
" to stick close to one another, and then, if this country
can be saved, your joint efforts will save it." [2]

Thus time, which heals so many sores and makes up
so many quarrels, had brought about a union which,
a few years before, would have seemed impossible ;
and the political situation was indeed fundamentally
altered by what had taken place. Permitted a choice
between an alliance with the Rockinghams or the
Grenvilles, Chatham had deliberately taken the latter
alternative, and the consequences might truly be
disastrous to the party thus left out in the cold. To
the more anxious of Rockingham's followers, it must
have seemed that the summer of hope had been suddenly
turned into the winter of despair ; and that fortune
had idly tempted them by the sight of a prize safely
placed beyond their reach. As early as July 9th, Burke
had begun to anticipate with alarm " a family system
which, in my opinion, precludes all possibility of a
good event " [3] and his fears must have been rather
intensified than diminished by what had since
happened. If the present was judged in the light of
the past it seemed only too likely that Chatham had
been driven to choose the Grenvilles by his hatred of
the Rockinghams ; and it was this thought which
struck terror into the hearts of many, Burke somewhat

---

[1] Hist. MSS. Comm. Lothian MSS., pp. 287-288.
[2] Grenville Papers, 4, 436.   [3] Burke's Correspondence, 1, 173-179.

bitterly complaining to Rockingham that no information could be gained " of the dispositions of Lord
Chatham, or of what he would have pass for his dispositions, with regard to your lordship and your connexion, and that past experience had informed us of
nothing but his enmity to your whole system of men
and opinions." [1]

Yet, much as Burke might dislike the man whom
he believed to be responsible for the evil condition of
the country and the government, he was not prepared
openly to affront either Grenville or Temple because
of their alliance with Chatham, and was even ready
to work with them as long as it was understood that
the union was confined to the question of the Middlesex
election. He took an active part in promoting the
Buckinghamshire petition which was approved by
Grenville and warmly supported by Temple,[2] enter-
tained at Beaconsfield Thomas Whately who was known
to enjoy Grenville's political confidence,[3] and was
largely instrumental in overcoming Rockingham's
objections to the practice of petitioning,[4] thus con-
ducting his leader into line, not only with the Grenvilles,
but also with Chatham who heartily approved this
method of bringing popular pressure to bear upon the
crown and the ministers.[5] But further than that Burke
refused to go, fearing to purchase temporary advantage
by the sacrifice of a principle ; and he did what he could

[1] Burke's Correspondence, 1, 194-197.
[2] Grenville Papers, 4, 440-452 ; Burke's Correspondence, 1, 191-194.
" Our petition," wrote Temple to Lady Chatham in October, " goes on here
to my heart's content. As Lord Shelburne is a great enemy to faction, he
would not permit his name to be used at High Wickham, nor his steward
to go round the town with the person who carried it round, notwithstanding
which, and a very adverse neighbourhood of gentlemen, thirty-two out of
fifty-four signed." Chatham MSS. P. R. O., 1st series, vol. lxii.
[3] Grenville Papers, 4, 440-452 ; Burke's Correspondence, 1, 186-191.
[4] Rockingham Memoirs, 2, 104-106.
[5] Grenville Papers, 4, 440-452.

to restrain the enthusiasm of the more ardent members of the party who, alive to the advantages of an united opposition, were anxious that direct overtures should be made to the Grenvilles and Chatham. Thus, when early in October Thomas Townshend pressed the adoption of such a policy, both Burke and Rockingham were emphatic in their opinion that it would be destructive to the cause which they had at heart.[1] " At this minute," wrote Burke, " your lordship has, undoubtedly, a very delicate game to play, in which you cannot disavow this supposed union without giving great advantage to the common enemy ; or admit too much of it, without the risk of putting yourself in the power of your allies, on the one hand, or giving them a pretence to charge you with breach of faith, on the other " ; and it is interesting to note that Temple also appears to have been fully aware of this doubtful attitude taken up by the leaders of the Rockingham party ; and, which is more surprising, to have been fairly satisfied with it. " Without seeming offended," wrote Burke, who had a long conversation with him, " the turn of his discourse indicated at times that he had heard of your lordship, and your friends, expressing a disrelish to their junto, though he did not speak out upon it so clearly, as to make me quite satisfied that this was his meaning. He said that as we had got to see one another, and to act together, he hoped there would be no retrospect, no charge, and no recrimination. That we had done each other a thousand acts of unkindness ; let us make amends by a thousand acts of friendship. He was of opinion that, let what would happen, the great point for us, and the country, would be to get rid of the present administration, which could only be effected by the appearance of union and

[1] Burke's Correspondence, I, 194-197 ; 207-214.

confidence. He said, and he repeated it, that, to be
sure, there was no treaty, expressed or implied, to bind
the parties in honour to one another, or to any measure,
except the establishment of the rights of the freeholders.
In everything else we were both free—' we were both
free to play the fool as much as we pleased, mark that.'
He said these last words with a good deal of emphasis.
. . . On the whole I was glad to find that we understood one another thoroughly, on the nature and
extent of our coalition ; which once being mutually
explained, will not render it necessary to say anything
upon it publicly, so as to give an advantage against
us to the common enemy." [1]

It is very much open to doubt whether such an
union, so narrow and contracted in its scope, and so
lacking in the spirit of trust and friendship, could ever
be really effective as a political force. January 9th,
1770, had been fixed for the meeting of parliament, and
if in reality the salvation of the country depended upon
the overthrow of the ministry, then, surely, Chatham,
the Grenvilles, and Lord Rockingham ought to have
agreed upon a comprehensive programme, and proclaimed their alliance to the world. That this was
not done, that old animosities were not completely
forgotten, does not appear to have been the fault of
either Chatham or his brothers-in-law, the burden of
responsibility resting more upon Rockingham and
Burke. As the session drew near, Chatham, with
something of his old fire, publicly announced his
intention of denouncing the ministers for their foreign,
their colonial, and their domestic policy, and expressly
stated that he would never sit at the council without
Rockingham and his supporters, for " he, and he alone,"
he is reported as saying, " has a knot of spotless friends

<hr>

[1] Burke's Correspondence, 1, 207-214.

such as ought to govern this kingdom." [1]   To Burke, moreover, Temple " expressed the most earnest desire of the union of all the parties, . . . wished that all memory of past animosities might be worn away, and stated very strongly, and, as I have since found, very truly, the hopes which the court built upon the supposed impossibility of such an union." [2]   Not an over effusive welcome, however, was extended to these friendly overtures. Burke, unable to rid himself of the suspicion which he had contracted against Temple and his brother, published abroad that his party was only united with the Grenvilles on the question of the Middlesex election,[3] and Rockingham found it difficult to believe that Chatham had sincerely abandoned his crusade against the party system. Early in the new year, shortly before the meeting of parliament, Rockingham gave John Yorke a frank account of the political situation. " He had been strongly pressed, he said," wrote Yorke to Lord Hardwicke, " on coming to town to admit the E. of C——m if he called upon him, and it was pretended that his lordship wished it. He said he was very reluctant, but yeilded (*sic*) at last ; and then asked those, who pressed him so warmly, what they would advise him to, in case his lordship should be suddenly taken with something that should induce him to desire the visit should be made to him, not by him : a fetch not unlikely. To which they answered that he ought not to go. In this he readily concurred, and since that has never heard a word of it." [4]

[1] Rockingham Memoirs, 2, 141-142 : 143-144.
[2] Burke's Correspondence, 1, 215-217.
[3] Burke's Correspondence, 1, 218-221.
[4] Add. MSS., 35375, f. 19. For a garbled version of the same incident, see Walpole's Memoirs, iv. 22-23.

From the tone of Rockingham's discourse, it is quite clear that he had not yet fully forgiven Chatham for the past, and, as John York shrewdly remarked, " this *novum fœdus* is rather *nullum fœdus*, and does not deserve to be celebrated even in a thatched cottage." [1] If the old Duke of Newcastle had still been alive, and permitted to exercise his influence, it is not improbable that the indirect overtures of Chatham and Temple would have met with a more eager response ; and although Burke might rather contemptuously remark, " how much the late Duke of Newcastle hurt himself in his interest very often, by his itch of negotiation," [2] it remained true that the opposition could hardly hope for victory without union and a proper understanding. The link of the Middlesex election though useful enough, was by no means sufficient to bind the parties closely together, and something more was needed before a firm and united front could be presented to the enemy.

That the administration was now tottering to its fall, and that Chatham was intent upon its destruction, there is little doubt. It would take but little to induce Grafton to desert a cabinet in which he was being outvoted and over-ruled, and in his autobiography he confesses that after his defeat over the repeal of the revenue act he formed the resolution, " to withdraw myself from my office, which was become very uncomfortable and irksome to me, on the first favourable opportunity that offered itself." [3] Such a determination on his part is more deserving of praise than censure ; but Camden and Granby were guilty of more dubious conduct. The lord chancellor, indeed, had ample cause for discontent, convinced as he was that

---

[1] Add. MS., 35375, f. 19.   [2] Burke's Correspondence, 1, 201-207.
[3] Grafton's *Autobiography*, p. 234.

the expulsion of Wilkes and the partial repeal of the revenue act were colossal blunders, but it is not easy to forgive him for his treachery towards Grafton and the king.   Instead of finding an honourable solution of his difficulties by resignation, he continued in the cabinet, and, at the same time, actively intrigued with Chatham against the very government of which he was a leading member.   It was not only that he abstained from attending the meetings of ministers : [1] when appealed to by Grafton for an opinion upon the legality of the petitions, he refrained from giving an answer till he had consulted with Chatham who took to himself the credit that " as to petitioning, his lordship was also very explicit as to the right, as well as to the illegality of all prosecutions for the exercise of it." [2] Nor is this the worst charge against him.   He does not seem to have concealed his dislike of his colleagues, but, on the contrary, blazoned it abroad ; [3] and, taking advantage of Grafton's good nature, agreed with Chatham to refrain from resignation for the express purpose of embarrassing and weakening the government. [4]   Granby, moreover, stands in the same condemnation, being guilty of intriguing with Camden

---

[1] Grafton's *Autobiography* p. 234, pp. 240-241.

[2] Grenville Papers, 4, 477-479.

[3] " The guns are now firing upon the river for Lord Mayor Beckford," wrote Rigby to the Duke of Bedford on November 9th.   " He will be attended by no officer of the state but the lord chancellor, who, I suppose, will be hallooed all through the city as a staunch friend of Wilkes.   The lord chancellor's conduct, since our conversation in Arlington Street, has by no means justified the opinion we held at that interview by his situation ; he is affectedly hostile every day to the ministry, and has a pride in showing it. I could give your grace many instances of it." Rockingham Memoirs, 2, 155.

[4] Notwithstanding all report, the opinion at Hayes is that lord chancellor will not be removed ; and he certainly will not have the unpardonable weakness to resign in such a crisis.   His lordship is firm, and in the rightest resolutions." Chatham's Correspondence, 3, 388-389.   For Grafton's hesitation, and the anxiety of the king and the Bedford party to remove Camden, see Grafton's *Autobiography*, pp. 245-246.

and Chatham to oppose the ministry, and to resign at a convenient opportunity.[1]

Such were the political conditions when the new session of parliament began on January 9th, 1770 ; and all men, and not least the king, realised that the fate of the ministry, and all that it involved, was hanging in the balance.[2] In the speech from the throne an allusion was made to the cattle disease which was prevalent at this time, a reference bitterly commented upon by Junius who savagely accused Grafton of attributing to the king of England " the misery of a ruined grazier and the whining piety of a methodist." Stress was also laid upon the disturbed conditions of the colonies, the failure of the measures, which had been taken to restore peace, being admitted. In the house of lords the address was moved by the Duke of Ancaster, but all men's eyes were fixed upon Chatham who had travelled up from Hayes in order to strike a blow for England and against the ministry. For over three years he had not attended a debate ; and, when last present, he had been first minister and the defender of the court against the aggression of factions. He returned a very different man, having learnt much by adversity, but still inflamed by that passionate love for England, which, whether he served king or party, or stood alone in splendid isolation, never forsook him. When he rose to speak, the peers realised that they were the privileged spectators of a historic event, and that they were about to listen, not to carping criticism, but to a declaration of policy.

[1] Chatham MSS., P.R.O., 1st series, vol. xxv., John Calcraft to Chatham, 22nd November 1769 : vol. lxii., Lord Temple to Lady Chatham, 21st November 1769 : Chatham Correspondence, 3, 388-391.

[2] Thus, two days before the session begun, George III. instructed Lord North to make preparations for an oratorical display in force by members of the ministry in the house of commons on January 9th. Correspondence of George III. with Lord North, 1, 10.

He called upon his hearers to consider the evils of the time, the universal discontent which prevailed in the country, the isolation of England in Europe, and the unhappy relations with the colonists who, though they had erred, ought not to be condemned unheard, and, as the champions of freedom, deserved a consideration which ordinary law breakers could not expect to receive. " Liberty," he characteristically remarked, " was a plant that deserved to be cherished." The grievances of America, however, did not form his main theme ; it was upon the discontent at home that he laid the greatest stress, declaring the general dissatisfaction to have its root in the expulsion of the legally elected member for Middlesex. " The privileges of the house of lords," he observed, " however transcendent, however appropriated to them, stood in the fact upon the broad bottom of the people," and, taking advantage of the licence allowed to the orator, he called upon the descendants of the barons of Runnymede to emulate their predecessors, and right the wrongs of a distressed nation. To point the way in this work of regeneration, he moved, as an amendment to the address, that, " we will, with all convenient speed, take into our most serious consideration, the causes of the discontents which prevail in so many parts of your majesty's dominions, and particularly the late proceedings in the house of commons, touching the incapacity of John Wilkes, Esq., expelled by that house, to be elected a member to serve in this present parliament, thereby refusing, by a resolution of one branch of the legislature only, to the subject his common right, and depriving the electors of Middlesex of their free choice of a representative."

Such an amendment could hardly have been expected to be carried, being, in fact, an indictment of

the ministry, but it amply fulfilled its purpose of bringing into the foreground of the discussion the one subject upon which the opposition was in agreement. Of
even greater moment, however, was the opportunity
afforded to Camden of expressing the discontent he
had long felt, and there could have been little surprise
when he declared that he was most strongly opposed
to the expulsion of Wilkes, and had never approved
it. In the house of commons an amendment, similar
to that moved by Chatham in the upper house, was
brought forward by Dowdeswell; and, though incurring the same fate of rejection, was supported by a
minority of one hundred and thirty-eight members,
which included not only Grenville and the followers
of Rockingham, but also Lord Granby who announced
that he repented of having voted for the expulsion
of Wilkes, and Dunning, the solicitor-general, who
defended the legality of petitions.[1]

The opponents of the government had no cause to
feel ashamed of the part they had played on the first
day of the session, even though in both houses their
amendments had not been carried. Indeed, they
had ample reason for jubilation, two cabinet ministers
and a law officer of the crown having declared in their
favour, and it was the ministry rather than the opposition that had suffered in the first encounter. Its
prestige, already diminished to almost vanishing point,
had incurred a serious blow ; and, if it was to continue
to survive, it must at least show that it was still able
to punish disobedience. The lord chancellor had long
been marked down for slaughter, and he had sealed
his doom by his frankness in debate. No sooner were
the words out of his mouth than Temple was prophesy-

---

[1] For the debates in the two houses, see *Cavendish Debates*, i. 434 ff.
Walpole's Memoirs, 4, 23-25. *Parl. Hist.*, xvi. 644 ff. ; 668 ff.

ing that he would be speedily dismissed for daring to
stand up in defence of English freedom; and, before
leaving the house, Camden himself privately told
Grafton that he was quite aware that he would be
deprived of his office for what he had done, but that he
did not intend to facilitate the task of the government
by resignation.[1] The forecast was correct, no time
being lost by the court in beginning the search for a new
occupant of the woolsack, and truly there was no time
to lose. The moment was critical, and great was the
need for urgent action. The enemy was clamouring
at the gates, the country had been aroused from its
political lethargy, the administration seemed to be
breaking into pieces; and it might well happen that
the opposition would be left in victorious possession
of the field.

At such crises George III. was wont to display a
capacity for rapid action, a courage and resolution,
which account in no small degree for his success as
a political commander. If not " pleased with the
tempest when the waves ran high " he was, at least,
able to rise to a sudden emergency; and it was when
he was most hard pressed that he revealed, if not the
arts of a great statesman, at least the cunning of a
successful politician. Nor was he found wanting
on this occasion. In consultation with Grafton, it
was agreed that the great seal should be offered to
Charles Yorke; and the decision was in no sense the last
despairing and almost haphazard throw of the ruined
political gambler. On the contrary, it was a deliberate
and carefully thought out study in temptation, an
attempt on the king's part to turn human weakness
and frailty to his own advantage.

The life of Charles Yorke had been saddened and

---

[1] *Parl. Hist.*, xvi. 644 ff.; Grafton's *Autobiography*, pp. 245-246.

embittered by a great ambition never satisfied. Of great eminence in the legal profession, of which his father had been so distinguished an ornament, he had set his heart upon becoming lord chancellor, and, frustrated in this hope, failed to find satisfaction in success which would have been more than sufficient for most members of the bar. It meant little to him that he had been attorney-general, for he had only regarded that office as a stepping stone to one still higher; but fortune had always crossed his path just as he was on the point of attaining his goal. At the beginning of the reign of George III. it seemed that he had only to wait for the prize to fall into his grasp. The whig party, of which his father was one of the leaders, was still supreme, and seemed likely to continue so, and Yorke, marked out for promotion by his birth, his political opinions, and his legal skill, could legitimately anticipate that in a few years he would be sitting where his father had sat. This pleasing prospect, however, was soon over-clouded. The whigs, ejected from office, were driven into opposition to the king; and Yorke had to make his choice between the court and his friends. After much hesitation, and with infinite sorrow and regret, he threw in his lot with the whig opposition, resigning the office of attorney-general in the autumn of 1763. By thus alienating the king, he seemed to have blasted all his hopes of promotion; and it was not long before he came to the conclusion that it was vain to struggle against the power of the crown, and that obedience was wiser than rebellion. After a twelvemonths' experience of opposition he made his peace with the court, taking no office, but accepting a patent of precedency which gave him rank between the attorney and solicitor-general. Thus, blowing neither hot nor cold, it is probable that he was little trusted by either party, and it is certain that he was treated but indifferently by both. When the Rockingham ministry was formed in the summer of 1765, Yorke had to content himself with his old office of attorney-general, Northington being retained as lord chancellor in order to gratify the king ; and when, a year later, Rockingham fell before Chatham, Lord Camden became chancellor, and Yorke, disgusted by such treatment, threw up his office of attorney-general.

That Yorke had very real cause for discontent, and a legitimate grievance against the Rockingham whigs and the king, cannot be denied. He might well feel aggrieved that Rockingham, when he had the opportunity, had not placed him upon the woolsack ; and, though he had consented to return to his old office of attorney-general when assured by George III. that he should be lord chancellor within a year, that pledge had not been fulfilled. It is not surprising, therefore, that, after the construction of Chatham's ministry, Yorke, though continuing to be nominally a member of the Rockingham party, was disposed to play an independent part in politics, and to think little of the interests of a faction which had thought so little of his own. Indeed, he often inclined to direct disagreement with the men who were commonly reported to be his close political associates ; and although he took an active part in the defence of the East India company, and supported the *nullum tempus* bill, he believed that the administration had acted wisely in expelling Wilkes, was of the opinion that the house of commons could disqualify for election to parliament, and was opposed to the policy, pursued by his friends, of encouraging the counties and boroughs to petition the court. At so great a variance did he feel with his supposed allies that he sometimes purposely abstained from attending the house of commons. " When the question arose," wrote Lord Hardwicke, "towards the close of the session, about the power of the house of commons to disqualify, he would never give his opinion upon it in public, though, to a few friends in private, if he was asked, he declared himself strongly for the power. After the house of commons had voted in Colonel Luthel (*sic*) the question of right was taken up again in a petition of some Middlesex electors, and, as I foresaw it was likely to become a very serious matter, I pressed him most warmly one morning . . . to go down to the house, and give his full opinion in the cause." [1]

In spite of his brother's advice, however, Yorke refused to reveal himself, and it would have been well if he had foresworn political ambition altogether. But that was a renunciation beyond his power to achieve. The prize of the lord chancellorship still dangled before his eyes, and hope was not yet dead. It soon became known that Camden was discontented with his situation, opposed in opinion to the court, and on the point of either resignation or expulsion ; and, in the spring or summer of 1769, Yorke had been warned that he might be called upon in the immediate future to take his place upon the woolsack. He failed to greet the prospect with the rapture which might have been expected, being the victim of conflicting impulses. Though he had always hoped to attain to the great position which his father had held, and was not called upon to be over-mindful of the feelings of Lord Rockingham and his followers, there were considerations sufficiently weighty to cause him to hesitate, and to doubt whether, after all, as a man of honour he could afford to satisfy the ambition of his lifetime. He had never explained, either to Rockingham or the world, what little sympathy he had with the party to which he was supposed to belong ' [1] and, if he accepted a place in the Grafton ministry, his action would be interpreted by the good as a sacrifice of honour to personal advantage, and by the bad as the triumph of policy over prejudice.[2] Moreover, he naturally shrank from linking his fortunes with a government so justly decried, and with whose policy on many questions he was entirely out of sympathy ; and, cursed with an over-sensitive nature, he feared the reproaches of his many friends in the Rockingham camp. They would not be likely to mince their words with the man who, while they were seeking to destroy the ministry, frustrated their expectations by stepping into the breach left by the fall of Camden ; and it was most improbable that they would lend an attentive or sympathetic ear to explanations of a course of conduct so detrimental to their interests. Convinced that Yorke was, at heart, one of themselves, they would regard him on the woolsack with abhorrence and detestation ; and, if he elected to satisfy his ambition, he would be compelled to suffer the contempt of many close and intimate friends, whose former affection would only serve to intensify their hatred.[3]

---

[1] " As well as I can recollect," wrote Lord Hardwicke, " Mr John Yorke and myself were clear . . . that he ought long ago to have explained himself to Lord Rockingham, that the world might not have run away with the idea that he particularly belonged to that connection." Add. MS., 35428, f. 1.

[2] On January 9th, in the house of lords, Lord Shelburne had expressed the hope that " there would not be found in the kingdom a wretch so base and mean-spirited, as to accept of them (the seals) on the conditions on which they must be offered." *Parl. Hist.*, vol. xvi. pp. 644 ff.

[3] Thus between Rockingham and Charles Yorke existed a close friendship ; and there is no reason to believe Mrs Yorke's assertion that this was insincere on Rockingham's part. " It was a fortunate thing," she wrote, " for a man of so middling a capacity as his lordship to have a director and adviser like Mr Yorke, to whom he could apply every moment, and without whom he

Thus, torn by opposing considerations, and of a high-strung temperament, Yorke dreaded what the future would bring forth, and, in a measure, must have prayed that he might never be called upon to make so critical a decision. Like many another man before and since, he found it difficult to know where the path of duty lay, and, as it gradually became clearer and clearer that Camden could not long continue in the cabinet, he sought advice from his brothers, Lord Hardwicke and John Yorke, and received divided counsel. While his elder brother was in favour of Charles accepting the offer of chancellorship, should the court make it, the younger was of a contrary opinion ; and thus he failed to get a clear lead when he most urgently needed one.[1] At the beginning of the year, 1770, he was as irresolute as ever ; and it was when he was in this mental condition that he received, at his Highgate residence on Friday, January 12th, a letter from the Duke of Grafton, asking for an interview.[2]

Though Grafton only asked him to call, saying nothing about the purpose of the meeting, Yorke was quite aware that the much dreaded summons had come :[3] and he was hardly in a fit state to meet it. The anxiety of the last few months, the state of continuous and harassing doubt, had begun to prey upon his mind and affect his health ; and he had only just returned from his country residence in Hertfordshire where he had been confined by illness.[4] The business of courts,

would have made no figure at all in his administration ; it was also useful to have a friend whose purse could so frequently supply the wants which his extravagance continually brought on him." Add. MS., 35428, f. 132.

[1] Add. MS., 35428, f. 1. [2] Add. MS., 35428, f. 124, f. 128.

[3] Add. MS., 35428, f. 132.

[4] " I have been confined by a violent cold and illness," he wrote to Grafton on January 12th, " at my house in Hertfordshire for some days, and did not reach Highgate till yesterday afternoon." Add. MS., 35428, f. 128 (rough draft).

however, cannot be delayed in the interests of the health of private individuals, and Yorke rallied his strength to embark upon the negotiation in which he was to meet his death. Arranging to wait upon Grafton on the evening of Friday, January 12th, he took his wife and his two brothers into his confidence, discussing with them the line of conduct he ought to pursue. From the tone of his remarks Mrs Yorke gathered the impression that he would probably refuse Grafton's offer;[1] but, unfortunately, we do not know definitely what advice was tendered by his two brothers on this occasion. Probably, they suggested that, at his first conference with Grafton, he should avoid committing himself finally in either direction, and thus gain time in which to ascertain the opinions of his friends. Such, at least, was the policy adopted by Yorke at his meeting with the prime minister on January 12th. " He received the offer of the great seal," wrote Grafton in his autobiography, " with much gratitude to his majesty, but hoped that he should be allowed to return his answer when he should have given it a day's consideration. Mr Charles Yorke remained with me between two and three hours, dwelling much on the whole of his own political thoughts and conduct, together with a comment on the principal public occurrences of the present reign. When he came to make remarks on the actual state of things, after speaking with much regard of many in administration, he said that it was essential to him to be informed from me whether I was open to a negotiation for extending the administration, so as to comprehend those with whom I had formerly, and he constantly wished to agree. My answer was that he could not desire more earnestly than myself to see an administration as com-

[1] Add. MS., 35428, f. 132.

prehensive as possible, and that this object could only be brought about by the re-union of the whigs, adding that I should be happy to have his assistance to effect it. Mr Yorke appeared to be pleased with this answer, and, after many civilities on both sides, we parted.[1]

Yorke had been given until the morning of Sunday, January 14th, to come to a final decision; and the time was not over-long. The problem, moreover, was as insoluble as ever, for the meeting with Grafton could hardly have had the effect of dissipating the doubts which clouded the prospective lord chancellor's brain. In reply to the suggestion that the Rockingham whigs should be introduced into the ministry, Grafton had returned an evasive answer of little or no meaning, but which might fairly be interpreted as conveying that the offer was to Yorke, and to him alone. Few men have ever been subjected to a severer trial, and it is at least to his credit that he sought to obtain a clearer conception of his duty by ascertaining the opinions of his friends. By Rockingham, with whom he had a meeting on the evening of Saturday, January 13th [2] he was told to decline the offer of the court; and from that quarter such advice might have been expected. Little as the marquis might esteem Chatham, he was certainly not entirely blind to his value as a political ally, and he could not but know that the great statesman would be most bitterly offended if a member of the Rockingham party succeeded Camden as lord chancellor. Indeed, no event could well be more unfortunate for the success of the opposition in the parliamentary struggle, and one may well believe that Rockingham used strong words of dissuasion.[3] John Yorke, as he had always been,

---

[1] Grafton's *Autobiography*, pp. 247-249 ; Add. MS., 35428, f. 116.
[2] Rockingham Memoirs, 2, 159-160.   [3] Add. MS., 35428, f. 132.

was of the same mind as the whig leader ; while Lord Mansfield, upon whom Yorke waited at his Hampstead residence, was of the opinion that it was his duty, as well as his interest, to come to the assistance of the court, and accept a gift which would hardly be offered again.[1] It is more difficult to be certain of the views expressed by lord Hardwicke, for, like Charles himself, he was the victim of conflicting impulses. Family pride and fraternal affection led him to wish that his brother's ambition should find satisfaction ; but, on the other hand, he feared the comments of Lord Rockingham and his friends. It was quite possible that, even if Yorke stepped into Camden's place, the ministry might still fall and the opposition triumph ; and Hardwicke not unnaturally felt that, if this came to pass, the last state of his house would be worse than the first, for mortal offence would have been given to the whigs, and Charles would have only taken his seat on the woolsack in order to vacate it. Thus, it is not surprising that he had some difficulty in making up his mind, and changed his opinion within twenty four hours [2] ; but there is no reason to doubt his own

---

[1] Add MS., 35428, f. 132.

[2] The following is Mrs Yorke's account of Hardwicke's conduct at this time, but it ought to be remembered that she was hostile to him :—" Lord Hardwicke was of a contrary opinion, as will appear by what follows. Lady Grey came to me on the Saturday morning. She began very soon to talk on this subject. I told her Ladyship that my mind was perfectly easy, for I had but one opinion, which was that Mr Yorke should not accept, for the reasons above mentioned, and that I believed such were Mr Yorke's own thoughts and determination. She replied that it was true, and that there was much to be said against it ; but she thought the reasons that might be urged for accepting were much stronger than the objections. . . . She ended, however, by saying that these were Lord Hardwicke's sentiments as well as her own. I was very much struck by what she said, especially of Lord Hardwicke, and told her Ladyship I thought my Lord was of a very different opinion, and had advised Mr Yorke to the contrary the night before ; at least I understood so from what Mr Yorke told me : indeed, replied Lady Grey, Mr Yorke must have misunderstood my lord very much if he thought so." Add. MS., 35428, f. 132.

statement that when Yorke visited him on the Sunday morning, before going on to Grafton, he agreed with him that the right thing to do was to decline. " He (Mr Y.) called upon me that morning (the 14th)," he wrote, " and seemed in great perplexity and agitation. I asked him if he saw his way through the clamorous and difficult points upon which it would be immediately expected he should give his opinion, viz., the Middlesex election, America, and the state of Ireland where the parliament had just been prorogued on a popular point. He seriously declared he did not, and that he might be called upon to advise measures of a higher and more dangerous nature than he should chuse to be responsible for. He was clearly of opinion that he was not sent for at this present juncture from predilection but necessity ; and how much soever the great seal had justly been the object of his ambition, he was now afraid of accepting it. Seeing him in so low and fluttered a state of spirits, and knowing how much the times called for a higher, I did not venture to push him on, and gave into the idea, he himself started, of advising to put the great seal in commission, by which time would be gained." [1]

Thus Yorke reached a determination, and it would have been well for him if it had been final. Taking the advice of his brothers, Lord Rockingham, and his wife, he declined the great seal in his interview with Grafton on the Sunday morning, and so strongly did he express his resolution of not joining the administration that the duke did not attempt to press him, contenting himself with asking him to wait upon the king before coming to a completely final resolution, a request with which Yorke undertook to comply.[2] The inter-

---

[1] Add. MS., 35428, f. 116.
[2] Add. MS., 35428, f. 116 ; Grafton's *Autobiography*, pp. 247-249. Grafton

view then ended, but, unfortunately, Yorke was unable
to dismiss the matter from his mind. He had promised
to see the king, and, still a prey to uncertainty and
doubt, he fell to brooding over what he had done.
He began to wonder whether he had missed a
great opportunity, and inflicted upon himself all the
tortures of morbid introspection. Unable to rest, he
still sought advice, being told by Lord Chief Justice
Wilmot, and by Lord Mansfield again, to accept the
promotion offered by the court. His mental agitation
revealed itself in a loss of sleep and appetite, symptoms
which had the unfortunate effect of causing his wife
to change her mind. Thinking that her husband
would be happier if he received what he had so eagerly
coveted for so long, and influenced by the opinion
of her friends, she now pressed the wretched man to
accept ;[1] and her well-meant but ill-advised suggestions
could only have had the effect of increasing his suspense
and misery. He was now no more certain of what he
ought to do than he had been when he opened Grafton's
letter of summons. Meeting him on the morning of
Monday, January 16th, Hardwicke found him resolved
to adhere to his refusal ; but in twenty-four hours
he veered about, and on the morning of Tuesday was
agitatedly talking about accepting.[2]

The audience with the king had been fixed for
Tuesday evening ; and by that time Yorke had again
changed his mind, being now resolved to refuse. The
accounts of the interview at court vary, but, in the midst
of much that is in doubt, it is at least certain that Yorke
formally declined the offer made to him.[3] On leaving

states that it was Yorke who asked to wait upon the king, but this is con-
tradicted in Lord Hardwicke's account, and, on the face of it, seem rather
unlikely.

[1] Add. MS., 35428, f. 132.   [2] Add. MS., 35428, f. 116.
[3] Lord Hardwicke and Mrs Yorke give conflicting accounts of the king's

the palace, he called upon Hardwicke and Rockingham, to inform them of what he had done, and authorised Hardwicke to publish the news to the world.[1]   Having transacted this business, he returned home, only to have a restless and disturbed night.   When he rose on Wednesday morning, he looked worn and ill ; but, instead of taking his wife's advice to leave town at once for the country, insisted upon attending the levée which was to be held that day.   " He said," in Mrs Yorke's words, " that it was proper that he should make his bow to the king." [2]

That obeisance was indeed to have a fatal consequence, and one would give much to know the secret of Yorke's determination to attend the levée.   It may well be that the king had refused to take a final answer on the Tuesday evening, and that it was in obedience to a royal command that Yorke went to court on the Wednesday morning[3] ; but, whatever was his motive for going, he went to his doom.   The king, aware that Granby had either resigned, or was immediately about to resign, the office of master of the ordnance,[4] deter-

conversation at this meeting.   According to the former " the king had not pressed him (Charles Yorke) so strongly as he expected, that he had not held forth much prospect of stability in administration, and that he had not talked so well to him as he did when he accepted the office of attorney-general in 1765.   His majesty ended the conversation very humanely and prettily, that after what he had said to excuse himself it would be cruelty to press his acceptance."   Mrs Yorke in her account states, " I gathered from what he did say, that the king would not take his answer, and had made use of much flattery and persuasion," and these remarkable words, " Mr Yorke, I cannot do without you ; I lay my commands upon you ; you must take the seals." It is, of course, possible that in her narrative Mrs Yorke confuses the two meetings with the king.   Add. MS., 35428, f. 116, f. 132.

[1] Add. MS., 35428, f. 116.   [2] Add. MS., 35428, f. 132.

[3] In a note, written in the year 1781, and placed at the end of his narrative, Lord Hardwicke states : " I have reason to think from what Lord H—gh hinted to me this winter that some means were used, which I was ignorant of, to bring my brother to court when the great seal was forced upon him."   Add. MS., 35428, f. 116.

[4] There is no evidence whether Granby resigned his office before or after

mined upon making a final effort to win Yorke. Calling him into the royal closet, he sought to persuade him to accept the chancellorship, and apparently did not scruple to employ methods of intimidation. According to Hardwicke, the king said, " my sleep has been disturbed by your declining, do you intend to declare yourself unfit for it ? " and still stronger afterwards— " if you will not comply, it must make an eternal breach between us." [1]

Such expressions, coming from the mouth of an occupant of the throne, were invested with a sinister and threatening import, and Yorke was well enough versed in the ways of courts to understand that, by refusing to assist the king in the hour of his need, he for ever precluded himself from being considered for the office of lord chancellor. He now knew that the king would never forgive what he elected to construe as a personal affront ; and that, were he to decline to bend to the will of the crown, all political and legal ambition was at an end. A strong and resolute man might have remained unmoved by such a threat ; but Yorke was emphatically neither strong nor determined. Changing his mind from day to day, and almost from hour to hour, he was in a most appropriate disposition to be cajoled and intimidated, and, with no will of his own to oppose to the imperious will of his master, he bowed before the storm, and accepted the great seal.

It was a great political and personal triumph for George III.; and he could justly claim that his achievement was the fruit of perseverance, though hardly of that virtue alone. He could boast that he had

Yorke was summoned into the closet ; but the point is not material, inasmuch as the king must have been quite aware of his intention.

[1] Add. MS., 35428, f. 116.

defeated the treacherous designs of the opposition, who had thought that the expulsion of Camden and the resignation of Granby would bring about the destruction of the ministry ; and with Yorke on the woolsack there was a good hope that the government might successfully withstand the attacks of the parties opposed to it. But the plans of kings, like those of ordinary men, are subjected to influences beyond their control ; and George III. was only to enjoy a three days' triumph which was to end in a dismal tragedy.

On leaving the court Charles Yorke called upon Lord Hardwicke to inform him of what he had done. He found Rockingham closeted with his brother, and both were deeply chagrined on learning that Yorke had submitted to the king's will ; and they had just cause for vexation. " I was hurt personally," writes Lord Hardwicke, " at the figure I had been making for a day before, telling everybody by his authority that he was determined to decline " ; [1] and, though Rockingham's personal pride might be unaffected, he understood how the weakness of one man had changed the whole prospect of the opposition. Neither of these two angry and astonished men minced their words, and a stormy scene ensued. They told the new lord chancellor to return to the palace and withdraw his consent ; but he refused, saying that his word was pledged. The conversation was lengthy and altercating, and John Yorke, who came in during the proceedings, united with Rockingham and Hardwicke in deploring what had happened. In spite, however, of the arguments rained upon him, Charles Yorke refused to give way ; and after a heated conversation of at least three hours [2] left his brother's house. On

[1] Add. MS., 35428, f. 116.
[2] Charles Yorke arrived at his brother's house at three o'clock in the after-

his arrival at home, he found that his wife had already heard the news which had quickly got into circulation ; and it is worthy of note that Yorke, in spite of the angry scene at Hardwicke's house, seemed in better spirits than he had been for some days past ; [1] a change doubtless due to the fact that he was no longer tortured by suspense, having taken a step from which there was no going back.   But his mind was by no means completely at rest ; and to his wife he confided his distress at the insults he had suffered at the hands of his two brothers and Rockingham.   In particular he complained of Hardwicke, who apparently had " exceeded all bounds of reason and even common civility.   I hope he will in cooler moments think better of it, and reconcile himself to me, and my brother John also ; for if I lose the support of my family, I shall be undone." [2]

Thus, no sooner had the old suspense ended than its place was taken by a new anxiety ; and Yorke was no happier than he had been before.   He now feared that, repudiated by his family and the Rockingham party as a whole, he would become a second Duke of Grafton, a servile instrument of the court.   From such a future he naturally shrank, for it was not with that design that he had accepted the great seal.   He had hoped that, though seated on the woolsack, he would maintain friendly relations with his kinsmen and political associates ; and that, gradually and by degrees, the administration would be extended so as to include some of those with whom he had formerly worked.   If, however, he was to be repudiated, put to the ban, and treated as a renegade, then all hope of happiness was gone ; and so greatly did this fear prey

noon, and had not returned to his house in Bloomsbury Square by six o'clock that evening.   Add. MS., 35428, f. 116, f. 132.

[1] Add. MS., 35428, f. 132.   [2] *Ibid.*

upon his mind that he besought his wife to visit Lord Hardwicke that very evening, and endeavour to soften him, arranging to call for her at his brother's house on his way home from the palace, where he was going to receive the great seal, and to kiss the king's hand on being made Baron of Morden in the county of Cambridge.

On this errand of mercy Mrs Yorke departed without delay, and was, apparently, having some success in appeasing Hardwicke's wrath, when Charles Yorke entered the room to conduct his wife home. Of what then followed the accounts vary. According to Mrs Yorke the quarrel between the brothers began again, angry words passed, and only when she burst into tears did they cease their bickering, and exchange some formal expressions of forgiveness.[1] According to Lord Hardwicke, however, " a warm word did not escape either of us " ;[2] and thus, confronted by conflicting versions, we are left in ignorance of what actually took place. But whatever happened, we know that the second meeting with his brother did nothing to relieve Yorke's fear that he would be deserted by his family. All that night he never closed his eyes, in spite of having taken a sleeping draught, but kept muttering to himself that he was utterly undone, and that it would have been kinder of his brothers " to have shot him through the head than have wounded him so deeply by their unreasonable anger."[3] Sometimes he cried out that he must return the great seal, for he could not live if he kept it ; and by six o'clock in the morning he was so ill and distraught that his terrified wife sent for a doctor who, having inspected his patient, promised to call again before the end of the day. Obliged to

---

[1] Add. MS., 35428, f. 132. [2] Add. MS., 35428, f. 116.
[3] Add. MS., 35428, f. 132.

rise in order to receive the numerous visitors who came to congratulate him upon his promotion, the new lord chancellor passed a day of misery and gloom. Amongst those who called was John Yorke whom he begged to take a place in the administration, murmuring, when the request was civilly but firmly declined, that " then it would be the ruin of him."[1] Lord Hardwicke did not appear, having gone into the country to compose his thoughts ; and his absence was unfortunate, for it must have confirmed Charles in his belief that he was about to be disowned by his kinsmen.[2] Those who saw him on this day were struck by his depression and settled melancholy. " I was myself," wrote his wife, " so ill with fatigue and anxiety that I was not able to dine with him, but Dr Plumptre did. When I went to them after dinner, I found Mr Yorke in a state of fixed melancholy ; he neither spoke to me or to Dr Plumptre. I tried every method to awake and amuse him, but in vain."[2]

Thus Yorke passed the first day of his life as lord chancellor ; and his condition could not but be a cause of anxiety to those to whom he was dear. In the evening the physician, Dr Watson, called again, and gave him a strong opiate which enabled him at least to get some sleep during the first part of the night. Prolonged rest, however, was denied him : " about the middle of the night he awaked in a delirium, when I again sent for Dr Watson. Towards the morning he was more composed, and at noon got up."[3] He had not been up for more than an hour, however, when he was seized, in Mrs Yorke's words, " with a vomiting of blood."[4] She was not with him at the time of the seizure, if indeed it can so be called ; but,

[1] Add. MS., 35428, f. 116.
[3] Add. MS., 35428, f. 132.
[2] Add. MS., 35428, f. 132.
[4] *Ibid.*

hurriedly summoned to his side, found him almost speechless, and only just able to gasp out the words, " How can I repay your kindness, my dear love ; God will reward you, I cannot be comforted." [1] These were the last words the unhappy woman heard from the lips of her husband who passed away about five o'clock in the afternoon of the following day, Saturday, January 20th.

From that time to this, a mystery has surrounded this tragic death ; and it is unlikely that it will ever be dispelled. Contemporaries were widely of the opinion that Yorke had taken his own life ; and the evidence available at the present day is not sufficient to prove or disprove this belief. We are certainly not driven to adopt the theory of suicide as the only possible solution of the problem. Yorke was not in good health when he arrived in London to embark upon the road which was to lead to his grave ; and it is clear that his condition soon became such as to give rise to the liveliest anxiety. It is therefore not improbable that he may have broken a blood vessel on the Friday afternoon, and, in a weak state of health, worn out by the acutest mental anxiety, been unable to rally his strength. Yet, on the other hand, there are certain suspicious circumstances connected with the last hours of his life, which undoubtedly lend colour to contemporary opinion. We do not hear of anyone being present when the reported " vomiting of blood " took place ; and it is significant, though perhaps nothing more, that Mrs Yorke, save for that brief and tragic meeting at which he spoke to her for the last time, was not allowed to see her husband until life was extinct.[2] What is however of more weight is the suspicious secrecy that was maintained about the illness. On

---

[1] Add. MS., 35428, f. 132. [2] *Ibid.*

the Friday evening Grafton called at Yorke's house by appointment, apparently in complete ignorance that anything had happened ; and his account of his visit is worthy of quotation : " By his own appointment," he writes, " I went to his house about nine o'clock in the evening, two days as I believe after Mr Yorke had been sworn in at a council-board summoned for that purpose at the queen's house. Being shown into his library below, I waited a longer time than I supposed Mr Yorke would have kept me without some extraordinary cause. After above half an hour waiting, Dr Watson, his physician, came into the room ; he appeared somewhat confused, sat himself down for a few minutes, letting me know that Mr Yorke was much indisposed with an attack of colic." [1] This account is of interest, giving as it does a glimpse of Watson who must have known the secret of the tragedy ; and his remark to the prime minister is of importance. None of the symptoms of her husband's illness described by Mrs Yorke are in any sense peculiar to, or even characteristic of, colic ; and it is possible that the physician, aware that his patient had not long to live, attributed to him a disease which would account for a speedy demise.[2]

So the problem stands ; and the real truth will never be known.[3]   In any case, however, Charles Yorke was

[1] Grafton's *Autobiography*, pp. 247-249.

[2] It is of interest that Hardwicke on Friday evening had apparently abandoned all hope of his brother's life. " I can only tell your lordship," he writes to Rockingham, " with the utmost anxiety and concern, that my dear and unhappy brother is much worse, and that I tremble for the event. God send me and his family strength of mind enough to bear against this too probable calamity. I abominate the court politics, and almost those of every sort." Rockingham Memoirs, 2, 164.

[3] The above account of the last days of Charles Yorke's life is based upon the narratives of Lord Hardwicke and Mrs Yorke (Add. MS., 35428, f. 116, f. 132). These have been used by Mr Basil Williams for an interesting and valuable account of the Yorke family (*Transactions of the Royal Historical*

killed by anxiety ; and no small part of the responsibility for his death falls upon the king who had not scrupled to employ intimidation, and yet had failed to attain his end. By the evening of Saturday, January 20th, the administration was indeed in a parlous condition. There was no lord chancellor, no master of the ordnance, and Dunning, the solicitor-general, had announced his intention of retiring from office. But worse was to follow, the Duke of Grafton informing the king on the morning of Monday, January 22nd, or perhaps earlier, that he was resolved to retire from an administration which indeed he ought to have abandoned many months before.[1] The last straw had been the unexpected death of Yorke, upon whose co-operation Grafton had relied to enable him to struggle against the forces opposed to him in his own cabinet.[2] Now that hope was gone, and Grafton's ministerial career was, characteristically enough, brought to an end by a dismal tragedy.

If George III. had been a wiser and a better man, less tenacious of the privileges of the crown, and more ready to listen to unpalatable lessons and wholesome truths, he might at this crisis have played a great

Society, 3rd series, vol. ii.) to which I am much indebted ; but it may not be out of place to say a few words about them. In many respects Lord Hardwicke's account is the better of the two. It was written within a twelve-month of the events it records, whereas Mrs Yorke did not begin her narrative until October 1772, and did not complete it until two years later. In consequence of this delay, her story is not free from error of fact ; and it is sometimes difficult to be certain that she is placing events in their right order. Moreover, it is perfectly clear that her affection for her husband strongly prejudices her against Hardwicke and Rockingham ; and her unsupported testimony on the conduct of those two men must be accepted with caution. On the other hand she is far more detailed than her brother-in-law, and is naturally able to give a far fuller account of her husband's state of mind during the last three days of his life.

[1] Walpole's Memoirs, iv., 40-41.

[2] " Recollect that the hopes of co-operation with Mr Yorke to bring about an essential addition of right principle, credit, and support, vanished of course with himself." Grafton's *Autobiography*, pp. 249-250.

and noble part by which he would have earned forgiveness for his many mistakes during the first decade
of his reign. He was now no longer an inexperienced
boy, but a ruler of mature years, whose political understanding had been sharpened and developed by use;
and his duty lay clearly before him. His ministry
was falling to pieces before his eyes, and it was his
business not to retard but to hasten the process of
dissolution, in order that a cabinet might be formed,
which would be both popular and efficient. And such
a task would be comparatively easy; for the men out
of whom a new administration might be constructed
lay ready to his hand. The followers of Chatham,
Rockingham, and Grenville were now no longer the
enemies they had once been; and the opposition, if
not at one on all points, at least enjoyed a degree of
unity which it had hitherto seldom attained. A
coalition ministry, composed of representatives of the
three parties in opposition, might, indeed, have been
a failure; but few would assert that the experiment
was not worthy of a trial; and it was not public interest
but private malice that caused George III. to turn
his back upon such a suggestion. He told Conway,
who found him on January 22nd in the deepest distress,
that he would employ neither Rockingham nor Chatham,
both of whom, he declared, " were engaged to dissolve
the parliament; but he would abdicate his crown
sooner. Yes," continued the king, laying his hand
on his sword, " I will have recourse to this sooner than
yield to a dissolution." [1]

Thus spoke George III., unable to overcome his
unconquerable hate of men who had dared to try to
thwart his will; and he was as good as his word. He
resolved to maintain his ministry against the onslaught

[1] Walpole's Memoirs, iv., 40-41.

of the opposition, if only a man could be found brave enough to take up the burden which Grafton was laying down. His choice fell upon Lord North, chancellor of the exchequer ; and in a letter, written on January 23rd, he fervently appealed for his assistance. " After seeing you last night," he wrote, " I saw Lord Weymouth who, by my direction, will wait on you with Lord Gower this morning to press you in the strongest manner to accept the office of first commissioner of the treasury ; my own mind is more and more strengthened with the rightness of the measure that would prevent every other desertion. You must easily see that if you do not accept, I have no peer at present in my service that I could consent to place in the Duke of Grafton's employment. Whatever you may think, do not take any decision, unless it is one of instantly accepting, without a farther conversation with me. And as to the other arrangements, you may hear what others think, but keep your own opinion till I have seen you." [1]

The appeal was fervent enough, and it was effective. With characteristic good-nature, North came to the rescue of the crown at the moment of dire peril ; and, at his master's bidding, accepted an office which he was to hold for twelve years to the destruction both of his country and himself.

[1] Correspondence of George III. with Lord North, i, 11-12.

CHAPTER VI

THE UNITED OPPOSITION

THE resignation of the Duke of Grafton in January, 1770, is a turning point in the political history of the reign of George III. ; and, though it did not appear likely at the time, was to prove a piece of rare good fortune for the king, marking as it does the beginning of an era happier for the court though more disastrous for the country. Nine years had elapsed since the king had taken his place upon the throne, and declared war upon the whig oligarchy ; and the contest had by no means been brought to a conclusion, or even suspended by a truce, when Grafton retired from office. It is true that the balance of success certainly lay with the crown which could claim many victories to its credit ; but the royal triumph, though startling, had not been overwhelming, and seldom had George III. enjoyed complete immunity from harassing political anxiety. Not infrequently it had seemed that the edifice, which he had so laboriously reared, was about to be shattered into the dust. The frequent changes of ministry, which had occurred since the beginning of the reign, testify, not only to the subservience of a parliament which supported with equal complacency four different administrations, but also to the difficulties which the king experienced in the exercise of his political influence. Bute had become impossible because of his unpopularity ; Grenville had

destroyed himself by his adherence to principle;
while Rockingham had been merely a stop-gap, and
Grafton no more than the unworthy and unfortunate
representative of a great statesman in whom the king
thought, for a brief period, that he had found salvation.
Nor had the search for a suitable instrument been the
only difficulty which hindered the complete execution
of the royal design. Refusing to acknowledge defeat,
clinging to hope in the face of great adversity, and ever
on the alert for a favourable turn of fortune, the
ostracised whigs had never abandoned their attack
upon the principles of personal government ; and if
George III. had succeeded in restoring the crown to a
position of greater authority than it had enjoyed since
the death of Queen Anne, he had also incidentally
promoted the development of a regular and systematic
opposition. But, fierce as the contest had been
in the past, no previous political crisis of the reign
had ever been so acute as that which was precipitated
at the beginning of 1770, when it became clear that the
administration, which had stood for four years as a
barrier between the king and his opponents, was
tottering to its fall. The dismissal of Camden and the
resignation of Granby deprived the cabinet of the only
two ministers who enjoyed in any degree the confidence
of the country ; and, by declining to continue in office,
Grafton publicly confessed his inability to defend any
longer the citadel of the royal power. For a few hours,
indeed, it had seemed that the situation was to be saved
by Charles Yorke ; but this expectation was suddenly
shattered by a dismal tragedy which, by the additional
horror of personal suffering, served to intensify the
political gloom. In such circumstances a ruler of less
courage and greater wisdom than George III. might
excusably have faltered, and, with the consolation

that he had made a good fight, submitted to a defeat which seemed inevitable ; but, to the king's credit as a political warrior, a policy of surrender was never part of his programme.   Throughout his reign he consistently regarded concession as lamentable weakness ; and the greater the danger the more he was resolved to overcome it.   Grafton might fail him, and Yorke might find, or be granted, an escape, but George III. was determined never to truckle to those who, while professing a desire to be his servants, were resolved to be his masters.   Chatham had sinned far too deeply to be forgiven, and if Rockingham and Grenville were less potent for mischief, they were equally guilty. All three in varying degrees had endeavoured to thwart the will of the crown ; and to confer office upon such men, to invest them with the dignity of royal advisers was, from the point of view of the king, clearly impossible.   Unprepared for such a complete surrender of the principles to which he had ever adhered since boyhood, he turned to North for salvation in this hour of peril.   And North was not found wanting.   Stepping into the breach at the royal command, he undertook the perilous task of defending the king against his enemies ; and his courage was rewarded with conspicuous success.   Never before or after in his reign did the king have a prime minister so fitted in every way for the work which he was intended to accomplish, and for twelve years North continued in office, serving only too faithfully his royal master.   Keeping the opposition at bay during the stormy session of 1770, and establishing his administration upon the secure though corrupt foundations of parliamentary support, he triumphed where Grafton had failed ; and it is pleasing to find that George III., for a time at least, was sincerely grateful to the man who had rescued him from a great disaster. When, seven years later, the king asked permission to be allowed to pay his minister's debts, he coupled his request with a reference to the circumstances in which North had accepted office, asserting that he could never forget his conduct " at a critical minute." " You know me very ill," he wrote in a confidential strain, rarely adopted by a sovereign to a servant, " if you do not think that of all the letters I have ever wrote to you, this one gives me the most pleasure ; and I want no other return but you being convinced that I love you as well as a man of worth as I esteem you as a minister." [1]

The new prime minister was indeed worthy of the king's affection. The eldest son of the first Earl of Guilford, he was still a comparatively young man when he succeeded Grafton, being under forty years of age ; but, in his case, the advantages of youth were not counterbalanced by a deficiency in political experience. For the last sixteen years he had sat in the house of commons for the family borough of Banbury, a seat which he continued to hold until he succeeded his father in the peerage in 1790 ; and he had been given every opportunity of acquiring a grasp of administrative business. Appointed a junior lord of the treasury in 1759 by his kinsman, the Duke of Newcastle, he resigned that office on the formation of the first Rockingham administration ; but in the following year he again entered official life, being created joint paymaster of the forces by Lord Chatham. In the autumn of 1767 he rose to far greater eminence, succeeding Charles Townshend as chancellor of the exchequer ; and, during the last months of the Grafton ministry, he practically acted as leader of the lower house in place of Henry Conway. Thus it was as no unknown man that he came

---

[1] George III.'s Correspondence with Lord North, 2, 82-83.

to the king's assistance, and his political opinions were such as to ensure him a favourable reception at court ; for he had distinguished himself by his steady and persistent advocacy of tory principles of government.   Speaking in the house of commons in 1769, he remarked that during the previous seven years he had never given his support to any of the popular measures ; [1] and such a boast could not but sound gratefully in the ears of George III.   Yet North was certainly something far more than a tory reactionary, a time-server, or hanger-on of the court, and his political success contributes one of the many triumphs of mind over matter.   In an age when charm of person and grace of demeanour counted for far more in politics than they do at the present day, his appearance was such as to make him the obvious butt of the caricaturist ; and it was well for his peace of mind that he was totally devoid of any personal vanity.   One of the most ugly and awkward of men, resembling much more the stage buffoon than the typical statesman, he was not only totally lacking in dignity of deportment but even in any of the physical attributes which are more useful than is commonly recognised to leaders of men. Gross and unwieldy in figure, with a swollen and inflated countenance, the ludicrous effect of which was heightened by a gaping mouth and great, bolting eyes, his appearance was close upon being actually repulsive ; and the disagreeable impression was not removed when he spoke, his voice being harsh and unmusical.   By a contemporary he was compared to a blind trumpeter ; but the author of this apt comparison also pointed out that within this rude and unattractive casket many rare and useful talents were concealed.   If not a great orator, North was undoubtedly a very quick

[1] *Cavendish Debates*, I, 299.

and ready debater; and in ability, industry, and tact, incomparably superior to his predecessor in office. In happier circumstances, and under a more enlightened master, he might have earned a respectable name as a statesman; for, if without great political insight or understanding, he was at least furnished with good sound common-sense, sufficient to have enabled him to steer safely through many difficulties. Moreover, to this useful attribute he added a temper so sweet that it was almost impossible to ruffle it, and a wit so ready and sparkling that it even amused those against whom it was directed. During the fierce debates upon the American war, North not infrequently met the attack of an embittered member of the opposition with a witty rejoinder which dissolved the house into laughter at the expense of the assailant; and, during the same period, it was not an unknown experience for a speaker, engaged in holding up the leader of the government to the scorn of all honest men and succeeding ages, to be suddenly disconcerted by discovering his victim peacefully sleeping upon the treasury-bench.[1]

Such were the characteristics of the man who was nominally to rule England for twelve years, to the country's undoing; and, in spite of his many attractive qualities and genuine political ability, it must be admitted that he was entirely unfitted to be the minister of a monarch determined to overstep the limits to which custom had confined a constitutional king. Indeed, the very virtues which caused him to be an adored father and charming companion, became serious defects when he entered into the service of

[1] Walpole's Memoirs, 4, 52-56; Walpole's Letters, 7, 361-363. An interesting sketch of Lord North is contained in Lord Brougham's *Statesmen of the Time of George III*.

the crown. A happy and amiable disposition, a reluctance to give pain, and a sense of humour, are such attractive qualities in a private individual that we are apt to rate them too highly; and it is open to question whether they are not serious drawbacks to a statesman who must needs encounter opposition, and who is hindered rather than assisted by a humorous appreciation of the littleness of the issues which men think great. For, however that may be, there is no doubt that these amiable characteristics of North, combined with his bias in favour of toryism, caused him to degenerate into a tool of the king who used him to rivet his will upon the people. The severe treatment, which he has received at the hands of historians, is, indeed, deserved, for out of his own mouth he stands condemned of continuing the American war, in deference to the royal will, long after he had become convinced that there was no alternative for this country but to make peace with the revolted colonists. Moreover, it is during his twelve years of power that the influence of the crown reached the zenith of its fortunes; and, though North might be in office, it was George III. who really ruled. Never again was the king to have a minister who combined such a readiness to serve with such skill in the parliamentary warfare; and it was not likely that, having wandered in the wilderness for nine years, he would lightly discard a servant so well suited to his needs !

Yet, difficult as it may be to forgive North for the evil that he wrought, it ought not to be forgotten that when he accepted office at the royal command, he conclusively proved that, whatever were his political defects, a lack of courage was not amongst them. The situation which confronted him was sufficiently adverse to have intimidated the most daring and reckless of men. It was quite possible that the new prime minister might be out of office in a few days, for panic and disorder prevailed in the ranks of the ministerialists, while the opposition, elated by the hope of victory, was eager to push the encounter to the final stage. Moreover, the enemies of the court were far stronger than they had hitherto been, for, without entering upon any formal treaty of alliance, Chatham, Rockingham, and the Grenvilles, had agreed to unite in defence of the rights of the electors, and to refrain from wasting their energy in bickering and discord. Fragile as such an union might be, it was at least an improvement upon what had gone before, and the opposition leaders were not so blind as to fail to see that the time had at last come for them to stand together against the throne. Before the parliamentary session was many days old, Chatham had visited Rockingham, thus proclaiming to the world that the feud, which dated from the summer of 1766, was dead ; [1] and Temple, who may fairly be taken as speaking for his brother as well as for himself, was warm in his approval of his new allies, informing Lady Chatham that " everything has passed very amicably betwixt Lord Rockingham, the Duke of Richmond, and me." [2] Such harmony had long been absent, and, now that it had come, boded no good to the court ; for though the ministers still possessed a numerical superiority in parliament, it was extremely uncertain how long they would continue to enjoy this advantage over an opposition inspired by the greatest statesman of the time, and resolved to take the tide of fortune at the flood. Restored to as much health as he ever expected to enjoy, and to all his old vigour,

[1] Walpole's Memoirs, 4, 39-40 ; Letters, 7, 356-359.
[2] Chatham's Correspondence, 3, 394-396.

Chatham was burning to destroy an administration which he believed guilty of trampling English liberty under foot; and it was impossible to forecast the effect of the onslaught that he was certain to make. It might well happen that the magic of his name and the splendour of his eloquence would arouse such a fury in the nation and such trepidation in parliament that North would lose his majority, and the king be compelled to admit the victorious opposition into office. Nor would Chatham stand alone in denunciation. Temple, who was never happier than when engaged in attack, might be trusted to be unsparing in the vitriolic scorn which he always had at his command; and both Shelburne and Camden, though so lately in the service of the court, were not likely to be over-merciful in their treatment of their former colleagues. In the house of commons, moreover, the contest was certain to be equally fierce and acrimonious, for there, Burke, Dowdeswell, Savile and Meredith were to be as constant in criticism as they had been in the past; and their efforts were to be ably seconded by a recent and unexpected recruit to the cause of freedom— Alexander Wedderburn, a native of Scotland, who had lately risen to parliamentary eminence, and proved himself a debater of the first rank. Though destined very shortly to be branded as a turn-coat, and to be held for ever in abhorrence by every good whig, Wedderburn at this time enjoyed a reputation for disinterested patriotism which he seems to have deserved as little as his subsequent ill-fame. Nothing in his previous career justified any other assumption than that he was an extremely able man, conscious of his own power, determined to advance in life, and the least likely of all men to starve his ambition for the sake of satisfying a principle. His consistency lay in the steadiness with which he sought his goal ; and, though the means might change, the end always remained the same. Trained in youth for the legal profession, he had abandoned the Scotch for the English bar where he had quickly won a name as a great equity lawyer. Entering parliament in the winter of 1761, he had enlisted under the banner of his countryman, Lord Bute, and appears for some years to have been a consistent advocate of tory principles of government, actively supporting George Grenville's administration, and going into opposition on the formation of the first Rockingham ministry. On the retirement of Bute from any active participation in political life, Wedderburn transferred his allegiance to George Grenville ; and he was doing no more than following in the footsteps of his leader when, in the session of 1769, he went into open opposition to the court, and warmly embraced the cause of Wilkes. His legal knowledge, and his undoubtedly great gifts as a parliamentary debater, rendered him a most valuable accession of strength to a party which needed all the assistance it could get ; and the enthusiastic welcome, which was given him by his new allies, is a tribute to the value which they placed upon his aid.

Thus, in both houses of parliament the government was called upon to meet the attack of some of the most brilliant debaters and distinguished politicians of the age ; and the battle began before North had actually taken office. On Monday, January 22nd, Lord Rockingham, acting in the closest concert with Chatham and Temple,[1] moved that on the following Wednesday

---

[1] Lord Temple's letter to Lady Chatham on January 16th, 1770, clearly shows that he and Rockingham were working together ; and we glean from Horace Walpole's letters that Chatham's visit to the marquis preceded the debate in the upper house. Chatham Correspondence, 3, 394-396 ; Walpole's Letters, 7, 356-359.

the house of lords should sit in committee to consider the state of the nation.   In what was for him an unusually lengthy speech, for, conscious of his own ineffectiveness as a debater, he but rarely spoke, he argued that the popular discontent had been provoked, not by any single act of the administration or legislature, but by years of consistent misgovernment.   The peace of Paris, the cyder tax, the treatment of the colonies, and the payment of the king's debts without inquiry into the past or guarantees for the future, were all cited to prove the ample excuse that existed for the national dissatisfaction ;   and although, as was inevitable, there was a reference to the expulsion and disqualification of Wilkes, Rockingham was careful to state that " he considered it only as the point to which all the other measures of the administration had tended," the crowning evil, but certainly not the sole source of mischief.   In thus seeking to explain the present by the past, Rockingham framed an indictment which was directed far more against the crown than against the particular administration which happened to be in power ; and still wider ground was taken by Chatham who, though forestalled in his intention of seconding the motion by Grafton who was anxious to show show little he had to fear from an inquiry,[1] was not to be prevented from expressing his opinions.   Paying more attention than Rockingham to the persecution of Wilkes, Chatham thundered against those who, in order to gratify the court, had cared as little for the law as the most despotic rulers in the past.   " The constitution," he exclaimed, " has been grossly violated.   The constitution at this moment stands violated.   Until that wound be healed, until that grievance be redressed, it

---

[1] Grafton's *Autobiography*, pp. 251-252 ;   *Parl. Hist.*, xvi., 747.

is in vain to recommend union to parliament; in vain to promote concord among the people." Then, rising from the particular to the general, he proceeded, in defiance of the prejudices of his class and time,[1] to enlarge upon the corrupt and unrepresentative character of parliament as the root evil from which all others sprang. Asiatic wealth, he argued, had brought in its train Asiatic methods of government, with the result that though " the constitution intended that there should be a permanent relation between the constituent and representative body of the people," it had become impossible for any candid man to affirm that " as the house of commons is now formed, that relation is in any degree preserved." Thus, out of the ashes of the Middlesex election rose parliamentary reform, and though the remedy proposed by Chatham may appear to us niggardly enough, confined as it was to increasing the county representation in order to counterbalance the corrupt influence of the boroughs, it was no small matter that the greatest statesman of the day had pointed out the plague spot in the constitution, and declared with emphasis that an unrepresentative parliament would always incline to be subservient to the court and tyrannical to the people.[2]

Succeeding ages have rightly recognised Chatham on this occasion as the herald of a future dawn ; but the judgment of history is frequently in conflict with the verdict of contemporaries ; and most of his hearers thought of the utterance as springing from the rage

---

[1] How an intelligent contemporary regarded parliamentary reform may be gathered from Walpole's remark that " Lord Chatham, not content with endeavouring to confound and overturn the legislature, has thrown out that one member more ought to be added to each county ; so little do ambition and indigence scruple to strike at fundamentals." Walpole's Letters, 7,.359-361.

[2] *Parl. Hist.*, xvi., 741 ff. ; Grafton's *Autobiography*, pp. 251-252.

of the baffled intriguer who, prevented from steering the ship of state where he would, was prepared to vent his disappointment by running it upon the rocks. Yet, though the ministers and their supporters paid but little heed to what was by far the most momentous remark made in the course of the debate, they were not oblivious to the danger which immediately confronted them. Much had been said, and more had been hinted, to cause the king and his advisers to view the future with alarm and anxiety. The directness of the attack and the harmony in the opposition's ranks were clear indications that a stormy time was ahead, and, as Rockingham's motion had been passed unopposed, the decisive battle might be expected in two days' time. The notice was short, and the forces of the government, disorganised, disheartened and confused, were in no way prepared for a fight to the death ; and, if nothing had happened to modify the situation, it is by no means unlikely that the ministers would have suffered a humiliating defeat. Fortunately, however, for them, Chatham was too ill to attend on the appointed day, and the committee of the house was therefore postponed until Friday, February 2nd.[1] Great was the advantage of this delay to the ministers, for not only were they given time for very necessary preparation, but they were also able to turn their attention to the house of commons where the hunt was equally up against the government. Resolved to lose no time in pressing the attack home, Dowdeswell on January 25th moved that " this house, in the exercise of its judicature in matters of election, is bound to judge according to the law of the land, and the known and established law and custom of parliament, which is part

[1] Lord Temple to Lady Chatham (undated), Pitt Papers, R. O., 1st series, vol. lxii. ; Chatham Correspondence, 3, 401-407.

thereof " ; and the motion was skilfully enough framed. It was hardly possible to allow it to pass unchallenged, bearing as it did such obvious reference to the action of the government in the Middlesex election ; and yet opposition seemed equally difficult, except on the clearly impossible ground that a single house of parliament was free from all restraints of law. Thus, driven between the horns of a dilemma, the ministry might possibly have remained there, had it not been rescued by North who contrived to wreck the motion by the addition of a clause stating that the disqualification of Wilkes was agreeable both to the law of the land and of parliament. By this amendment North skilfully turned the position taken up by his opponents ; and, as was only natural, the motion so amended was fiercely opposed by those who were responsible for it in its original form. The struggle was protracted, and it was only after a debate lasting until three o'clock in the morning that the ministers carried the day. Their triumph, however, was not great, and whatever joy there was over the result was to be found among the vanquished rather than among the victors. The government had only prevailed in a very full house by the comparatively small majority of forty-four ; and, what was of still greater significance, the defeated minority included some who were reckoned as habitual supporters of the ministry. Country gentlemen like the Ridleys of Northumberland, and a well known adherent of the court like Lord Percy, Bute's son-in-law, had thrown in their lot with the opposition ; and one enthusiastic follower of Chatham warmly congratulated his leader upon the " fine increase to minerity " (sic).[1]

---

[1] John Calcraft to Chatham, January 26th, 1770 ; Pitt Papers, R. O., 1st series, vol. xxv.   For a general account of the debate, see Walpole's Memoirs,

It was two days after this debate in the commons that Grafton informed the king that he could no longer continue in his service. For nearly four years he had borne the burden of an office which he had been reluctant to accept when it was first offered him ; and few men have been equally unfortunate in their experience of administrative life. Almost everything he touched had turned to disaster, and he neither inspired confidence in those whom he served, nor fear in those whom he opposed. By some he has been depicted as a tyrant anxious to strike down liberty wherever he detected it, and by others as a weak, helpless creature, unstable as water and shifting as sand. Thus, decried by friends and foes alike, he has come down in history with a sorry reputation ; and it is only comparatively lately that it has been understood that he was, to a very great extent, the plaything of cruel circumstance. His many faults of character, his indolence, his selfish love of pleasure, and his irresolution, indeed unfitted him to be the ruler of the country in a perilous moment of its history ; but, aware as he was of his own deficiencies, it is extremely unlikely that he would have set out upon the fatal journey had he foreseen the accidents which were to befall him on his way. The totally unexpected collapse in Chatham's health imposed on him a burden which he was totally unable to bear ; and from that time he plays the sorry part of a victim of forces which he was too weak to resist. Flouted by Charles Townshend, dominated by the king, and overpowered by the Bedford faction, Grafton might have saved himself from much ignominy and mental suffering by timely resignation ; and for the fact that he did

4, 42-44 ; *Parl. Hist.*, xvi., 785 ff. ; Add. MS., 35609, f. 141 ; Walpole's Letters, 7, 361-363.

not take this easy road out of all his many difficulties, George III. and Chatham must be held responsible. It was they who had urged him to stay, who had impressed upon him that his duty consisted in remaining at his post, and the advice they gave recoiled upon themselves. If Grafton had not continued in office, it is extremely unlikely that Chatham, on his recovery, would have found so much to deplore in the state of the nation ; and the king had little reason to be satisfied with a servant who had brought the administration to the condition in which it was at the beginning of 1770. It must have been with a heavy heart that North undertook to repair the damage which Grafton had wrought ; and he might well think that the mischief had been allowed to go too far. " In the meantime," wrote Walpole about this time, " Lord North is first minister. He is much more able, more active, more assiduous, more resolute and more fitted to deal with mankind. But whether the apparent, nay, glaring timidity of the duke may not have spread too general an alarm is more than probable." [1]

Such was the opinion of a well-informed and sagacious contemporary, but no great insight was needed to perceive the difficulties which attended the undertaking. The most superficial observer might have seen that the new prime minister was in the unfortunate position of a general who takes command in the middle of the battle ; and no sooner had he kissed the king's hand for office than he was compelled to face the full fury of the storm. Elated by the comparative success of his previous motion, Dowdeswell, on January 31st, moved that " by the law of the land, and the known law and usage of parliament, no person, eligible by common right, can be incapacitated by vote

[1] Walpole's Letters, 7, 361-363.

or resolution of this house, but by act of parliament only." No challenge of the legality of what the ministry had done could well be more direct ; and, if the motion was carried, it could hardly fail to be a death-blow to the administration. Nor was it over-sanguine on the part of the opposition to believe that there was a reasonable chance of success. The recent reduction in the usual ministerial majority, the changes in the cabinet, and the not unimportant fact that, whatever experience and success North had previously had, he was a novice as prime minister, might easily lead men to believe that the government was doomed, and to throw in their lot with what they expected to be the triumphant opposition.

If events had followed this course, if North had failed in what may not unfittingly be described as his Marengo, then the debate on January 31st would have become historic, and, perhaps, marked the beginning of a new era in the reign. The lengthy campaign between the crown and the whig party was not destined, however, to have such a dramatic end ; and great was the disappointment in the ranks of the opposition when, after Dowdeswell's resolution had been debated until one o'clock in the morning, a motion, put by Lord North, that the chairman might leave the chair, was carried by two hundred and twenty-six to one hundred and eighty-six votes.[1] The ministerial majority was, it is true, slightly less than it had been on January 25th ; but the cause of mortification to the opposition was that it was no smaller. An administration which, in the most adverse circumstances, had prevailed by a majority of forty, might well be expected to in-crease its numerical strength as it became more firmly

[1] Add. MS., 35609, f. 143 ; *Parl. Hist.*, xvi., 800 ff. ; Walpole's Memoirs, 4, 50, ff.

established in power ; and the chagrin felt by the supporters of the defeated motion was certainly not unjustified. Writing to Chatham on the day following the battle, Rockingham remarked with no little bitterness that the earl " would not be much surprised at the majority last night having been two hundred and twenty-six, as his lordship must have seen for some years past that it is neither men nor measures but something else which operates in these times "; [1] but the disappointment, which was felt by Rockingham and his friends, was more than counterbalanced by the joy at the court that so critical a day had passed off so successfully. " I am greatly rejoiced at the conclusion of the debate," wrote George III. to Lord North ; [2] and though an impartial and critical observer like Horace Walpole declined to believe that the ministry was out of the wood,[3] men of more enthusiastic temperament were ready to jump to the conclusion that all danger was over. " You have no doubt observed with surprise," wrote Edward Sedgwick to his friend, Weston Underwood, " that contrary to all experience and probability, the critical resignation of the Duke of Grafton did not at all diminish the number of the majority on the great day of battle, but on the contrary that number was increased by two,[4] and everything since looks as if the present ministry were to continue with Lord North at the head of the treasury." [5]

The whigs had, therefore, failed in the lower house, and no happier fortune attended their efforts in the

---

[1] Chatham Correspondence, 3, 414-415.

[2] Correspondence of George III. with Lord North, 1, 13.

[3] Walpole's Letters, 7, 363-366.

[4] On January 25th the numbers on a division had been 224 to 180.

[5] Hist. MSS. Comm. Weston Underwood MSS., 421. It should be noted, however, that this letter was written after the debate in the upper house on February 2nd, which may account for its sanguine tone.

house of lords, where, on February 2nd, the day fixed for the peers to go into committee upon the state of the nation, Lord Rockingham moved a resolution similar to that which Dowdeswell had failed to carry in the house of commons. The motion, which was debated until past midnight, and most eloquently supported by Chatham, was finally rejected by ninety-six to forty-seven votes ; and no sooner had the division been taken than Lord Marchmont, regardless of the lateness of the hour, moved that " any resolution of this house, directly or indirectly impeaching a judgment of the house of commons, in a matter where their jurisdiction is competent, final, and conclusive, would be a violation of the constitutional rights of the commons, tends to make a breach between the two houses of parliament, and leads to general confusion." On this question the battle began again and was continued until two o'clock in the morning, an unusually late hour for the house to sit. Hard words were spoken, Camden being bitterly reviled by Weymouth and Sandwich for having concealed from them, while yet their colleague, his real opinion upon the legality of Wilkes' disqualification ; a charge upon which the ex-lord chancellor defended himself but weakly. But the debate was not confined to merely personal recriminations ; with more than even his usual oratorical vigour, Chatham besought the peers, by the noble blood which ran in their veins, and by their noble ancestors who had fought so bravely in the cause of freedom, not to regard with cynical indifference the violation of the cherished law of England ; and then, as though bowing his head to the inevitable, suddenly cried out that " if the constitution must be wounded, let it not receive its mortal stab at this dark and midnight hour." The appeal, however, fell upon deaf ears ; and when Marchmont's motion was put to the vote it was carried in the affirmative.[1]

In both houses of parliament, therefore, the ministry had more than stood its ground against its enemies ; and if North only continued as he had begun, George III. might count upon a notable triumph over what he persisted in believing to be the forces of faction. And, as the month of February drew to a close, it became more and more apparent that the hope which the opposition had cherished of storming the royal closet at the point of the sword, was fast fading into the light of common day. When on Monday, February 12th, Dowdeswell asked leave to introduce a bill for the disenfranchisement of certain of the lower revenue officers, permission was refused by seventy-five votes, a majority far larger than the government had expected upon a proposal which might be expected to commend itself to the approval of many ; [2] and when, a few days later, Dowdeswell's resolution of the previous 25th of January, as amended by North, was reported to the house, it was successfully carried by the government against the opposition by a majority of seventy-eight.[3] As often happens, those who had been beaten sought to explain away their failure by assigning every reason except the true one ; and Calcraft ingeniously argued that the decline in the numerical strength of the opposition was merely temporary and accidental. " We rather gain than lose," he wrote

[1] *Parl. Hist.*, xvi., 813 ff ; Grafton's *Autobiography*, 251-252 ; Walpole's Memoirs, iv., 58-59.

[2] " The motion was popular and constitutional, but the old artillery of the court, the tories, were played against the proposal, and it was rejected by 263 against 188." Walpole's Memoirs, iv., 60. George III. also remarks in a letter to North that, " as the question proposed by Mr Dowdeswell was well calculated to catch many persons, I think it has been rejected by a very handsome majority." Correspondence of George III. with Lord North, 1, 14. For an account of the debate *see Parl. Hist.*, xvi., 833, ff.

[3] *Cavendish Debates*, 1, 488 ff. ; Parliamentary History, xvi., 807 ff.

to Chatham, " though sickness, loss of relations, idleness and the ridotto prevented our friends' attendance ; had not these accidents interfered, we should have turned two hundred which we have strength to do." [1] But explanations such as these are too common to gain easy acceptance ; and, to the discerning and unprejudiced observer, it was quite clear that the opposition was rapidly losing ground in the house of commons. Nor was the prospect any brighter in the upper house ; for when on February 12th Chatham moved that a capacity for election to parliament did not depend finally upon a determination of the house of commons, the motion was defeated by the previous question being put and carried.[2] Seeing the ministry thus triumphant in both houses men came to the conclusion that the tide of good fortune had turned definitely in favour of the court. " In good truth," wrote Walpole, towards the end of the month, " that stock (Wilkes) is fallen very low. The court has recovered a majority of seventy-five in the house of commons ; and the party has succeeded so ill in the lords that my Lord Chatham has betaken himself to the gout, and appears no more." [3] Such was the general opinion ; and in a letter, written on the day after the debates in both houses on February 12th, Simon Fraser, regardless of grammar, remarked how " to-day the countenances of the friends of government is cleared up, and all partys agree that we shall have no change this winter." [4]

It is far easier to state the fact of North's success than to assign the cause ; and it may be partly for this reason that little attention has hitherto been paid to

[1] John Calcraft to Lord Chatham, Pitt Papers, R.O., 1st series, vol. xxv.
[2] Walpole's Memoirs, iv., 60.
[3] Walpole's Letters, 7, 366-369.
[4] Hist MSS. Comm., 11th Report, Appendix, Part iv., p. 407.

an achievement which, quite apart from its permanent value, was at least a triumph of no mean skill. The simple explanation of bribery and corruption is certainly not an adequate solution of the problem, for there is no evidence that Grafton was hindered in the working of this part of the machinery of government, or that North was given greater facilities than his predecessor enjoyed. In one respect, however, North was far more favourably situated than Grafton for the purpose of dispensing the loaves and fishes of official life ; for, as a member of the house of commons, he was more in touch with the popular assembly in which, after all, the most momentous battles of the administration had to be fought. Even a veteran and experienced leader like Newcastle had found it almost impossible to control the lower from the upper house, to marshal the battalions in support of the ministry, and to know which of the representatives of the people needed to be rewarded for their devotion ; and what a Newcastle had found difficult, a Grafton was certainly not likely to achieve. Yet, when every allowance has been made for the advantage which North enjoyed from being a commoner, it remains true that he owed his triumph not a little to his own skill, vigour, and perseverance. Whereas Grafton had been listless, indifferent, weary of the contest, and almost convinced that victory was as fatal as defeat, North conscientiously believed that the time had come to make a resolute stand against the forces of faction both at home and in the colonies. It was the change of the believer for the cynic that worked the miracle, and the triumph of North was the triumph of faith. He may have been misguided, but at this stage of his career he was at least sincere in believing that in defeating the opposition he was preserving the court from the fury of disappointed political factions, and safeguarding the English constitution from oligarchical perversion. It was in this sign that he conquered.

Yet, great as was his courage, it must be remembered that he profited not a little by the disabilities under which his antagonists suffered, and the mistakes of which they were guilty. In electing to continue the contest against the court upon the old question of the Middlesex election, Chatham and his associates were doubtless inspired by a sound political instinct, for there was no doubt that the treatment of Wilkes had stirred the indignation of the country, and therefore made a good rallying cry against the court; but, unfortunately for the opposition, the topic had been so much discussed and debated that it was difficult to say anything new upon it, and there were indications of a growing indifference in the country. Few political questions indeed maintain their supremacy over the popular imagination for any length of time, and nothing perhaps is quite so extinct as a controversy which is a twelve-month old. Wilkes had served his turn, and it would have been well if the opposition had been able to enlist the sympathy of the nation in some less well-worn theme. But this was impossible, for upon the only other topic of interest and importance then before the country, the treatment of the colonies, the members of the opposition were certainly not in agreement; and so they were compelled to continue upon a dusty and well-trodden road for want of knowing where else to go. The Middlesex election, with all its numerous ramifications, was their only bond of union; and the link was certainly not too strong. While both Chatham and Rockingham believed that Wilkes had been illegally disqualified, they differed as to the method of procedure to be adopted for righting the wrong, Chatham favouring a far more democratic course of action than Rockingham with his aristocratic prejudices approved ; and although this divergence of opinion was, for the time being, successfully suppressed, signs are not wanting that no little diplomacy and skill were needed from the first to avert the disruption of the so recently concluded alliance. Thus, only with extreme reluctance and hesitation had the followers of Rockingham agreed that a motion for the increase of the navy, which had been originally fixed to be made by Lord Craven on February 19th, should be postponed until March 2nd, in order that Chatham, who was suffering from gout, might be able to attend ; and Temple was highly indignant that the delay, which he demanded on behalf of his brother-in-law as a right, should only be grudgingly granted as a boon. " Our friends give themselves too many airs of taking the lead," he wrote to his sister. " I matter not the outward trappings, but really we must not be dragged by the Duke of Richmond." [1]

[1] Lord Temple to Lady Chatham, February 19th, 1770 ; Pitt Papers, R.O., 1st series, vol. lxii. In another letter to Lady Chatham, he gives an interesting meeting at Rockingham's house, summoned to consider the policy of postponement. " The intention of going on without my dear sister's lord and master," he wrote, " was indeed at last checked, but the resolution was firmly taken, and not without much reluctance departed from. My Lord Rockingham is very polite, but be it then known unto your ladyship that above one dozen of our lordships met in Grosvenor Square in consequence of my proposition. . . . Lord Rockingham came to sit by me. He added many, many arguments to those he had used in the morning for not changing the day, and not without art. Upon my saying it was Lord Chatham's own proposition ; it had been talked of in the house of lords by the Duke of Richmond, Lord Rockingham, and Lord Chatham, and they scarce knew who first dropped the hint. The council sat. The Duke of Manchester opens strongly . . . for going on, the Duke of Richmond supports it at large—Lord Coventry and Lord Bucks declares a contrary opinion ; Lord Shelburne joyns with them, and adds the warmest testimonies of respect and devotion to Lord Chatham. Lord Suffolk speaks strongly for putting off, Lord Lyttelton is of the same opinion, and finally your humble servant, with great modesty and submission to the determination of that most respectable assembly. . . . At last some of the opposite grandees confer in corners, and the result is consent to put

By the weakness of his opponents, therefore, as well as by his own skill, North had contrived to carry the government successfully through a crisis of its fortunes ; and from the end of February until the middle of April, when parliament rose for the Easter holidays, he·more than held his own against those who had thought in their pride that their hour had at last come. The parliamentary history of these weeks is no narrative of the varying fortunes of war, of battles lost and others won, but a fairly steady record of the triumph of the ministry. When on the last day of February Grenville moved for an account of all the civil list expenses, which had been incurred during the past year, to be laid before the house, the proposal was rejected by ninety-seven votes,[1] and Rockingham had no better fortune when, a fortnight later, he introduced the same motion into the upper house, supported though he was by Chatham who, in the course of his speech, made such a pointed reference to the truth and sincerity of the late king as to suggest that he was rather at a loss to detect these virtues in the present occupant of the throne.[2]

Nor were the ministers content with standing upon the defensive, merely repulsing the attacks of the opposition : assured of their own strength, they were now prepared to carry the war into the enemy's camp, and they did not have to wait long for a fitting

it off, but the Duke of Richmond lays in his claim never to do it again, which I do not understand to be agreed to as a general proposition, though it will be hard to procure their assent to a further delay than Wednesday sennight for this question. . . . This event, I am satisfyed, has proved very mortifying, but really they presume too far, and occasional checks must be given." Pitt Papers, R.O., February 18th, 1st series, vol lxii. See also Rockingham to Temple, February 18th, *ibid.*, and Chatham Correspondence, 3, 419-423.

[1] *Parl. Hist.*, xvi., 843 ff. ; *Cavendish Debates*, 1, 475 ff.

[2] *Parl. Hist.*, xvi., 849 ff.; Grenville Papers, 4, 508 ff. Rockingham Memoirs, 2, 168-169.

occasion. On Wednesday, March 14th, Beckford, the lord mayor, accompanied by the sheriffs, had waited upon the king with a remonstrance which, as addressed to the throne, may fairly enough be termed insolent and dictatorial. Though styled " the humble address, of the city of London, in Common Hall assembled," it was anything but humble, and more of an ultimatum than an address. " May it please your majesty," it began, " we have already, in our petition, dutifully represented to your majesty the chief injuries we have sustained. We are unwilling to believe that your majesty can slight the desires of your people, or be regardless of their affection, and deaf to their complaints : yet their complaints remain unanswered, their injuries are confirmed, and the only judge removeable at the pleasure of the crown has been dismissed from his high office, for defending in parliament the laws and the constitution." After this minatory preamble the remonstrance proceeded to rehearse the grievances under which the people suffered, to declare that in depriving the electors of Middlesex of their just rights, the house of commons had been guilty of an illegality " more ruinous in its consequences than the levying of ship-money by Charles the First, or the dispensing power assumed by James the Second," and, to implore the king, in order that these wrongs might be redressed, to dissolve his parliament, and to dismiss his evil advisers.[1]

Such uncourtly language and such unfortunate historical parallels were not likely to be pleasing to any sovereign, and least of all to the one to whom they were addressed ; and, if those responsible for the wording of the remonstrance thought to intimidate the king by scantily-draped threats, they clearly

[1] *Cavendish Debates*, I, 517-518.

showed that they did not understand the man with whom they were dealing. It is at these moments of his career that George III. commands respect by his resolute bearing; and in his short answer to the remonstrance, he flung back the defiance which had been offered him. Calmly declaring that he had always made the law of the land the rule of his conduct, a statement all the more startling because it was absolutely sincere, he expressed his regret that any of his subjects should have been so misled as to offer a remonstrance which " I cannot but consider as disrespectful to me, injurious to my parliament, and irreconcileable to the principles of the constitution." [1]

It was this affront to the royal dignity that the ministers determined to bring to the notice of the house of commons, thus indirectly attacking the parliamentary opposition; and in so deciding it seems that they were not guilty of any rash or precipitate action. On the contrary, they deserve commendation for an adroit stroke of policy, designed far more to embarrass their enemies than to defend the king's honour. It must have been a matter of fairly common knowledge that Chatham, inasmuch as he was known to be a personal friend of the lord mayor, extending to him a confidence which few shared, approved of the remonstrance; and it might also be fairly anticipated that neither Rockingham nor his friends viewed with pleasure or approbation such an obvious attempt to subject parliament and the crown to the pressure of a mob. Thus, by a weapon taken out of the enemy's armoury, the ministry might destroy the alliance which at one time seemed so threatening, and at all times could not fail to be dangerous; and it was

[1] *Cavendish Debates*, I, 517-518.

probably in this hope [1] that on Thursday, March
15th, Sir Thomas Clavering was instructed [2] to move
for copies of the remonstrance and the king's answer
to be laid before the house. The success was even
greater than probably the ministers had anticipated,
the address being carried by the very substantial
majority of one hundred and sixty-three; "a vast
majority," wrote Walpole to a friend, " in the present
circumstances, and composed of . . . many who abandoned the opposition." [3] Nor is it difficult to perceive
the cause of this notable defection, for few speakers
on the opposition benches were sufficiently indifferent
to a reputation for moderation, to defend a remonstrance which certainly had not failed in the matter
of plain speaking. The lord mayor and the two sheriffs,
Townshend and Sawbridge, having already deeply
committed themselves, naturally enough did not
scruple to avow their full responsibility for the offending
document, and their pride in their achievement;
but the majority of the members, with more to
lose, maintained an attitude of greater caution and
reserve. Thus Wedderburn, who was certainly never
afraid of either giving or receiving hard words, confined
himself, for the most part, to a defence of the undoubted
right of the subject to petition; and Grenville warned
his hearers to take example by what had happened
in the case of Wilkes, and to refrain from entering
into a contest with the city of London from which they

[1] " Every temptation is, or will be, forthwith, held out to Lord Rockingham,"
wrote one of Lord Chatham's correspondents, two days before the debate.
Chatham Correspondence, 3, 423-427.

[2] Sir Thomas Clavering had the reputation of being unconnected with any
party; but, as Walpole points out, " the gentleman's independence was a
little sullied by the command of Languard Fort being . . . conferred on his
brother Colonel Clavering, a meritorious officer, to whom it had been promised,
but which made the connection of the elder brother with the court observed." Walpole's Memoirs, iv., 70.

[3] Walpole's Letters, 7, 369-372.

might well find it difficult to emerge with dignity. But the greatest caution, as had been anticipated, was displayed by the Rockingham whigs. Though Burke both spoke and voted against Clavering's motion, he was careful to state that, in so doing, he did not commit himself to a belief in the decency of the remonstrance ; and much the same line was taken by Lord John Cavendish, a member of the same party. Discouraged by such a half-hearted defence, it is not surprising that the opposition suffered a numerical declension ; and, a few days later, events followed much the same course when, the papers having been laid before the house in the interval, a resolution condemning the remonstrance, and a loyal address to the crown, were proposed, both being carried by large majorities.[1]

The ministers therefore had triumphed, but if they thought that they had done all they had set out to do, they were guilty of a mistake. Though they had been victorious in parliament, and made a demonstration of strength, they had not succeeded in dividing the opposition. It is true that the politicians of the city were deeply disgusted at the poor show their remonstrance had made in the house of commons, and attributed the blame to the Rockingham party ; [2] but Chatham was not to be separated from allies whom he still regarded as indispensable to the success of his designs. Experience had taught him to rate political union at a higher value than formerly; and, though probably aggrieved by what had happened, he perceived that for the opposition to quarrel would be to play the ministerial game. Thus, when he heard that some of his friends, and among them Lord

---

[1] *Cavendish Debates*, 1, 516 ff. ; *Parl. Hist.*, xvi., 874 ff. ; Walpole's Memoirs, 4, 68 ff.; Walpole's Letters, 7, 369-372; Hist. MSS. Comm. Weston Underwood MSS., 422.

[2] Chatham Correspondence, 3, 438-439.

Shelburne, were beginning to think of the Rockingham whigs as false allies, he was emphatic in the expression of his desire for union and harmony to continue. " I am a stranger to any particular incident at Lord Shelburne's," he wrote to John Calcraft, " not being supplied with over-much communication. I deeply lament any tendency towards jealousies or animosities between different parts of the combined forces, who stand for the public, and upon the maintenance of whose union all hope of good depends. If that transcendent and indispensable object shall be thrown away, I shall esteem nothing worth pursuing with a moment's thought. . . . May a temper of more manly wisdom, and some public-spirited candour and indulgence prevail amongst those who happen to differ in particular points, than that which seemed just bursting forth. As for Lord Rockingham, I have a firm reliance on his zeal for liberty, and will not separate from him." [1]

Thus, in a truly statesmanlike spirit did Chatham speak, averting by wise counsel the catastrophe for which the court had schemed ; but the fact that his intervention was necessary testifies to the reality of the danger. North, indeed, had been successful both in defence and offence, and these operations had not exhausted his activity ; for, while thus engaged, he had carried, in accordance with the decision arrived at by the cabinet in the previous year, the repeal of Townshend's revenue act, with the exception of the tax upon tea which was retained as an assertion of England's right to levy impositions upon the colonies for the purpose of obtaining a revenue. If North had failed in this part of his task it would indeed have been a boon to the country ; but it was probably the easiest

[1] Chatham Correspondence, 3, 438-439.

part of his achievement, for it was extremely difficult
for the opposition to make any effective resistance.
An amendment for the total repeal of the act was,
indeed, introduced ; but it only served to illustrate
the difference of opinion existing in the ranks of the
opponents of the government. Grenville, who refused
to believe that a partial repeal would satisfy the
Americans, or that a total repeal was anything but an
unworthy concession to rebellion, declined to vote ;
and though Wedderburn supported the amendment
on the ground that the " duties contended for are not
worth a single debate," he angrily denounced the
doctrine advanced by one speaker that, though
England had an undoubted right to levy taxes upon
the colonies, she ought never to exercise it. " What,
sir," he scornfully declared, " declare that you have
a right, and at the same time declare that the exercise
of it would be impolitic and unjust." In denouncing
such a position as illogical, Wedderburn was undoubtedly right ; but, unfortunately in so doing,
he was obliged to bear hardly upon his allies, the
Rockingham whigs. For, having passed the declaratory act when in power, they could not deny the
abstract right of parliament to tax the colonies ; and
it was by no means easy for them to show that, though
the right existed, it was inexpedient to exercise it.
Thus, when Sir William Meredith contended that the
existence of the declaratory act dispensed with the
necessity of retaining the tax upon tea, the argument
was hardly convincing since there is a world of difference between theory and practice ; and though it has
been said that " notwithstanding all the weight of
ministerial influence, the majority was only sixty-two
for continuing the whole act," [1] the assumption,

---

[1] *Cavendish Debates*, I, 500, note I.

underlying this remark, that it was only with difficulty
that the administration gained the day, is certainly
not justified, a majority of that size being very little
below the ministerial average for the session. Indeed,
North could fairly claim that he had been assisted to
victory by being more consistent than his critics ;
but, if the force of logic was with him, the strength
of wisdom was with them. Though unable to make
points in argument, and open to the charge of inconsistency, they at least understood that the most
ardent spirits among the colonials were not to be
logic-driven into submission, and were determined
not to forego the Englishman's privilege of not having
his money taken out of his pocket without his own
consent. Moreover, the belief in the futility of a
partial repeal seems to have been shared by some
who supported North's bill, to judge by the remark
of one adherent of the government who confessed
that " there is little reason, I fear, to expect that it
will satisfy the Americans : so long as they deny
the authority of parliament to tax them at all, they
will say their burthen is indeed lightened, but that
their grievance remains, while a single farthing is
imposed on them by that authority." [1]

Successful as North had been by the time that
parliament rose for the Easter recess, it would be
untrue to imagine that his triumphal progress had
been unchecked ; for he had indeed suffered one mis-
adventure which, less skilfully handled, might have
been converted into a serious catastrophe. Convinced
by a long and intimate acquaintance with parliament,
and by a very recent experience, that the most crying
abuse of the age was the trial of election petitions by

[1] Hist. MSS. Comm. Weston Underwood MSS., 420-421 ; *Parl. Hist.*,
xvi., 852 ff. ; *Cavendish Debates*, 1, 483 ff. ; Walpole's Memoirs, 4, 63-64.

the house of commons, George Grenville introduced a bill by which the exercise of this right was transferred from the whole body to a select committee which was to be authorised to hear evidence given upon oath. Every impartial man was bound to admit that the reform was in the interests of justice and impartiality, the house of commons having clearly shown itself unfit to continue to enjoy a privilege which it had consistently abused from the time that a seat in parliament became a coveted honour. As is well known, the trials of election petitions had for long been conducted without any reference to impartiality or fairness, being merely considered as tests of party strength ; and the scandal of the Middlesex election was but one of a long series of similar, though less flagrant, instances of the assertion of might over right. Thus Grenville's measure was designed to remedy a crying evil ; and it might be thought that the advantages, which would ensue from it, were so abundantly clear as to render any opposition to it impossible. But such was not the case. With consciences dulled by habit, many men failed to see the iniquity of a system to which they had long been accustomed ; and neither the court nor the ministers were likely to favour a reform which, whatever its abstract value, could not fail to circumscribe their influence. Thus, though supported by all the parties in opposition, Grenville was not by any means able to count upon an easy victory ; and his bill did not pass unchallenged through the lower house. Hardened placemen like Rigby and Dyson, who never shocked their contemporaries except when they pretended to be honest, were inveterate in their opposition, and North quite frankly and honestly avowed his dislike of the change. But the scandal, which the bill sought to remedy, was so glaring and disgraceful that the conscience of the house was touched ; and even trusty and habitual supporters of the ministry began to desert their colours on the plea that they could not vote against their convictions. When Sir William Bagot announced his intention of supporting the bill, he spoke for a good many of the country gentlemen ; and when it was proposed to adjourn the consideration of the measure for two months, the motion was rejected by sixty-two votes. A less adroit party-leader than North might at this critical juncture have made a fatal blunder, and, by continuing his resistance to the bill, given the opposition the very triumph which they sought. Having the wisdom, however, to perceive that he could not carry his majority with him, and acting like the experienced commander who declines to give battle when the enemy has taken up an impregnable position, he withdrew from the attack,[1] and allowed the bill to become law without any further serious opposition.[2]

Thus, by skilfully changing his tactics in the middle of the struggle, North had averted disaster, and could retire to enjoy the Easter holidays with the comfortable assurance that the most difficult part of his work was over. The session, indeed, was not yet ended, but, as far as it had gone, he had outwitted the opposition, repaired the evil which Grafton had wrought, and freed

[1] " My brother's bill," wrote Temple to Lord Chatham on April 2nd, " is this day passed in the house of commons; the court having given up the design of opposing it on the third reading, which they fully intended, as it was said yesterday." Chatham Correspondence, 3, 439-440. See also *Parl. Hist.*, xvi., 923-924.

[2] " I made a shift, however," wrote Temple to Lady Chatham on April 3rd, " to go to the house, and get a first reading to our favourite bill. It is to be read a second time on Thursday ; all thoughts of opposition to it are entirely vanished, so that I would not by any means have my lord's zeal and kindness make him so much as think of setting his foot amongst us." Pitt Papers, R.O., 1st series, vol. lxii. See also Grenville Papers, 4, 515-516. For a general account of the parliamentary debates see *Parl. Hist.*, xvi., 902-904, 907-924 ; *Cavendish Debates*, 1, 475 ff., 505 ff.

the king from the harassing anxiety which had weighed upon him at the beginning of the year. But, if North had ample cause for self-congratulation, his opponents, on the contrary, needed no little ingenuity to discover any source of consolation. The most sanguine of them could not but acknowledge that their hopes had been blasted, and their efforts frustrated ; and the Duke of Richmond was probably not alone in thinking that it was vain to continue struggling after the tide of fortune had turned so decisively against them. Having withdrawn into the country, and disheartened by what had happened, Richmond began to grudge the necessity of returning to London after the Easter holidays were over, informing Rockingham of his suspicion that they " would all think it best to give over opposition for this year, as many people will be, like myself, very unwilling to go to town, nay more so, for I am persuaded that many good friends will not attend." [1] Such a suggestion sprang from no craven spirit, but from a natural weariness of a vain expenditure of energy ; and if there was an inclination towards despair in the ranks of the opposition, it is hardly surprising. But there was one man at least who was convinced that the hour had not yet come to refrain from denouncing the government, and that man was Chatham. A policy of surrender, of tame acquiescence in accomplished events, had never been part of his political creed ; and he was resolved, though success might be out of the question, never to relax in his attack upon the ministry. A great wrong having been committed, there was to be no rest until reparation had been made, and a stain removed from the annals of parliament. Never before, save at the outset of his political career, had Chatham been so

[1] Rockingham Memoirs, 2, 177-179.

active in opposition ; and contemporaries, whose memories did not go back to the days of Walpole and the war of Jenkins' ear, were astonished to find him playing what they thought to be such an uncongenial and unaccustomed rôle.[1]

Thus it was Chatham who infused courage into the faint hearts of his allies, and decided that the fight must continue ; and that he was right is beyond all doubt. An opposition which abandons the contest confesses to abject failure, and suffers a far severer loss of dignity and prestige than any defeat, however humiliating, can inflict upon it. This is axiomatic ; but skill was needed as well as courage, and, if the campaign was to continue, it was necessary to determine the method of attack. It was here that the difficulty came. The experience of the past two months had shown that the possibilities of the Middlesex election, as a political cry against the government, were fully exhausted ; and yet no new cry was at hand. If the parliamentary warfare was not to cease, there was nothing to be done but to prolong the discussion of a topic of which most men were thoroughly weary ; and easy though it is to blame the opposition for a lack of resource, the existence of any alternative course is certainly not obvious. If the country was weary of the Middlesex election, it was frankly in-different to all other possible political questions of the day ; and thus the opposition had either to repeat what already had been said, or to say what nobody wanted to hear. The former alternative 'was chosen and proved a failure, but it is by no means certain that any other policy would have been less disastrous.

---

[1] " Lord Chatham continued, for two months together in a more active opposition to the ministry than I had ever known in his lordship." Grafton's *Autobiography*, p. 252.

Driven between the horns of a dilemma, the opponents of the court were in a situation which could hardly be more unfavourable ; and it may fairly be urged in their defence that, in continuing to thunder against the past illegalities of the government, they were not sinning against their own sincere convictions. They, at least, rallied to a fight on behalf of a cause in which they believed.

Before parliament had risen for the Easter recess, Chatham had given notice of his intention to introduce a bill reversing the proceedings of the house of commons upon the Middlesex election ; [1] and, after the holidays were over, he lost no time in fulfilling his pledge. During the last days of April he was in active correspondence with Rockingham, and a draft of the bill having been approved at a meeting of the whig lords on Sunday, April 29th,[2] Chatham introduced it into the house of lords on Tuesday, May 1st. The expectation of victory had, of course, been absent from the first, but the opposition had reason to be disappointed with the results of the venture. A motion, appointing the bill to be read a second time, was easily defeated by the ministry, only forty-three peers being rallied in support of it ; and against Camden, who spoke on behalf of the bill, the court put up Lord Mansfield whose legal reputation was at least equal to that of the ex-lord chancellor.[3] Yet, great as the rebuff was, Chatham does not appear to have been unduly cast down, for, three days later, he brought forward a motion condemning the royal answer to the city remonstrance as a direct and flagrant contradiction to " the clearest

---

[1] *Parl. Hist.*, xvi. 924.

[2] Chatham Correspondence, 3, 445-449 ; Rockingham Memoirs, 2, 174-177 ; Lord Rockingham to Chatham, April 29th, 1770, Pitt Papers, R.O., 1st series, vol. liv.

[3] *Parl. Hist.*, xvi. 954 ff. Walpole's Memoirs, 4, 81.

rights of the subject, namely, to petition the king for redress of grievances ; to complain of violation of the freedom of election ; to pray dissolution of parliament ; to point out malpractices in adminis- tration ; and to urge the removal of evil ministers." This minatory resolution, however, supported though it was, like the bill which had preceded it, by all sections of the opposition, encountered no happier fate, being defeated by a slightly larger majority.[1]

These onslaughts upon the government may well have been inevitable, but it is undeniable that they served to illustrate the ineffectiveness of the opposition and the growing strength of the administration. However gallantly a party may struggle, it is not likely to win recruits by revealing the diminution in its strength, for the scripture maxim that " to him who hath shall be given " is as true in politics as elsewhere. But, great as was the disappointment, consolation was not entirely absent, for, in spite of certain difficulties and a real divergence of opinion upon particular questions, the opposition had, at least, preserved internal harmony. If that was destroyed, if Chatham or Grenville quarrelled with Rockingham, and the leaders of the different parties, breaking apart from one another, fought as rival tribal chieftains, then, indeed, the last state of the opposition would be worse than the first, and a crowning mercy be vouchsafed to the court. And towards the close of the session it appeared not improbable that the work of destruc- tion would be completed by this crushing and final disaster. Though fully aware of the dangers which beset such a course, Chatham was determined, before the session came to an end, to propose an address to

[1] *Parl. Hist.*, xvi. 966 ff. Hist. Comm. MSS. Weston Underwood MSS., 423-424.

the crown praying for the dissolution of parliament. In so doing he would undoubtedly be playing into the hands of the more extreme politicians in the city and elsewhere, who asserted that, by the exclusion of Wilkes and the intrusion of Luttrell, the house of commons had destroyed its legal position, and forfeited all claim to the respect and even to the obedience of the nation ; but it is wrong to assume that Chatham was merely playing the demagogue. It is far more reasonable to believe that he was influenced by sincere conviction, and conscientiously believed that only by a new parliament, untainted with illegality, could the evils of the state be redressed. " I could never," he emphatically declared about this time, " in any case wish a friend of mine to go into the king's service, unless a new parliament was called, it being in my sense an illusion, little short of infatuation, to imagine that this house of commons, the violators of the people's rights, would ever become the safe instrument of a system of administration founded on the reparation of the violations, and on a total extinction of the influence which caused them." [1]

In accordance with this opinion, so strongly expressed, Chatham was determined upon an address for dissolution, and would have taken this step earlier in the session had he not feared the opposition of Rockingham and his followers.[2] Though apparently as convinced as Chatham that a new parliament ought to be called, the Rockingham whigs were fearful that if they supported such an address as Chatham proposed, they might identify themselves, too closely for their comfort, with the democratic party ; and their alarm was increased by Chatham's declaration that " a surmise more than begins to spread, that zeal for this indis-

[1] Rockingham Memoirs, 2, 180-182.　　　　[2] *Ibid.*

pensable measure is slackening every hour " and that
he knew " of no adequate means to prevent the fatal
effects of such an umbrage taking possession of the
public, but a motion of dissolution in the house of
lords." [1] By these remarks a weight was attached
to public opinion which Rockingham was unable to
admit, and in his answer he clearly implied that, though
Chatham might submit to popular pressure, he himself
was not to be mob-driven. " I cannot just now,"
he wrote, " recollect my thoughts so fully as to be
able to write to your lordship a decisive opinion on the
subject of the letter I had the honour to receive from
you. As yet I have not seen the Duke of Richmond,
the Duke of Portland, and some other lords whom I
wish much to talk with on the matter. From some
information I have, I should doubt whether in general,
among the lords in opposition, an address for the
dissolution of parliament would be a measure which
they would incline to. It does not strike me that it
is particularly called for ; because I cannot admit
that, though some people may throw out suspicions
or reflections that there is lukewarmness, or that we
or others do not adhere to the measure of dissolution,
and various surmises, etc., yet I must hold an opinion,
that it is neither for your lordship's honour, nor for
ours, to suffer ourselves to be sworn every day to keep
our word." [2]

From this interchange of letters it is clear that
there was a danger of dissension in the opposition
camp. Chatham, as was his wont, refused to abandon
his design in deference to what he must have thought
were the craven fears of his allies, and bravely asserted
the existence of " arguments amounting to a political

---

[1] Rockingham Memoirs, 2, 180-182.
[2] Chatham Correspondence, 3, 455-456.

demonstration in favour of the motion, . . . upon the supposition that dissolution, universally liked or not, is the measure *sine qua non* ; " [1] but, insistent though he might be, he found it no easy task to convince others of the pressing character of the necessity. After having conversed with Rockingham and some other members of the same party, Temple informed his brother-in-law that they were " much averse to the dissolution motion, though firm as to the thing," and expressed the opinion that " the sacrifice will be great if they yield to our wishes." [2] Critical as the situation undeniably was, the peril was less than it might appear at first sight, since all were convinced that nothing could be more disastrous to the cause they had in common than a quarrel; and it is seldom that differences cannot be settled when there is a predisposition towards peace. Rockingham's objection to the proposal was sensibly diminished on learning that Chatham was more influenced by personal conviction than by popular pressure ; [3] and the question was finally settled at a meeting held at Rockingham's house on the evening of Sunday, May 13th. Although no record survives of this conference, what evidence we have strongly points to the fact that Chatham carried his point, and secured the consent of his allies. [4]

[1] Rockingham Memoirs, 2, 183-184.

[2] Temple to Chatham, Friday, 1770; Pitt Papers, R.O., 1st series, vol. lxii.

[3] " Your lordship's last letter, putting the matter on your lordship's own opinion of the propriety of now moving the address, is, I assure your lordship, of much more weight with me, and may be with others, than the argument in the former letter, where your lordship, in part, put it on the necessity of clearing up some doubts which some have spread or attempted to propagate among the public." Chatham Correspondence, 3, 456-457.

[4] The evidence for this belief is a letter written by Chatham to Rockingham on Monday, May 14th, and which runs as follows : " Lord Chatham presents his compliments to Lord Rockingham, and hopes the following words will answer his lordship's doubts: . . . though Lord Chatham still thinks the other mode preferable, he defers with pleasure to Lord Rockingham's wish, and concludes it will better meet the Duke of

Having no time to lose, for the session was fast drawing to a close, Chatham moved the address on Monday, May 14th, the day after the meeting at Lord Rockingham's. It would be interesting to know how far he was supported by those who had so reluctantly given their consent to the scheme ; but, unfortunately for the historian, all strangers, with the exception of sons of peers and members of the house of commons, were excluded from the debate ; and the very meagre account in the parliamentary history contains nothing but a very brief summary of Chatham's speech and a simple record of the defeat of the motion.[1]

Five days later, parliament was prorogued until the following autumn, and North was given time to recover from the strain of four months of arduous conflict. By his success he had more than justified his appointment ; and in him George III. could feel that he had a servant who might be trusted to defend the court to the death, and yet never claim more independent authority than the crown was willing to grant. Meanwhile the opposition had nothing to look back to but a record of consistent failure only relieved by the fact that the alliance between the factions had stood the undoubtedly severe test of an unsuccessful campaign. Yet the continuance of this harmony in the future could not be predicted with any certainty ; for though Walpole was guilty of exaggeration when he informed a friend that " disunion has appeared between all parts of the opposition,"[2] he was not, as has been seen, very far from the truth. It is true that hitherto disruption had been averted by the existence of a conciliatory spirit ; but when allow-

---

Richmond's ideas." Rockingham Memoirs, 2, 185. This letter, which is misdated Wednesday, May 14th, obviously implies that an understanding had been arrived at on the Sunday evening.

[1] *Parl. Hist.*, xvi. 978-979.   [2] Walpole's Letters, 7, 375-377.

ance has been made for the frailty of human nature, and the ease with which misunderstandings arise, it must be admitted that no great ingenuity or perversity was needed to provoke a quarrel and destroy the alliance It was by no means improbable that Chatham might throw in his lot with the democratic section of the opposition, and completely identify himself with those whom Burke so contemptuously referred to as the " bill of rights people." [1] These more extreme politicians clamoured for constitutional remedies far too searching and drastic to be approved by what had come to be recognised as the official whig opposition ; and Rockingham and his followers, thinking more of restricting the influence of the crown than of submitting themselves to the power of the people, were certainly not prepared to listen favourably to the cry for parliamentary reform, the exclusion of placemen from the house of commons, and for triennial parliaments   In their eyes such remedies were almost worse than the disease they were designed to cure, since, damaging as they might be to the authority of the crown, they would be equally damaging to the influence of the aristocracy ; and in his pamphlet " Thoughts on the cause of the Present Discontents," which was published in April, 1770, Edmund Burke gave an eloquent exposition of the political opinions held by the party of which he was so illustrious a member.   In this famous political tract, probably the best known of all his writings with the exception of the more famous " Reflections on the French Revolution," Burke said much which might give offence to Chatham as well as to the extreme wing of the opposition.   Declaring that he had " no sort of reliance upon either a triennial parliament, or a

[1] Burke's Correspondence, 1, 228-231.

place bill," he emphasised, over and over again, the importance of party as an indispensable part of the machinery of government, and as a panacea for all the evils which weighed upon the country. " Party," he remarked in a passage which has become hackneyed from frequent quotation, " is a body of men united, for promoting by their joint endeavours the national interest, upon some particular principle in which they are all agreed " ; and in another place he declared that " whoever becomes a party to an administration, composed of insulated individuals, without faith plighted, tie, or common principle . . . abets a faction that is driving hard to the ruin of his country. He is sapping the foundations of its liberty, disturbing the sources of its domestic tranquillity, weakening its government over its dependencies, degrading it from all its importance in the system of Europe."

Burke's pamphlet has been so universally and justly acclaimed as a work of genius, rich in political philosophy and in the wisdom which observes eternal principles underlying ephemeral events, that criticism cannot but appear somewhat misplaced if not audacious ; and yet, while allowing that the world would have been considerably the poorer if Burke had never written, his discretion in choosing the exact moment that he did for publication is, to say the least, open to doubt. A malicious critic might well contend that Burke had no object in thus giving his opinions to the world but to break up the alliance between the different parties in opposition ; and although it is in the last degree improbable that this was either his intention or desire, it nevertheless is true that, though fully aware of the differences of opinion existing between the factions nominally in alliance, and alive to the fact that Chatham found much to object to in the modera-

tion of Lord Rockingham, he did ˙nothing to spare
the susceptibilities of allies whose assistance, he must
have known, was essential to the success of the cause
he had at heart.   Chatham could not but be offended
by the insistence upon the necessity of party, and by
the reference to the evil wrought by the man ·who
practised the principle of " men not measures " ;   and
he would be no better pleased by the slur cast upon
the politicians who advocated drastic and extreme
measures of reform.   It is true that he had discouraged
the clamour for triennial parliaments, but he had raised
the cry for reform from his place in the house of lords,
and was hand in glove with Beckford, the leader of
the opposition party in the city.[1]   Yet neither he nor
his friends had been spared, and it is to his credit,
both as a man and as a statesman, that he refused to
take offence at what he might well have resented as an
outrage.   Though, as Burke narrates, " the bill of
rights people . . . have thought proper at length to
do us, I hope, a service by declaring open war upon
all our connexion,"[2] Chatham declined to be responsible for civil strife in the opposition camp.   " A good
harmony," wrote the author of the offending pamphlet,
" subsists, at least in appearance, between the capital
members of opposition " ;[3] but, if this was the case,
the credit was due much less to him than to Chatham.
It is true that, a few months later, Chatham, in a letter
to Rockingham, complained how " a pamphlet of last

---

[1] On the occasion of the presentation of the second remonstrance of the
City to the Crown, on May 23rd, Beckford violated all custom and precedent
by delivering a speech which had not been previously submitted to the king ;
and it is worthy of note that Chatham waxed enthusiastic over this breach
of very necessary etiquette.   He declared that he was rejoiced " to hear
that my lord mayor asserted the City with weight and spirit," and told
Beckford himself that " the spirit of old England spoke, that never to be
forgotten day."   Chatham Correspondence, 3, 459-460, 462-463.
[2] Burke's Correspondence, 1, 228-231.   [3] *Ibid.*

year, however well intended, I find has done much hurt to the cause ; " [1] but this seems to have been the only murmur that escaped his lips. Such restraint is all the more striking from not being habitual.

Yet, content though Chatham might be silently to suffer the pin-pricks of a man whom he probably thought of too little importance to be taken into serious consideration, it ought not to be assumed that he had no fault to find with the Rockingham party, or that he was content to be driven rather than to lead. " Moderation, moderation," he wrote at the end of July, " is the burden of the song among the body. For myself, I am resolved to be in earnest for the public, and shall be a scarecrow of violence to the gentle warblers of the grove, the moderate whigs and temperate statesmen." [2] Such was not the utterance of a man who was prepared to submit to dictation ; and warm though he might be in the expression of his personal approval of Rockingham,[3] it is not unreasonable to imagine that he found much to lament in the latter's course of procedure. It seemed to him that the interval between the two parliamentary sessions was being wasted, that nothing was being done ; and it was with unfeigned pleasure that he heard that the Yorkshire freeholders intended to draw up a remonstrance for presentation to the crown. Eagerly did he wait the execution of this design [4] which

---

[1] Rockingham Memoirs, 2, 193-195. Twenty-two years later Burke, on discovering this letter among Rockingham's papers, wrote on the back of it, " I remember to have seen this knavish letter at the time. The pamphlet is itself, by anticipation, an answer to that grand artificer of fraud. . . . Oh ! but this does not derogate from his great, splendid side. God forbid ! " Whatever Burke thought to be Chatham's " great splendid side," we may be certain that it was not the aspect which he presented to the Rockingham Whigs.

[2] Chatham Correspondence, 3, 469.   [3] Ibid.

[4] Ibid., 3, 471-472.

acquired no little importance from the fact that, as Rockingham's influence was predominant in Yorkshire, any political action in that county must be associated with his name, if not actually sanctioned by him. Through the freeholders of Yorkshire Rockingham would speak ; and even Burke, with all his prejudice against extreme measures and playing into the hands of the mob, was in favour of the plan.[1] Yet, in spite of Chatham's anxiety and Burke's advice, the design failed of execution ; for when the freeholders met on September 25th, and a remonstrance was proposed, Sir George Savile, the member for the county, and Lord John Cavendish preached the gospel of moderation and restraint so effectively that nothing was done. That the fiasco was due to Rockingham's influence it is almost impossible to doubt ;[2] and Chatham must have been strengthened in the conviction that the only fruit of a policy of moderation was consistent inaction.

Thus the opposition did nothing but mark time, a perilous exercise for those who, if they do not advance, must necessarily fall back ; and the approach of the parliamentary session, which had been fixed to begin on November 13th, must have given Rockingham and his friends as little pleasure as it gave the ministers anxiety. The opposition alliance still existed, but no one could predict how long it would continue, for there were already, as has been seen, signs of approaching discord. The future was indeed dark and uncertain, and it was at the moment when the fate of his country and his party was most in doubt that George Grenville was removed from the stage of political life. For long

[1] Burke's Correspondence, 1, 231-243.
[2] Walpole affirms that Rockingham was intriguing with the court, a statement which has neither evidence nor probability to support it. Walpole's Memoirs, 4, 116-117.

his health had been failing, and his death, which took place on November 13th, came as a shock, but not as a surprise, to those who knew him. Mourned sincerely by his friends, and the subject of an eloquent eulogy by Burke, Grenville has been more the victim of censure than of praise, having come down in history with a very unenviable reputation. Condemned on all sides : by the admirers of Chatham for his inability to appreciate the merits of his great brother-in-law ; by the whigs for his colonial policy ; and by the tories for his treatment of the king ; he has incurred the wrath of all parties, and, with few to defend, there have been many to find fault. And, unfortunately for him, faults are not difficult to find, for few statesmen have been more unhappy in achievement, or more unattractive in character. By imposing the stamp act he laid the foundation of the quarrel with the American colonies, and by arresting Wilkes he converted a worthless, though witty, scribbler into a national hero. Moreover, these mistakes sprang, not from a temporary aberration of judgment, but from deep-rooted defects in his character. Grenville was in no wise fitted to be a ruler of men ; and though, if he had practised at the bar, it is not unlikely that his name would be quoted with reverence and respect, as a statesman he was doomed from the first to fail. His legal cast of mind and his narrowness of vision totally incapacitated him for grasping the broad issues of the problems which presented themselves for solution ; and he thought to rule a great country as a schoolmaster rules a class. Whether in power or in opposition he never ceased from being the pedagogue, desiring to enforce law and to maintain discipline. Thus Wilkes must be punished for his libel upon the king, the Americans coerced for their resistance to the stamp act, and the Rockingham whigs censured and distrusted for their acquiescence in colonial rebellion. There was to be no policy but the enforcement of law, and no object but the maintenance of order. Yet, unattractive as such a conception of government, and the man who holds it, are, it must be allowed that, if Grenville was often objectionable, he was always consistent. Untouched by respect of persons or considerations of expediency, he meted out the same measure to all, and when the house of commons violated the law, he granted it no more mercy than he had shown to the Americans. He was emphatically a man of principle, and this was no mean glory in an age of political opportunism. It is true that such men as he do not easily inspire affection, for they are apt to be intolerant of differences, and destitute of any diplomacy in handling either their friends or their enemies ; but they are not unworthy of the respect so habitually denied them. It is easy for dazzling opportunists to despise those who are not brilliant but only sincere, and the taunt which Napoleon hurled against Mounier has been often repeated in varying forms ; but virtue, even though it is unattractive, deserves recognition ; and the tribute paid by Burke was the offering of one righteous man to another. In an evil hour for his fame Grenville abandoned his ambition of becoming speaker of the house of commons, an office for which he was in every way suited ; and both he and the nation have paid to the full the price of his mistake. He was not even happy in the opportunity of his death which was to prove a crushing blow to the unity of the opposition. When Lord George Sackville, one of Grenville's followers, heard that his leader was ill, he significantly remarked that " if any accident should happen to him, it will require very serious consideration what part we are then to take " ; and two days later he wrote to a friend, " If poor Mr Grenville dies, what is to be the object of opposition ? I hope not to make Lord Chatham minister. If it is, you cannot suppose I shall be very sanguine in such a cause." [1] Such were the clouds which gathered round the bedside of the dying statesman.

[1] Hist. MSS. Comm. Stopford Sackville MSS., i., 131-132.

CHAPTER VII

THE DOWNFALL OF THE OPPOSITION

It is not improbable that when parliament was prorogued in May, 1770, until the following autumn, Lord North indulged himself in the pleasant fancy that he had seen the worst of his troubles ; and that, whatever the future had in store, it was hardly likely to bring that incessant and harassing anxiety which had attended him in the early stages of his career as first minister. To all appearances the government bark had safely navigated the point of danger, and passed into clear unruffled waters. At peace both at home and abroad, the nation seemed about to be granted a welcome immunity from the unrest and disorder which had so long and so grievously disturbed it ; and no great insight was needed to perceive that Lord North, able to count upon the most intimate confidence of his sovereign, and assured of a majority in both houses of parliament, was far more firmly seated in power than any previous minister of the reign, with the exception of Lord Bute, had been. Nor was it only by reason of the inherent strength of his own position that North was justified in regarding the future with equanimity ; he could, in addition, count upon deriving no little benefit from the very probable decline in the vigour and effectiveness of the opposition. Though led by Chatham, and united in the desire to dislodge the ministry, the various

368

whig factions had clearly failed to obtain the end for which they had fought ; and there was no reason to believe that disaster in the past would be redeemed by success in the future. On the contrary, there was every indication that the whigs, unless they were prepared to relinquish the contest, and publicly confess to failure, had no alternative but to continue along the downward path upon which they had already started. Internecine strife, for so long their bane, though temporarily stilled by the hope of victory, might easily spring into new life when the prospect of a speedy triumph had faded ; and, unfortunately, this old and deep-rooted evil was likely to be aggravated rather than diminished by the loss of George Grenville. For, strange and paradoxical as it may appear at the first glance, the death of Grenville was to prove a grievous and irreparable blow to the opposition ; and the states-man, who, when alive, had wrought so much harm to the cause of unity, was to work still further mischief when dead. It was very possible that his followers, bereft of their master, might decline to promote the triumph of either Rockingham or Chatham ; for, like the *comites* of the ancient German chieftain, they had fought more for their leader than for victory ; and with his death departed their chief incentive to continue the struggle. Though no man could predict with any degree of assurance their future course of action, it was, at least, certain that the disciples of Grenville, by no means inconsiderable either in numbers or in ability, had imbibed too much of their master's teaching to sacrifice principles for the sake of maintaining unity, and, perhaps, too little to refrain from sacrificing them for their own personal advantage.

By the date of Grenville's death, however, that pleasing prospect of rest and quiet, which had greeted

the wearied ministers at the close of the ·previous
session, no longer existed ; for when all had seemed at
peace, the danger had suddenly arisen of the country
being engulfed into a great European war. In a
moment the whole political scene was changed, and
the future charged with risk and peril. Both the
king and North were well aware that their success
in the past had been largely due to the difficulties
under which their opponents suffered ; and that not
the least of these difficulties had been the lack of any
popular cry against the government, The grievances
of Wilkes, and the illegalities connected with the
Middlesex election, had been worn almost threadbare
by lengthy and reiterated discussions ; and the
opposition sorely needed a new ground of attack against
the court, sufficiently important to awaken the passions
and arouse the interest of the people. It seemed that
this precious boon was now about to be granted.
Shortly before the meeting of parliament, news reached
this country that Port Egmont, an English settlement
upon one of the Falkland Islands, had been attacked
and, taken by a Spanish force in the previous June ;
and immediately upon the receipt of this intelligence,
it was understood that, unless ample reparation was
made for what had every appearance of being a
flagrant and wanton insult, England had no alternative
but to resort to the sword. Thus an armed conflict
seemed imminent, and it is not easy to exaggerate
the influence of this sudden and unexpected transformation of the political situation upon the fortunes
of the opposition. Great and deplorable as the
catastrophe of an European war would be, it might
yet bring in its train salvation for the enemies of the
court. If England was either engaged in, or upon
the verge of, hostilities, the cry would be raised for

Chatham, the statesman who had guided the country so triumphantly through the difficulties of the Seven Years' War, to be once more placed at the helm ; and it was by no means improbable that such a cry would penetrate through the walls of parliament. Corrupt and venal as the average member of the house of commons was, the lust for illicit gain had not completely dried up every noble instinct in his composition ; and it might well happen that, convinced that the country was threatened by a great danger, he would refuse to continue to sell his support to the government, and, in the exercise of his vote, allow himself to be guided by considerations of patriotism rather than by those of pecuniary profit. Nor would all danger of the destruction of the administration be removed if war was happily averted by diplomacy. Following in the wake of those who had compassed so successfully and so unscrupulously the overthrow of Sir Robert Walpole, it would be comparatively easy for the opposition to represent that peace had been purchased by the humiliation of England, that the ministers had truckled to the pride of Spain, and that the prestige of the country had been materially and needlessly diminished. Reckless and unfair as such accusations might be, they would, nevertheless, probably find a ready hearing with a people quite prepared to believe the worst of the ministers, and to accept their incompetence as an article of faith ; and thus, whether war was declared or peace maintained, the future of the administration might be materially affected by a trivial encounter on a desert island in a remote region of the globe.

Though discovered towards the close of the sixteenth century, the Falkland Islands had, hitherto, played but a very insignificant part in the world's history. Claimed by Spain as part of that dominion in the new world assigned to her by papal decree, they were for many years left to their native wildness and desolation, having nothing wherewith to attract colonists and settlers to whom were open far more fertile and accessible regions. Situated off the east coast of South America, and in nearly the same latitude with the mouth of the Strait of Magellan, the Falkland Islands, in extent little more than half the size of Ireland, present a dreary and desolate aspect. Everywhere covered by a peaty soil entirely unsuitable for vegetation, nearly barren of trees, and the prey of almost incessant wind and rain, it is hardly surprising that for well over a century the rights of Spain over such a desert spot were allowed to pass unchallenged.[1] About the middle of the eighteenth century, however, the period when the predatory instincts of European nations began to assume their modern form, it was suggested that a settlement upon these islands might be serviceable for purposes of trade and useful in time of war ; and, in accordance with this advice, an English

---

[1] Darwin's *A Naturalist's Voyage round the World*. An interesting account of these Islands was given by Captain Hunt in his report to the government, dated July 1770. " Near the seashore," he wrote, " the soul is of a black spongy nature, and, in general, not above eighteen inches deep, and then you come to a cold yellow clay. The valleys, where it was swampy, we found good turf ; the other parts of it, and the sides of the hills,. afforded good herbage ; and we found the sheep, goats, and hogs, that we put on shore, to thrive very well upon it, though the surface is much like our heaths or moors. We planted cabbages, potatoes, turnips, lettuce, radishes, and several other things, some of which sprang up, but, in general, they failed, owing, in my opinion, to the poorness of the soil. There is no wood growing upon the Islands ; but a few shrubs, and a kind of brushwood, and great plenty of sedge growing near the seashore, which give the cattle good shelter in the bad weather. There is but two sorts of fish—the mullet and the smelt—which are very scarce in winter, and not plenty in summer. At our first coming to Port Egmont, we found great plenty of wild geese, which now are so scarce that we were obliged to go a considerable distance to get any number of them. From the month of September till the latter end of November, we get great quantities and great variety of eggs." Calendar of Home Office Papers, 84-85.

expedition was fitted out in the year 1748, with a view of founding an establishment in this hitherto neglected region. At once the Spanish ambassador protested against the enterprise as a direct violation of his master's territorial rights, and although the expedition was abandoned, this change of plan was not made in deference to the Spanish claim, the validity of which was stoutly denied by the English ministry of the day. From that time, the disputed question of ownership was allowed to rest until the year 1764, when Choiseul, the French minister, taking possession of the most easterly of the Falkland Islands, founded a settlement which he named Port Louis ; and two years later his example was followed by the English who, occupying the island to the west of that seized by the French, erected a fort which, in honour of the then first lord of the admiralty, was given the name of Port Egmont.[1]

It is highly probable that both France and England were well aware that, in so acting, they were running counter to the claims put forward by the Spanish court ; and they had not to wait long for a protest to be made. France was the first to be called to account, the Spaniards lodging a formal remonstrance against the establishment of Port Louis ; and Choiseul, unwilling to offend an ally whose assistance against England had been useful in the past, and might be still more useful in the future, promptly surrendered the French settlement which, passing into the hands of Spain, was renamed Port Soledad. This somewhat tame submission on the part of the French court was decidedly unfavourable to England who was thus deprived of her partner in a policy of very doubtful legality ; and, as might have been anticipated, the Spaniards, having succeeded in ousting the French,

---

[1] Stanhope's *History of England*, 1713-1783, vol. v. 276-277.

were by no means prepared to allow the English to enjoy their recent acquisition undisturbed. Towards the end of the year 1769, Captain Hunt of the frigate *Tamar*, then stationed off Port Egmont, received several messages from the Spanish governor of Port Soledad, the main purport of which was to protest against the English occupation of what was claimed as Spanish territory; and, unfortunately, in his replies to these remonstrances, Hunt displayed much of the frankness of a sea-captain and little of the tact of a diplomatist. Instead of contenting himself with a polite denial of the Spanish claim, and a firm assertion that the island belonged to England by the double right of discovery and occupation, he proceeded to unnecessary and unjustifiable lengths, and, returning threat for threat, menaced the Spaniards with eject-ment from Port Soledad. Such minatory language was not likely to make the Spaniards more willing to acquiesce in the English occupation, and, when he left for England shortly afterwards, Hunt must have realised that the seeds of a conflict had already been sown. On his arrival home in June, 1770, he duly reported to the government his passage of arms with the Spanish governor; but his information came too late to be of any practical value to the ministry. Possibly alarmed lest the threat uttered by Hunt might be speedily translated into action, the Spaniards resolved to be first in the field; and much about the same time that Hunt arrived in England, a Spanish force, consisting of five frigates, which had set sail from Buenos Ayres early in May, under the command of Buccarelli, the governor of that city, appeared off Port Egmont, and called upon the garrison to surrender. Resistance was out of the question, the assailants having a decided advantage both in numbers and equipment; and the English, having perfunctorily fired a few shots, hoisted a flag of truce, and surrendered the island and fort into the hands of the Spaniards.[1]

When every allowance has been made for the wound inflicted upon Spanish pride by a foreign establishment in the Falkland Islands, and for the apprehension aroused by Hunt's idle words, it still remains difficult to defend the assault upon Port Egmont, smacking as it does more of piracy than the conduct of a civilised European power. Friendly relations existed between England and Spain, and no notice had been given that such an avowed act of hostility was in contemplation. It is, of course, quite possible, as was alleged at the time by Prince Masserano, the Spanish ambassador in England, that Buccarelli had acted entirely on his own responsibility, and without any specific orders from the government at Madrid; [2] but the actions of subordinates are sometimes

[1] Annual Register for 1771, 232-234.

[2] Calendar of Home Office Papers, 63-64. In a speech delivered in the house of lords on January 22nd, 1800, the Earl of Carnarvon, who asserted that he had received his information from D'Ossun, the French ambassador to the Court of Madrid, gave a rather different version of this incident. " Where can be found," he remarked, " in the history of mankind, a more atrocious instance of insidious treachery, or more perfidious breach of faith, than that which took place on the treaty of peace which preceded, and was disturbed by the capture of Falkland's Island ? At the very moment that Spain and France signed peace with this country, an order was signed by the minister of Spain, in concert with the Duke de Choiseul, to attack Falkland's Island on a given date some years after, in order to produce a rupture, resolved on, at the very instant of executing a treaty, professing perpetual amity ; at the time when this sealed order was opened and put in execution, it suited the interests and views of neither court, and produced equal astonishment in both. M. D'Ossun, then ambassador from France to the Court of Spain, from whom I heard this anecdote, was directed to remonstrate against this act of aggression, which embarrassed the court of Paris ; he found equal surprise at Madrid, for the order was forgotten by both, nor was recollected till the attack was defended by the production of the order." *Parl. Hist.*, vol. xxxiv. p. 1239. See also Adophus' *History of England*, from the accession to the decease of King George the Third (1840), vol. i. p. 441.

fraught with momentous consequences, and, at one time, it seemed extremely likely that an obscure Spanish colonial governor was to enjoy the very doubtful honour of having precipitated an European conflict. English dignity had incurred a dire affront, and, unless the ministers were prepared to face a storm of national indignation far exceeding in fury that which had greeted Walpole on the conclusion of the famous Spanish convention, they must demand instant reparation for so grievous an injury and so public an insult. Yet a request of this character, however moderately expressed, was not unattended with danger, for it was clear that Spain believed that she had suffered as well as inflicted a wrong, and it was by no means certain that she would be ready to grant all that England asked. The evil-doer is not always prepared to atone for his guilt, or to confess that his crime was without provocation ; and, great though the power of England might be, it was not improbable that Spain, counting upon the assistance of France, might prefer to save her pride by incurring the risks of war. Much indeed would depend upon the attitude of France at this critical juncture. Connected as she was with Spain by the Pacte de Famille of 1761, and still smarting under her humiliation by England in the Seven Years' War, it was quite possible that France might elect to throw in her lot with her Bourbon neighbour, and, in that event, there would be but a remote chance of maintaining peace.

It was, therefore, no easy task which fell to the lot of Lord Weymouth, the secretary of state for the southern department. Though fully alive to the very serious influence that an outbreak of war might exert upon the course of domestic politics, he was also aware that an ignominious peace might be equally disastrous, and that salvation could only be procured by a settlement, possible for Spain to accept, and, at the same time, satisfactory to English pride. Strait and confined indeed was the diplomatic road which the secretary of state was called upon to tread if he was to reach the goal of " peace with honour " ; and those acquainted with his habits during that large part of the day and night which he devoted to his pleasures might well be appalled to think that so narrow a path was to be trodden by so drunken a debauchee. Yet, such apprehensions did Weymouth some wrong, for a plentiful indulgence in vice had not entirely ruined his good natural ability. Called upon to make a great effort, he appears, for a time at least, to have risen to the occasion, and to have expended upon diplomacy some of that energy which was commonly devoted to less arduous, though perhaps more diverting, pursuits. Nor can be he accused of failing to perceive the importance of the issue, or of procrastination ; and he deserves no little credit for his handling of an exceedingly difficult and delicate negotiation. It was early in September that he learnt, both from Masserano and from James Harris, then a youthful chargé d'affaires at the court of Madrid, and only on the threshold of a diplomatic career which was to bring him both renown and a peerage, that a Spanish force had set sail from Buenos Ayres with hostile intentions against Port Egmont ;[1] and he wasted no time in stating the redress which England expected to receive, the Spanish ambassador being promptly informed that peace could only be preserved by the formal disavowal of Buccarelli's action, and

---

[1] Diaries and Correspondence of the Earl of Malmesbury, 1, 59 ; Calendar of Home Office Papers, 63-64.

the restoration of Port Egmont; and Harris being instructed to lay the same demands before Grimaldi, the minister of the king of Spain.[1]

In formulating such requirements, Weymouth was certainly not guilty of opening the negotiation in an unduly aggressive or hostile spirit ; for, unless prepared to admit without further parley that England had no right to a single inch of territory in the Falkland Islands, it was incumbent upon the cabinet to proclaim, from the outset, the complete absence of any justification for Buccarelli's action, and to demand reparation in no uncertain tone. Yet, firm though Weymouth's attitude might be, he certainly was not blind to the urgent necessity of a careful scrutiny of French diplomacy. He was well aware that the reception accorded in Spain to the English demands would largely depend upon the opinions which prevailed at the court of Madrid upon the stability of the Pacte de Famille ; and it is significant that the letter to Harris was first sent to Robert Walpole, a nephew of the great prime minister, and secretary to the English embassy at Paris, who, in the absence of Lord Harcourt, the ambassador, was instructed to communicate its contents to Choiseul, and then despatch it to Spain.[2] The motives which inspired this somewhat tardy method of procedure are not difficult to perceive. Before plunging deeply into the negotiation with Spain, it was advisable for Weymouth to ascertain how far there was a danger of England being called upon to meet the combined onslaught of the two Bourbon powers ; for, though Choiseul had already intimated that he hoped war would be averted, and a friendly

---

[1] Calendar of Home Office Papers, 63-64.
[2] Weymouth to Walpole, September 12th, 1770. Foreign State Papers, R.O., 281.

settlement reached,[1] it was by no means certain that he would continue in the same pacific state of mind when he learnt the degree of reparation which England expected.   Yet, from the point of view of this country, no conversation could have been more re-assuring than that which took place between Choiseul and Walpole at Versailles on the morning of September 16th. " When I had read the letter to Mr Harris," wrote Walpole to the secretary of state, " the Duc de Choiseul expressed himself highly satisfied with it, and desired me to leave it with him, that he might the more easily be able to communicate it to his most Christian majesty in its very words.   He said that Marquis Grimaldi could not do better than subscribe his name to your lordship's letter, that he would write immediately to Marquis Grimaldi, and would adopt the sentiments and language of it ; and would recommend it very warmly to Marquis Grimaldi to direct a memorial to be presented to the court of England in answer to what is demanded ; wherein the conduct of Monsieur Buccarelli should be disavowed in the strongest terms, an engagement made to re-establish the affairs of the settlement at Port Egmont, and that even an indemnification should be promised to be made to the sufferers ; and he would desire that this might be done immediately, that the alarm and apprehension upon this occasion might entirely cease." [2]   No utterance could have been more friendly or pacific, and Choiseul did not confine himself to words alone.   Two days after the conversation at Versailles, he told Walpole that, with the approval of Louis XV., who was in entire sympathy with the English demands, he had already

[1] Walpole to Weymouth, September 12th, 1770 ; Foreign State Papers, R.O., 281.
[2] Walpole to Weymouth, September 16th, 1770 ; Foreign State Papers, R.O., 281.

written to Grimaldi, " exhorting him in the strongest manner, and with all the reasons he could think of, to procure from his Catholic majesty a declaration under his own hand, acquiescing in what the court of England demanded, and to despatch this without loss of time." [1]

Thus Choiseul breathed peace and conciliation ; but it is a penalty attaching to all statesmen and diplomatists that their words, and even sometimes their actions, are not always sufficient to carry conviction ; and the question of the French minister's sincerity must inevitably arise. It has been contended with no little plausibility that Choiseul was, in reality, playing a double game, that, while he professed to be seeking for peace, he was engaged in scheming for war, and that the only object of his pacific utterances was to lull England into a false and delusive belief in the security of her own position. Weighty arguments can be urged in support of such a view. It can be said that the time had come for the two Bourbon powers to unite in humiliating the country under whose supremacy they had suffered, that the interests of France were closely engaged in fomenting a quarrel, and that Choiseul's personal predominance, inasmuch as he was no longer as influential at court as he once had been, depended upon the outbreak of a war which he might utilise to render himself indispensable, and to regain his control over the king. Moreover, it is known that as late as the month of July, 1770, he had instituted inquiries into Spain's readiness for war, and given every indication of being anxious to strike without delay a blow against the power of England ; [2] and it

---

[1] Walpole to Weymouth, September 18th, 1770 ; Foreign State Papers, R.O., 281.

[2] Le Règne de Louis XV., H. Carré (1909), 390.

can, therefore, be contended that, though not absolutely convicted, the French minister falls under grave suspicion of having been guilty of duplicity in expressing his desire for the maintenance of peace. No mistake, however, is greater than to attribute consistency to statesmen, who, as experience shows, are generally quite willing to trim their sails to the changing breeze ; and there is good reason to believe that, whatever may have been his disposition in the previous July, Choiseul in September was by no means desirous of war. It is not of much weight, perhaps, that both Robert Walpole, and, later, Lord Harcourt, testified strongly to his sincerity, for diplomatists are not proof against deception ;[1] but when we learn that Choiseul advised the Spanish ministry to avoid a contest, even at the cost of a surrender to England,[2] the testimony of Walpole and Harcourt becomes credible and easy of acceptance. Nor is it difficult to account for this sudden change in French policy. A little reflection had convinced Choiseul that, attractive as was the idea of a war with England, the internal condition of France rendered it impossible to carry such an enterprise to a successful conclusion. Confronted by a depleted treasury, and precluded from imposing fresh taxes by the quarrel between the French crown and the parlements, which was then at its height, he realised that, even with the assistance of Spain, France was in no condition to undertake the subjugation of a nation which, though she might be destroyed, would be certain to make a long and desperate resistance ; and that, therefore, it was in accordance with the best interests of his country

---

[1] Walpole to Weymouth, September 18th, 1770 ; Harcourt to Weymouth, November 18th, 1770 ; Foreign State Papers, R.O., 281.

[2] *Le Règne de Louis XV.*, H. Carré, 390.

to endeavour to avert an European war for which she was not ready, but in which she could not but be involved.

Yet, though the weight of France might be thrown into the scale for peace, it was by no means certain that Spain would follow tamely in the wake of its ally, and there was a real danger that the lesser power would draw the greater, and Choiseul be compelled by the Pacte de Famille to take part in a war for which he had no liking. So much, therefore, depended upon the reception accorded at Madrid to the English demands that no little interest attaches to the first meeting between Grimaldi and Harris, which took place on Tuesday, September 25th. In accordance with the instructions communicated to him by Weymouth, Harris informed the Spanish Minister of the reparation England demanded, and stated that, if the request was not fulfilled, war would be inevitable. Such a communication was certainly plain and straight-forward enough, but it did not have the effect of elicit-ing equal frankness on the part of Grimaldi. It is true that he expressed his regret for what had happened, his anxiety for the maintenance of peace, and his desire for a speedy settlement ; but he laid a very unpleasant emphasis upon the very doubtful status of the English in the Falkland Islands, and roundly asserted that Buccarelli had only acted in accordance with " the established laws of America," a statement which might be taken to imply that it was the duty of all the Spanish governors in that continent to defend their master's dominions against foreign aggressions. From remarks so general, and, therefore, so obscure, it was almost impossible to gather Spain's probable course of action, and Harris learnt but very little more from his second meeting with Grimaldi, which took place three days later. " He said," wrote the English chargé d'affaires, " he had laid my memorial before the king, and that his majesty was resolved to do everything in his power to terminate in an amicable manner this affair ; that, therefore, he admitted our demand, and that he assented to it in every point consistent with his honour, which, as well as ours, was to be considered : that . . . orders had been given to Prince Masserano to lay before your lordship the several ideas which had been suggested on this head ; and, as they only differed in the terms, and not essentially, he trusted some of them would be adopted. I begged his excellency would tell me, in general, in what those terms consisted ; he said they were various ; we might choose those we liked best ; that it was needless to tell them to me, since I might be satisfied they differed only in the mode, not in the effect, from our demand. I then asked him if I might consider this as an answer to my memorial ; he said I might, and that he hoped my court would look upon it as a favourable one, since nothing could induce them to condescend so far but their great desire of maintaining the good harmony between the two courts." [1]

A careful reading between the lines reveals the essentially unsatisfactory character of this vague and ambiguous communication. It was certainly not a hopeful sign that Grimaldi had refused to admit Harris into his confidence, and it was very significant that, though he attempted to minimise the difference, the Spanish minister allowed that what his government was prepared to give, did not quite coincide with what England had asked. Indeed, the very noticeable stress laid upon the honour of the country, the justification of Buccarelli's action, and the doubtful legality of the

---

[1] Diaries and Correspondence of the Earl of Malmesbury, i, 59-63.

English occupation pointed to the fact that the Spanish government, convinced that the wrong-doing had not been exclusively on one side, was more prepared to conclude a bargain than to sue unconditionally for surrender. Such was, indeed, the case, and when Masserano, having received his instructions from Madrid, submitted the proposals of his government to Weymouth, it at once became clear that the two countries had made little or no progress towards an agreement. Instead of undertaking that the English demands should be fulfilled without delay, the Spanish Ambassador proposed the conclusion of a convention under which both countries would be pledged to make certain concessions. Thus Spain, on her part, was to disavow Buccarelli's conduct, and to promise to restore Port Egmont, but, in return for receiving this reparation, England was to admit that Buccarelli had acted in accordance with his general instructions and his oath as governor, to disavow the threat of Captain Hunt, which was alleged by Spain to have provoked the attack upon Port Egmont, and to agree that in restoring the English settlement the king of Spain in no way acknowledged that England possessed any legal right to territory in the Falkland Islands.[1]

It is clear that such proposals were very far from complying with the demands of England; and Weymouth and his colleagues in the cabinet were justified in expressing their profound dissatisfaction with the attitude adopted by Spain. From the first

[1] Weymouth to Harris, October 17th, 1770 ; Foreign State Papers, R.O., 185. In their original form Masserano's instructions contained a suggestion that both countries should evacuate the Falkland Islands, but Choiseul, realising that England would never assent to such a proposal, contrived to obtain its withdrawal. It may be to this incident that a curious tale told by Grafton in his *Autobiography* refers. Walpole to Weymouth, October 7th and October 9th, 1770 ; Foreign State Papers, R.O., 281 ; Grafton's *Autobiography*, 255-256.

they had acted on the not unreasonable assumption
that they were entitled to receive unconditional reparation ; and they now discovered that this point of
view was not shared by the court of Madrid.   Both
the idea of a convention, and of making any concessions,
however trivial, were entirely unpalatable to the
ministry with the fear of the parliamentary opposition
and public opinion before its eyes ; and the terms were
decisively and unhesitatingly refused.   " I was ordered
to tell the Spanish ambassador," wrote Weymouth to
Harris on October 17th, " that when the king's moderation condescended to demand of the court of Madrid
to disavow the proceedings of the governor of Buenos
Ayres, and to restore things precisely to that situation
in which they stood before the rash and unwarrantable
undertaking of the governor, as the smallest reparation
for the injury received that he could possibly accept,
his majesty thought there was nothing left for discussion except the mode of carrying that disavowal
and that restitution into execution.   I was also ordered
to say that his majesty adheres invariably to his first
demand ; and that, without entering into the insurmountable objections to the matter of this proposed
convention, the manner alone is totally inadmissible ;
for his majesty cannot accept under a convention that
satisfaction to which he has so just a title without
entering into any engagements in order to procure it ;
that the idea of his majesty becoming a contracting
party upon this occasion is entirely foreign to the case,
for, having received an injury, and demanded the
most moderate reparation of that injury, his honour will
permit him to accept, that reparation loses its value
if it is to be conditional, and to be obtained by any
stipulation whatsoever on the part of his majesty." [1]

---

[1] Weymouth to Harris, October 17th, 1770 ; Foreign State Papers, R.O., 185.

The immediate consequences of the refusal of the English ministry to continue the discussion along the lines suggested by Spain, was the temporary suspension of the negotiation, no further progress between Weymouth and Masserano being possible until the latter had received fresh instructions from his government. Thus the situation was critical in the extreme, for it apparently lay with Spain to determine whether the peace of Western Europe was to be broken, and it was by no means easy to foresee what she would do. According to D'Ossun, the French ambassador in that country, the court of Madrid was in favour of a bellicose policy, and was supported in this by public opinion;[1] while Harris believed that Spain was in no condition to embark upon hostilities, was genuinely desirous of peace, and feared " nothing so much as our breaking with them."[2] Yet even Harris, sanguine though he was, admitted the existence of a warlike party in the government and nation, and narrated how, early in October, Grimaldi had told him that the king of Spain " was not so reduced as to suffer himself to be menaced," and that " he had a powerful ally who would indisputably share his fate."[3] From such conflicting accounts the truth is not to be easily disentangled, but it may be that the key to the puzzle lies in Grimaldi's boast that France would be certain to come to her ally's assistance. It is clear that Spain, inasmuch as she had already offered to fulfil the demands of England, was not desirous of provoking a conflict at all cost ; but it is equally clear that she was keenly desirous of saving her pride, and of receiving something in return for the concessions she was pre-

---

[1] *Le Règne de Louis XV.*, H. Carré, 390.

[2] Diaries and Correspondence of the Earl of Malmesbury, 1, 63-66.

[3] Harris to Weymouth, October 11th, 1770 ; Foreign State Papers, R.O., 185.

pared to make ; and, therefore, it was only too probable
that, if the English ministers continued to demand an
unconditional surrender, Spain, trusting in French
support, might prefer the burden of a war to the loss
of her dignity.

If this interpretation of the situation be correct, the
outlook was certainly not very hopeful. The English
ministry, fearful of its own safety at home, was not
likely to recede from its original position ; and, if compromise was outside the range of practical politics, there
appeared to be no solution of the problem but the blunt
and clumsy method of resort to armed force. It is
not surprising that Choiseul was appalled at such a dire
prospect. Convinced that it was not a suitable time
for entering upon hostilities with England, and equally
convinced that he could not allow Spain to embark upon
a war alone, he saw the only salvation for himself and
his country in peace, and strained every nerve to promote an amicable settlement. With Walpole he discussed the terms which Masserano had offered and
Weymouth rejected, seeking to represent them in as
favourable a light as possible. With some show of
plausibility he contended that Spain had really
granted all that England had ever asked, that the
demand for the conclusion of a convention was of little
or no account, and that the failure of the two countries
to come to a speedy agreement had been rather the
fruit of a misunderstanding than of a real difference of
opinion. Moreover, in order to promote a settlement,
he undertook, with the approval of the Spanish
ambassador in France, to recommend Grimaldi both
to tell Harris that the English demands would be
fulfilled and to instruct Masserano to sign a declaration embodying a similar assurance. More he could
hardly do, and Walpole was sanguine enough to believe

that Choiseul had sufficient influence over the Spanish government to avert the catastrophe of an European war.[1] Such an expectation, however, seriously underestimated the difficulties of the French minister's task. Grimaldi was clearly chagrined by the summary rejection of his offer, somewhat petulantly remarking to Harris that " we have allowed ourselves to be in the wrong, we have offered the most ample reparation ; surely it is very hard in the point wherein we are insulted (meaning the menace of Captain Hunt), you will not listen to our solicitations, although they are such as you might acquiesce in without the least diminution of the satisfaction we give you."[2] Such a declaration did not testify to a conciliatory disposition, and the situation, already quite critical enough, was rendered no easier by the fact that all three countries were busily preparing for war.

It was on October 29th that Harris waited upon Grimaldi to learn what steps the Spanish government proposed to take, now that its first offer had been refused ; but it was not until November 7th that he received the information he sought. Nor when it came was it hopeful for peace, Harris being told by Grimaldi that though Spain was willing to abandon the idea of a convention, and to allow England to select the mode of giving the promised satisfaction, she still required that, her honour should be safeguarded, and that " the affair should be ultimately and decisively terminated."[3] The meaning of these studiously vague and ambiguous phrases was fully revealed by Masserano in the many conversations he had with Weymouth after Monday, November 19th, the day on which he received his new

[1] Walpole to Weymouth, October 21st, 1770; Foreign State Papers R.O., 281.

[2] Diaries and Correspondence of the Earl of Malmesbury, 1, 66-68.

[3] Calendar of Home Office Papers, 104-106.

instructions from Madrid. The suggestion of a convention was not, indeed, again put forward, but Weymouth, much to his disgust, was not slow to discover that this was a concession more in appearance than in reality, inasmuch as the principle of reciprocity was maintained. Thus, the conduct of Buccarelli, though to be disavowed, was again to be excused as having been provoked by Hunt's menaces, and though Masserano was authorised to sign a declaration such as England had demanded, he was only to do so on the understanding that immediately afterwards a negotiation should be set on foot between the two countries with a view of settling their rival claims in the Falkland Islands. To such terms it was clearly impossible for the ministry to accede, and Weymouth met them with a definite refusal.[1]

[1] The general trend of these conversations between Weymouth and Masserano can be gathered from various sources. In a letter to Weymouth, dated November 14th, Walpole, writing from Paris, mentions that " the courier arrived from Spain yesterday morning with dispatches for the Duc de Choiseul, the Spanish ambassador here, and Prince Masseran. . . . I saw the Duc de Choiseul last night. He and the Spanish Ambassador think the contents of their dispatches are good . . . that the court of Madrid gives Prince Masseran full powers to negotiate upon the affair with his majesty's ministers, and he is ordered to make a declaration whereby he will disavow the enterprise of Monsieur Buccarelli, though he is at the same time to excuse his conduct in that the menace of Captain Hunt was the cause of it. He is then by the same declaration to consent to the re-establishment of his majesty's subjects in the Falkland Islands, as has been required, and is to desire that his majesty would be disposed to enter into a negotiation on the *fond* of the matter, as soon as the declaration shall be made and accepted." Foreign State Papers, R.O., 281. In a letter to Lord North, dated November, 23rd, George III. wrote, " I saw Lord Weymouth on his coming from the Spanish ambassador; the project produced this day differed but little from that of Wednesday. Lord Weymouth has renewed the demand of the governor of Buenos Ayres being disavowed, and the island restored, unattended by any discussion on the right." Correspondence of George III. with Lord North, 1, 210. " I cannot account," wrote Walpole to Harris on December 1st, " for such unreasonable behaviour in the court of Spain, and can neither see the justice or the prudence of it. The obstinacy in not at once granting what the honour of our nation justly requires makes me think that court more in the wrong than what I have all along wished, or been inclined to do, for where is the difficulty of disavowing the conduct of a giddy

Thus, for a second time, the negotiation reached a deadlock, and the clouds of war loomed larger than ever upon the political horizon. Choiseul, who had flattered himself that peace was within sight, was aghast to hear that the Spanish offer had been summarily rejected; and promptly begged Lord Harcourt, who had now returned to his ambassadorial duties, " to write immediately to your court that we may know their final determination, what they want, and what they wish, that I may make a last effort to obtain the satisfaction they desire." [1]   But, though willing to make this final attempt to bring about a peaceful solution, he appears to have cherished but little hope of success, bitterly exclaiming to Harcourt that " this paltry island . . . will probably draw us into a war, as contrary to our several interests as to our inclinations," [2] and in a dispatch to D'Ossun, dated December 4th, he took for granted that war was inevitable.[3]   Nor was he at all singular in this opinion, for in England there was an equally strong conviction that there was but a very slender prospect of the maintenance of peace. Harcourt was told by Lord Weymouth that now his most important work was to procure intelligence of military and naval preparations in France; [4] and Harris was instructed that " as Prince Masserano continues to hold a language which gives very little reason to expect just satisfaction for the insult committed in the midst of profound peace . . . it is thought proper

officer, and putting things in the situation they were before the undertaking. . . . Our court, therefore, keeps firmly to its two first propositions, and will hear of no foreign matter whatever." Diaries and Correspondence of the Earl of Malmesbury, 1, 68-70.

[1] Harcourt to Weymouth, November 27th, 1770; Foreign State Papers, R.O., 281.

[2] Ibid.

[3] Le Règne de Louis XV., H. Carré, 390.

[4] Weymouth to Harcourt, November 28th, 1770; Foreign State Papers, R.O., 281.

that Coates should be dispatched to you with this information, in order that you may take such method, as you shall think most advisable, to apprise, as privately as possible, the lieutenant-governor of Gibraltar of this uncertain state of affairs, and of letting him know that general Cornwallis and other officers belonging to that garrison are ordered to their posts, and are to embark immediately." [1] Moreover, in addition to sending these significant instructions to its representatives abroad, the ministry made active preparations at home.   In order that Ireland might be put into a state of defence, the lord-lieutenant of that country was officially warned that " the language which the Spanish ambassador holds is unpromising with regard to peace " ; [2] an order in council was approved, placing an embargo on all provision ships in Irish port ; [3] and the lieutenant-general of ordnance was instructed " to report on the state of the ordnance stores of all kinds, and particularly the quantity of gunpowder ready for use on any emergency ; and also as to the quantity of stores abroad, etc., and as to the supply of the different articles necessary for the demands which may possibly be made in case of a war with France and Spain." [4]

It was while the negotiation was passing through this critical and dangerous stage that parliament assembled, the session having been begun on November 13th ; and it was tolerably certain that, difficult as the

[1] Weymouth to Harris, November 28th, 1770 ; Foreign State Papers, R.O., 185.

[2] Calendar of Home Office Papers, 93.   [3] *Ibid.* 97.

[4] Calendar of Home Office Papers, 96.   The lieutenant-general of ordnance at this time was Henry Conway.   On the resignation of Lord Granby, in January 1770, the mastership of ordnance had been offered to Conway who had declined it on the plea that, having lived in friendship with Granby, he did not wish to profit by his fall.   Conway, however, consented to discharge the duties of the mastership without possessing either the title or emoluments of the post.

ministerial task had been in the past, it was likely to
be still more difficult in the future. Never are the
dangers associated with the existence of a systematic
parliamentary opposition so great as when the international situation is complicated and the clouds of
war hang low over Europe ; for then arises the peril
that the opponents of the administration of the day,
impelled partly by hunger for office, and partly,
perhaps, by the honest conviction that only by a
transference of power can the country be saved, will
resort to reckless and irresponsible criticism, advocate
violent measures and indiscreet revelations, and, in
their haste to destroy the government, run the risk of
precipitating an European conflict which but for them
might have been avoided. Such had been the fatal
policy pursued by the enemies of Sir Robert Walpole,
and such was the line of conduct which commended
itself to the opposition in the autumn of 1770. Convinced that they had received a clear call for battle, that
no time could be more favourable for an united attack,
and that it was incumbent upon every patriot to denounce the ministers for having failed to prepare for
a struggle which was certain, both Rockingham and
Chatham were keenly anxious for an onslaught to be
made, and were desirous of working together in the
closest harmony.[1] It would be wrong, however, to
imagine that they were encouraged to undertake this
venture by any hope of immediate victory ; their
intention was rather to disseminate the belief, both in
and out of parliament, that the country was in danger
of descending from that proud eminence upon which
she had once rested, and of falling an easy prey to the

---

[1] After an interview with Rockingham, shortly after parliament met,
Chatham declared that " my esteem and confidence in his Lordship's upright
intentions grow from every conversation with him." Chatham Correspondence, 3, 480-481.

joint attack of the two Bourbon powers. It was by raising a panic in the nation that they hoped to drive North and his colleagues from office ; and it is difficult to find any sufficient excuse for their conduct. Both Rockingham and Chatham were experienced statesmen who could not but know that they would best serve their country by assisting rather than thwarting the ministers at this critical juncture, that a quarrel over the possession of a barren island was not a sufficient justification for a European war, and that no useful purpose could possibly be served by spreading abroad alarming rumours about the incompetence of the government and the defenceless condition of the country ; but, like other politicians before and since, they placed the interests of party above the welfare of the state, and hoped to obtain an end, which they thought to be good, by means which they must have known to be unjustifiable.

The storm did not break at once, the first day of the session being quiet enough ; but this calm at the beginning was largely due to the absence of Chatham, Temple, and the followers of Grenville,[1] who abstained from attending out of respect to the dead statesman.[1] Nor were signs of a tempest in the future altogether wanting. No fault, indeed, could be found, even by the most bellicose member of the opposition, with the speech from the throne, the king being made to declare that he would not relinquish his preparations for war until he had received " proper reparation for the injury, as well as satisfactory proof that other powers are equally sincere with myself to preserve the general tranquillity of Europe " ;[2] but, though the speech might

[1] Walpole's Letters, 7, 418-421.
[2] It is worthy of note that Choiseul at first interpreted the king's speech as tantamount to a declaration of war ; Harcourt to Weymouth, November 20th, 1770 ; Foreign State Papers, R.O., 281.

be generally approved, the address of thanks was not allowed to pass without encountering some hostile and pungent criticism.   Various members of the opposition complained that they had not been told of the steps that had been taken to put the country into a state of defence ; and Sir Charles Saunders, a follower of Lord Rockingham, who, for a brief period, had held the office of first lord of the admiralty in Chatham's administration, expressed his regret that preparations for war had not been begun upon the arrival of Hunt in England at the beginning of June.[1]

Unfair as much of this criticism was, it has the interest of being indicative of the line of attack that the opposition intended to follow.   The contest against the government was waged in both houses, but it was in the upper house that the fight was fiercest.   On Thursday, November 22nd, the Duke of Richmond, having previously consulted with Chatham, introduced three motions, so framed that, if they were carried, the ministers would be obliged to reveal how far they had been aware of the danger which threatened Port Egmont before the actual news of its fall was known in England ; and the debate certainly made up in acrimony whatever it may have lacked in effectiveness. Thus Richmond, while energetically disclaiming any desire to complicate the negotiations, modestly declared that he was content merely to reveal to the world the sloth and treachery of the royal advisers ; and Chatham, exclaiming that " something must be done, my lords, and immediately, to save an injured, insulted, undone country," thundered in fury against " those servants of the crown, by whose ignorance, neglect, or treachery this once great flourishing people are reduced

---

[1] Cavendish Debates, 2, 37-54 ; *Parl. Hist.*, xvi. 1030-1081 ; Walpole's Memoirs, iv. 128-130 ; Chatham Correspondence, 3, 489-492.

to a condition as deplorable at home as it is despicable abroad." Nor was Shelburne behindhand in denunciation; for although he discarded the bludgeon for the rapier, he was equally, if not more, effective in criticism, remarking with withering sarcasm that a war would be but a small price to pay for the downfall of the ministry.[1]

Yet, in spite of the scorn thus so lavishly heaped upon the government, the opposition only numbered twenty-one on a division, and this very meagre figure was not exceeded when on Wednesday, November 28th, Chatham, acting on a suggestion thrown out by Rockingham,[2] moved that Captain Hunt should be summoned to the bar of the house, and that the ministers should state when they first learnt that the Spaniards intended to take Port Egmont by storm.[3] Nor was the Duke of Manchester any more successful when, in accordance with a plan suggested by Chatham, and approved by Rockingham,[4] he moved that a strong naval force should be stationed at Gibraltar, Minorca, and Jamaica, only fourteen votes being given for the motion.[5] Moreover, in the house of commons the ministry was equally victorious. On Thursday, November 22nd, Dowdeswell moved for " copies of the intelligence received by his majesty's ministers previous to the twelfth of September . . . touching any hostility commenced or designed to be commenced by the crown of Spain against any part of the British dominions," but his motion was easily rejected, the previous question being carried by two hundred and

---

[1] *Parl. Hist.*, xvi. 1081-1119 ; Walpole's Memoirs, 4, 133-136 ; Walpole's Letters, 7, 423-424.
[2] Chatham Correspondence, 4, 26-29.
[3] Walpole's Memoirs, 4, 139-140.
[4] Chatham Correspondence, 4, 46-48.
[5] Walpole's Memoirs, 4, 150-151 ; *Parl. Hist.*, xvi. 1321-1322.

twenty-five votes to a hundred and one;[1] and when, a week later, he asked for information about the state and disposition of the Spanish fleets, only forty-three members were found to vote against a motion for adjourning the debate.[2]

Such were the first-fruits of a crusade from which so much had been expected ; and it was indeed a barren harvest. Victory, indeed, had not been expected by those who had planned and executed this venture, but they certainly had not anticipated such a complete and overwhelming repulse. An opposition, which dwindled rather than increased in numbers, was not likely to acquire that national confidence so essential to its success ; and Chatham can hardly be blamed for believing all to be lost, and concluding, in the bitterness of his soul, that the times were " pollution in the very quintessence."[3] Yet the catastrophe was by no means inexplicable. It must have been clear to impartial observers that the designs of the opposition were far more factious than patriotic, and that, even assuming that no adequate preparations for war had been made, it was not a fitting time to proclaim the fact to the world at large.[4] Such considerations, however, though they may be held to account for the con-

---

[1] Cavendish Debates, 2, 57-88 ; Parl. Hist., xvi. 1119-1124.
[2] Cavendish Debates, 2, 177-184.
[3] Chatham Correspondence, 4, 31-32.
[4] In the course of a debate in the house of commons, on December 12th, the opposition represented the navy as being in a deplorable condition, and, on the previous day, Chatham declared in the house of lords that half our ships were rotten. It would have been better to have deferred making such accusations until peace was assured, but they certainly were not devoid of truth. Sir Edward Hawke, though a distinguished naval commander in his day, had not proved himself in his old age an efficient first lord of the admiralty, and there appears to be no doubt that, though on paper our navy was adequate, many of our ships were unseaworthy and much undermanned. For some interesting details about the navy at this time, see a speech by Lord Sandwich in 1775, reported in Parl. Hist., xviii. p. 280 ; and also Walpole's Memoirs, iv. 136-137 ; Cavendish Debates, 2, 194-213.

spicuous failure of the opposition to win new recruits, cannot be advanced to explain the actual declension in its numerical strength, which is rather to be attributed to that lack of unity, the cause of so many of its disasters in the past.   Close and cordial as were the relations between Rockingham and Chatham,[1] they had failed to rally the full strength of the opposition to their support.   Both Temple and Camden had declined attending the debates in the upper house ;[2] and, what was of far greater moment, the conduct of the former followers of George Grenville had been strangely hesitating and uncertain.   It would not be true to describe them as having broken with the opposition, but there is no doubt that they were pursuing a policy of waiting upon events, and by no means anxious to bind themselves by words to definite allegiance either to Chatham or Rockingham. Wedderburn and Lord George Sackville had, indeed, supported Dowdeswell in the house of commons, but other members of the same party were conspicuously absent when Chatham moved for Captain Hunt to be

[1] According to Horace Walpole (Memoirs, 4, 133-136), Chatham, in the debate on November 22nd, spoke with contempt of the opposition, and declared his freedom from any party connections ; but this statement appears to be a very decided exaggeration.   Quite apart from what we know of the intimate relations between the two opposition leaders at this time, there is nothing in the account of the debate in the Parliamentary History to show that Chatham bore in any way hardly upon the Rockingham whigs.   It is true that he spoke warmly in favour of impressment, a practice which the Duke of Richmond had opposed ; and that he remarked that " an administration formed on an exclusive system of family connections, or private friendships, cannot, I am convinced, be long supported in this country " ; but he also referred to " men who, if their own services were forgotten, ought to have a hereditary merit with the house of Hanover," and, though he denounced the practice of restricting admission to high office to the members of a few great families, he expressly said that " no man respects or values more than I do that honourable connection which arises from a disinterested concurrence in opinion upon public measures, or from the sacred bond of private friendship and esteem."   Parl. Hist., xvi. 1081-1119.

[2] Chatham Correspondence, 4, 29-30 ;   31-32 ;   Walpole's Memoirs, 4, 139-140 ;   Walpole's Letters, 7, 423-424.

called to the bar of the house ; [1] and, although Lord
Lyttleton had spoken in support of the Duke of
Richmond's motion, it is to his credit that he differentiated himself from all the other speakers against
the government by expressing the opinion that it was
not becoming in wise and responsible statesmen to
" intimidate the people by our fears when we ought to
fire them by our resolution."

From these scattered hints it may be gathered
that the Grenvilles had by no means enthusiastically
co-operated with the other parties in opposition, and
upon them must rest no small share of the responsibility
for the fiasco. But, unfortunate as the enterprise
had been, the hope of ultimate victory was not quite
dead ; for, were the peace of Europe to be broken,
Chatham might once again come into power upon the
shoulders of the people. And, to the dismay of all wise
men, war now appeared to be almost inevitable. The
rejection of the second Spanish offer was followed by
that ominous calm which so often precedes the storm.
The negotiation with Spain was discontinued,[2] and, in
each of the three countries most intimately concerned,
preparations for war were actively hurried on. Harris,
though still retaining his belief in Grimaldi's pacific
disposition, began to fear that the warlike party in
Spain would carry the day,[3] and Choiseul, convinced

[1] Walpole's Memoirs, 4, 139-140.

[2] Thus, on December 21st, Lord Rochford, who had succeeded Weymouth
as secretary of state for the southern department, informed Lord Harcourt
that " negotiation has long been at an end between us and the Court of Spain."
Foreign State Papers, R.O., 281.

[3] " M. Grimaldi, however," wrote Harris to Weymouth on December 17th,
" I am convinced will strain every nerve to accommodate this affair. . . .
Nevertheless, I fear the restless and ambitious temper of Monsieur D'Aranda,
who has, on one hand, represented to the king that the honour of the Spanish
nation would be exposed by acceding to our propositions, and, on the other,
painted the state of both its army and it finances in the most flattering and
. . . false colours ! I fear, I say, these arguments will have more weight

of the futility of endeavouring to maintain peace, definitely determined upon hostilities. Aware that he no longer enjoyed the favour of the king, and believing Spain to be resolved upon war, he thought to re-establish himself in his former omnipotence by remaining faithful to the Pacte de Famille, and uniting with Spain to humiliate the pride of England. He was not blind to the dangers which beset the road he had chosen. He knew that Louis XV. was averse to war, and that his political opponents, who were seeking to drive him from office, were of the same opinion ; [1] but he thought to persuade the king that nothing could be done to avert a conflict between England and Spain, and that France was compelled, both by honour and by interest, to come to the assistance of her ally and neighbour. If his arguments carried conviction, great would be his triumph ; for he might well hope that one immediate consequence of the outbreak of war would be the return of his former political supremacy. Engaged in a great conflict with the old enemy, England, neither Louis XV. nor his people would be inclined to dispense with the services of the most experienced statesman which France possessed.

It was just when the international situation had assumed this aspect of extreme gravity that Lord Weymouth astonished his countrymen by abandoning office, resigning the seals on December 16th, 1770. For this dramatic and unexpected retreat no really adequate explanation has ever yet been given. It has

than they ought ; and greatly obstruct, if not totally prevent, an amicable conclusion of this affair." Foreign State Papers, R.O., 185.

[1] " I am informed," wrote Harcourt to Rochford on December 16th, " that the king continues extremely averse to the thoughts of a war ; and the party in opposition make no difficulty of declaring that a war . . . will complete the ruin of it." Foreign State Papers, R.O., 281. See also *Le Règne de Louis XV.*, H. Carré, p. 390.

been asserted that Weymouth fell a victim to the peace party in the cabinet, and that, for refusing to give way to Spain, he was driven from office by Lord North and the king, who had been converted to a policy of conciliation by the fear that a war with the two Bourbon powers might involve the return of Chatham to power.[1] Such an explanation, however, is exceedingly difficult to accept. If the English demands had been diminished in extent after Weymouth's departure from the cabinet, it would, doubtless, be reasonable to assume that his resignation was due to a division of opinion in the ministry; but no such modification took place, and, therefore, little faith can be placed in an interpretation which is both unsupported by evidence, and in conflict with well-established fact. What is far more probable is that Weymouth, believing war to be inevitable, and realising that his indolent and profligate habits rendered him totally unfit to occupy an office of great responsibility in a moment of stress, adopted the unheroic course of seeking safety in retirement;[2] and though it is not possible to bring forward any evidence in support of this view, it is at least not inherently improbable. But, amidst much which is so doubtful, we know at any rate that no abatement in the English demands followed upon Weymouth's resignation. To fill his vacant place Lord Rochford was transferred from the secretaryship of state for the northern department which was given to Lord Sandwich; and Rochford proved himself as determined as ever his predecessor had been, to obtain reparation for the insult to England. At a cabinet meeting on December 19th, it was decided to recall Harris[3] who, in a dispatch

[1] Walpole's Memoirs, 4, 157-158. For a slightly different account, see Almon's *Anecdotes and Speeches of the Earl of Chatham*, 2, 249-250.

[2] Walpole's Memoirs, 4, 158.

[3] Calendar of Home Office Papers, 102.

written by Rochford, two days later, was instructed to
leave Madrid after formally taking leave.[1]

The withdrawal of the English representative at the
Spanish court could only be interpreted as a preliminary
to a declaration of war ; and it may fairly be assumed
that the cabinet was led to adopt this extreme measure
by the conviction that any further delay was useless,
and that the sooner war began the better.   It is not
easy to censure such pessimism, seeing how black the
outlook was ; but, nevertheless, the ministers stand
convicted of having neglected some very essential
factors in the situation.   They took for granted, not
only that Spain was bent upon hostilities, but that
France would come to her assistance ; and in this
latter particular they were guilty of a fundamental
error.   It was not the French king but Choiseul who
had decided upon war ; and the last word did not rest
with him but with his master.   Were he to fail to
persuade Louis XV. that war was the only alternative,
it was extremely probable that Spain, deprived of the
hope of French assistance, might show herself far more
ready to come to terms with England ; and it was this
possibility that the ministers failed to include in their
reckoning.   They thought that war was inevitable,
whereas, as a matter of fact, it was not.   Louis XV.
was well aware that the outbreak of hostilities would
involve the cessation of his conflict with the parlements,
and, consequently, a decline in the prestige of the crown ;
and, compelled to come to a final determination, he
decided for peace abroad and war at home.   He gave
orders for a letter to be written to the King of Spain,
imploring him to make every possible sacrifice in the
cause of peace; commanded D'Ossun to use all his
influence to promote a speedy settlement with England ;

[1] Diaries and Correspondence of the Earl of Malmesbury, i, 71-73.

and, having taken these steps to avert the approaching war, dismissed Choiseul from office on December 24th, 1770.[1]

Four days later, the news of Choiseul's fall was known in England ;[2] and though amateur politicians were at first puzzled to determine the precise influence of this cabinet revolution upon the international situation,[3] the ministers were not long in learning that it was likely to be a very powerful factor in the promotion of peace. " It has been intimated to me," wrote Harcourt to Rochford on December 26th, " by a person well acquainted with this court, that, as soon as the new minister is appointed for the foreign affairs, I shall receive the strongest assurances of the pacifick disposition of this court,"[4] and this cheering intelligence was confirmed by a change for the better in the attitude of Masserano,who now, in the words of a well-informed contemporary, " declares that he expects daily orders from his court to give us the satisfaction we demand."[5]

Thus, at the bidding of an aged voluptuary, the clouds of war began to disperse, and the English ministers had good reason to regret their hasty action in recalling Harris. It might well happen, for such is the instability of the foundations upon which the peace of nations and the happiness of thousands rest, that the prospect of a happy settlement might be suddenly

[1] *Le Règne de Louis XV.*, H. Carré, 389-391.

[2] Harcourt to Rochford, December 24th, 1770. For the date of the arrival of this dispatch, see Walpole's Letters, 7, 430-432.

[3] The Duc de Choiseul is fallen. . . . There ! there is a revolution ! there is a new scene opened. Will it advance the war ? Will it make peace ? These are the questions all mankind is asking. Walpole's Letters, 7, 430-432. It is interesting to notice that Chatham still persisted in believing war to be certain. Chatham Correspondence, 4, 64-65.

[4] Harcourt to Rochford, December 26th, 1770 ; Foreign State Papers, R.O., 281.

[5] Thomas Bradshaw to the Duke of Grafton, January 5th, 1771 ; Grafton's *Autobiography*, 260-261. Bradshaw was a secretary of the treasury and enjoyed Grafton's intimate confidence.

blasted by a trivial question of diplomatic etiquette. When on January 3rd, 1771, the Spanish ambassador was informed that a dispatch had already left England, instructing Harris to return home, he did not disguise his deep annoyance, and declared that, " should he now receive full power to acquiesce in our demand, he should look upon himself as tied up till he knew the sentiments of his court relating to the recall of Mr Harris," [1] but, fortunately, he did not continue in this unbending attitude. With the authorisation of his government which, now that it could no longer depend upon France, was prepared to come to terms,[2] he signed, on January 22nd, 1771, a declaration by which the conduct of Buccarelli was disavowed and the restoration of Port Egmont was promised, but, at the same time, it was expressly stated that " the engagement of his said Catholick majesty to restore to his Brittanic majesty the possession of the fort and port called Egmont cannot or ought in any wise to affect the question of the prior right of the sovereignty

---

[1] Rochford to Harcourt, January 7th, 1771 ; Foreign State Papers, R.O., 282.

[2] When the Spanish ministry dispatched this authorisation to Masserano, it was not aware that Harris had been recalled ; and this statement can be proved by a comparison of dates. It was not until January 12th, that Harris informed Grimaldi that he had been recalled, and in a dispatch to Rochford, dated the same day, the English ambassador in France states : " The night before last a messenger arrived from Spain, and yesterday morning the Spanish ambassador had an audience of the king that lasted one hour and a half. I am assured that the Spaniards will acquiesce to our demands, and that the Prince de Masserano will have orders to signify as much to your lordship." It may, I think, be taken as fairly certain that this messenger was on his way to England with instructions to Masserano, and it is obvious that he must have left Spain some days before Harris informed Grimaldi that he had been recalled. Moreover, according to Walpole, it was at the advice of the French king that Masserano consented to make use of the full powers granted to him, and we have on the same authority, the doubtful, though dramatic, story that two days after the Spanish ambassador had signed the declaration, he received orders commanding him to return to Spain without delay. Foreign State Papers, R.O., 282 ; Diaries and Correspondence of the Earl of Malmesbury, 1, 71-73 ; Walpole's Memoirs, 4, 175.

of the Malouine Islands, otherwise called Falkland Islands." [1]

This happy conclusion to a negotiation which at one time seemed about to end in a rupture between three great nations and the horrors of an European war, was approved by all wise men ; but to Chatham and his political allies, their eyes blinded by the passions aroused by domestic strife, it was more an occasion for sorrow than for joy. They had not unreasonably hoped that the outbreak of war would give the signal for the downfall of the ministry, and they were now called upon to undergo the mortification of witnessing the conclusion of a settlement which only by blind and embittered partisanship could be represented as dishonourable or inadequate. Nor was the blow any easier to bear from coinciding with another and a greater misfortune—the defection of several of the leading members of the Grenville party. Such a secession had for long been regarded as possible and even probable. Almost from the very beginning of the session, sinister, and unfortunately well founded, rumours had been circulated that Wedderburn was about to make his peace with the court,[2] and there is good reason to believe that the ministers were well aware of their adversary's readiness to be bought.[3] Nor had Wedderburn been the only object of suspicion. Writing to Mann at Florence about the middle of

---

[1] Annual Register for 1771, p. 238.

[2] Chatham Correspondence, 4, 20-23 ; 30-31. Wedderburn stated his own point of view in a letter to Lord Clive, written on November 14th, 1770. " I have not yet been, " he wrote, " in the house of commons ; and if people would impute my absence to its true cause, a real indifference to all that passes there at present, I should continue for some time in the same ignorance. . . . It is possible, I believe, even in these times, for a man to acquire some degree of credit, without being enlisted in any party ; and, if it is, the situation, I am sure, is more eligible than any other that either a court or an opposition have to bestow." Quoted in the Cavendish Debates, 2, 81-82.

[3] Correspondence of George III. with Lord North, 1, 45.

January, 1771, Horace Walpole had mentioned that " Mr Grenville's friends point due west to St James's "[1] and before his letter reached its destination what he hinted at had come to pass. In a letter to Lord Temple, dated January 22nd, 1771, Lord Suffolk, who was commonly looked upon as Grenville's successor in the leadership of the party, announced that he had that day formally accepted the office of lord privy seal ;[2] and, a few days later, it was announced that Wedderburn had been appointed solicitor-general, that Thomas Whately, who was well-known to have enjoyed Grenville's closest confidence, had been named a commissioner of the board of trade, and that to Augustus Hervey, afterwards Lord Bristol, had been given a lordship of the admiralty.[3] At the same time, moreover, some important internal changes were made in the ministry. The great seal, which had been in commission since the dismissal of Camden, was given to Henry Bathurst who was raised to the peerage as Lord Apsley ; and though, as a lawyer, Bathurst was beneath contempt, being probably the most insignificant man who has ever sat on the woolsack, he could be trusted to stand by the court which had rewarded him so richly for his services. Onlookers might be astonished at the sight of the greatest prize of the legal profession being given to a notoriously incompetent lawyer, but no surprise was felt at the promotion of Edward Thurlow, who had already given ample proof of having great abilities and few scruples, from the office of solicitor to that of attorney-general. Nor could any objection be taken to the appointment of Lord Sandwich as first lord of the admiralty in place of Sir Edward Hawke now almost in his

[1] Walpole's Letters, 8, 1-3.　　[2] Grenville Papers, 4, 529-530.
[3] Chatham Correspondence, 4, 74-76 ; 80-82.

dotage ;[1] though it was possible to doubt the wisdom of transferring Lord Halifax, who, according to Horace Walpole, " knew nothing, was too old to learn, and too sottish and too proud to suspect what he wanted,"[2] from the comparatively sinecure office of lord privy seal to be secretary of state in place of Lord Sandwich.

The internal reconstruction of the administration, important though it was, attracted far less attention than the admission of Wedderburn and his friends into office, and it was round these new recruits that the interest centred. All of them were denounced as vile and self-seeking apostates, but Wedderburn above the rest. Yet that shrewd Scotchman, and those who stood with him in the same condemnation, were certainly not incapable of making a rational defence, being able, indeed, to bring forward arguments of undoubted force in support of their action. It must in fairness be remembered that when George Grenville and his followers had thrown in their lot with the opposition, they had been impelled to take this step, partly by the wish to speeden the downfall of the government, so that room might be made for a cabinet in which Grenville should have the predominant influence, and partly by a sincere desire to take their part in protecting the rights of electors against the oligarchical usurpation of the house of commons. The death of Grenville, however, and the apathy with which the nation had come to regard the once burning question of the Middlesex election, now rendered it

---

[1] " The admiralty, in which he had formerly presided with credit, was the favourite object of Lord Sandwich's ambition : and his passion for maritime affairs, his activity, industry, and flowing complaisance, endeared him to the profession, re-established the marine, and effaced great part of his unpopularity." Walpole's Memoirs, iv. 170.

[2] Walpole's Memoirs, iv. 173.

impossible for either of these ends to be attained ; and, therefore, the causes, which had originated and maintained an alliance, essentially artificial, ceased to be operative.   But, on the other hand, the old sources of dissension, the difference of opinion upon colonial policy, and the jealousy between the rival parties, still existed in undiminished vigour ; and it is, therefore, hardly surprising that, after the death of their leader, and the collapse of any widespread interest in the wrongs of Wilkes, some of Grenville's followers sought for admission into a government with which they had really far more in common than with their supposed allies.   Yet, though justified by reason, the secession proved a death-blow to the Grenville faction which from this time ceased to exist as an independent political party.   Some of its members elected to play, for a time at least, an independent part, alternately criticising and supporting the court, and others preferred to follow in the wake of Wedderburn ; but each man did what was right in his own eyes, and that which had been a political organisation, endowed with an unity and coherence of its own, was dissolved into separate and disconnected fragments.

Thus with Grenville died his party, and the loss to the opposition was wellnigh irreparable, reduced as it now was to the followers of Chatham and Rockingham. Moreover, the danger was not remote that even this alliance might break asunder.   Temple had retired from public life on the death of his brother ; [1] and Camden, though friendly enough with the Rockinghams, was aggrieved with Chatham with whom he declared himself to be no longer connected.[2]   If dissension broke out in this reduced and attenuated band, it would,

---

[1] Chatham Correspondence, 4, 37 ; Grenville Papers, 4, 530-531.

[2] Rockingham Memoirs, 2, 197-198 ; Walpole's Memoirs, iv. 140-141.

indeed, be vain to continue the struggle ; and it was somewhat difficult to see how the unity, so much desired, could be retained unless a new cry against the government could be discovered upon which all were agreed.   Experience shows, however, that when a grievance is needed it can generally be found ; and just as the convention with Spain in 1739 had been converted into a weapon of attack against Walpole, so now the opposition agreed to unite in throwing ridicule and scorn upon the declaration recently signed by the Spanish ambassador and approved by the cabinet.   For such a policy it is almost impossible to find any sufficient excuse.   Spain had fulfilled the original demands of England, the dignity of the nation had been preserved, and a totally unnecessary, and therefore entirely wicked, war averted; and though many and weighty are the crimes with which North and his colleagues can be truly charged, it ought never to be forgotten that, at least in one instance, they co-operated to prevent the catastrophe of useless blood-shed.   But their very virtue was an offence in the eyes of men who had seen in a war their own salvation ; and directly it was known that the declaration was to be submitted to both houses of parliament on Friday, January 25th, the preparations for attack were begun. In letters to his friends Chatham was unsparing in his objections to the terms which the ministers had accepted, declaring that the article which reserved the question of the right of sovereignty in the Falkland Islands, was " lower and more abject, as well as more dangerous in consequence and extent than I could imagine even our ministry could have furnished hearts to conceive, heads to contrive, or hands to execute " ; [1]

---

[1] Chatham Correspondence, 4, 73-74.   His bitterness may have been increased by the belief, for which Barré was responsible, that the article in

and roundly asserting, without a shadow of evidence to support his theory, that " the whole will be found to be an ignominious collusion with the present views of France." [1] So thinking, he naturally accepted with eagerness an invitation to attend a meeting of the opposition peers, which was to be held at the Duke of Richmond's house on the evening of Thursday, January 24th, and warmly encouraged his devoted follower, Calcraft, to attend an assembly of members of the house of commons, summoned by Dowdeswell for a similar purpose.[2]

At these conferences projects were discussed and plans settled ; and the design of the opposition was well expressed by the Duke of Richmond who told Chatham that " it seems necessary, after the late defection, that we should show no languour, but by some spirited conduct tell the world, as early as possible, that we remain steady and firm in the cause we have undertaken." [3] Thus the ministerial foreign policy

question was secret and implied that England had consented to evacuate Port Egmont at some future date.   A few years later, it was asserted that in a dispatch to his government, dated 16th March 1771, the Comte de Guines, then French ambassador in England, stated " que les ministres anglais annonant qu'immédiatement après le retour des vaisseaux chargés de reprendre possession des Isles Falkland, leur premier soin sera d'envoyer l'ordre de les abandonner." Called upon for an explanation by Horace St Paul, then secretary to the English embassy at Paris, the Comte de Guines, in a letter dated May 16th, 1775, replied : " M. le C. : de Guines vient de s'assurer par lui-même du contenu de la dépêche du 16 Mars, il ne peut en envoyer l'extrait litteral à monsieur le colonel St Paul, mais il a l'honneur de l'assurer qu'en parlant du discours que nous tenaient alors les ministres de sa magisté Brittanique, il eût dit en propres formes : *à la resérve cependant de milord Rochford.*" If the secretary of state for foreign affairs refrained from giving any promise to abandon the Falkland Islands, it may with safety be assumed that the utterances of the other ministers on this point were entirely unofficial, and made upon their own responsibility.   *Colonel St Paul of Ewart,* edited by George G. Butler (1911) vol. ii. pp. 75, 133-134 ; Chatham Correspondence, iv. 71-72.

[1] Chatham Correspondence, 4, 76-77.
[2] Chatham Correspondence, 4, 78-79 ; 82-86.
[3] *Ibid.,* 78-79.

was the occasion, but not the cause, of the attack ; and
never was a better demonstration given of factious
criticism and perverted ability than on Friday,
January 25th, when the Spanish declaration was laid
before parliament. No blame, indeed, attaches to
the opposition for calling for papers connected with
the negotiation ; for no harm could ensue, now that a
settlement had been reached, from a publication of
documents which, a few weeks before, could not have
been safely revealed ; and the request was willingly
granted. Nor is the Duke of Richmond to be censured
for moving that all the memorials which had passed
between England and France should be laid before
the house, since he could justify his demand by the
popular, though entirely baseless, belief that France
had been allowed to interfere in the negotiation, and
had practically dictated the terms of the settlement.[1]
But what, indeed, was worthy of blame was the violent
and factious tone adopted by the opposition speakers.
Thus Richmond, instead of being content with Rochford's plain and truthful statement that no Anglo-
French memorials could be produced as none existed,
proclaimed the truly startling doctrine that the word
of a minister ought never to be accepted by the nation ;
and in this wild contention he was supported by
Chatham who, though he refrained from giving
Rochford the lie direct, asserted that he knew as a
positive fact that France had interfered in the negotiation. In the house of commons, moreover, the same

---

[1] It is necessary carefully to discriminate between influence and participation. It is, of course, true that France very materially influenced the negotiation, but this was inevitable from her position as a possible ally of Spain in
the event of war. It is not true, however, to say that she interfered ; and
there is an interesting dispatch from Rochford to Harcourt, dated December
21st, 1770 (Foreign State Papers, R.O., 281), which illustrates the care taken
by the English ministers to safeguard against any suspicion of French
mediation.

recklessness in accusation was displayed, the most notable speech being made by Dowdeswell who declared that the declaration was shameful, that the satisfaction obtained was miserably disproportionate to the length of the negotiation, that it was impossible not to believe that Spain, from the very first, had been willing to grant such meagre reparation ; and that, if the ministers had never intended to ask for more, they had grossly deceived the people in making preparations for a war which could never have been a serious possibility.[1]

Such were the charges, the offspring of ignorance and faction, produced by the opposition ; and the campaign of misrepresentation was not confined to a single day. When the papers, which had been demanded, were laid before the house of commons on February 4th, the cry was again raised that France had interfered in the negotiation, and no heed was paid to North's denial of the charge. " Sir," said Dowdeswell, " we know the court of France has interfered ; and we ought to know in what way the elder branch of the house of Bourbon has interfered " ; and the same accusation was repeated in slightly varying forms by nearly every speaker on the opposition side. Thus Barré proclaimed that it was " the public opinion of all Europe that the whole transaction is by France alone," and Burke, going still further, declared that he knew, " from a better source than common rumour, that France has interfered, not as a mediator but as a party." [2]   Nor did even this attack exhaust the activity and satisfy the venom of the opposition ; and when, on February 13th, an address of thanks for the

---

[1] Cavendish Debates, 2, 218-226 ;   *Parl. Hist.* xvi. 1336-1345 ; Chatham Correspondence, 4, 86-88.
[2] Cavendish Debates, 2, 231-243.

settlement of the dispute with Spain was moved in the house of commons, Dowdeswell seized the opportunity to make a lengthy and violent assault upon the ministers. According to him their crimes were, indeed, many. They had neither prepared for the attack upon Port Egmont, nor obtained compensation for the protracted refusal of Spain to do justice to this country ; and, filling the cup of their iniquity, they had approved a declaration, the terms of which were so vague and ambiguous as to give neither satisfaction for the past nor security for the future.[1] In the upper house the government was subjected to the same ill-informed and vindictive criticism, but, unfortunately, we know little of the debates in that assembly at this time. It seems that Chatham was foremost in the fray, speaking for two hours to an amendment to the address of thanks on February 14th ;[2] and, a few days earlier, the Duke of Bolton had moved that the instructions, which had been given to Hunt when he was sent to the Falkland Islands, should be laid before the house, in the hope, it has been asserted, that the publication of these orders, which were excessively minatory, would so outrage the Spanish court as to induce it to refuse to ratify the declaration, and provoke it into embarking upon a war with England.[3]

Yet, in spite of all their labours, the opposition failed in their crusade. They aimed at bringing discredit and disgrace upon the government, and they did not attain the end they sought. It was not their bitterest grief that they had been easily outvoted in both houses, for that had been a foregone conclusion : it was of much greater moment that they had been so

[1] Cavendish Debates, 2, 272-306.
[2] Walpole's Memoirs, 4, 182-183 ; *Parl. Hist.*, xvi. 1379-1385.
[3] Walpole's Memoirs, 4, 179.

entirely unsuccessful in stirring up any national discontent against the ministry. Like Carteret before them, they had endeavoured to fan the war fever, to disseminate the belief that the honour and welfare of the country had been sacrificed, and that nothing could be more disastrous that a peace purchased at so high a rate ; but the people, to whom they appealed, refused to listen to them. Their case was, indeed, too bad to be rendered even plausible by the eloquence of Chatham and the reasoning of Burke ; and it may be that because they failed, the iniquity of their conduct has been generally overlooked. Baffled intriguers, however, cannot plead the frustration of their plans as an excuse for their actions ; and though Chatham's opposition to Sir Robert Walpole has sometimes been pardoned on the ground of his comparative youth, it is instructive to remember, in connection with this plea, that he was guilty of an even less defensible display of factious opposition when well advanced in years and one of the most famous and experienced of European statesmen.

Having thus failed to plunge the country into war, the opposition, if it was to continue, was obliged to find another grievance against the government ; and this time the discovery was not easy to make. All the possibilities of the Middlesex election had long been exhausted ; and although this much over-debated question was again raised in both houses in the course of the session, the futility of such a revival was made quite obvious. Only twenty supporters rallied to the side of Chatham, when, in the house of lords on December 5th, he moved that the judgment of the house of commons upon the capacity to be elected a member of parliament was neither final nor conclusive ; [1] and

[1] *Parl. Hist.* xvi. 1302-1312 ; Walpole's Memoirs, iv. 140-141.

when, a few weeks later, Sir George Savile asked leave of the commons to introduce a bill dealing with the rights and privileges of electors, he suffered the indignity of addressing a half-empty and inattentive house, many members having paired or withdrawn to neighbouring coffee-houses in order to avoid hearing arguments which they already knew by heart.[1] It was, indeed, time decently to inter the Middlesex election, especially as another question of almost equal importance had lately arisen and awaited discussion. It is by no means an unimportant part of the functions of a parliamentary opposition to defend the subject against that tendency towards arbitrary and oppressive conduct which exists, in more or less degree, in every government ; and Chatham and his friends were now given an opportunity to play this rôle. It was open to them to make amends for past failures and mistakes by nobly standing up in defence of what, in spite of many drawbacks and unhappy consequences, is one of the surest guarantees of constitutional liberty, the freedom of the press.

During the year 1770, public attention had been attracted to the very unsatisfactory character of the existing law of libel ; and, in order to understand the awakening of this widespread interest in a subject which might well be thought too technical and abstract to evoke much enthusiasm, it is necessary to go back to the publication, in the *Morning Advertiser* of December 19th, 1769, of Junius' famous letter to the king. With almost unparalleled malice and spleen this vindictive and anonymous letter writer drew his sovereign's

---

[1] *Parl. Hist.*, xvi. 1355-1358 ; Cavendish Debates, 1, 245-250. According to the Parliamentary History " one reason the numbers were but small on either side, was that this point, having often been debated, several paired off, and the question being put before it was expected, many gentlemen were absent in the coffee-houses."

attention to the consequences of nine years of personal government. He showed how the affections of England, of Ireland, and of the Colonies had been so successfully alienated that the king was obliged to depend upon the Scotch whose loyalty was now so great that " one would think they had forgotten that you are their lawful king, and had mistaken you for a pretender to the crown." Yet, cruel as such gibes were, they appear almost innocent in comparison with the threats and admonitions with which the epistle closed. Covering the indecency of his language with a certain mock reverence and respect which doubled its offensiveness, Junius informed the king that before he could hope to subdue the hearts of his subjects, " he must gain a noble victory over his own, that the pretended power, which robs an English subject of his birthright, may rob an English king of his crown " ; and that a prince, who elected to model his conduct upon that of the Stuarts, might well profit by the example of their fate.

Such threatening and denunciatory words could easily be construed as an incitement to rebellion and sedition ; and George III. and his advisers are hardly to be blamed for resorting in self defence to the weapon of the law. Unfortunately, however, the chief offender was beyond their reach, being concealed in that well-contrived obscurity from which he has never completely emerged ; and the victims of the royal vengeance were the subordinate agents in the crime, the printers and publishers of the offensive letter. Of these sufferers the most famous were Henry Woodfall, the printer of the *Morning Advertiser*, and John Almon, a bookseller, who had sold a reprint of the libel. Both were arrested and brought to trial ; and in the course of the legal proceedings against them, Lord Mansfield ruled, though not for the first time, that a printer or publisher was responsible for the actions of his subordinates, and that, in cases of libel, the jury was restricted to returning a verdict upon the mere facts of printing and publication, leaving it to the bench to determine the all important question whether what had been printed or published was actually a libel. In both trials, the lord chief justice laid particular stress upon the latter point, carefully instructing the jury, in the case of Woodfall, that " as for the intention, the malice, the sedition, or any other harder words which might be given in informations for libels, public or private, they were merely formal words, mere words of course, mere inferences of law, with which the jury were not to concern themselves."

In proclaiming such a doctrine Lord Mansfield was able to defend himself both by precedent and reason. Many eminent lawyers in the past, and among them the great Lord Hardwicke, had upheld a precisely similar view ; and it is impossible to contend that such a limitation of a jury's province was entirely unreasonable. It may fairly be argued that though the united opinion of twelve average and uninstructed men may be of great weight upon a subject which demands for its understanding no particular knowledge or training, it is to the experts we look when a highly specialised topic is under discussion ; and that twelve grocers are no more qualified to determine the libellous character of a publication than they are to decide the question of the authorship of St John's Gospel. Many are the men who have discovered to their cost how dark and intricate the law of libel is ; and it may well appear the height of unreason to expect the untrained and ignorant layman to find his way through a labyrinth which has sometimes puzzled even a lawyer. Yet, in spite of the undoubted weight of such arguments, and supported though they were by many precedents, the opinion expressed by Mansfield had for many years been challenged, even in legal circles. The greatest opponent of the lord chief-justice was Lord Camden who had always maintained that it was the business of the jury to decide the criminality of a libel as well as the fact of its publication, and that this privilege was guaranteed by the law of the land. Public opinion, moreover, had always supported that party in the controversy to which Camden belonged, and for very obvious and cogent reasons. It was abundantly clear that if the judiciary alone was to decide whether publications were libellous or not, the much boasted freedom of the press would quickly become very little more than a mere empty vaunt. Few would dare to criticise the actions of the government, or to voice the grievances of the nation, if they were to be left to the mercy of judges who, appointed by the crown, and by reason of their training and environment far more in sympathy with the maintenance of authority than with the assertion of freedom, would be only too likely to affix the stigma of libel to every writing which ran counter to the wishes of the court or tended to provoke discontent against the government. Free criticism, it was urged, would be quickly stifled, and the press converted into an engine of royal tyranny; and the only possible safeguard against such a danger was to allow a reputed libeller that privilege of being tried by a jury of his fellow-countrymen, which was not denied to the lowest criminal.

It is evident that much of the disagreement between the two schools was due to a fundamental difference in their point of view. Mansfield, and those who shared his opinions, not unnaturally resented the claims of the layman to interfere in what they regarded as the province of the lawyer; whereas Camden, paying perhaps too little heed to the necessity of specialised knowledge in legal administration, thought almost exclusively of the great constitutional question which was at stake. It seemed to him far more important that the press should be free than that the law of libel should be scientifically applied; and there can be no doubt that he was substantially in the right. The practical, and, therefore, the real value of any system of law depends upon the degree to which it promotes and develops a well-ordered and vigorous national life, and it is certain that if the judicial bench were able to control the most powerful organ of political criticism that has ever existed, constitutional growth, if not impossible, would, at least, be rendered exceedingly difficult. Therefore, if the law of libel really was as Mansfield had always stated it, it must be changed in the interests of the nation as a whole; for men had come to perceive that what was scientifically true might easily be politically dangerous, and that it was necessary for them to take steps to prevent their liberty being sacrificed to the pedantry of lawyers. Thus, in Woodfall's trial, the jury, circumventing rather than defying the instructions it had received from Lord Mansfield, returned a verdict of " guilty of printing and publishing " only; and when Miller, another printer, was charged at the Guildhall, the jury disregarded both the weight of evidence and the elementary principles of justice by returning a verdict of " not guilty."

A conflict between law and public opinion is always attended by serious danger, and when such discord arises, the easy and natural remedy to adopt is to bring the law into conformity with the national will. Un-

fortunately, however, it was in the last degree unlikely
that a ministry which depended upon the court, and
upon the court alone, would make a change which
must result in the multiplication of its already numerous
critics ; and, therefore, what the administration would
not attempt, the opposition must. Indeed, there
was much to induce Chatham and Rockingham to essay
the task which the ministry declined. If they succeeded, their names would be for ever linked with an
important constitutional development ; and, if they
failed, they would, at least, enjoy the satisfaction
which comes from a gallant struggle against a combination of ignorance and interest, and could count with
security upon the gratitude of contemporaries and the
admiration of posterity. Thus, inaction would indeed
be fatal ; but it would be still worse if, after having
engaged in battle upon behalf of the nation, the leaders
of the opposition turned their swords against one
another, and saved the enemy the trouble of destroying
them by bringing destruction upon themselves. Yet
it was this miserable fate which befell them ; and
never was a greater opportunity missed, or a catastrophe more complete. The only result of the crusade
to reform the law of libel was the complete collapse
of the party which had undertaken it. Henceforth,
dissension between the followers of Chatham and
Rockingham was open and avowed ; anything approaching an united opposition ceased to exist ; and
the parliamentary conflict was stilled until the days
when England was on the verge of war with the colonists.

The tragedy of the disaster was rendered all the
greater by being totally unnecessary ; for the difference
of opinion, which separated the two parties in opposition,
was comparatively slight, and could easily have been
adjusted by the timely exercise of a little tact and

forbearance. Both were agreed in considering the
law of libel, as interpreted by Mansfield, to be a serious
menace to the freedom of the press, and, as this was the
main point at issue, it might be thought that little
room was left for any serious disagreement. History,
however, teaches that embittered quarrels, both
between nations and individuals, often spring from
very trivial causes, and it was over the method to be
adopted to attain an end which all desired that there
arose the dispute which wrecked the opposition.
Taking what may fairly be called the common sense
view of the situation, Rockingham and his supporters
desired to remove the prevalent doubt and uncertainty
upon a very important legal point by introducing a
bill definitely giving the jury the right to decide whether
a publication was libellous or not. It was not, they
might truly say, for them, mere politicians and lay-
men, to arbitrate between such eminent jurists as
Camden and Mansfield upon a question of law ; but,
at the same time, it was their duty as statesmen to
endeavour to end the confusion which arises when
lawyers disagree. Thus, having no desire to inquire
into the past, to plunge into a controversy for which
they were not equipped, or to censure Mansfield
for expressing a belief which, they were well aware,
he could support by far better arguments than ever
they could produce, they sought a remedy for the
future, and approached the problem, not as lawyers
which they were not, but as statesmen which they
were. Yet, it was by this very wisdom and restraint
that they incurred the wrath of the ally who could
frustrate their plans and defeat their hopes. Chatham
who, though he had the insight of genius, could never
think clearly or logically, was entirely unable to distinguish between the legal and the constitutional

aspect of the question. Rightly convinced that the doctrines, enunciated by Mansfield, were inimical to freedom and alien to the spirit of the constitution, he at once concluded that the lord chief-justice was guilty of a grievous error. To him it seemed far more likely that the man, who was well known to favour autocratic methods of government, should twist and pervert the law to his own evil ends than that the law itself should be an engine of tyranny and oppression. So thinking, he could not favour the design of a legislative change, for that might be well construed as a confession of weakness, as an admission that Mansfield was right and Camden was wrong : what he sought to promote was an inquiry into the administration of the law of libel, confidently believing that such an inquisition would reveal the evil deeds of wicked judges, and establish, once and for ever, the true doctrine that the freedom of the press, though assailed by those who had most to fear from it, enjoyed the protection of the law of the land.

Thus, the antagonists of the court inclined once more to range themselves under opposing banners ; and the line of demarcation between the followers of Chatham and Rockingham became unpleasantly well-defined. It is certain that a great deal of difficulty in the future might have been avoided if a plan of campaign had been discussed and settled between the two parties ; and there is reason to believe that this very obvious method of adjusting differences was ruled out of consideration by Chatham and his followers, who were determined to act independently of men whom they were already beginning to regard with distrust and suspicion. It was in accordance with this most unfortunate resolution that though Chatham and his friends had originally intended that the campaign

should be opened by Charles Cornwall, a very insignificant member of the opposition, moving for the
institution of an inquiry into the administration
of justice, the idea was promptly abandoned when it
was found that Cornwall felt himself pledged in honour
to communicate his intention to the Rockinghams.
An equally effective, though more roundabout, method
was contrived ; for when it was discovered that Captain
Constantine Phipps, an independent member of parliament, intended to move for leave to introduce a bill
dealing with the attorney-general's power of filing
informations *ex officio* for libel, it was at once arranged
that Cornwall, in speaking to the motion, should press
for an inquiry into the administration of justice on
the ground that far more mischief was being wrought
by the judges than by the attorney-general ; and that
then Phipps should extend his proposition in order to
meet this criticism.[1]

This was an ingenious contrivance, and, save in
one particular, successfully executed. On November
27th, 1770, Captain Phipps moved that " leave be given
to bring in a bill to explain, amend, and render more
effectual, the act of the 4th and 5th of William and
Mary, to prevent malicious informations in the court
of king's bench," and after the motion had been
seconded by Sir William Meredith, and opposed by
Welbore Ellis, Cornwall rose to play his pre-arranged
part of the friendly and sympathetic critic. While
allowing that the public mind was strangely agitated,
Cornwall contended that this did not spring from any
abuse of the power lodged in the hands of the attorney-
general, but rather from juries being told that " upon
the trial of a libel . . . they were only judges of the
fact, not of the law " ; and that, therefore, the agitation

---

[1] Chatham Correspondence, 4, 20-23.

in the nation would best be allayed by the appointment of a committee to inquire into the administration of justice. According to the original programme, Phipps ought then to have consented to amend his proposal ; but, with the natural pride of a father, he found it impossible, when the time came, to mutilate his own offspring, and retorted upon Cornwall by asserting that " if it should be proved, that there is a power within the letter of the law, which militates against the constitution, why, before we correct the evil, should we go into so serious an inquiry, as whether the administration of justice is correctly administered or not ? " Yet, though Phipps had proved himself unexpectedly obdurate, and no motion for an inquiry was made, Cornwall's interposition was certainly not without value as a preparation of the ground for future operations, and as a test which, from Chatham's point of view, divided the sheep from the goats. Thus Dunning, who had once been solicitor-general in Grafton's ministry, and had only recently joined the opposition, and Serjeant Glynn, a leading member of the " Bill of Rights " Society, and a consistent opponent of the court, won Chatham's good opinion by their denunciation of Mansfield's doctrines and their enthusiastic support of Cornwall's suggestions ; and it equally did not pass unnoticed that Dowdeswell had remained silent, and that Burke, though he pressed for an inquiry, had been frank enough to admit that juries might be corrupt as well as judges.[1]

" If Burke's picture of juries, and of that mode of justice," wrote Chatham, on receiving an account of the debate, " be to be adopted, I will separate from so unorthodox a congregation " ;[2] and this was certainly

---

[1] *Cavendish Debates*, 2, 89-116 ; *Parl. Hist.*, xvi., 1127-1211 ; Chatham Correspondence, 4, 30-31.

[2] Chatham Correspondence, 4, 31-32.

no idle threat. Aware that in Dunning and Glynn he had supporters of established legal reputation,[1] and determined to be no longer fettered by what he deemed the sickly moderation of the Rockingham party, Chatham resolved to push on the campaign in complete independence of his former allies ; and, using Shelburne as his go-between, persuaded Glynn to father the resolution which Cornwall had abandoned.[2] Consequently, on Thursday, December 6th, Glynn moved " that a committee be appointed to inquire into the administration of criminal justice, and the proceedings of the judges of Westminster Hall, particularly in cases relating to the liberty of the press, and the constitutional power and duties of juries." The rejection of this motion was, of course, a foregone conclusion, but the debate afforded an interesting illustration of the very clearly marked divergence in opinion between the two parties in opposition. All Chatham's followers who joined in the discussion were unanimous in denouncing Mansfield's conception of the law of libel, not only as antagonistic to freedom, but as actually illegal. Thus Glynn declared that " these doctrines . . . have no authority from our laws and constitution," and Calcraft scornfully remarked, " What does it signify to have proved that the arraigned doctrines are conformable to precedent, since they have not been proved conformable to the principles of the constitution " ; while Alderman Oliver, who seconded the motion in a short but extremely violent speech, boldly accused Lord Mansfield of maladministration. On the other hand, it was very noticeable that all the members of the

---

[1] " Mr Dunning's visit yesterday," wrote Chatham on December 3rd, " has filled me with the highest satisfaction. He is another being from any I have known of the profession. . . . Mr Dunning is not a lawyer, at the same time that he is the law itself." Chatham Correspondence, 4, 41.

[2] Chatham Correspondence, 4, 35-36.

Rockingham party who spoke were careful, while supporting the motion, clearly to dissociate themselves from the opinions expressed by Glynn and his friends. Thus Sir George Savile argued that he favoured an inquiry because, confused by the division of opinion among the experts, he was anxious to have his doubts cleared up, and Burke had the honesty to avow that if Lord Mansfield " has erred, he has erred in the best company." [1]

" Upon the whole," wrote Chatham in reference to this debate, " the day was a good and great one for the public," [2] and it is very significant that he should find pleasure in what might have been expected to produce a very different emotion. Doubtless it was well that a protest should be made against an interpretation of the libel law, which ran counter to the spirit of the constitution, but it would have been still better if such a protest had come from an opposition which was agreed, not only upon principles, but also upon a programme. Only seventy-six votes had been given for Glynn's motion, and such an attenuated minority suggests that not a few of the Rockingham party had not troubled to attend the debate. Nor can they be blamed for their absence, for, unconsidered and unconsulted, they were under no obligation to support a method of procedure which they did not approve. To them it seemed that to institute an inquiry into the administration of justice was not only to shake the foundations upon which all ordered government rests, but also to convert what ought to be a crusade on behalf of the freedom of the press into a malicious assault upon a single individual. There was good reason to believe that Chatham and

Cavendish Debates, 2, 121-148 ; Parl. Hist., xvi., 1211-1301.
[2] Chatham Correspondence, 4, 45-46.

his friends were aiming far too much at making a personal attack upon Lord Mansfield ; and this suspicion gained no little support from the proceedings of the opposition in the house of lords. When, on Friday, December 7th, Mansfield informed the peers that he wished the house to be summoned for the following Monday, as he had an important communication to make, it is very probable that Chatham believed that he had succeeded in driving the lord chief-justice out into the open, and that the latter was about to commit the serious indiscretion of making a public defence of his conduct. In this expectation, however, he was disappointed, for, when Monday came, Mansfield did no more than inform his hearers that he had left a copy of the judgment of the court of king's bench in Woodfall's case with the clerk of the house. As there was no motion, there could be no debate ; and although, on the day following, Camden, instigated by Chatham,[1] sought to entrap Mansfield by addressing to him six questions upon the law of libel, the lord chief-justice rightly refused to be interrogated without notice ; and, though he gave a general promise that the topics raised by Camden should receive discussion, stoutly declined to name any particular day for the debate.[2]

The motion for an inquiry having been rejected in the lower house, and Camden being determined not to renew the attack upon Mansfield,[3] it seemed that Chatham was at the end of his resources, and that it was now the turn of the Rockingham whigs to move

[1] According to Horace Walpole, Camden confessed that "Lord Chatham had driven him into the attack on Lord Mansfield, which he did not like, and in which at last he declared he would meddle no further : he did not care to have all the twelve judges against him." Walpole's Memoirs, 4, 149.

[2] *Parl. Hist.*, xvi., 1312-1317, 1321-1322 ; Walpole's Memoirs, 4, 143-144, 146-148.

[3] Chatham Correspondence, 4, 97-99.

in the matter. That they would steer a different course was certain, for they had not approved of the method hitherto adopted ; and Rockingham was only expressing the opinion of the majority of his followers when he said, " I early thought that the mode of proceeding in the house of lords, by debates, queries, questions, etc., between Lord Camden and Lord Mansfield, would ultimately end in nothing advantageous to the public," and that " the inquiry into the proceedings of the courts of law in the house of commons seems to have been instituted more to gratify popular clamour than for any expectation or plan of public security to ensue." [1] Indeed, realising that Mansfield was by no means singular in his interpretation of the law, and that by far the larger proportion of the judiciary sympathised with him rather than with Camden, the Rockingham whigs fully appreciated the futility of an inquiry, and sought to effect the needed change by statute. In this they showed greater wisdom than Chatham had displayed. Nothing could be more detrimental to the public welfare than the prevailing uncertainty on a legal question of great importance for the community at large ; and the Rockinghams are deserving of credit for their determination to introduce a bill which, if carried, would dissipate all doubt, and establish beyond dispute the freedom of the press by giving the jury the right to decide the criminality of a libel.

No time was lost in preparing a bill on these lines, the work being entrusted to the experienced hand of William Dowdeswell ; and it speaks volumes for the forbearance of the Rockingham whigs that they were

[1] The Duke of Richmond refers to " those doubts which the opinion of seven judges of the king's bench, countenanced by that of perhaps all the judges now living, has created in the minds of many well-meaning people." Chatham Correspondence, 4, 97-99.

willing to ask Chatham, who had so recently treated them with such scant courtesy, to co-operate with them in this enterprise.   They realised, if he did not, how evil must be the consequences of disunion and dissension ; and, in the absence of Rockingham, who was prevented from coming to London by his wife's ill-health, the Duke of Richmond waited upon Chatham to learn his views.   The reception he encountered was certainly not encouraging.   It is true that Chatham was prepared to abandon his original design, and to support the introduction of a bill ; but he suggested that Camden and not Dowdeswell should be entrusted with the conduct of this measure, which, moreover, should be so framed as simply to declare that by the existing law, a jury was fully competent to determine the criminality of a libel as well as the fact of its publication.[1]   It is not difficult to perceive the motive of Chatham's preference for a declaratory over an enacting measure. He was resolved never to admit that Mansfield, and those who agreed with him, were justified by law, and he feared that the introduction of a bill, such as the Rockingham party had designed, might be used as an argument in support of the position occupied by the lord chief-justice.   It is certain that this was by no means an imaginary danger, for it might fairly be contended that if the law of libel was really as Chatham and Camden represented it, no statutory change was necessary : and that the only possible

---

[1] There is no direct account of this interview ; but Rockingham, after having heard from Richmond, wrote to Dowdeswell that " the conduct Lord Chatham holds in this matter shows very plainly that, at the bottom, one cause of difference between our friends and him arises from a jealousy that our friends might get credit.   The proposal that the bill you had given notice you should move, should be altered, and put into Lord Camden's hands, was a very evident mark that he could accommodate a little on the main point where the public were concerned, if he and his friends were to appear in public as the leaders of the business."   Rockingham Memoirs, 2, 200-203.

logical deduction to be drawn from the introduction of an enacting measure was that Lord Mansfield was justified by law in having consistently confined the scope of the jury's verdict.

Political progress, however, is not governed by dialectic however skilful ; and the Rockingham whigs refused to be convinced by these arguments, preferring to dispense with Chatham's assistance rather than accept it upon such terms. " If you yield now, the horseman will stick to you while ever you live," [1] wrote Burke to Dowdeswell who, indeed, did not need much persuasion to remain firm ; and both Rockingham and Richmond were sincerely convinced that it would be fatal, both to their credit and to their political utility, to surrender to Chatham.[2] Nor was their refusal dictated by pride of party alone. By making the alteration in their measure which Chatham demanded, they would pledge themselves to a definite belief in either the ignorance or villainy of Lord Mansfield ; and this they were not prepared to do. " We wish," wrote the Duke of Richmond to Chatham, " to leave the past just where it is, and shall be well satisfied if this bill can be carried through, and thereby security obtained on this great point for the future. Your lordship and the friends of this bill all mean alike the support of this material part of the constitution ; we differ only in the means, and I think not very widely. I shall, therefore, ever lament, if your lordship should think it necessary to go so far as to oppose those honest endeavours, for which we are pledged to the public, and which, after repeated and mature deliberation, we think ourselves bound to pursue." [3]

---

[1] Burke's Correspondence, 1, 251-252.
[2] Rockingham Memoirs, 2, 200-204.
[3] Chatham Correspondence, 4, 97-99.

It is sad to record that this dignified and almost pathetic appeal did not meet with the response which it deserved. Either on the very day that he received Richmond's letter, or the day following, Chatham informed Barré that " Mr Dowdeswell peremptorily will move his bill concerning juries in the course of next week ; when the friends of the constitution will, it is hoped, strenuously resist this compound of connection, tyranny and absurdity " ; [1] and to Calcraft he expressed the hope that the bill would " meet with the reception from the public which such a task-master deserves." [2] Moreover, taking his cue from his leader, Barré, when asked by Dowdeswell to attend a meeting at Sir George Savile's house, declined the invitation cn the ground that it was impossible for him " to make part of a company which was to discuss a measure which I not only disliked, but thought myself bound to oppose " ; [3] and if this sort of spirit were to continue to animate the followers of Chatham, it seemed likely that when Dowdeswell introduced his bill into the house of commons, he would be fiercely attacked by many influential members of the opposition, whose votes would go to swell the ministerial majority. Such a complete breach, however, was averted by a timely meeting between Rockingham and Chatham, at which, though no reconciliation between the two points of view was affected, it was probably arranged that Chatham's followers should vote for the introduction of Dowdeswell's bill on the understanding that they should be completely at liberty to oppose it at a later stage. " I have seen," wrote Chatham to Shelburne on March 2nd, " Lord Rockingham, who has entered

[1] Chatham Correspondence, 4, 100.
[2] Chatham Correspondence, 4, 103-104.
[3] Chatham Correspondence, 4, 100-102.

largely, in his candid and temperate manner, into the reasons for pursuing Mr Dowdeswell's bill. Your humble servant remained . . . unconvinced, and next week, I believe Thursday, it will come on. I fear much the consequence, and false comments, if our friends of the long robe should take the plan of saying nothing the first day. A silent disapprobation of a bill simply enacting, will not be distinguishable from the disapprobation of ministry to any assertion of the juror's rights. The wrong bill, it seems to me, should be admitted to be brought in, in order to make it right, that is, declaratory, in the committee." [1]

Such a compromise, to give it a name which it hardly deserves, was essentially unsatisfactory ; and the debate in the house of commons on March 7th, when Dowdeswell asked leave to introduce his bill, illustrated the deep division of opinion between those who ought to have stood united. Not by their votes, which, for the most part, they gave against the ministry, but by their words did the followers of Chatham betray their dislike of Dowdeswell's measure. Barré, Calcraft and Dunning chorused their disapproval of the bill and their fervent intention to amend it in committee, and there were some who went further than they did. Thus James Grenville, a nephew of the dead statesman, declared that he could not give his vote for Dowdeswell's motion as he would never admit " the dangerous proposition that juries are judges of the fact, but not of the law," and Sir William Meredith, once a loyal and enthusiastic member of the Rockingham party, seconded a motion for adjournment which was proposed by Constantine Phipps, and carried by two hundred and eighteen votes to seventy-two. Such a substantial victory was all the more gratifying to the court from

[1] Chatham Correspondence, 4, 108-109.

having been obtained without a single member of the government, with the exception of Conway who was more of the body than of the soul of the administration, raising his voice in the discussion. " I sincerely rejoice at the very good conclusion of yesterday's debate," wrote George III. to his first minister, " and at nothing more than the wisdom of leaving the opposition, as they were divided in their sentiments, the whole altercation ; besides, if gentlemen can let their reason guide them to differ with their friends on what they might deem a popular question, it is to be hoped they will by this be encouraged to hold on future occasions the same propriety of conduct." [1]

Nor was it only at court that there was joy, for something not unlike scornful exultation prevailed amongst the followers of Chatham. " You see, my lord, what a glorious day yesterday was for the opposition, and particularly for its leaders," wrote Barré to Chatham on March 8th. " Nothing under the humour of a Swift or a Rabelais can describe it to you. I went down to the house very angry with them, but in less than an hour they forced me to pity them. Poor things ! They told me that they never would do the like again." [2] Such contemptuous pity was characteristic of the vitriolic Barré, but the same bitter tone can be detected in the milder Calcraft's almost gleeful utterance that " Mr Dowdeswell, Mr Burke, and their few followers were completely disgraced." [3] Yet, it is difficult to see any justification for joy over what, from the standpoint of the vigour

---

[1] Correspondence of George III. with Lord North, 1, 62. For the debate see Walpole's Memoirs, 4, 188 ; *Parl. Hist.*, xvii., 43-58 ; *Cavendish Debates*, 2, 352-377 ; Letters of the first Earl of Malmesbury (1870), 1, 219-220 ; Chatham Correspondence, 4, 109-114.

[2] Chatham Correspondence, 4, 109-114.

[3] Calcraft to Chatham, March 8th, 1771 ; Pitt Papers, R. O., 1st series, vol. xxv.

and effectiveness of the opposition, was nothing short of a crowning disaster. Henceforth, the supporters of Chatham and Rockingham were divided by a gulf which, if not unbridgeable, was, at least, unbridged. A fatal breach had been effected, and the history of the concluding weeks of the session, though not without interest, is doleful reading enough. A detailed account of the famous struggle between the commons and the city of London is hardly necessary, since the tale has already been brilliantly told ; but it cannot be entirely overlooked, affording as it does such ample illustration of the lack of union and co-operation between the enemies of the court. Few pages in eighteenth-century history are more familiar than those which record the ignoble attempt to prohibit the publication of the parliamentary debates, the apprehension of the printers who dared to disobey the orders of the house, their discharge by the city magistrates, and the committal of the lord mayor and Alderman Oliver to the Tower of London ; but it is not so well known that in the various stages of this lengthy, tedious, and essentially futile struggle, the followers of Rockingham and Chatham, while certainly united in opposing a policy which could only end in loss of dignity and the outburst of popular passion, acted so independently of one another as to make their resistance of little or no account. At the very height of the contest Chatham was informed by Calcraft that " opposition are in great want of a leader and a general system " ; [1] and the same thought was probably in George III.'s mind when, a few weeks earlier, he told North that " there being so many of the principal persons of the opposition in the minority this day, and yet the number amounting only to nineteen, appears rather extra-

[1] Chatham Correspondence, 4, 125-127.

ordinary." [1] But this phenomenon might have occasioned less surprise to the king if he had known, like Calcraft, of the absence of a " general system." There are no traces of any meetings between the two parties during this struggle, of any elaboration of plans in common, or of any general programme of attack ; and negative though such testimony may be, it throws no little light upon the parlous condition into which the opposition had fallen. " I need not say, my dear friend," wrote Chatham to Calcraft, " how little is left to keep up my animation towards public affairs : the desultoriness and no plan of our friend in Pall Mall ; [2] the poor weakness of Lord Camden ; the no-weight of such advice as I can give, either in the city or Grosvenor Square [3] are circumstances not very encouraging " ; and this was a cry from the heart. Despair, indeed, reigned, and although, before the session was brought to an end, Chatham moved an address for the dissolution of parliament, this was but the last and final rally before the complete abandonment of all hope. On all sides he encountered disappointment. Lord Camden whom he suspected unjustly of carrying on an intrigue with the government, expressed his strong disapproval of the address, [4] and was supported by Lord Lyttleton ; [5] and Temple, though he approved, refused to emerge at his brother-in-law's bidding from that political seclusion to which he had condemned himself for some time past. [6]

The downfall of the opposition was indeed complete, and when parliament re-assembled in January, 1772,

---

[1] Correspondence of George III. with Lord North, 1, 58-59.
[2] Lord Temple.   [3] Lord Rockingham.
[4] Chatham Correspondence, 4, 161-162.
[5] Chatham Correspondence, 4, 163-164.
[6] Grenville Papers, 4, 533-534. Chatham Correspondence, 4, 154-155, 163-164.

Chatham was not found in his place. Writing from his Somersetshire home, he told Shelburne that he did not see " that the smallest good can result to the public from my coming up to the meeting of parliament. A headlong self-willed spirit has sunk the City into nothing : attempting powers it has no colour of right to, it has lost the weight to which it is entitled. In another quarter, the narrow genius of old-corps connection has weakened whiggism, and rendered national union on revolution principles impossible ; and what but such an union can have any chance to withstand the present corruption." [1] He was, indeed, only too right in his assertion that an united opposition existed no longer, and that it was vain to continue the battle against the administration. There is no doubt that George III. had won the greatest victory of his reign, and England now stood upon the threshold of that era of personal government which was destined to be productive of so much mischief. All the persistence, the courage and the gallantry which had been expended upon the struggle against North and his predecessor, Grafton, seemed wasted ; and the political ideals, which George had cherished from the first and never abandoned in the hour of greatest adversity, were about to find complete realisation. Thus the curtain is rung down upon a triumphant king and the defeated whigs ; and the grouping of the characters at the close of this act in the political drama was certainly not accidental. The opposition had failed very largely because it deserved to fail, and neither Rockingham, Chatham nor Grenville can escape their share of the responsibility for the disaster. All three in their different ways helped unconsciously, but none the less effectively, to promote the triumph of the

[1] Chatham Correspondence, 4, 186-187.

court. Rockingham, not marked out by nature for a political career, was but a poor substitute for Newcastle as a leader of a party ; and neither Chatham nor Grenville, though the one had genius and the other most exemplary industry, ever really grasped the essential conditions of success in parliamentary warfare. Yet to argue that it would have been better if the battle had never been waged, would be to overlook much of permanent value in the struggle. No little instruction can be gleaned from blunders and mistakes in the past ; and a study of this brief though critical period in the reign of George III. enforces the old lesson contained in the well-known adage, " united we stand, divided we fall." It is easy enough for us to see how fatal were the consequences of the division of the whig party into three separate and, too often, rival camps ; but it may well be that we are able to appreciate the value of political unity because we have been instructed by events in the past. In the early days of George III., those who consistently opposed the court were constitutional pioneers, hewing their way through many obstructions, and compelled to make their own road as they went along ; and if they sometimes went astray, and were lost in the desert, their journey was not in vain ; for by their labours they lightened the task of those who came after them.

INDEX

Abhorrers, in the reign of Charles II., 276 and *n.* 1.

Albemarle, George Keppel, third Earl of, and the fall of the Rockingham ministry in 1766, 36 ; and the overtures to the Bedford party in December 1766, 97 ; opposed to reduction of land tax, 106 ; and the Duke of Bedford's motion on 10th April 1767, 134 ; prepared to forego his claims to be commander-in-chief, 156, 157 *n.* 1 ; and the negotiation of July 1767, 160-162 ; his visits to Woburn, *ibid.* and 183 and *n.* 4 ; his theory to account for failure of negotiation, 174 ; his anxiety for union with Bedford party, 177 ; see also 156 *n.* 1, 181, 187.

Aldborough, borough of, and general election of 1768, 213 and *n.* 4.

Almon, John, libel suit against, 415-416.

America, South, 372.

American colonies and the question of taxation of, 38, 46, 55, 96 ; discontent in, after repeal of stamp act, 107-108, 128 ; views of English parties upon, 108-110 ; proper policy to be pursued towards, 128-129 ; Shelburne's sympathy with, 51, 130 ; attitude of Lord Chatham and Camden towards, in 1767, 130-131 ; ministerial policy towards, in 1767, 129-145 ; taxation of, by Charles Townshend, 141-145 ; included in secretaryship of state for the southern department and then transferred, 161, 192 ; attitude of George Grenville towards, 167-168, 175 ; influence of dispute with, upon domestic politics, 176 ; resistance of, to revenue act, 232-234 ; parliamentary action against, in session of 1768-69, 247-255 ; Chatham's defence of, in 1770, 294 ; and repeal of the revenue act, 347-349 ; see also 47, 121, 123, 162, 169, 293, 305, 323-324, 328, 365, 415, 419.

Ancaster, Peregrine Bertie, third Duke of, moves the address in the House of Lords, 1770, 293.

Anne, Queen, 319.

Apsley, Henry Bathurst, first Lord, becomes lord chancellor, 405.

Archer, Lord, 202.

Archer, Mr, 202.

Arthur's club, 23 ; meeting of Rockingham and Gower at, 135.

Austria and Frederick the Great, 71.

Bagot, Sir William, 351.

Bailey, Abraham, the Duke of Newcastle's steward, 215 *n.* 1.

Banbury, borough of, represented in parliament by Lord North, 321.

Barré, Isaac, and the American colonies, 248 ; and John Wilkes, 271 ; and the Falkland Islands, 408 *n.* 1, 411 ; and the law of libel, 430-432.

Barrington, William Wildman, second Viscount Barrington, secretary

whigs, 186-191 ; their accession to ministry, 191-192, 192-193, 195-197 and *n.* 1, 235 ; and John Wilkes, 227, 228, 229, 230, 260 ; their antagonism to Shelburne, 234-235 ; and Lord Rochford, 236 ; opposed to Camden, 237 *n.* 4 ; and the American colonies, 245 ; see also 63, 147, 332.

Bengal, conquest of, 90.

Bennet, curate at Aldborough, 213 and *n.* 4.

Bentinck, William Henry Cavendish, third Duke of Portland ; see Portland.

Berkeley Square, the Jesuit of, nickname of Lord Shelburne, 51.

Bernard, Sir Robert, 277 *n.* 2.

Bertie, Peregrine, third Duke of Ancaster ; see Ancaster.

Bessborough, William Ponsonby, second Earl of, resignation of, 80-84 ; attempts to reconcile the Rockingham whigs with Chatham, 82-84 ; appointed to approach Lord Gower, 97 ; his opinion of the Rockingham whigs, 98 ; and Bedford's motion on 10th April 1767, 134.

Blackstone, Dr, and John Wilkes, 270-271.

Bolingbroke, Henry St John, first Viscount, political philosophy of, 4-5 ; and George III., 212 ; see also 63.

Bolton, Harry Paulett, sixth Duke of, and the Falkland Islands, 412.

Boroughs, treasury and rotten, 11 ; sale of, at general election of 1768, 212-213 and 213 *n.* 1 and 2 ; and Chatham, 329.

Boston, and Townshend's revenue act, 232, 249 ; and Sons of Liberty of, 256 ; see also 247, 252.

Boulton, Henry Crabb, a director of the East India Company, 125.

Bradshaw, Thomas, secretary of the treasury, 402 *n.* 5.

Brett, Sir Piercy, appointed to a place on the board of admiralty, 87.

Bridgewater, Francis Egerton, third Duke of, 187, 189, 191.

Bristol, George William Hervey, second Earl of, 242 *n.* 1.

Bristol, Augustus Hervey, afterwards third Earl of, supports nullum tempus bill, 210 ; accepts a lordship of the admiralty, 405.

Buccarelli, the governor of Buenos Ayres, 374 ; and the attack upon Port Egmont, 374, 375 and *n.* 2, 377, 378, 379, 382, 384, 389 and *n.* 1, 403.

Buckinghamshire, John Hobart, second Earl of, his opinion of the Duke of Richmond, 40 and *n.* 1 ; his opinion of Charles Townshend, 185 *n.* 1 ; see also 280 *n.* 2, 341 *n.* 1.

Buckinghamshire, petition of, in 1769, 287 and *n.* 2.

Buenos Ayres, 374, 377, 385.

Burke, Edmund, and the party system, 14 ; elected to a seat in parliament in 1766, 22 ; defence of the first Rockingham ministry, 36 ; secretary to Lord Rockingham, 37 ; estimate of Chatham's ministry, 55 ; attacks the indemnity bill, 89 *n.* 2 ; and the East India Company, 94, 104, 203 ; opposed to opposition to land tax, 106-107 ; his allusion to Charles Townshend, 117-118 : and the negotiations in July 1767, 174 ; his influence over Rockingham, 178 ; his partiality for Conway, 178 *n.* 2 ; his opinion of Chatham's administration, 196 ; and the nullum tempus bill, 210 ; and colonial policy, 251, 253 ; and the Middlesex election, 261-263, 267-271 ; and the popular agitation for Wilkes, 276, 277 *n.* 1, 278, 364 ; and co-operation with Grenville in 1769, 280, 287-290 ; his

INDEX

Fitzroy, Augustus Henry, third Duke of Grafton ; see Grafton.

Fletcher, Henry, and the Cumberland election, 248 *n.* 2.

Florence, Sir Horace Mann at, 404.

Fox, Henry, first Lord Holland ; see Holland.

Fox, Stephen, eldest son of Lord Holland, and the meeting at Devizes, 278.

France, war and peace with France, 7, 18, 28, 30 ; and Frederick the Great, 72 ; Wilkes in, 219 ; annexation of Corsica by, 231-232, 234 ; and the Falkland Islands, 373, 375 *n.* 2, 376, 378-382, 386-391, 389 *n.* 1, 398-399, 402 and *n.* 3, 403 *n.* 2, 409-411, 410 *n.* 1 ; see also 70.

Frankland, Frederick Meinhardt, 215.

Fraser, Simon, 338.

Frederick the Great, King of Prussia, 27 ; project of an alliance with, during the first Rockingham ministry, 39 ; Pitt in favour of, and Lord Egmont opposed to an alliance with, 55 ; Chatham's overtures to, 69-72 ; and the Russian alliance, 71.

Frederick, Prince of Wales, 11 *n.* 1.

Gage, William Hall, second Viscount Gage, and the parliamentary election at Lewes in 1768, 215.

General warrants ; see warrants.

Genoa, loss of Corsica by, 231-232.

George II., decline of influence of the crown under, 2, 12-13, 32, 152 ; and the Duke of Newcastle, 15 ; his opinion of Lord Weymouth, 198 ; death of, 41.

George III., his accession and constitutional opinions, 1-5, 3 *n.* 1, 5 *n.* 1 ; his attack upon the coalition ministry, 5-8 ; and ministerial relations with George Grenville, 8-10 ; and the overthrow of the whig party, 10-12, 15-16 ; and John Wilkes, 26-27, 218-222, 227, 230, 260, 275 ; and William Pitt in 1761, 28-29 ; his fear of a coalition between Pitt and Newcastle, 33 ; his dislike of George Grenville, 33-34, 35, 39, 149, 320 ; negotiations with the Rockingham whigs in May 1765, 34 ; his negotiations with Pitt in June 1765, 34 ; and the offer of the chancellorship to Charles Yorke, 43-44, 296, 306 and *n.* 3, 307-308, 307 *n.* 3 ; and the first Rockingham ministry, 35-37 ; his refusal to create peers, 37 ; his objection to the Duke of Richmond as secretary of state, 40-41 ; his situation in the summer of 1766, 41 ; he dismisses the first Rockingham ministry, 42-44 ; and the formation of Lord Chatham's administration, 44 and *n.* 2, 45 ; Chatham's confidence in, 55-56 ; his dislike of the system of party government, 86-87 ; visited by Grafton and Northington in May 1767, 146 ; his appeals to Chatham, 146-147, 150, 151 ; in favour of overtures being made to the Rockingham whigs in June 1767, 149 ; visited by Grafton on 3rd July 1767, 150-151, 150 *n.* 3 ; his conspicuous courage, 151-152 ; and negotiations with the whig opposition, 152-175, 164 *n.* 1, 172 *n.* 1 ; his opinion of Lord Sandwich, 192 *n.* 2 ; his original distrust of the Bedford party, 196-197 ; his conciliatory disposition towards, 197 ; ministerial relations with Lord Chatham, 199 ; his opinion of Lord Hillsborough, 199 ; advantage accruing to, from the accession of the Bedfords to the ministry, 199-200 ; and the "patriot

Henry VIII., 252-253.
Herbert, Henry, first Earl of Carnarvon ; see Carnarvon.
Hertford, Francis Seymour Conway, first Earl of, persuades Henry Conway
not to resign office, 85, 172 ; and the negotiations of July 1767, 165 *n.* 1.
Hertfordshire, 301 and *n.* 4.
Hervey, Augustus, afterwards third Earl of Bristol ; see Bristol.
Hervey, George William, second Earl of Bristol ; see Bristol.
Highgate, 301 *n.* 4.
High Wickham, 287 *n.* 2.
Hill, Wills, first Earl of Hillsborough; see Hillsborough.
Hillsborough, Wills Hill, first Earl of, secretary of state for the colonies, 192,
199 ; his character, 199; George III.'s opinion of, *ibid.*; and the American
colonies, 252 ; and the repeal of the revenue act, 254, 255 *n.* 1.
Hobart, John, second Earl of Buckinghamshire ; see Buckinghamshire.
Holland, Henry Fox, first Lord, his denunciation of Shelburne, 51 ; his
favourable opinion of Gower, 199 *n.* 1 ; see also 278.
Home, Hugh, third Earl of Marchmont ; see Marchmont.
Honiton, attack upon the Duke of Bedford at, 279.
Howard, Henry, twelfth Earl of Suffolk ; see Suffolk.
Hunt, Captain, and the Falkland Islands, 372 *n.* 1, 374, 384, 388-389, 389 *n.* 1,
394, 395, 397, 412.

Indemnity act, 74-75, 88-89, 89 *n.* 2.
India, conquest of, 28, 90 ; see also East India Company.
Inglewood Forest, lease of, granted to Sir James Lowther, 206-208.
Ireland, 305, 415.
Italy, Wilkes in, 219.

Jacobites, political influence of, 12.
Jamaica, 395.
James I., 209.
James II., 1, 343.
Jenkins, Robert, and the Spanish war, 353.
Jenkinson, Sir Charles, appointed to a place on the admiralty board, 87.
Jesuit of Berkeley Square, nickname of Lord Shelburne, 51.
Johnson, Dr Samuel, his estimate of George Grenville, 10 *n.* 1.
Jones, Mr, president of the Bill of Rights Society, 277 *n.* 2.
Junius, 20, 274, 293, 414-415.

Keppel, Augustus, resignation of, 84, 86, 87 ; and the land tax, 107 ; and the
negotiations of July 1767, 167 ; his visit to Woburn in the autumn of
1767, 183.
Keppel, George, third Earl of Albemarle ; see Albemarle.

Lambeth, 258
Land tax, 105-107, 106 *n.* 1.
Languard Fort, command of, given to Colonel Clavering, 345 *n.* 2.
Legge, William, second Earl of Dartmouth ; see Dartmouth.